MENTAL ILLNESS AND SOCIAL POLICY

THE AMERICAN EXPERIENCE

MENTAL ILLNESS AND SOCIAL POLICY

THE AMERICAN EXPERIENCE

Advisory Editor
GERALD N. GROB

THE BEGINNINGS
of
MENTAL HYGIENE
in
AMERICA

Three Selected Essays
1833 - 1850

ARNO PRESS
A NEW YORK TIMES COMPANY
New York • 1973

Reprint Edition 1973 by Arno Press Inc.

MENTAL ILLNESS AND SOCIAL POLICY:
.The American Experience
ISBN for complete set: 0-405-05190-5
See last pages of this volume for titles.

Manufactured in the United States of America

————————◆————————

Library of Congress Cataloging in Publication Data
Main entry under title:

The Beginnings of mental hygiene in America.

    Mental illness and social policy: the American
experience)
    Reprint of the 2d ed., 1833, of Remarks on the
influence of mental cultivation and mental excitement
upon health, by A. Brigham, published by Marsh, Capen,
& Lyon, Boston; of the 2d ed., 1850, of Mental hygiene,
by W. Sweetser, published by G. P. Putnam, New York;
and of the 4th ed., 1840, of Hints for the young in
relation to the health of body and mind, by S. B.
Woodward, published by G. W. Light, Boston.
    1. Mental hygiene—United States—Addresses, essays,
lectures. I. Brigham, Amariah, 1798-1840. Remarks
on the influence of mental cultivation and mental
excitement upon health. 1973. II. Sweetser, William,
1797-1875. Mental hygiene. 1973. III. Woodward,
Samuel Bayard, 1787-1850. Hints for the young in
relation to the health of body and mind. 1973.
IV. Series [DNLM: WM B417 1850F]
RA790.B435   613   73-2385
ISBN 0-405-05193-X

Contents

REMARKS

ON THE INFLUENCE

OF

MENTAL CULTIVATION

AND

MENTAL EXCITEMENT

UPON HEALTH.

BY AMARIAH BRIGHAM, M. D.

Is not that the best education which gives to the mind and to the body all the force, all the beauty, and all the perfection of which they are capable ? PLATO.

S' il est possible de perfectionner l'espece humaine, c'est dans la medicine qu'il faut en chercher les moyens. DESCARTES.

𝔖econd 𝔈dition.

BOSTON:

MARSH, CAPEN & LYON,

1833.

BOSTON:
Printed by James B. Dow,
122 Washington-St.

PREFACE

TO THE SECOND EDITION.

———

THE favor with which the first edition of this work was received by the public, has been extremely gratifying to the author, not only by confirming his belief of the importance of the truths it contains, but by giving promise that they will be regarded, in the education of the youth of this country.

The inutility, and even the danger of very early attempts to cultivate the minds of children to a high degree, are beginning to be acknowledged, not only in this country, but also in England. An article in a recent number of the *Christian Observer*, denounces in strong terms this dangerous practice ; and from various parts of our own country, I have been assured that experience has convinced many of the most intelligent and reflecting people, that it has been prosecuted to an injurious extent.

Public attention is now awakened to the importance of manual labor and exercise for scholars, in high schools and colleges. I rejoice at this ; but I still believe there is far more injury caused by too much *mental labor* required of children, when young, and by efforts to suppress their natural gaiety and love of amusements, than by neglect of exercise in after life. This is more particularly true as regards females.

1*

The author has endeavored to improve the present edition of this work by the correction of some verbal errors, and the addition of some new matter, particularly upon the influence of mental excitement in producing diseases of the heart ; upon *self-education*, and upon the *Sunday Schools* of this country.

He would again express the hope that his countrymen, and particularly those who have the care of youth, would give more attention than they have hitherto, to the study of anatomy and physiology ; — sciences which he regards as of the utmost value to mankind, and which ought to be understood by every individual.

Hartford, Ct., June 15th, 1833.

PREFACE

———

THE object of this work is to awaken public attention to the importance of making some modification in
the method of educating children, which now prevails
in this country. It is intended to show the necessity
of giving more attention to the health and growth of
the body, and less to the cultivation of the mind, especially in early life, than is now given ; to teach that
man, at every period of his existence, should be considered both as a spiritual and material being — as influenced both by physical and moral causes, and that
therefore all plans for his improvement should be formed, not from a partial view of his nature ; but from a
knowledge of his moral, intellectual, and physical powers, and of their development.

The importance of Physical Education, or the perfect development of the organs of the body, appears in
modern times to be nearly forgotten. This forgetful-
ness has, no doubt, been occasioned by modern discoveries, inventions and improvements in the mechanic arts, which have rendered the employment of the
physical strength of man less necessary than it was in
past ages, and produced a general conviction that
' knowledge *alone* is power.' The invention of gun-
powder, in particular, has contributed very greatly to

this neglect of physical education. So little regard, however, is now paid to this subject, that the connexion between the mind and body is by many entirely overlooked, and the necessity of well-developed organs for the manifestation of good mental powers, seems to be generally unknown. But, as exclaimed the eloquent Dupaty, on seeing the magnificent Anatomical Museum at Florence, ' Philosophy has been in the wrong, not to descend more deeply into physical man ; there it is that the moral man lies concealed.'

The people of the United States ought to become the most vigorous and powerful race of human beings, both in mind and body, that the world has ever known. Living in a climate which permits the fullest development of all the powers of human nature — enjoying entire freedom — possessing an abundant supply of the best nutriment, and of everything necessary to promote the increase and healthy action of their physical powers — exempt from those influences which tend to repress the mental and physical improvement of the people of most other countries, they certainly ought to reach the highest perfection of which humanity is capable. But to effect this, all that belongs to human nature should be regarded in education ; the whole man should be improved. And not only should all his powers be developed, but they should be developed harmoniously, and at the proper time.

An improvement in female education has become very necessary in this country. It is lamentable, and in fact alarming, to find that the females of the United States, especially those in cities, and those belonging to the most wealthy class, are in general more delicate and feeble than those in several countries of Europe.

From my own observation, I am confident that a far greater proportion of the females seen in the cities of this country, are pale, slender, and apparently unhealthy, than of those seen in the large towns of England and France. The truth of this remark is abundantly confirmed by our own and foreign travellers. But there is no other country where females generally receive so early and so much intellectual culture, and where so little attention is paid to their physical education. Unless there is a reform in this respect, the general feebleness of the females in this country will be increased. Besides, there is danger of ultimately regarding extreme delicacy as requisite to beauty, and thus a false and most dangerous error may be encouraged. No people will long hold a high rank among the nations of the earth, where such an opinion extensively prevails, and where females are generally feeble.

It is not, however, the object of this publication to discountenance, in the least degree, any judicious efforts to cultivate the human mind. On the contrary, I wish to awaken a more general attention to this subject. But I would not have this attention confined to children, and to that age when the human system requires all its energies to perfect the organization. Education should be made the business of life, and the multiplication of books has now placed the means of acquiring knowledge within the reach of all.

I have endeavored, also, in this work, to point out what I conceive to be the most frequent cause of the ill health of literary men in this country ; and to show that only by carefully developing and judiciously exercising the organs of the body, and especially the brain, can mental labor be long performed with energy, without injury to the health.

I hope also that my remarks may serve to awaken some attention to the study of human *Anatomy* and *Physiology*; on which all plans of education ought to be founded. The general neglect of these sciences is one of the most extraordinary facts of the kind that this inquiring age presents. Not to know the composition of most inorganic substances, and not to understand the mechanism of the steam-boat or the spinning-jenny, is considered disgraceful, by men who live and die totally ignorant of the far more curious and wonderful mechanism which their own bodies present.

This work is given to the public with the hope that it will be read with candor, and that the facts adduced, though presented in a very imperfect manner, will have their proper weight. If they do, I shall confidently expect that it will prove of some service to the cause of education in this country.

A. B,

Hartford, Nov. 21st, 1832.

CONTENTS.

INFLUENCE OF

MENTAL CULTIVATION

UPON HEALTH.

———

THE influence which the exercise of the intellectual faculties has upon the health, growth, and proper
development of the body, is a subject of interesting inquiry to every rational being.

The peculiarly intellectual character of the present
age, the high mental excitement which pervades all
classes of society, and of which the child partakes in
its very infancy, render it more important now, than
has ever been before, for men, and particularly for
the inhabitants of the United States, to possess correct views upon this subject. In this country, where
the Government and Institutions are of the most liberal character, where the highest honors and distinctions are put into one common market, and made the
rewards of personal merit, men are constantly stimulated to mental industry. The accidental circumstances of fortune, parentage, or the favor of the great,
have here but little control; the power to gain high
and desirable stations is to be derived from knowledge;
and nobility and dignity of character belong only to
those who possess enlarged and cultivated minds.

2

Hence we find, that, by all classes of the community, the culture of the mind is considered as the first and most important pursuit, especially for those in early life. The parent whose own education was deficient, soon perceives its value, in the influence and power with which it rewards those around him who do possess it, and is willing to make great exertions to enable his children to acquire that knowledge which it was his misfortune not to have obtained. Though he has never expected, for himself, any other station in society than that of a daily laborer in the field or the work-shop; yet he aims to prepare his son for a different fortune, and aspires to place him among the most distinguished of the learned, or among the rulers of his country. Conscious that without education such an elevation cannot be attained, he becomes earnestly desirous of the mental improvement of his child : he watches over his infancy with intense anxiety, endeavoring to call forth and strengthen at an early period those powers of mind which will enable him in future years to sway and delight mankind.

This prevalent eagerness for intellectual improvement in our republic, leads to a constant search after new and sure methods by which the education of children may be promoted. Hence we so frequently hear novel plans proposed for the earlier and more rapid development of the infant mind, and see machines invented for accelerating the progress of babes in the acquisition of what is called 'useful knowledge.' Bookstores are filled with innumerable works of instruction for children, and parents anxiously resort to every method which will enable their offspring to become prodigies in mental endowments, while in every other respect they remain weak and delicate infants.

When such feelings and opinions prevail extensively, respecting the importance of developing and cultivating the mental powers of young children, it would not be surprising if, to accomplish that which is thought to be so desirable an object, some injudicious if not dangerous methods should be adopted. It becomes important, therefore, to examine occasionally and see whether parents and teachers, in their great eagerness to produce good results, are not sometimes too regardless of the injury which some of the methods employed may produce.

Many physicians of great experience are of the opinion, that efforts to develope the minds of young children are very frequently injurious; and from instances of disease in children which I have witnessed, I am forced to believe that the danger is indeed great, and that very often in attempting to call forth and cultivate the intellectual faculties of children before they are five or six or seven years of age, serious and lasting injury has been done both to the body and the mind. The danger arises from parents and teachers forgetting or disregarding this important fact, that, although the mind is immaterial and indestructible, it is yet allied to a material body, upon the healthy state of which the intellect is dependent for vigor and power.

Of the nature or essence of mind we are ignorant. — We believe it is distinct from matter. We do know, however, that it manifests itself solely by the aid of material organs, and that a well-formed and healthy condition of these organs is as essential to correct and powerful mental action, as well-developed and healthy lungs are for the performance of free and perfect respiration, or a sound state of the eye and the ear for seeing and hearing. In consequence of this intimate connexion between the mind and body, we cannot doubt that mental labor calls into action some organ, and that, if continued for a great length of time, it will fatigue, and may injure this organ, and unfit it for its accustomed duties, just as too much excitement of the heart or stomach will injure these organs, and derange the circulation and digestion.

If these observations are true, (and that they are I think can be abundantly proved,) every person will perceive, that in cultivating the mental powers of children, we should be less anxious to ascertain how rapidly and to how great an extent they may be developed, than how much the delicate organ or organs by which the mind acts may be excited without injury to the body or the mind.

Very different views, I am aware, respecting the education of children, prevail in this country. In most schools, the importance of a sound body, and a well-developed organization to the production of correct and long-continued mental action has been overlooked; and both parents and teachers have chiefly labored to discover the quickest methods of developing the minds of children, without once thinking that mental labor itself could injure any part of the corporeal system.

But in commencing the inquiry as to the influence which the cultivation of the mind has upon the health of the body, it will be necessary first to ascertain what part or organ of the human system is called into action by mental labor, and then to trace the effect which this labor has upon that part of the system, and upon other organs of the body, at different periods of life.

SECTION I.

THE BRAIN THE MATERIAL ORGAN BY WHICH THE
MENTAL FACULTIES ARE MANIFESTED.

EVERY part of the human system has undoubtedly
been created for the performance of some action; as
the heart for the circulation of the blood, the eye for
seeing, the ear for hearing, the nerves for sensation, the
bones to sustain, and the muscles to move the body.

That action which nature intended a certain organ
to perform, cannot be executed by another organ; the
ear cannot supply the place of the eye, or the nerves
perform the duties assigned to the muscles. The particular action or duty assigned to several organs of the
body we know by the evidence of our senses. We can
see and feel the heart beat and the muscles contract.
But as regards the action or function of other organs,
we have not the same evidence. We do not see the
action by which the liver secretes the bile, nor that by
which the eye conveys to us a knowledge of outward
things, and of their different colors, &c. We do not
know, from the evidence of our senses, that any action
at all is excited in these organs to produce such results; still we are confident that the liver does produce
the bile, and that the eye sees. So as regards mental
action, we do not, to be sure, witness it. We never
see the mind at work. So far as we can discover by
our senses, the most profound thoughts of the philoso-

2*

pher, or the finest conceptions of the poet, produces no action of the brain. The mental operation which determined Cæsar to pass the Rubicon, or Napoleon the heights of St. Bernard, could not be perceived to increase or change the action of the brain; yet such facts do not force us to believe that the mind acts independently of this organ. We do not doubt that the stomach is in action, when it separates from the numerous articles which compose an epicure's dinner, or from the coarse and simple fare of the Esquimaux, those particles and those only which are nutritious, and appropriates them to the support of the body, although this action cannot be perceived by us. Neither do we doubt the formation of bile from the blood by the liver, as has been hinted, nor the action of numerous other organs of the body, though we can derive no knowledge concerning their operations through the senses : they are just as mysterious to us as the manner in which the brain modifies thought by its action.

The brain is one of the largest organs in the body : it is better supplied with blood than any other, and is better protected. These facts show that nature designed it to answer very important purposes ; and unless it is the organ by which mental operations are performed, there is but little for it to do, and that little comparatively trifling. That it is, however, the ' material organ of all the mental faculties, scarcely, at this period of science, requires to be proved.' * To ' discipline the mind,' means, therefore, to call into regular and repeated action certain portions of the brain, and to enable them to manifest easily and powerfully cer-

* Elements of Pathology, by Caleb Hillier Parry.

tain mental operations : this process is like that of exercising other organs of the body, thus giving them increased facility in the performance of their respective functions.

There is much proof that the brain consists of a congeries of organs, each of which, in a healthy state, manifests a particular faculty of the mind, and that the power of each faculty chiefly depends on the size of its appropriate organ. I allude to these facts, however, only for the purpose of directing the inquiries of others to them. My present aim is simply to show that the brain, considered as a whole, is the instrument by which the mind operates ; and I hope to impress this fact deeply upon the minds of all those who are engaged in the education of youth.

As a first proof, I will refer to that belief in the dependence of the mind upon a sound state of the body, which is forced upon us by almost daily occurrences. We see that severe blows upon the head are followed by an entire deprivation of intellect ; sensation and volition are destroyed, at the same time no part of the system is injured but the brain, and the action of other organs goes on as usual. When a person is thus, by a blow or by a fall, deprived of his reason, the bystanders by an instinctive impulse look to the head to find the injury. No one ever supposes that an injury of the hand or foot will affect the mind and derange its operations, but all uniformly expect such a result when the brain is wounded ; and this general expectation is founded upon observed facts.

Insanity furnishes further evidence that the brain is the organ by which the mind acts ; for this is not a disease of the immaterial mind itself, but of the brain, and often resulting from some injury. Such a diseased state of the organ of the mind, of the very instrument of thought or of some part of it, deranges the intellectual faculties, just as a diseased state of the stomach deranges digestion. The immortal and immaterial mind is, in itself, surely, incapable of disease, of decay and derangement ; but being allied to a material organ, upon which it is entirely dependent for its manifestations upon earth, these manifestations are suspended or disordered when this organ is diseased.

If the mind could be deranged, independently of any bodily disease, such a possibility would tend to destroy the hope of its immortality which we gain from reason ; for that which is capable of disease and decay may die. Besides, it would be natural to expect that mere mental derangement might be cured by reasoning, and by appeals to the understanding. But attempts to restore the mind in this manner generally prove useless, and are often injurious ; for insane persons feel that their understandings are insulted whenever opposition is made to their own hallucinations and to the evidence of their senses. It is fortunate for them, that the true nature of mental derangement has of late been acknowledged in practice, and that in all attempts to benefit and cure this unfortunate class of beings, they have been assigned to the physician, and treated for corporeal disease.

The phrase *derangement of mind*, conveys an erroneous idea ; for such derangement is only a symptom of disease in the head, and is not the primary affection. It is true, that moral and mental causes may produce insanity, but they produce it by first occasioning either functional or organic disease of the brain. On examining the heads of those who die insane, some disease of the brain or its appendages is generally found. I am aware of the statement by many writers, that they have examined heads of the insane, and found no trace of organic disease. But, until late years, there has not usually been great accuracy in such examinations, and slight organic disease might have been overlooked. Even admitting that there was no organic disease in the cases described by these writers, there was undoubtedly functional disease inappreciable by the senses ; just as there is often great disorder of the stomach and derangement of digestion which cannot be discovered by dissection. There are in fact no diseases which are independent of affected organs, although the affection may not always be evident to the senses.

Although mental derangement may perhaps sometimes occur in individuals who after death exhibit no trace of organic disease, I think such cases are more rare than has generally been supposed. Dr. Haslam says, that insanity is always connected with organic alterations of the brain. Greding has noticed thickening of the skull in one hundred and sixty-seven cases out of two hundred and sixteen, besides other organic disease. Spurzheim says he *always* found changes of structure in the heads of insane people. M. Georget dissected a great number of brains, and his experience is conformable to that of the authors above-mentioned.* Mr. Davidson, House Surgeon to the Lancaster County Lunatic Asylum, examined with great care the heads of two hundred patients who died in the asylum, ' and he scarcely met with a single instance in which traces of disease in the brain or its mem-

* Medico-Chirurgical Review, 1827.

branes were not evident, even when lunacy was recent, and a patient died of a different disease.' *

Dr. Wright, of the Bethlem Lunatic Hospital, states, that in one hundred cases of insane individuals, whose heads he examined, all exhibited signs of disease; in *ninety* cases the signs were very distinct and palpable; in the remaining ten they were fainter, but still existed in some form or other, — such, for instance, as that of bloody points, when the brain was cut through.†

One of these writers for the prize offered some years ago by the celebrated Esquirol, for the best Dissertation on Insanity, observes, that he examined the heads of more than one hundred individuals who died from insanity, and comes to the following conclusions : —

1st. That in the brains of those who die of insanity, changes of structure will always be found.

2d. That these changes are the consequences of inflammation, either acute or chronic.

3d. That there exists a correspondence between the symptoms and the organic changes ; and that the names monomania, mania, &c. ought only to be employed as representing degrees and stages of inflammation of the brain.‡

These references to the intimate connnexion between insanity and disease of the brain have been made, because I propose to show hereafter, that whatever strongly excites the mind or its organ, whether it be study or intense feeling, tends to produce this awful calamity. I shall proceed now with additional evidence that the brain is the material organ of thought.

* Observations on Mental Derangement, by Andrew Combe, M. D.

† Medico-Chirurgical Review, 1828.

‡ Archives Generales de Medicine, 1825.

This appears then farther, from the fact, that pressure on the brain suspends all the operations of mind. If a person receives a blow upon the head which depresses a portion of the skull upon the brain, his intellect is suspended or deranged until such pressure is removed. Cases like the following are not uncommon. A man at the battle of Waterloo, had a small portion of his skull-bone beat in upon the brain, to the depth of half an inch. This caused volition and sensation to cease, and he was nearly in a lifeless state. Mr. Cooper raised up the depressed portion of bone from the brain, and then the man immediately arose, dressed himself, became perfectly rational, and recovered rapidly.*

The following case occurred in Hartford, within a few weeks: — H. O., a young man, fell in the evening through the scuttle of a store, but arose immediately, mentioned the fall to some of his acquaintance, and transacted business during the evening. Next day he was found in bed in nearly a senseless state, and soon became incapable of speaking, hearing, seeing, or swallowing, and appeared to be dying. There was no evidence of any fracture of the skull, and but very slight appearance of any external injury whatever. A small swelling over the right ear, and the conviction that he could live but a few minutes in the state in which he then was, determined his medical advisers to perforate the skull.

I removed a small portion of the bone beneath the slight swelling over the ear, by the trephine, and found more than a gill of clotted blood, which had probably

* Principles of Military Surgery, by John Hennen.

flowed gradually from a wounded blood-vessel. On removing this blood, the man immediately spoke, soon recovered his mind entirely, and is now, six weeks after the accident, in good health, both as to mind and body.

Richerand mentions the case of a woman whose brain was exposed, in consequence of the removal of a considerable portion of its bony covering by disease. He says he repeatedly made pressure on the brain, and each time suspended all feeling and all intellect, which were instantly restored when the pressure was withdrawn. The same writer also relates another case, that of a man who had been trepanned, and who perceived his intellectual faculties failing, and his existence apparently drawing to a close, every time the effused blood collected upon the brain so as to produce pressure.* Professor Chapman, of Philadelphia, mentions in his Lectures, that he saw an individual with his skull perforated and the brain exposed, who was accustomed to submit himself to the same experiment of pressure as the above, and who was exhibited by the late Professor Westar to his class. His intellect and moral faculties disappeared, on the application of pressure to the brain : they were held under the thumb, as it were, and restored at pleasure to their full activity by discontinuing the pressure.†

But the most extraordinary case of this kind within my knowledge, and one peculiarly interesting to the physiologist and metaphysician, is related by Sir Astley Cooper in his Surgical Lectures.

* Richerand's Elements of Physiology.
† Principles of Medicine, by Samuel Jackson, M. D.

A man, by the name of Jones, received an injury of his head, while on board a vessel in the Mediterranean, which rendered him insensible. The vessel, soon after this accident, made Gibraltar, where Jones was placed in the hospital, and remained several months in the same insensible state. He was then carried on board the Dolphin frigate to Deptford, and from thence was sent to St. Thomas's Hospital, London. He lay constantly on his back, and breathed with difficulty. His pulse was regular, and each time it beat, he moved his fingers. When hungry or thirsty, he moved his lips and tongue. Mr. Cline, the surgeon, found a portion of the skull depressed, trepanned him, and removed the depressed portion. Immediately after this operation, the motion of his fingers ceased, and at 4 o'clock in the afternoon (the operation having been performed at one,) he sat up in bed ; sensation and volition returned, and in four days he got out of bed and conversed. The last thing he remembered was the circumstance of taking a prize in the Mediterranean.* ' From the moment of the accident, *thirteen months and a few days*, oblivion had come over him, and all recollection had ceased. He had, for *more than one year*, drank of the cup of Lethe, and lived wholly unconscious of existence ; yet, on removing a small portion of bone which pressed upon the brain, he was restored to the full possession of the powers of his mind and body.' †

It is curious to notice, that often an injury of the brain impairs only that part of the mental faculties. Such instances give great support to the Phrenological

* Lectures of Sir Astley Cooper, by Frederick Tyrrell.
† Scalpel, 1824.

3

views of Gall and Spurzheim, who contend for a plurality of organs in the brain, and a separate and peculiar function to each organ, as, one organ for comparison, another for language, another for tune, &c.

Dr. Beattie mentions the case of a learned man, who, after a blow on his head, forgot all his Greek, a language he was well versed in before the injury. His mind and memory were not affected in any other respect. Another person, mentioned by Dr. Abercrombie, lost all recollection of his having a wife and children, for several days after a similar injury, while his memory of the accident and of recent circumstances was perfect.

Sir Astley Cooper mentions, from personal knowledge, the case of a German sugar-baker, with disease of the brain, who, in the early stage of his complaint, spoke English, but, as his disease advanced, forgot this language, and remembered only the German. The same author relates the case of a man at St. Thomas's hospital, who, after a blow upon his head, was found talking in a language unknown to all, until a Welsh woman, who entered the hospital, recognized it as Welsh: the blow upon his head had caused him to forget the English language.

Dr. Conolly relates a still more remarkable case of a young clergyman, whose head was severely injured a few days before that on which he was to have been married. He recovered as to his health, and lived until the age of eighty; but from the time of the injury his understanding was permanently deranged, though he retained the recollection of his approaching marriage, talked of nothing else during his whole life, and expressed impatience for the arrival of the happy day.

But we see analogous affections resulting from fevers, and other diseases which affect the brain. Dr. Rush says that many of the old Germans and Swiss in Pennsylvania, who had not spoken their native language for fifty or sixty years, and who had probably forgotten it, would often use it in sickness; and he explains it by supposing that the stimulus of the fever in their brains revived their recollection.

He refers also to the case of an Italian, who was master of the Italian, French and English languages, but who, in a fever which terminated his life in the city of New York, spoke English in the commencement of his disease, French only in the middle, and on the day of his death Italian.

Numerous cases are related, of persons, who, from disease affecting the brain, forget names and events, times and places, but retain a perfect recollection of persons and numbers. As like symptoms arise from blows on the head, and often from fevers, we cannot doubt that the brain is very similarly affected in both cases. Insanity is known frequently to arise from blows on the head, and fevers often make people insane for years, who are suddenly restored to the full possession of their mental powers, just as Jones was restored by trepanning, after remaining a year in an insensible state.

Numerous instances similar to those which I have related, are found in works on mental derangement, and they all tend to prove that a well-developed and sound brain is absolutely necessary for correct and powerful operation of the mind. Many of them are exceedingly interesting, and very difficult to explain, except on the ground adopted by Gall and Spurzheim, and eloquently developed and illustrated by Messrs. Combe.*

These writers divide the intellectual faculties into two classes — the *knowing* and the *reflecting*. The knowing faculties are *individuality, form, size, weight, coloring, locality, order, time, number, tune*, and *language;* the reflecting faculties are *comparison* and *causality*. Each faculty has a separate and material instrument or organ in the brain; and memory belongs to each faculty : hence there are as many kinds of memory as there are organs for the knowing and reflecting faculties. They say, moreover, that memory is only a degree of activity of the organs : hence from disease or other causes, increasing the activity of the organs, the recollection of things is far more vivid at one time than at another. This enables us to explain those cases that frequently occur, in which, from some injury of the brain, a person loses the memory of words, but retains that of things. Dr. Gregory mentions the case of a lady, who, after an apoplectic attack, recovered her recollection of things, but could not name them ; others forget the names of their most intimate friends, whose persons they perfectly recollect. I have a patient at the present time, whose memory is good as respects everything but places : he recollects perfectly, persons, names, events, &c., but does not recollect his own or his neighbors' houses, or the place in which he has resided for many years.

Further proof of the connexion between the state of the brain and that of the mind, might be adduced from the many instances of idiots and cre-

* See System of Phrenology by George Combe, and Observations on Mental Derangement, by Andrew Combe, M. D.

tins, who are all nearly destitute of intellect, and defective in the organization of their heads. There have been many examinations of the heads of such individuals, says Esquirol, and they have usually been found to be of vicious formation. The same writer adds this important remark, 'that idiots and cretins sometimes manifest great intelligence in early life, and give promise of possessing superior mental powers; but these premature beings soon become exhausted, their intellects remain stationary, and the hopes they excited soon vanish.'*

The general proposition which I wish to establish, is made evident, also, from the fact that whatever excites the mind, excites and stimulates the brain.

This we know from experience in a severe headache. We perceive the pain to be increased by intense study or thinking, and that mental application determines more blood to the head. So true is it that mental excitement produces an increased flow of blood to the head, that surgeons are very careful to preserve a quiet state of mind in those whose heads are wounded. Sir Astley Cooper, speaking of such injuries, says, that if any mental power remains, all excitement of the brain should be avoided; and relates the following case. 'A young gentleman was brought to me from the north of England, who had lost a portion of his skull just above the eyebrow. On examining the head, I distinctly saw the pulsations of the brain, which were regular and slow; but at this time he was agitated by some opposition to his wishes, and directly the pulsations of the brain were increased, and became more violent, and more blood rushed to the brain. If, therefore, you omit to keep the mind free from agitation, your other means will be unavailing in injuries of the head.'*

The same author mentions another similar case ; that of a young man, who had an opening in his skull from a wound, through which he could see an increased action in the brain, whenever anything occurred, even in conversation, to agitate the mind of the patient.

The following case is related by M. Broussais. M. Thavernier, a captain in the —— regiment, forty-two years of age, moderately stout, but well formed, received in the middle of the Palais Royal, in May, 1815, ninety days before his death, a letter containing *bad news*. Whilst perusing it, he remained motionless as if thunderstruck, and the left side of his face became paralysed, and drawn to the opposite side. He was taken to Val de Grace, and attended to. At this time he had complete paralysis of the arm, thigh, and leg of the right side, and was unable to speak. After using various remedies for more than two months, he began to improve, and became so much better as to be able to stand up, and to speak, although with difficulty.

In this state of improvement, M. Thavernier received another letter, said to be from his wife : he read it, and instantly there occurred loss of speech, general immobility, abolition of sense, and complete apoplexy. He died in three days after this attack, and, on examining the head, there was found engorgement of blood in the sinuses, and several abscesses were observed in the substance of the brain, and other marks

* Lectures on Surgery, &c.

of organic disease. M. Broussais considers this a case of chronic inflammation of the brain induced by a moral cause.*

The same general fact, that mental excitement stimulates the brain, is proved by numberless cases, and forms the basis of correct treatment of diseases of the brain, and especially of insanity.

This disease is generally produced by morbid excitement of some portions of the brain, and requires for its cure that this disordered organ should be left in absolute repose. Hence arises the benefit of Asylums for Lunatics, where this unhappy class of persons have no cares, no wants to provide for, and where their minds are not excited, but soothed by kind words and gentle and affectionate treatment.

Sometimes the increased flow of blood to the head is such as wonderfully to increase the powers of the mind. Pinel, and other writers on insanity, relate cases of patients, who possessed but weak minds when in their usual state of health, but who exhibited very superior powers of intellect during paroxysms of insanity, which determined more blood to the head than ordinarily. Similar facts I have noticed in the insane : sometimes the memory seems to be wonderfully increased ; at other times, imagination, or wit, &c. ; and thus many of the insane are supposed to possess uncommonly brilliant mental powers. I have known an insane person, during a paroxysm of insanity, which usually occurred about once a month, exhibit a very animated countenance, and repeat correctly and with great force and dignity, passages from Shakspeare and

*History of Chronic Phlegmasiae, by F. J. V. Broussais. Vol. 1.

other writers, but who in the intervals of these paroxysms, appeared stupid, thoughtless, and forgetful.

Many instances are on record, of the development
of genius by disease during childhood. The celebrated Novalis had his great mind apparently created by a
very severe disease when he was in his ninth year.*
An increase of power may be given to the brain by an
increased determination of blood to it, just as the senses
are often rendered more acute, by disease and partial
inflammation ; or it may arise from the repose allowed
the brain during disease, and its feeble powers not being
overtasked and injured by mental application.

I might adduce many more cases to prove the very
intimate connexion between the brain and the mind,
that it is a defective brain which makes the idiot, and
a diseased brain which causes delirium and insanity ;
and that all the various states of mind produced by alcohol or by opium, &c., arise from the disordered action which these articles produce in the brain; that the
weak mind manifested by the infant, and the feeble
mind by the aged, are produced by a small and unde-
veloped, or an enfeebled and diseased brain, and not
by a change of the immaterial mind itself. But cases
enough have been cited to prove these truths. And if
we do admit that the brain is the organ by which the
mind acts, we must acknowledge the necessity of
guarding this organ most carefully, of exercising it with
extreme caution, of not endangering its delicate structure at any period of life by too much labor, or preventing its full development by too little ; for the regular exercise of all the organs of the brain is necessary

* Foreign Review.

to prepare them for the active and powerful manifestation of the mental faculties.

The healthy condition and proper exercise of the brain, are therefore far more important than of any other organ of the body, for we might as well expect good digestion with a diseased stomach, or good music from a broken instrument, as a good mind with a disordered, enfeebled, or improperly developed brain. And yet, how little regard has been paid to these important truths, in the cultivation of the mind! While people are exceedingly fearful of enfeebling and destroying digestion, by exciting and overtasking the stomach, they do not appear to think they may enfeeble or derange the operation of the mind by exciting the brain, by tasking it when it is tender and imperfectly developed, as it is in childhood.

SECTION II.

CONDITION OF THE BRAIN IN EARLY LIFE — EFFECT
ON THE MIND — OF EXCITEMENT AND ENLARGE-
MENT OF THE BRAIN BY DISEASE — MENTAL PRE-
COCITY USUALLY A SYMPTOM OF DISEASE.

SINCE at first, no organ is fully developed, and prepared for the powerful execution of its appropriate
function, let us inquire at what time of life, nature has
prepared the brain for the performance of the important office of manifesting the mind.

Let us begin with the infant, and ascertain what is
the condition of its brain in early life.

The brain of a new-born infant weighs about ten
ounces;* that of an adult, generally, three pounds and
a half, apothecaries' weight, frequently a little less. —
But if the mind of an adult has been long devoted to
thought, if he has been engaged in constant study, his
brain is usually increased beyond this weight. The
brain of Byron, for instance, is said to have weighed
four 'pounds and a half; and that of the illustrious
Cuvier, four pounds thirteen ounces and a half. The
size of this organ increases from the time of birth till
manhood, remains stationary from this period until old
age, and then diminishes in bulk and weight. † The

* Meckel's Anatomy, Vol. 2.
† Andral's Pathological Anatomy, Vol. 2.

relative size of its different portions constantly varies during several of the first years of life, and it is not until about the seventh year that all its parts are formed.* During childhood it is 'very soft, and even almost liquid under the finger, and its different parts cannot be clearly distinguished.'† Still at this time it is supplied with more blood, in proportion to its size, than at any subsequent period. It then grows most rapidly, and more rapidly than any other organ : its weight is nearly doubled at the end of the first six months ; and hence the nervous system, being connected with the brain, is early developed, and becomes the predominating system, in youth. At this period of life, however, which is devoted to the increase of the body, it is necessary that the nervous system should predominate ; for this system is the source of all vital movement, and presides over, and gives energy to those actions which tend to the growth of the organization. — Besides, 'Infancy,' says Bichat, 'is the age of sensation. As every thing is new to the infant, every thing attracts its eyes, ears, nostrils, &c. That which to us is an object of indifference, is to it a source of pleasure. It was then necessary that the nervous cerebral system should be adapted by its early development to the degree of action which it is then to have.'‡

But this great and early development, though necessary for the above purposes, very much increases the liability to disease : it gives a tendency to convulsions, and to inflammation and dropsy of the brain, and

* Meckel.
† Bichat's General Anatomy, Vol. 1.
‡ General Anatomy.

to other diseases of the nervous system, which are most common and fatal in childhood.

It is, therefore, deeply important, that the natural action of the nervous system should not be much increased, either by too much exercise of the mind, or by too strong excitement of the feelings, lest at the same time the liability of children to nervous diseases be increased, and such a predominance given to this system as to make it always easily excited, and disposed to sympathize with disorder in any part of the body; thus generating a predisposition to hypochondriasis and numerous afflicting nervous affections.

Mental excitement, as has been shown, increases the flow of blood to the head, and augments the size and power of the brain, just as exercise of the limbs enlarges and strengthens the muscles of the limbs exercised. The wonderful powers of mind which an infant or child sometimes manifests, and by which he surpasses ordinary children, do not arise from better capacity in the mind itself of the child, but, in fact, from a greater enlargement than usual of some portion or the whole of the brain, by which the mind is sooner enabled to manifest its powers. This enlargement takes place whether the mental precocity arises from too early and frequent exercise of the mind, or from disease, and it must arise in one of these two ways. But in my opinion, mental precocity is generally a symptom of disease ; and hence those who exhibit it very frequently, die young. This fact ought to be specially remembered by parents, some of whom regard precocity, unless accompanied bv *visible* disease, as a most gratifying indication; and, on account of it, task the memory and intellect of the child. Sometimes, however, it is accompanied by visible deformity of the head, and then the fears of parents are greatly awakened. Take for instance the disease known by the name of rickets. Every person understands that this is a disease of childhood, and, according to the best medical authorities, it arises from the irritation or inflammation of some organ, and frequently of the brain. Its most characteristic symptoms when it affects the brain, are an enlargement of the head, and premature development of the intellectual faculties. On examining the heads of those who have died of this disease, the brain is found very voluminous, but ordinarily healthy. Meckel observes that its mass is increased in rickets; an effect gradually produced, without disorganization of the brain by increased action in its blood-vessels, and the consequent transmission to it of more blood than usual. Being thus augmented in size, increased mental power is the consequence of this augmentation. 'One of the most remarkable phenomena in the second stage of rickets,' says M. Monfalcon, 'is the precocious development, and the energy of the intellectual faculties. Rickety children have minds active and penetrating; their wit is astonishing; they are susceptible of lively passions, and have perspicacity which does not belong to their age. Their brains enlarge in the same manner as the cranium does.' He adds, 'this wonderful imagination, this judgment, this premature mental power which rickets occasion, has but a short duration. The intellectual faculties are soon exhausted by the precocity and energy of this development.' *

* Dictionare des Sciences Medicales, Vol. 46.

I do not say or believe, that cautious tasking of the minds of young children will frequently cause this disease, but I believe there is great danger that it will produce the same unnatural growth of the brain, and this will give rise to an exhibition of superior mental power, and be followed, as in the case of rickets, by permanent weakness, or loss of mental energy. That an increase of mental power results from other diseases besides rickets, which stimulate the brain, is evident in many instances ; as in fevers that affect the head, in inflammation of the brain, and insanity. The following cases are in point. ' I have often,' says Pinel, ' stopped at the chamber door of a literary gentleman, who, during his paroxysms, appears to soar above the mediocrity of intellect that was familiar to him, solely to admire his *newly acquired* powers of eloquence. He declaimed upon the subject of the revolution with all the force, the dignity and purity of language, that this very interesting subject could admit of. At other times he was a man of very ordinary abilities.'

The memory sometimes receives a wonderful addition of power from an increased flow of blood to the head, caused by some slight irritation, or stimulation of the brain. Dr. Abercrombie relates the case of a boy, who was trepanned for a fracture of the skull, at the age of four. He was at the time in complete stupor, and after his recovery retained no recollection of the operation. At the age of fifteen, during the delirium of a fever, he gave a correct description of the operation, and the persons that were present at it, with their dress and other minute particulars. It is added, that he had never been heard to allude to it before, and no means are known by which he could have acquired a knowledge of the circumstances he mentioned. I have myself seen repeated instances of the increase of the power of memory during delirium, paroxysms of fever, and other affections which determined more blood than usual to the head.

Intoxication sometimes increases the energy of the intellectual faculties, and revives the memory. Mr. Combe mentions the case of a porter, who, in a state of intoxication, left a parcel at a wrong house, and, when sober, could not recollect what he had done with it. But the next time he became stimulated with liquor, he recollected where he had left it. Shakspeare, no bad authority, says that ' wine makes the brain apprehensive, quick, and inventive ;' and another author of celebrity truly observes, ' that wine, up to a certain point, rather tends to steady the intellect, and that a few glasses advantageously affected his own.'* This effect, almost all persons have experienced. They have perceived that their mental and moral faculties were greatly and rapidly changed by alcohol, or wine, or opium, or some other substance which affects the circulation. Who has not felt that transient joy, happiness, or courage, is a marketable commodity, ' that extacies can be corked up in bottles, or peace of mind sent in gallons by the mail coach.'

From such facts we learn, that the varying states of the organization have a powerful influence upon the intellectual and moral faculties; and that to affect the mind beneficially, and to increase and perpetuate its energy, it is necessary to give constant attention to the

* Confessions of an English opium-eater.

agents that act upon the body, and watch that they do not injure the mind by too much excitement of the physical system, nor prevent the proper development of its powers, by too little; for wine, and all other unnatural stimuli, though they may for a short time quicken and give energy to the intellect, ultimately depress and enfeeble it; and on the other hand, long-continued low diet, and a want of sufficient nutriment for the body debilitates the mind.

I proceed to mention additional cases, to prove that mental power is increased by the action of the brain. During an attack of delirium, many people have learned to read and write with great rapidity, but have been unable to do either after their reason returned, and increased determination of blood to the brain had ceased. Another attack of insanity, however, revived their memory, and their ability to read and write. Many people have their recollection of past events wonderfully restored by dreams. Several instances of this kind are related by Dr. Abercrombie, in his ' Inquiries concerning the Intellectual Powers ; ' but I think they must be accounted for on the ground of increased activity of certain portions of the brain, during sleep. In somnambulism, which differs but little from dreaming, some persons have been able to recollect things long forgotten, and to talk in a language of which they possessed no knowledge when awake, but with which they had in early life some partial acquaintance. This wonderful power of the memory has been frequently exhibited, by a few, when under great excitement; and, in ignorant and fanatical times, has induced a belief in the gift of tongues. Those who had learned but little of a language when young, and

had totally forgotten it, were now, when in a convulsive state, able to speak it fluently; while others were
able to repeat long passages from books that they had
never read but once, and had not seen for many
years.* Similar effects have been produced by
animal magnetism, which, as every one knows, powerfully affects the imagination. During the state of
' extase,' caused by *magnetism,* the memory has been
often surprisingly perfected; and some have been rendered able to speak in a language they had long forgotten. This state was always accompanied by symptoms that showed an increased determination of blood
to the head. All had slight convulsions, the face became red, the eyes bright, and after a while humid.†

Like effects are produced by disease. They are
not rare, says M. Bertrand, in all diseases which
greatly excite the brain. M. Moreau (de la Sarthe)
says, in the *Encyclopedie Methodique,* (Art. Medicine
Mental,) that he had the care of a child twelve or
thirteen years of age, who knew only the first elements
of the Latin language, and yet suddenly, during the
excitement of a nervous fever, became capable of
speaking this language with fluency.

But the most remarkable and instructive case within my knowledge, one that serves to show the influence
of the organization and action of the brain on the mental and moral character, and which appears to me
very deserving of the consideration of the metaphysician, is related in the *American Journal of Medical*

* See interesting accounts of the Possedes; Trembleurs des
Cevennes; Convulsionnaires de Saint-Medard; Malades exorcises
par Gasner, &c., in Magnatisme Animale par Bertrand.
† Bertrand. Magnetisme Animale.

Sciences, for 1829, by Professor Horner, of the University of Pennsylvania.

Master William M., the fourth child of his parents, was born in Philadelphia on the 4th of June, 1820. At birth, his head was of ordinary size, but very soon, after an attack of dropsy of the brain, it began to grow inordinately. After he began to walk, its size was so great that he attracted much attention; and he was apt to fall, especially forwards, from readily losing his equilibrium. His health was generally good.

Dec. 12th, 1828, he fell against a door, and bruised his forehead; in an hour afterwards he vomited, became very sick, and died the next evening. During his short sickness he had no head-ache, and complained only of his stomach.

On examining his head, the day after his death, it was found to be considerably larger than that of a full-grown person, measuring twenty-eight inches in circumference. The lateral ventricles contained a great quantity of transparent serum, which had distended the brain to a very great degree, and produced much of the enlargement of the head. The appearance of all the parts of the brain it is not necessary to particularize. Many parts, especially those at the base of the brain, were healthy, and the small blood-vessels were generally congested with blood.

The following interesting account of this child's mental and moral faculties, was furnished by Dr. J. K. Mitchell, the family physician. 'When 15 months old, the child spoke well, and, at 18 months, was able to sing a variety of musical airs with tolerable correctness, and always exhibited a strong predilection for music. His intellectual faculties generally were very

respectable, and his powers of observation rather remarkable. But his memory, both of language and
sentiments, was such as to excite surprise in those
who took pains to converse with him. The following
example of his powers of recollection may not be
amiss. A customer of his father having been absent
two years, returned, and, on his entrance into the shop,
saluted as an acquaintance, its inmates ; but they had
forgotten him. On turning to little M., the latter immediately called him by name, inquired kindly about
him, and then told him that he had not been to see
them for two years.

Of a grave and quiet temperament, he preferred the
society of his seniors, and took little interest in the
common pastimes of childhood. Only sedate children
were agreeable to him. For so youthful a person, his
sentiments and affections were of a lofty character.
Seeing the distress of his mother, when commercial
affairs took his father to Europe, the child, then five
years of age, said, ' Father will soon be back : if he
don't come again, I will be a husband to my mother,
and will work for her, and take care of her when she
is old.'

For two years before his death, little M. became
affected by religious impressions, which grew stronger
and stronger, until his death. Often advising others,
he presented in his own conduct, a fine exemplifica-
tion of his principles, being distinguished among the
children of the family and the school, for love of truth,
and general sincerity of character. At length, even
while in full health and vigor, he spoke of death as a
thing to be desired ; and when dying, expressed
pleasure at the approaching crisis.'

The following, in my opinion, is the true explanation of the surprising mental powers exhibited by this boy. Disease or some other cause, irritated his brain; this irritation attracted more than an ordinary quantity of blood to the head, and thus excited, and unnaturally or prematurely developed, certain portions of the brain; and just in proportion as these were developed, his mental powers were increased.

A similar case of enlargement of the head from dropsy, accompanied by great power of memory, is related by Dr. Monro, in the second volume of the Medical Transactions of the London College of Physicians; and cases like the following are not rare in medical books, or in practice. L. H., aged 14, had always appeared in delicate health, without having any serious disease. He exhibited more *maturity of understanding* than is common at his age, and preferred study to the usual amusements of children. At the age of 13, he had scrofulous swellings, then disease of the head, and finally convulsions, of which he died. On opening his body, the brain was found very *large;* its vessels turgid with blood.* In the substance of the brain was found a small tumor of the size of a walnut, and of a red color. Mental application did not, in this case, probably, produce the disease; but the disease itself, by increasing the determination of blood to the brain, caused the early comparative *maturity of understanding.* I have referred to it to show that disease, and constant excitement of the mind in childhood, have similar effects upon the brain, and each may unfit it for the long continuance of its appropriate functions.

*Merat, Journal de Medicine, Vol. X

I have repeatedly seen cases very similar to the above as to the symptoms, in connexion with scrofulous diseases, and premature development of the mind. Dangerous forms of scrofulous disease among children, have repeatedly fallen under my observation, for which I could not account in any other way, than by supposing that the brain had been exercised, at the expense of other parts of the system, and at a time of life when nature is endeavoring to perfect all the organs of the body. And after the disease commenced, I have witnessed, with grief, the influence of the same cause, in retarding or preventing recovery. I have seen several affecting and melancholy instances of children, five or six years of age, lingering awhile with diseases from which those less gifted readily recover ; and at last dying, notwithstanding the utmost efforts to restore them. During their sickness, they constantly manifested a passion for books, and mental excitement, and were admired for the maturity of their minds. The chance for the recovery of such precocious children, is in my opinion small, when attacked by disease ; and several medical men have informed me that their own observations had led them to form the same opinion ; and have remarked, that in two cases of sickness, if one of the patients was a child of superior and highly cultivated mental powers, and the other one equally sick, but whose mind had not been excited by study, they should feel much less confident of the recovery of the former than of the latter. This mental precocity, results from an unnatural development of one organ of the body, at the expense of the constitution, as is thus explained by two of the most celebrated men of the medical profession. ' It is a fundamental law of the

distribution of vital powers,' says Bichat, 'that when
they are increased in one part, they are diminished in
all the rest of the living economy ; that the sum is never augmented, but that they are necessarily transported from one organ to another, and therefore to increase
the powers of one organ, it is absolutely necessary they
should be diminished in the others.'* 'Extra development and sensibility of the brain,' says Dr. James
Johnson, ' cannot take place, but at the expense of
some function or structure in the animal or organic system ; when, therefore, an undue share of the vital energy of any individual is directed to a particular organ
or system, a proportionate subduction is made from
some other organ or system ; and this is a most un-
doubted and most important truth, which is little understood, and less attended to by the world in general.' †

It is thus, that a child is made an intellectual prodigy. The premature development of mind, is owing
to the premature development of the brain, occasioned
by undue excitement, and the robbing of other organs
of their natural share of vital energy. But, as Dr.
Johnson says, this is a 'truth little attended to by the
world in general.' Most parents are ignorant of it,
and are generally anxious for the early cultivation of
the minds of their children. To effect this object,
they are assisted by teachers, who undertake, with
the aid of books, maps, machinery and pictures, to
make children of only a few years of age understand
a vast many truths in Chronology, History, Geometry,

* Physiological Researches upon Life and Death.
† Influence of Civic Life on Health, &c.

and many other sciences; to mature very rapidly
their understandings, and surprisingly quicken their
reasoning powers. And when a child from much instruction, or from disease, has reached this superior
mental condition *Memoirs*, and *Anecdotes of his Life*
are published (for such children seldom live many
years,) for the sake of instruction and example.*
Such publications have been extensively circulated ;
they have been greatly approved, and probably have
had much influence with parents in the education of
infants.

Much of the thoughtlessness of parents, regarding
the injury they may do their children by too early
cultivating their minds, has arisen from the *mystery* in
which the *science of mind* has been involved, and ignorance of the connexion between the mind and body ;
for we find them exceedingly anxious and careful
about the health of their children in other respects.
Entirely forgetful of the brain, they know there is danger in exercising many other parts of the body too
much, when they are but partially developed. They

---

* See Memoirs of John Mooney Mead, who died April 8th, 1831,
aged 4 years, 11 months, and 4 days. He was 'taught hymns before he could speak plainly,' 'reasoned with,' and constantly instructed until his last sickness, during which, ' when the parents
and physician thought him getting better. the disease, *without
any assignable cause*, suddenly put on a violent and unexpected
form.' The Memoir was ' examined by several judicious persons
—ministers and others, all of whom united in the request that it
might be published ; and all agreed in the opinion, that a knowledge of *the manner in which the child was treated, together with the
results* would be profitable both to parents and children, and a benefit to the cause of education.' I sincerely hope they will be ; but
by producing a very different impression from that which the Memoir is designed to make ; and by teaching parents to avoid adopt-
ing a similar course with the children committed to their care.—
See also Memoirs of Addison Pinneo, Mary Lothrop, Nathan W.
Dickerman, and notices of numerous other young intellectual
prodigies, which are to be found in bookstores, in Magazines, and
various Periodicals for children.

know that caution is necessary with children in respect to their food, lest their delicate digestive organs should be injured by a too exciting and stimulating regimen. A parent would be greatly alarmed if his little child, by continued encouragement and training, had learned to eat as much food as a healthy adult. Such a prodigy of gluttony might undoubtedly be formed. The method of effecting it, would be somewhat like that of enabling a child to remember, and reason, and study, with the ability and constancy of an adult. Each method is dangerous, but probably the latter is the more so, because the brain is a more delicate organ than the stomach.

The activity of most of the organs of the body can be very greatly increased; they can be made to perform their functions for a while with unusual facility and power. I will dwell upon this fact a little. A child, for instance, may be gradually accustomed to eat and digest large quantities of stimulating animal food. I have seen an instance of this kind, and when I remonstrated with the parents on the impropriety and danger of allowing a child but two years old, such diet constantly, I was told that he was uncommonly robust; and indeed he appeared to be in vigorous health; but soon after this he had a long inflammatory fever, of an unusual character for children, which I attributed at the time, to the stimulating diet allowed him. This diet appeared also to have an effect upon his disposition, and confirmed the observation of Hufeland, that 'infants who are accustomed to eat much animal food become robust, but at the same time passionate, violent and brutal.' A child may also be made to execute surprising muscular movements, such as walking on a rope, and other feats ; but these are learned only by long practice, which greatly developes the muscles by which the movements are executed. From frequent and powerful action, the muscles of the arms of blacksmiths and boxers and boatmen, those of the lower limbs of dancers, and those of the faces of buffoons,* become strikingly enlarged when compared with the muscles in other parts of the body. Every employment in which men engage brings into relatively greater action particular parts of the system ; some organs are constantly and actively exercised, while others are condemned to inactivity. To make, therefore, one organ superior to another in power, it is necessary not only to exercise it frequently, but to render other organs inactive, so as not to draw away from it that vital energy which it requires in order to be made perfect.

The important truth resulting from these facts, that *the more any part of the human system is exercised, the more it is enlarged, and its powers increased,* applies equally to all organs of the body ; it applies to the brain as well as the muscles. The heads of great thinkers, as has been stated, are wonderfully large ; and it has been ascertained by admeasurement, that they frequently continue to increase until the subjects are fifty years of age, and long after the other portions of the system have ceased to enlarge.†
'This phenomenon,' says M. Itard, ' is not very rare,

---

* People who are in the habit of indulging anger, very often develope certain muscles of the face to such a degree as to impart to the countenance an expression of ill-nature, when they are not in anger.

† Dictionaire des Sciences Medicales, Vol. 22, Art. Hydrocephale.

even in the adult, especially among men given to study, or profound meditation, or who devote themselves, without relaxation, to the agitations of an unquiet and enterprising spirit. The head of *Bonaparte*, for instance, was small in youth, but acquired, in after life, a development nearly enormous.'

I would have the parent, therefore, understand that his child may be made to excel in almost anything ; that by increasing the power of certain organs through exercise, he can be made a prodigy of early mental or muscular activity. But I would have him at the same time, understand the conditions upon which this can be effected, and its consequences. I would have him fully aware, that in each case, unusual activity and power is produced by extraordinary development of an organ ; and especially that in early life, no one organ of the body can be disproportionately excercised, without the risk of most injurious consequences. Either the over-excited and over-tasked organ itself will be injured for life, or the development of other and essential parts of the system will be arrested forever.

From what has been said hitherto, we gather the following facts, which should be made the basis of all instruction ; facts which I wish often to repeat. *The brain is the material organ by which all the mental faculties are manifested ; it is exceedingly delicate, and but partially developed in childhood ; over-excitement of it when in this state, is extremely hazardous.*

SECTION III.

TEACHERS of youth, in general, appear to think,
that in exciting the mind, they are exercising something totally independent of the body, — some mysterious entity, whose operations do not require any corporeal assistance. They endeavor to accelerate, to
the utmost, the movements of an extremely delicate
machine, while most unfortunately they are totally
ignorant or regardless of its dependence on the body.
They know that its action and power may both be
increased for a while, by the application of a certain
force; and when the action becomes deranged, and
the power destroyed, they know not what is the difficulty, nor how it can be remedied. Fortunately they
do not attempt to remedy it themselves, but call in
the physician, who, if he affords any relief at all, does
it by operating on a material organ. If medical men
entertained the same views as teachers, they would, in
attempting to restore a deranged mind, entirely overlook the agency of the body, and instead of using
means calculated to effect a change of action in the
brain, would rely solely upon arguments and appeals

to the understanding. For if the mind may be cultivated independent of the body, why may not its disorders be removed without reference to the body?

Instructers of youth, and authors of books for children, would do well to acquaint themselves with human Anatomy and Physiology, before they undertake to cultivate and discipline the mind. The neglect of these sciences on their part, is a most lamentable evil. If they had been understood, I am confident that innumerable books for children, which have been highly recommended and esteemed very useful, would never have been published; books, which instead of being blessings to the community, have, I fear, done incalculable injury. Few things, I think, will be more surprising to future generations than the fact, that those whose business it is, in this enlightened age, to cultivate the human mind, were ignorant of the organ by which the mind acts, and of course were inattentive to the condition of that organ. It will appear strange hereafter, that many, through the medium of books, ventured to dictate the manner in which the mind should be disciplined and tasked; and when it became disordered, acknowledged its dependence on an organization of which they were ignorant, and expected to have it restored by those who, in all attempts to remedy it, act upon the bodily organization. Should teachers of youth venture thus, like Phaeton, to guide the chariot of the sun, while ignorant of the power they endeavor to superintend, and of the means of controlling its irregular action?

As reference has just been made to books for children, it seems a fitting opportunity to enlarge a 'little upon this topic. They are then *excessively abundant.*

Some are announced as purposely prepared, ' for children from *two* to *three* years old.' Many are for the week-day infant school; some for the ' Sabbath infant school;' some to teach children History and Geography; others to instruct them in Geometry, Theology, and Metaphysics. 'The Child's,' 'The Girl's,' 'The Boy's,' Books have been multiplied on almost all subjects, until they have become nuisances. Where is the proof that they have ever benefited a single child ? Do the youth now, of the age of 15, who have used such books most of their lives, who committed to memory innumerable truths, and were taught to reason when at the age of 3 or 4, possess more active and independent minds than their parents possessed at the same age ? Does their mental power *now* show the *good* effect of their early and extraordinary culture ? Do not the numerous slender, delicate, and pale-faced youths who are seen in our colleges, and in boarding schools for girls, exhibit the *bad* effects of this system ? I ask again, where is *any* evidence that books, put into the hands of children before the age of seven or eight, are of any lasting benefit, either to the body or the mind ? I have shown that they may do immense injury.

But apart from the injury which such books produce, by too early exciting the mind and feelings of children, many of them are very objectionable, on account of the nonsense and falsehood which they contain. Some, designed *for children from two to three years of age,* contain such trash as the following : ' Englishmen love roast beef and plum pudding. The Dutchman loves cheese and red herring. The Frenchman loves soup and sallad. The German loves ham;

and pompernicle,' &c. &c.* Surely children of any age are better without such knowledge than with it. Other ' Books,' ' Lessons,' ' Manuals,' and ' Tales for Infants ' and for ' Infant Schools,' contain much that is questionable as to its truth, much that infants had better not know, and much that is far above their comprehension. Some contain garbled accounts from Scripture, of the creation of man, and his apostacy, and other religious truths which no child can understand, or profit by, if he could understand them ; the full account given in the Bible is far better. Other books for infants contain ' Lessons in Geometry, Botany, Astronomy,' &c. &c.†

The method of teaching little children varies in different schools ; but that is everywhere considered the *best*, which forces the infant mind the *fastest*. In some schools, the *memory* is chiefly cultivated, and children are taught innumerable facts. Here we see those who are scarcely able to talk, exhibited as wonderful children. They are declared to be deserving of the highest praise, and prophesied about as giving promise of great distinction in future, because they are able to tell us who was the oldest man, and many other equally useful and important facts. They are also able to tell us many truths in Astronomy, Geometry, Chemistry, &c. &c., of which the innocent beings know about as much as do parrots of the jargon they deliver. In other schools, teachers are opposed to such practice ; and say that a child should learn nothing but

---

* See Lessons for Children, two or three years old.

† See Lessons for Infant Sabbath Schools, 1831. Infant School Manual, 1830, and a vast number of other books for *infants*, with which bookstores abound.

what he understands; that the memory should not alone be cultivated ; therefore they teach children that Methuselah was not only the oldest man, and nine hundred and sixty-nine years of age, but that he was the son of Enoch, and the grandfather of Noah, and that a year means 365 days, and a day 24 hours ; and all this they teach, in order, as they say, that a child may *fully understand* what he learns. Other teachers say, that it is very wrong to *compel* a child to learn — very wrong indeed ; and that he should learn no more than he will cheerfully : but though they do not gain their purpose by exciting *fear*, they awaken other passions of the strongest kind in the child, by a system of *rewards* and of *praise*. Now of all these methods, if there is any preference, it should be given to the first ; for that is the least objectionable which has the least tendency to develope the mind, and awaken the passions prematurely. They must all, however, be wrong, if they call into action an organ which is but partially formed ; for they do not conform to the requirements of the laws of nature, and wait for organs to be developed, before they are tasked.

I beseech parents, therefore, to pause before they attempt to make prodigies of their own children. Though they may not destroy them by the measures they adopt to effect this purpose, yet they will surely enfeeble their bodies, and greatly dispose them to nervous affections. Early mental excitement will serve only to bring forth beautiful, but premature flowers, which are destined soon to wither away, without producing fruit.

Let parents not lament, because their children do not exhibit uncommon powers of mind in early life, or because, compared with some other children, they are

deficient in knowledge derived from books. Let them
rather rejoice if their children reach the age of six or
seven, with well-formed bodies, good health, and no
vicious tendencies, though they be at the same time
ignorant of every letter of the alphabet. If they are in
this condition, it is not to be inferred that their minds
are inferior to those of children who have been constantly instructed. It is a great mistake to suppose
that children acquire no knowledge while enaged in
voluntary play and amusements.

They thus do acquire knowledge as important as
is ever acquired at school, and acquire it with equal
rapidity. Many think that the child who has spent the
day in constructing his little dam, and his mill, in the
brook, or the stream that runs in the gutter ; or in rearing his house of clods or of snow, or in making himself a sled or cart, has been but idle, and deserves
censure for a waste of his time, and a failure to learn
anything. But this is a great error of judgment ; for,
while he has thus followed the dictates of nature, both
his mind and body have been active, and thereby improved. To him anything which he sees and hears
and feels is new, and nature teaches him to examine
the causes of his various sensations, and of the phenomena which he witnesses. For him, the Book of
Nature is the *best book*, and if he is permitted to go
forth among the wonders of creation, he will gather
instruction by the eye, the ear, and by all his senses.

He is for a while just as ignorant that stones are
hard, that snow will melt, that ice is cold, that a fall
from the tree will hurt him, and a thousand other common facts, as he is of a ' parallelogram,' or ' perime-
ter,' or the ' diameter of the sun,' or the ' pericarpium

of flowers,' or of many other similar things, which some think important for infants to know.* If his time is constantly occupied in learning the last, he will grow up ignorant of many common truths, and fail in the best of all learning, *common sense.*

The child, when left to himself, manifests a true philosophical spirit of inquiry. The story related of the celebrated Schiller, who, when a boy, was found in a tree, during a thunder storm, trying to find where the thunder and the lightning came from, is an instance of the natural tendency of every child to self-education. This tendency it is highly important to encourage, for it involves the cultivation of that spirit of inquiry, 'which is far more valuable than limited acquirements in knowledge ; a spirit which teaches us to distinguish what is just in itself, from what is merely accredited by illustrious names ; to adopt a truth which no one has sanctioned, and to reject an error of which all approve, with the same calmness as if no judgment was opposed to our own.' † But this spirit will never be acquired, when the child is taught from his infancy to depend upon others for all he knows, to learn all he does learn as a task, and not from the desire of ascertaining the truth and gratifying his curiosity.

Let not the parent, therefore, regret that his child has passed his early hours out of school ; for in all probability the knowledge he has gained while running and exercising in the open air at play, is more valuable than any he would have gained at school. At all events, he has gained what is far, very far more valu-

* See Infant School Manual.
† Brown's Philosophy.

able than any mental acquirements which a child may make, viz. a sound body, well-developed organs, senses that have all been perfected by exercise, and stamina which will enable him in future life to study or labor with energy and without injury.

The remarks which I have made relative to the danger of too early exerting and developing the minds of children, are not made without some knowledge of the education of children in various parts of our country.

That children *do* have their mental powers prematurely tasked, is a fact which I know, from personal observation. I have seen a course like the following pursued in many families in various parts of the country, and I know that this course is approved of by many excellent persons. Children of both sexes are required, or induced, to commit to memory many verses, texts of scripture, stories, &c. before they are three years of age. They commence attending school, for six hours each day, before the age of four, and often before the age of three; where they are instructed during three years in reading, geography, astronomy, history, arithmetic, geometry, chemistry, botany, natural history, &c. &c. They also commit to memory, while at school, many hymns, portions of the Scriptures, catechisms, &c. During the same period, they attend every Sunday a Sabbath school, and there recite long lessons : some are required to attend upon divine service at the church twice each Sunday, and to give some account of the sermon. In addition to these labors, many children have numerous books, journals, or magazines to read, which are designed for youth. I have known some required to give strict attention to the chapter read in the family in the morning, and to give an account of it; and have been astonished and *alarmed* at the wonderful power of memory exhibited on such occasions by children when but five or six years of age. I have known other children, in addition to most of the above performances, induced to learn additional hymns, chapters of Scripture, or to read certain books, by the promise of presents from their parents or friends.

The foregoing account fails to describe the amount of mental labor required of many children in intelligent and respectable families.

The injurious and sometimes fatal effects of such treatment have been already mentioned. But I cannot forbear again to state that I have myself seen many children who were supposed to possess almost miraculous mental powers, experiencing these effects and sinking under them. Some of them died early, when but six or eight years of age, but manifested, to the last, a maturity of understanding which only increased the agony of a separation. Their minds, like some of the fairest flowers, were 'no sooner blown than blasted.' Others have grown up to manhood, but with feeble bodies and a disordered nervous system which subjected them to hypochondriasis, dyspepsia, and all the Protean forms of nervous disease. Their minds, in some cases, remained active, but their earthly tenements were frail indeed. Others of the class of early prodigies, and I believe the most numerous portion, exhibit in manhood but small mental powers, and are the mere passive instruments of those who in early life were accounted far their inferiors. Of this fact I am assured, not only by the authority of books, and my own observation, but by the testimony of several celebrated teachers of youth.

The history of the most distinguished men will, I believe, lead us to the conclusion, that early mental culture is not necessary, in order to produce the highest powers of mind. There is scarcely an instance of a great man, one who has *accomplished* great results, and has obtained the gratitude of mankind, who in early life received an education in reference to the wonderful labors which he afterwards performed. The greatest philosophers, warriors, and poets, those men who have stamped their own characters upon the age in which they lived, or who, as Cousin says, have been the ' true representatives of the spirit and ideas of their time,' have received no better education, when young, than their associates who were never known beyond their own neighborhood. In general their education was but small in early life. *Self education*, in after life, made them great, so far as education had any effect. For their elevation they were indebted to no early *hot-house culture*, but, like the towering oak, they grew up amid the storm and the tempest raging around. Parents, nurses, and early acquaintances, to be sure, relate many anecdotes of the childhood of distinguished men, and they are published and credited. But when the truth is known, it is ascertained that many, like Sir Isaac Newton, who, according to his own statement, was ' inattentive to study, and ranked very low in the school until the age of 12 ; ' or, like Napoleon, who is described, by those who knew him intimately when a child, as ' having *good health*, and

in other respects was like other boys,' * do not owe
their greatness to any early mental application or discipline. On the contrary, it often appears, that those
who are kept from school by ill health or some other
cause in early life, and left to follow their own inclination as respects study, manifest in after life powers of
mind which make them the admiration of the world.†

* Memoirs of the Dutchess of Abrantes. This lady says, ' My
uncles have a thousand times assured me that Napoleon in his
boyhood had none of that singularity of character attributed to
him.'
† Shakspeare, Moliere, Gibbon, T. Scott, Niebuhr, W. Scott,
Byron, Franklin, Rittenhouse, R. Sherman, Prof. Lee, Gifford,
Herder, Davy, Adam Clarke, &c. The last named person was
a very unpromising child, and learned but little before he was
eight or ten years old. But at this age he was ' uncommonly
hardy,' and possessed bodily strength superior to most children.
He was considered a ' grievous dunce,' and was seldom praised
by his father but for his *ability to roll large stones ;* an ability
however which I conceive a parent should be prouder to have his
son possess, previous to the age of seven or eight, than that
which would enable him to recite all that is contained in all the
Manuals, Magazines, and *books for infants* that have ever been
published.

6

SECTION IV.

OF the danger of developing the minds of children
to a great degree at a very early age, I have no doubt
from my own observation ; but I cannot expect to produce a change in public sentiment on this subject by
the publication of my own views and opinions, especially in those parts of the country where parents are,
generally, strenuous advocates for infant schools and
early mental excitement; but I request all who have
the care of children, and are desirous of giving them
sound minds and sound bodies, to consider attentively
the observations of those whose situations in life, great
learning, and experience, have eminently qualified them
to be high authorities on this subject. Let us then
inquire what are the opinions of learned and experienced medical men, as regards the cultivation of the
infant mind.

The celebrated Tissot, a learned and practical
physician, honored by sovereigns, and the friend and
intimate companion of Zimmerman, and Haller, and
the most distinguished men of his time ; published a
work on the *Health of Men of Letters*, which has
been greatly commended, and in Europe has had

great influence. In this work he says, ' The effects of study vary much, according to the age of the student. Long continued application, in infancy, destroys life. I have seen young children, of great mental activity, who manifested a passion for learning far above their age; and I foresaw, with grief, the fate that awaited them. They commenced their career as prodigies, and finished by becoming idiots, or persons of very weak minds. The age of infancy is consecrated by nature to those exercises which fortify and strengthen the body, and not to study, which enfeebles it, and prevents its proper increase and development.' After referring to instances observed by himself and others, of disease and death caused by great mental application in youth, he adds, ' I have elsewhere mentioned the injury that peasants do their children, by requiring of them more bodily labor than they ought to perform. But those injudicious parents who require from their children too much labor of the intellect, inflict upon them an injury far greater. No custom is more improper and cruel than that of some parents, who exact of their children much intellectual labor, and great progress in study. It is the tomb of their talents and of their health.' He concludes with this advice. ' The employments for which your children are destined in after life, should regulate their studies in youth; not requiring (as is the custom with many parents) the most study in early life, of those who are to be devoted to literary pursuits, but on the contrary, the least.' ' Of ten infants,' says he, ' destined for different vocations, I should prefer that the one who is to study through life, should be the least learned at the age of twelve.'

Let us ascertain what views are entertained respecting early mental culture, in those countries which have produced the most learned men. It is probably true that no other country has ever produced or now contains so many profound scholars as Germany. In truth, the Germans have so far surpassed the people of other nations, in whatever relates to the cultivation of the intellect, that Madame De Stäel very justly styled their country 'the Land of Thought.' We may therefore derive great advantage in this enquiry from the opinions of the Germans, for the course they have adopted cannot be bad, since we find their scholars and learned men generally healthy, and remarkable for longevity. Besides, the effect of mental cultivation upon the health, the importance of Physical Education in early life, and the best method of perfecting both the mind and body, have for a long time been subjects of much inquiry, and engaged the attention of the most learned men in that country. Some of their most distinguished medical men have devoted great attention to this subject, and published their views and opinions. From some of their works I will make a few extracts. Upon this subject, perhaps there can be no better authority than that of the distinguished Hufeland, physician to the king of Prussia, who, by his learning, and acquaintance with the greatest scholars of the age, is eminently qualified to decide upon this subject. In his valuable work on the *Art of Prolonging Life*, he observes, 'Intellectual effort in the first years of life is very injurious. All labor of the mind which is required of children before their seventh year, is in opposition to the laws of nature, and will prove injurious to the organization, and prevent its proper development.'

Again, he says, ' It is necessary that we should not begin to exercise the faculties of the mind too early ; it is
a great mistake to suppose that we cannot commence
their cultivation too soon ; we ought not to think of attempting this while nature is wholly occupied with the
development of organs, and has need of all the vigor
of the system to effect this object. If children are
made to study before this age, the most noble part of
the vital force is withdrawn from perfecting the organization, and is consumed by the act of thought ; from
which it necessarily results, that the bodily development is arrested or disturbed, digestion is deranged,
the humors deteriorated, and scrofula produced. In
fine, the nervous system thus acquires a predominance
over all others, which it preserves for the remainder of
life, producing innumerable nervous complaints, melancholy, hypochondria, &c. It is true, however, that
diversity of character requires different methods in this
respect. But in all cases the course to be pursued is
directly opposed to that which is usually adopted. If
a child shows at an early age a great propensity for
study, instead of animating and encouraging him to
proceed in this course, as most teachers do, it is necessary to moderate his zeal, for *precocity of mind is
nearly always disease,* or shows an unnatural propensity, which it is most prudent to correct. A child of
more dull intellect, whose thoughts are slow, may, on
the contrary, apply to study at an earlier period of life,
for in him this exercise is necessary for the proper development of the mental faculties.'

Doctor Spurzheim, whose inquiries upon this subject
have been very extensive, and who has for many years
devoted himself to the task of ascertaining the influ-

ence of the organization upon the mental and moral faculties, thus remarks, in his *Essay upon the Elementary Principles of Education :* ' Many parents anxiously strive to cultivate the intellect of their children, and neglect to fortify their constitution. They believe that children cannot too soon learn to read and write. Their children, therefore, are obliged to remain many hours in school, breathing an impure air, while they ought to be developing the organs of the body by exercise. The more delicate the children are, and the more their affections and minds are precocious, the more important it is that the above error should be avoided ; if it is not, premature death is often the consequence of this infraction of the laws of nature. We often see, also, that those much admired in infancy for their genius, waste all their energies in youth, and at a mature age, possess but ordinary minds. Experience demonstrates, that of any number of children, of equal intellectual powers, those that receive no particular care in infancy, and who do not learn to read and write until the constitution begins to be consolidated, but who enjoy the benefit of a good physical education, very soon surpass in their studies those who commence study earlier and read numerous books, when very young. The mind ought never to be cultivated at the expence of the body.; and physical education ought to precede that of the intellect ; and then proceed simultaneously with it, without cultivating one faculty to the neglect of others ; for health is the base and instruction the ornament of education.' *

* The above is taken from the French edition of this valuable work. A later edition in English, with additions, has been published, which I have not seen. The learned and estimable author

That these views respecting early education, have
had, and continue to have a practical influence in Germany, I have been assured by those long resident in
that country, and by Germans who have been educated there. By a learned and accomplished German
lady, now resident in this country, and who in her own,
enjoyed the best opportunities for knowing the views of
the most intelligent class, I was assured, ' There is
but one voice in Germany, upon this subject, and that
is, — very early learning affords no advantage to the
mind, and does essential injury to the body.'

Italy has produced many great and distinguished
scholars ; and the same instructions upon early education have been given by some of her most learned
men. Sinabaldi, in his great work on the *Science of
Man*, or *Anthropologie*, thus speaks of education in
early life : — ' We ought not to fatigue the memory of

of the above, is now in this country, and proposes to lecture upon the interesting science of Phrenology ; a science to which he
has given a philosophical character, and which, by his labors, he
has advanced to its present high standing. I cannot but believe
that his visit to this country will be productive of great good, by
directing the attention of the public to the immense importance of
physical education ; a branch of education the almost entire neglect of which, in this country, threatens dangerous and lasting
consequences. As to the correctness of the Phrenological system,
I am not qualified to determine ; but so far as I have had an opportunity of observing, I think it explains the phenomena of the
morbid action of the brain far better than any other.

I leave this note as it was in the first edition, though the work
referred to has been reprinted in this country. I still hope, that
although its illustrious author lived but a few months after his arrival in this country, that his visit will be of great service to it,
and that he will ere long be accounted a great benefactor.

In a letter which I received from him but a few days before the
illness which terminated his life, he remarks upon the uncommon
mental activity of the people of this country, and expresses his
belief that the science which he taught would do great good here,
and would ' contribute to a reform in education.' I trust that he
has awakened a spirit of inquiry on this subject, that will not sub-
side until the benefits he predicted are realized.

children by precepts, fables and histories, of which they are not in a state to comprehend either the signification or morality. To force the memory, before that mysterious organ the brain is developed, is the same thing as to fatigue the muscles while imperfect, by long-continued walking or by hard labor, which will produce a general languor, and arrest forever the complete development of the organs of the body. Children at this age ought to be guided wholly by example. In one word, this first epoch of life, from birth to the age of seven, ought to be entirely consecrated to the perfect development of the organization of children, and, by the agency of physical education, to render them as healthy, robust and strong as the nature of man will permit.'

In France, the education of youth has engaged the attention of many learned and distinguished men. Numerous treatises upon the subject have been published, urging the importance of physical education. M. Friedlander, in a late work dedicated to M. Guizot, thus speaks of early instruction : — ' Fromt he highest antiquity we have this rule, that mental instruction ought not to commence before the seventh year.' M. Friedlander thinks this rule is correct, and says that our climate, which necessarily confines children much of the time within doors, has led to the idea of teaching them early, and thus making them prodigies. He gives the following table for the hours of rest and labor, which he says is adopted by many instructers.

Age.	Hours of sleep.	Hours of exercise.	Hours of occupation.	Hours of repose.
7	9 to 10	10	1	4
8	9	9	2	4
9	9	8	3	4
10	8 to 9	8	4	4
11	8	7	5	4
12	8	6	6	4
13	8	5	7	4
14	7	5	8	4
15	7	4	9	4

M. Ratier, in an essay on the Physical Education of Children, which was crowned by the Royal Society of Bordeaux in 1821, thus speaks of early mental instruction : — ' The labor of the mind, to which some parents subject their children not only too soon, but in a wrong direction, is often the cause of their bad health, and causes nearly all those who are distinguished by precocity of the intellectual faculties, to perish prematurely ; so that we seldom see a *perfect man;* that is, one who exhibits an equilibrium of the Physical, Mental and Moral faculties.' M. Julien, late editor of the Revué Encyclopedique, in his large and valuable work on *Physical, Moral* and *Intellectual Education,* remarks, — ' All the pages of this work repel the double reproach, of wishing to hasten the progress of the intellect, and obtain premature success, or retard the physical development of children, by neglecting the means necessary to preserve their health. We have constantly followed the principle of Tissot, who wished that infancy might be consecrated to those exercises which fortify the body, rather than to mental application which enfeebles and destroys it.' Again he observes, 'The course to be adopted with children for the first ten years of life, is neither to press or torment them; but by plays, exercise of the body, entire liberty wisely regulated, and good nourishment, to effect the salutary and progressive development of the Physical, Moral and Intellectual faculties, and by continual amusement and freedom from chagrin, (which injures the temper of children) they will arrive at the tenth year without suspecting that they have been made to learn anything: they have not distinguished between study and recreation; all they know they have learned freely, voluntarily, and always in play. The advantages obtained by this course, are good health, grace, agility, gaiety, and happiness; a character frank and generous, a memory properly exercised; a sound judgment, and a cultivated mind.'

In a late work which holds a deservedly high rank in France, entitled Medical Gymnastics, by Charles Londe, similar views are inculcated, and the true Physiological reasons assigned; — that the moral and intellectual man depends upon the physical; that the mental faculties depend upon certain organs, and the exercise of these organs, developes them in accordance to a general law, — that 'the more an organ is exercised, the more it is developed, and is able to execute its functions with more facility. Thus habit, education, and other like causes, do not change the moral and intellectual character, without acting on the physical man, or changing the action of organs; repressing some, and increasing others.'

Professor Broussais, a man of great learning and genius, and one of the most distinguished physicians of the present age, thus alludes to this subject. 'Intellectual labors give rise, in early life, to effects corresponding with the actual state of the individual constitution. Thus the brain, the growth of which is not complete, acquires, by the exercise of thought, an extraordinary energy and volume; the moral faculties become truly prodigious: but this advantage is sadly counterbalanced by cerebral inflammations, which give rise to hydrocephalus, and by a languor in the rest of the body, the development of which remains imperfect.

'It is easy to conceive what a number of evils must result from a kind of life so little in harmony with the wants of youth; hence we rarely see all those prodigies of premature intellectual education prospering. If encephalitis does not carry them off, they infallibly perish with gastritis or scrofula; most generally, all these evils oppress them at once; and if they do not sink under them in infancy, they carry along with them in mature age, an irritability which does not allow of their resisting the morbific influences, in the midst of which man is necessarily forced to live. They are seen to decay and die, in the prime of life, if they are not destroyed, in spite of all the efforts of the art, by the first violent inflammation that attacks them.' *

Similar opinions have been inculcated in England, by some of the most distinguished medical men of that country; and particularly by the celebrated Dr. James Johnson, in several of his valuable and interesting works. I ought, however, to remark, that the Treatise of Locke on Education has had, in England, great influence;

---

* Treatise on Physiology applied to Pathology.

and undoubtedly has done much injury, by teaching the importance of 'reasoning with children at a very early age.' The practice has no doubt been carried much beyond what he intended ; and its injurious effects are of late often alluded to. Writers on Mental Alienation, state, that early and frequent attempts to *reason* with children, increases, if it does not create a predisposition to insanity ; * and its inutility has been satisfactorily and abundantly shown by several writers, and particularly by Rosseau in his Emile, or Treatise on Education ; a work exceedingly defective and absurd in some respects, but abounding with many important and practical truths upon education. The work has had a great and beneficial influence in Europe, but appears to be but little known in this country.

The evil effects of the course recommended by Locke, have been noticed, as I have said, by the medical men in England. A late writer on Dropsy of the head, observes, ' the present plan of education, in which the intellectual powers are prematurely exercised, may be considered as one of the causes of the more frequent occurrence of this disease.' †

Another writer, in a recent and valuable work, has also alluded to this subject, and in a manner that ought to awaken the attention of parents and teachers. He says, ' It is undoubtedly too much the custom of the modern system of education to stimulate the infant intellect to premature, and therefore prejudicial exertion. The recommendations enforced by Struve, should never be forgotten ; and if they are forgotten by pa-

* Voison, on the Moral and Physical causes of Mental Maladies.
† Medico-Chirurgical Review, 1826.

rents, it is the imperative duty of the medical practitioner to point out the necessity of complying with them. We should operate upon the tender intellect of a child, by the gentlest progression. It must surely be more judicious to complete the instrument previous to its use, than to employ it in an imperfect state. It is the same with children as adults. In the cultivation of the mental powers, we are always to bear in mind the capability of the individual to answer the demands which are made upon him for exertion. It is not only irrational, but it is frequently destructive, to impose either upon the mind or body, but particularly upon the former, a load which it is incapable of supporting. It may be a source of consolation to those parents who are too apt to lament any apparent loss of time in the very early periods of life, that early acquirements are not to be gained without destruction of health, and that the future progress and mental powers of the individual depend upon the foundation which is laid in infancy, by judiciously adapting the studies of the child to its age and constitution. By premature efforts to improve the powers of the intellect, the organ in which they reside is exhausted. The practitioner, then, cannot too forcibly reprobate the pernicious enforcement of precocious studies. The injurious effects arising from the folly and false vanity of parents, who are ambitious of holding forth their children as specimens of extraordinary talent, are constantly presenting themselves to our view, in a train of nervous symptoms, and of susceptibility to ordinary impressions, which frequently pave the way to decided paroxysms of convulsions.' *

* Practical Observations on the Convulsions of Infants. By John North.

7

The same dangerous consequences, resulting from the premature development of the intellect, have often been noticed by medical men in the United States, and one of the most distinguished has thus happily referred to them, in a recent and able work.

'In an early age, before the organism has acquired its proper development, the brain its perfect consolidation, or the organs are confirmed in the order of their existence, premature exercises of the intellectual faculties are the source of many disorders. By the undue excitement of the brain, its organic functions are augmented unnaturally, the organic actions of the organs of nutrition, secretion, &c. are enfeebled ; the muscular system is stunted and debilitated ; the nervous system becomes morbidly irritable ; and the brain subject to a variety of affections. Those highly gifted with precocious intellects possess miserable health, and are generally short-lived ; they are cut off by chronic inflammations and disorganization of their viscera, or by acute inflammation of the brain.' *

* Principles of Medicine, founded on the structure and functions of the animal Organism. By Samuel Jackson, M. D.

NOTE. — The inutility of early cultivating the mind, and its evil results, have been noticed by observing men, not belonging to the medical profession. Cobbett. in his *Advice to Young Men*, a work abounding with most excellent remarks upon the *rearing* and education of children, observes, ' The mind, as well as the body, requires time to come to its strength ; and the way to have it possess, at last, its natural strength, is not to attempt to load i too soon ; and to favor it in its progress, by giving to the body good and plentiful food, sweet air, and abundant exercise, accompanied with as little discontent or uneasiness as possible. It is the first duty of a parent to secure to his children, if possible, sound and strong bodies.'

A distinguished and popular American author has advanced, in a late work of fiction, the following just opinion upon this subject . ' Knowledge should only keep pace with the natural growth of the human faculties. When I see a little urchin, who ought to be enjoying nature's holiday, and strengthening his constitution by wholesome exercise to bear the vicissitudes of the world in after times, kidnapped and sent to school, to sit on a bench for four or five hours together, employed in learning by rote what he is unable to comprehend, I cannot help contemplating him as the slave and the victim of the vanity of the parent, and the folly of the teacher. Such a system is only calculated to lay a foundation for disease and decrepitude, to stint the physical and intellectual growth, and to produce a premature old age of body and mind.'—*Paulding. Dutchman's Fire-side, Vol. I.*

SECTION V.

INFLUENCE OF MENTAL CULTIVATION AND MENTAL
EXCITEMENT, IN PRODUCING INSANITY, NERVOUS
AFFECTIONS, AND DISEASES OF THE HEART.

INTELLECTUAL cultivation, and powerful mental excitement, have a very important bearing upon one of
the most appalling and deplorable diseases which
afflicts humanity ; a disease which now prevails to a
great extent in this country, and is, I apprehend, increasing with fearful rapidity. The disease I allude to
is *insanity*, or disorder of the organ of the mind, which
produces a derangement in the manifestation of the
mental faculties.

We have no means of determining, correctly, the
number of insane persons in the United States ; but if
there are as many in the other states of the Union as
in Connecticut, the whole number cannot be less than
fifty thousand, or *one in every two hundred and sixty-
two* of the population, as is evident from the following
facts. In the year 1812, a committee was appointed
to ascertain the number of insane persons in the state
of Connecticut. This committee addressed letters to
physicians, and other persons in every town in the state,
requesting correct information upon this subject. They
received answers from *seventy towns*, and, after much
deliberation and inquiry, reported, they were ' satisfied

there were *one thousand* individuals within the bounds of the state, mentally deranged, and that the condition of many of them was truly deplorable.' On mentioning this statement, recently, to the distinguished physician of the *Retreat for the Insane*, at Hartford, and my surprise at the great number reported by the Committee, he assured me, it was less than he believed the actual number of insane persons in Connecticut. But if we admit there were 1000 individuals mentally deranged in 1812, or 1 in every 262 of the inhabitants, then there were more than twice as many in this deplorable condition as in any country in Europe, in proportion to the population. The number of the insane in England has increased within the last twenty years; still there are but about 14,000 in that country, one half of whom are idiots.

In Scotland, the proportion of insane to the population, is 1 to 574; and in the Agricultural districts of England, 1 to 820.* There is, however, more insanity in England than in any other country of Europe.

An inquiry, therefore, into the *causes* of so much insanity in this country becomes very important; and these causes must be sought among the agents that act upon the brain. I have already shown that insanity is a disease of the brain, and that whatever powerfully excites this organ, may so derange its action as to produce derangement of the mind. Sometimes it is occasioned by a *blow* or *fall* upon the head, at other times by inflammation or fever, which produces an unusual determination of blood to the brain. But far oftener this disease is occasioned by *moral causes*, by too

* Holiday.

7*

violent excitement of the mind, producing morbid action in some parts of the brain.

Thus we find that insanity prevails most in those countries where people enjoy civil and religious freedom, where every person has liberty to engage in the strife for the highest honors and stations in society, and where the road to wealth and distinction of every kind is equally open to all. There is but little insanity in those countries where the government is despotic. The inhabitants of such countries possess but little mental activity compared with those who live in a republic, or under a representative government. There is but little insanity in China, and travellers state that there is but little in Turkey. The disease is uncommon in Spain and also in Russia, out of the large cities. In France there is much less in the country than in the cities.* Humboldt states that he saw very few cases of mental derangement among the American Savages. In such countries the spirit of inquiry and improvement is seldom awakened, or is soon stifled when it is ; and the inhabitants exhibit but little more mental excitement than the brute creation.

In all countries, the disease prevails most among those whose minds are most excited. Aristotle noticed, in his day, the great prevalence of insanity among statesmen and politicians. It is said, the disease prevails most among those whose minds are excited by hazardous speculations, and by works of imagination and taste ; and but little among those whose minds are exercised only by calm inquiry. The registers of the Bicetre, in France, show, that the insane of the educated classes consist chiefly of priests, painters, sculp-

* Esquirol. Art. Folie. Vol. 16. Dictionaire des Sciences Medicales.

tors, poets, and musicians ; while no instance of the disease in naturalists, physicians, geometricians or chymists has occurred.*

In all ages and countries, insanity has prevailed most in times of great moral and mental com motion. The crusades, and the spirit of chivalry that followed them, the reformation of Luther, the civil and religious discords of Europe, the French Revolution, the American Revolution, greatly multiplied cases of insanity.† So true is it, that moral and mental causes excite this disease, that Esquirol says, he ' could give the history of the Revolution, from the taking of the Bastile until the last appearance of Bonaparte, by that of some Lunatics, whose insanity relates to the events which have distinguished this long period.'

Not only do the commotions which powerfully affect the minds of people occasion immediate insanity in adults, but they *predispose the next generation to this terrible disease ;* and this is a fact that deserves great consideration. Esquirol says that many women, strongly affected by the events of the Revolution, bore children, whom the *slightest cause rendered insane.* He is supported by others in this opinion, *that strong mental emotion of the mother predisposes the offspring to insanity.*

Children do not, indeed, often become insane, though they do occasionally, from strong mental excitement, and injudicious development of the moral faculties. Esquirol has seen children rendered insane by jealousy, by fear, and the severity of their parents; and Pinel has made the same observation. The former relates the case of a child, ' endowed with pre-

* Conolly.   † Esquirol, Rush, Voison.

cocious intelligence, with a head uncommonly large,' and who became mentally deranged at the age of eleven. He states, also, that he has known many students, animated by a desire to surpass their comrades, to become insane after pursuing severe studies. M. Foville says, he has seen a child of ten years of age, whom the assiduous reading of romances rendered insane. This child at last believed himself one of the heroes of the works he had read, and passed most of his time in striking the walls, trees, &c., which he took to be his enemies.*

But though mental excitement may not often produce insanity during childhood, it may predispose a person to this disease ; and I believe it does, by giving an early predominance to the nervous system. The following facts support this opinion. Van Swieten says, that nearly all insane persons have had convulsions when young ; and I have seen repeated instances in which premature exercise of the mental faculties appeared to be the predisposing cause of convulsions. I now know several boys, with large heads, and who are remarkable for the maturity of their understandings, and the great proficiency they have already made in their studies, whom slight exciting causes throw into convulsions.

In view of these few brief facts respecting *Insanity,* we are forced to believe, that among the causes of the great prevalence of this disease in this country, are the following : —

First, Too constant and too powerful excitement of the mind, which the strife for wealth, office, political

* Dictionaire de Medicine et de Chirurgie Pratiques, Vol. 1.

distinction, and party success produces in this free country.

Second, The predominance given to the nervous system, by too early cultivating the mind and exciting the feelings of children.

Third, Neglect of Physical education, or the equal and proper development 'of all the organs of the body.

Fourth, The general and powerful excitement of the female mind. Little attention is given in the education of females, to the physiological differences of the sexes. Teachers seldom reflect, that in them the nervous system naturally predominates ; that they are endowed with quicker sensibility, and far more active imagination, than men ; that their emotions are more intense, and their senses alive to more delicate impressions ; and they therefore require great attention, lest this exquisite sensibility, which, when properly and naturally developed, constitutes the greatest excellence of women, should either become *excessive* by too strong excitement, or suppressed by misdirected education. If here was the proper place, it would be easy to show that efforts to make females excel in certain qualities of mind which in men are considered most desirable, — to make them as capable as men, of long-continued attention to abstract truths, would be to act contrary to the dictates of nature, as manifested in their organization, and would tend to suppress all those finer sensibilities, which render them, in everything that relates to sentiment and affection, far superior to men.

But in general the mental peculiarities of the female mind are not regarded in education. Their intellectual powers are developed to the greatest degree, and thus their natural sensibility is changed or rendered excessive. This excessive sensibility is not always counteracted by bodily labor and exercise; for there is probably no country where women belonging to the wealthy class, exercise so little, especially in the open air, as in this. But they here participate more, perhaps, than in any other country, in the excitement of parties and sects, which, in beings whose nervous system is easily excited, is very likely to produce strong emotions; and, as I have shown, such emotions may have deplorable effects upon their offspring.

It is fearful to contemplate the excited state of mind which everywhere prevails throughout this republic, and the vast amount of *machinery*, if I may so say, which is in operation, to increase and perpetuate such excitement; and the little attention that has hitherto been given to the dangers it may produce. The following facts in reference to the city of Hartford, are probably applicable to many, if not most of the towns of the same size in the United States. This city contains about 7000 inhabitants. Nearly all, if not all, the children of the city, commence attending school as early as the age of three or four, and attend six hours each day, for several years. Nearly all attend school on the Sabbath, also.* Most families have a library,

* About 1200 children, between the ages of four and sixteen, belonging to the city of Hartford, attend school on the Sabbath, both in the forenoon and afternoon. Most of these children attend at church also. Thus they are kept at school and at church at least six hours every Sunday. I regard this confinement of the body and the application of the mind, as too great for young children any day of the week, and when we call to mind the fact, that most of them, especially the younger portion, attend school the other six days of the week, it appears to me, that every candid and reflecting person must perceive that it is a practice that ought in a great degree to be abandoned.

and books for children, besides newspapers and other periodicals. There are nine large churches in the city, belonging to six different denominations, exclusive of one for colored people. These are all well filled twice, and frequently three times, every Sunday. Besides, there are religious meetings on other days, amounting, in the various churches, to twenty or thirty during the week. There are two lyceums, or literary associations, both of which meet once a week, and are open to all, without expense. At one, are weekly debates, usually on some political or historical subject ; and at the other is a lecture every week, on such subject as the lecturer pleases. Both of these are well attended. Every week, *seven* large political newspapers, advocating the interests of three different parties, are published in Hartford; and also *five* large religious newspapers ; no two of which belong to the same sect. Several other periodicals are published here, but not weekly. In addition to the papers published in this town, men

I know, from my own observation and inquiry in Manchester, and other large towns in England, that Sunday Schools *there*, are among the best institutions ever devised. And I have no doubt they are of great service in many towns and sections of this country. I hope, in such places, Sunday Schools will be continued ; and that wherever children cannot attend school on other days in the week, that increased efforts will be made to have them instructed on Sunday. But I cannot believe that those children who attend school during the week, and at the church on Sunday, should also *attend school on that day*. I know not of any good reason for it, nor of any evidence that such a course has been serviceable to children.

Much has of late been said, and very justly, I think, of the necessity of resting from accustomed labor one day in seven, in order to preserve health. Why is not such rest necessary for children also ? But if Sunday Schools are to be continued, for those children who attend school every other day of the week, I hope that the afternoon session will be discontinued ; an alteration which has very wisely and very recently been made by the directors of the Sunday School attached to the largest religious society in the city of Hartford.

of business take one or more of those published in the larger cities, and most of the Reviews and Magazines of this country, and of England, are received here and read.*

The papers published in Hartford are not circulated at a great distance, but are intended for the population of the town and vicinity ; as the large villages in every section have papers published in their own town. From this statement, it is evident that the inhabitants of Hartford are supplied with more mental excitement from periodical literature, than many of the largest towns in Europe ; yes, even far more than is afforded to the inhabitants of Naples, Madrid, and Moscow.

If, therefore, constant mental excitement is ever or in any country dangerous, it is so now in this country, and cannot fail ultimately to have most disastrous consequences, demanding the attention of the patriot and the philanthropist.

It is a common and just observation, that the permanency of our republican institutions depends upon the intelligence and the virtue of the people ; but there may be other causes besides ignorance and vice, slowly and silently operating upon the physical man. which will *as certainly lead to the ruin of the country.* The decline of the Roman empire was marked by the general predominance of a nervous temperament, especially among the Roman ladies.

Cobbett attributes our superiority to the British, in the late war, to the greater strength of our soldiers. This

* On inquiry at the post-office, I learn that 80 daily, 110 semi-weekly, and 432 weekly newspapers, published in other places, are taken by the inhabitants of Hartford. Besides, more than $300 are annually received at the same office for postage on papers and pamphlets that are received irregularly.

superiority we should be careful to preserve, by the proper physical education of both sexes, when young; and by cultivating every part of man's nature, and not the mind exclusively.

There is another, and I fear a more frequent and fatal disease than that of insanity, caused by mental excitement; and which, judging from my own observation, and the records of cases in modern medical journals, appears to be increasing with frightful rapidity. I allude to organic diseases of the heart. The heart is a vital organ, and its sound state is essential to the possession of good health. When we reflect, therefore, upon the powerful influence which the feelings have upon this organ, the change from its natural action, caused by anger, fear, love, joy, avarice, ambition, envy, revenge, and all those passions and feelings that agitate civilized society, we shall not wonder that the diseases of the heart have increased in modern times. This disease has also increased in all countries during times of great political and moral commotion. Corvisart says, 'it was more frequent in the horrible times of the French Revolution than in the usual calm of social life.'

Testa, in a late work on diseases of the heart, states the same fact as regards agitated Italy. This author considers the powerful and irregular operation of the passions, as the most frequent cause of organic disease of the heart. Whoever reflects upon these facts, must feel the importance of cultivating a quiet state of mind in order to preserve good health. This is important at all times of life, but particularly so during childhood. It should be recollected that the early development of the mental powers of children awakens the passions

8

and appetites earlier than they would be, but for this premature mental cultivation, and therefore excites the heart while it is in a tender and delicate state. 'At Hofwyl more than one instance has occurred, in which it was necessary to diminish the amount of a pupil's intellectual efforts, in consequence of the alarming tendency to sensuality which it produced.' * But not only does strong mental emotion greatly endanger children, but it is to be feared that the emotions of the mother may predispose her offspring to disease. This is the opininion of Corvisart, Esquirol, and many other very accurate observers. I must therefore repeat what I have elsewhere said, that the powerful and constant excitement of the minds of the females of this country, together with their neglect of proper physical education, threatens dangerous consequences. Whoever notices their general attendance at meetings where strong feelings are awakened, and perpetuated for weeks and months, by very frequent meetings, especially in the night; and witnesses their violent emotions, and knows anything of the effect of excited mind and agitated feelings upon a delicate bodily organization, must, on reflection, fear, not only for the injury which such procedure must inflict upon the females themselves, but for that which may be entailed upon the generation to come. I believe these few hints are, at the present time, deserving the serious consideration of all who have influence to perpetuate or allay the excitement alluded to.

* Annals of Education, 1833.

SECTION VI.

THE remarks which I have made respecting the danger of too early cultivating the intellectual faculties,
do not fully apply to the development of the moral
qualities ; though in regard to them some caution is
necessary ; for danger is to be apprehended from strongly exciting the feelings of children and awakening their
passions.   In endeavoring to call forth and cultivate
those moral qualities which are good, and to suppress
the bad, we should constantly keep in mind, that the
brain is not only the seat of the intellectual faculties,
but is also the agent by which the passions, the affections, and all the moral qualities, are manifested.   That
this is true, is shown in the same way as I have proved
that the brain is the material organ of the mind.   Insanity alone furnishes abundant proof.   This disease
of the brain as often deranges the moral as the intellectual faculties.   Some insane persons are remarkable
for great irascibility, others for pride, courage, hatred
&c., while others are affectionate, timid irresolute,
and melancholy.   Dr. Rush mentions the case of a
young lady who was insane for a considerable time,
during which she hated her father : after some time
she recovered a sound mind in every other respect
but this ; and at last her complete recovery was marked
by a return of her filial attachment.   This state of
mind undoubtedly arose from deranged action of some

portion of the brain, produced, perhaps, by neglecting to develope every part of the brain in a proper manner, or from inattention to the premonitory symptoms of this disease ; for insanity is usually preceded by some slight irregularity in the intellectual or moral faculties. ' Some of the insane,' says Esquirol, ' are distinguished from infancy, for excessive pride, anger, melancholy,' &c. These tendencies not having been arrested or counteracted by the judicious development of opposite qualities, the action of the brain finally became more irregular, and then what is called insanity was produced. But to the accurate observer, partial insanity existed long before this, though the conduct it occasioned was considered merely singularity, eccentricity, &c. But this singularity, or, as some call it, perversity of disposition, arises from the predominance of the action of some organ of the brain, and may often be corrected by care and attention.

The great object, therefore, in moral education should be, to call into repeated action those organs that manifest the good qualities, and increase their activity and power. For this purpose, it is necessary to study the characters of children when quite young ; and when certain moral qualities appear to predominate, that are likely to produce bad traits of character, great efforts should be made to develope and call into activity opposite qualities : when a child appears exceedingly selfish, he should be taught and accustomed to practise benevolence. In this manner, it is as certain that the moral qualities which are most desirable may be cultivated and made predominant, as that the memory may be increased by exercise.*

* Voison.

Such effects cannot, however, be produced by *precepts* alone. Children should be induced to *practise* the virtues which it is intended they shall possess, and by *practice* they should be endowed with good propensities and good habits. If parents would but feel that it is as essential to teach a child to practise the virtues that are desirable, as it is to cultivate the mind, and would give as much attention to the early development and proper exercise of the affections and passions, and take that pains to develope all the natural excellencies of his character they do to accelerate his progress in knowledge, we should soon see a great and pleasing change in the dispositions and conduct of men. But now, in very many families, the greatest praise is not bestowed upon those children that are merely *good*, but upon those whose minds are most active and premature.* In schools, much of the

---

* ' How many parents do we see, who, after teaching their sons, by example, everything which is licentious in manners, and lavishing on them the means of similar licentiousness, are rigid only in one point — in the strictness of that intellectual discipline, which may prepare them for the worldly stations to which the parental ambition has been unceasingly looking for them, before the filial ambition was rendered sufficiently intent of itself! To such persons, the mind of the little creature whom they are training to worldly stations for worldly purposes, is an object of interest only as that without which it would be impossible to arrive at the dignities expected. It is a necessary instrument for becoming rich and powerful; and, if he could become powerful, and rich, and envied, without a soul, they would scarcely feel that he was a being less noble than now. In what they term education, they have never once thought, that the *virtues* were to be included as objects; and they would truly feel something very like astonishment, if they were told that the first and most essential part of the process of educating the moral being, whom Heaven had consigned to their charge, was yet to be begun — in the abandonment of their own vices, and the purification of their own heart, by better feelings than those which had corrupted it, — without which primary self-amendment, the very authority which is implied in the noble office which they were to exercise, might be a source, not of good, but of evil, to him who was *unfortunately* born to be its subject.' — *Brown's Philosophy, Vol. 2.*

praise and censure, reward and punishment, connected with early mental culture is calculated to awaken rivalry, envy and hatred. Moral culture is sacrificed, in early life, to intellectual, and the bad passions are called forth to aid the mind's improvement; and then what originates from a faulty or neglected moral education is considered the fault of nature itself. But nature has not had fair play.

Example is also of great importance in the education of children, in consequence of their natural propensity to imitation. The influence of this strong propensity is not sufficiently attended to by parents and teachers. Dugald Stewart has very ably treated this subject, and shown its great importance in education.* Not only should the propensity of the youth to imitation be regarded in teaching 'accomplishments, and everything connected with grace, but in forming the moral character also. Every person knows that ' the imitation of any *expression* strongly marked by the countenance and gestures of another person, has a tendency to excite, in some degree, the corresponding

---

* See his Elements of the Philosophy of the Human Mind, Vol. 3. Chapter on the Principle of Law of Sympathetic Imitation. The whole chapter is very deserving of attention. After remarking that this principle has important effects in relation to our moral constitution, he adds, 'The reflection which Shakspeare puts into the mouth of Falstaff, with respect to the manners of Justice Shallow and his attendants, and which Sir John expresses with all the precision of a philosophical *observer*, and all the dignity of a moralist, may be extended to the most serious concerns of life. 'It is a wonderful thing to see the semblable coherence of his men's spirits and his : they, by observing of him, do bear themselves like foolish Justices ; he, by conversing with them, is turned into a justice-like serving-man. Their spirits are so married in conjunction, with the participation of society, that they flock together in concert, like wild geese. It is certain that *either wise bearing or ignorant carriage is caught, as men take disease ;* therefore, let men take heed of their company.'

passion in our own minds;' * and when it is considered how prone children are to imitation, we shall feel the importance of habitually exhibiting, both in looks and actions, only such feelings as we wish them to possess. Parents who are constantly manifesting fretful and unhappy dispositions, will do much towards producing like dispositions in their children. From these observations, those who have the care of educating children, cannot fail to see the importance of the examples they set them; they will also reflect that whatever is inculcated upon children by precept is of trifling consequence, compared with that which they learn by example; and if they wish to have their children possess a spirit of benevolence, kindness or humility, they must cherish an dcultivate these virtues in themselves, and be particularly careful not to let any contradiction exist between their expressed opinions of the value of these dispositions and their own habitual conduct.

* Stewart.

SECTION VII.

THE CULTIVATION OF THE MIND AT A PROPER TIME OF LIFE, NOT INJURIOUS BUT BENEFICIAL TO HEALTH.

THIS is evident, first from theory. In order to have good health, it is necessary that every organ of the body should not only be well developed, but should also be exercised. We know that if the muscles of the body are not exercised, they not only cease to grow, but that they shrink, and their power, energy, and activity are diminished. This is also the case with the brain, and every other organ of the body. If the functions of the brain are not exercised, the brain diminishes in size. Hence idiots usually have a diminished, *atrophied* brain.* When any organ diminishes for want of proper exercise, the whole system sympathizes, and thus the health becomes impaired. From this view of the subject I cannot doubt but that the exercise of the intellect tends to procure and perpetuate sound health.

But this is also proved by facts. Literary men, says M. Brunaud in his *Hygiene des gens des lettres,* have in all countries usually been long-lived. The class of learned men who have lived more than *seventy years,* includes the most distinguished that have ever existed.†

* Andral's Pathological Anatomy.
† See Table at the end of the volume.

Of one hundred and fifty-two *savans*, taken at hazard, one half from the Academy of Belles Lettres, the other from that of Sciences of Paris, it was found that the sum of years lived among them was 10,511, or above *sixty-nine* years to each man. Many of the most learned men now living, are very aged.*

The general increase of knowledge and civilization, has greatly increased good health, and prolonged human life. The discovery of the *kine pock*, by Jenner, the invention of the *safety lamp*, by Sir H. Davy, and other scientific discoveries, undoubtedly save tens of thousands of human lives yearly. The increase of knowledge has also led men, in modern times, to build hospitals and charitable institutions for the sick, the young, and the aged ; and thus life has been preserved and prolonged. The march of mind has also dispelled numerous superstitions, which formerly destroyed, in one way and another, an immense number of human beings.†

Intellectual cultivation has contributed to the preservation of the lives of men, by giving a predominance to the reasoning powers over the sensual. Thus we find that the inhabitants of the most civilized countries live the longest. Savages are usually more feeble than

* The declaration of American Independence was signed by 56 delegates — 35 from the Northern, and 21 from the Southern States. But *one* survives, and only *two* have died from accident. The whole number of years lived by these delegates, not including the two mentioned, is 3,609 ; or 66 years and 9 months each. Those from the northern states average 70 years and a half, and those from the states at the south, a little less than 60.

† It has been computed, that, in the course of *one century*, 100,000 human beings were put to death for witchcraft in Germany, 30,000 in England, and more in Scotland. This delusion respecting witches, was chiefly dispelled by the increase of science. — *See Scott, and others, on Witchcraft.*

civilized nations. 'Le Pere Fauque, who lived much among them, says he scarcely saw an old man; Raynal asserts the same of the savages of Canada ; Cooke and La Perouse of those of the north-west coast of America; Mungo Park of the Negroes ; and Bruce of the Abyssynians.'*

In all countries, the mortality has lessened in proportion to the advance of civilization, and is now the greatest in those regions where the inhabitants approach the nearest to the barbarous state. 'At Geneva, good mortuary tables have been preserved since 1560. From these it appears, that, in the seventeenth century, the probability of life was about eleven and a half years ; in the eighteenth century it increased to above twenty-seven years. In the space of about three hundred years, the probability of life to a citizen of Geneva, at his birth, has become five times greater. The *mean life*, in one century, was eighteen years ; in the next it grew to twenty-three ; and finally, during the present century, from 1815 to 1826, it amounts to thirty-six years.' † The expectation, or mean term of life of a Roman citizen, from the time of Servius Tullius to Justinian, was *thirty years ;* but, according to Mr. Finlayson, the expectation of life for the easy classes of England is 1 in 50, and for the whole mass of the population, 1 in 45.

England is superior in salubrity to any other country in Europe. The average mortality throughout the whole of England and Wales, has been, of late years, about 1 in 60 ; but in 1810 it was 1 in 50 ; in 1800

* Foreign Quarterly Review.

† Elements of Medical Statistics, by F. Bisset Hawkins, M. D. London, 1829.

it was 1 in 47 ; and in 1780 the ratio of death was 1 in 40.* In London, the annual mortality in the middle of the last century was 1 in 20 ; it is now 1 in 40. That of Glasgow is 1 in 44.† In the first half of the 18th century, the proportion of deaths to births, in London, was as 3 to 2 ; but since 1800, the number of deaths is less than that of births, as 12 to 15. Other countries and cities in Europe have likewise improved in the ratio of mortality. In *France*, in 1780, the deaths annually were 1 in 30 ; but, during the eight years previous to 1824, 1 in 40, or one fourth less. From the census of the population in 1817, it appears that the average annual difference between the deaths and the births for the eight following years, is nearly 200,000 in favor of the latter. ‡

Much of this decrease of mortality is no doubt owing to the increase of wealth, which has supplied all classes with the necessaries of life better than formerly ; but as much, I apprehend, is owing to the increase of knowledge, and to the abandonment of vicious habits, — to the predominance which education has given to the rational over the sensual man.

* Pembrokeshire and Anglesey have one death yearly, in 83 individuals — the lowest rate of mortality that has been known in Europe. There is perhaps no section of the United States where the annual mortality is less than this. In several towns on Connecticut River, in the state of Massachusetts, the average annual mortality for the last fifteen years, is 1 in 81. Our large cities are not more healthy than many of the largest in England. The average number of deaths in Philadelphia for the last ten years, is 1 in 38.85, annually ; but for the fourteen years previous, the mortality was as low as 1 in 47.86 of the population. — *See Emerson's Medical Statistics, American Journal of the Medical Sciences*, 1831.

† Hawkins.

‡ Discours sur les Ameliorations Progressives de la Sante Publique, par l'influence de la civilization. Par F. Berard.

Notwithstanding the still great prevalence of sensuality in civilized countries, history shows that formerly it was far greater, and more general, and has decreased as civilization has advanced. For proof of this, examine historically the prevalence of almost any sensual and vicious propensity, the indulgence of which tends to shorten life, and it will be found to have been formerly far greater than now. Take the vice of drunkenness, which, as every one knows, has destroyed innumerable human beings; and history will show, that in proportion as men and nations have become enlightened, they have regarded this vice as more odious. Savages are generally prone to intoxication. They regard drunkenness as bliss, and will part with anything they have for rum.

The ancient Greeks worshipped Bacchus, the god of wine ; and in Silenus we see the image of drunkenness ; and in many of their statues we observe representations of most beastly intoxication. So great, for a while, were the evils from intemperance, in Greece, that some rulers condemned to death those found intoxicated. Lycurgus destroyed all the vines of the country, and made slaves drunk, and exhibited them in this state, in order to deter youth from intemperance. The Romans had more than two hundred different kinds of intoxicating liquors, and drank them to excess. The ancient Germans, and the former inhabitants of all the northern countries were greatly addicted to drunkenness. For centuries, no one thought of the impropriety of drinking to excess : the only concern respecting intoxicating liquors, was how to procure them ; and for this purpose they roamed about like the beasts of the forests, and even invaded Italy to procure them by force.

On the revival of literature, after the dark ages, intemperance in drinking was exceedingly prevalent; but, as men became more enlightened, they had recourse to measures calculated to prevent it. And it is a curious fact, that in the fifteenth and sixteenth centuries, *Temperance Societies* were formed by the most intelligent and influential men, for the purpose of stopping intemperance in drinking. One was called the Society of St. Christopher, others were called Temperance Societies, and the members of one took the appropriate name of the *Golden Band.* These societies were productive of great good; they augmented industry, and contributed to the improvement of manners, and the establishment of good order.

As respects intemperance in England, if we go back but one hundred years, we shall find it far more general than at present. One hundred years ago there was scarcely a store in London where intoxicating liquors were not kept for sale. The physicians of London at that time stated to Parliament, that the victims of intemperance were exceedingly numerous; and this caused the number of dram-shops to be limited by law. The French were once exceedingly addicted to intoxication : their rulers enacted many and severe laws to repress the habit; destroying all the vines of the country — imprisonment — whipping — cutting off the ears of those found intoxicated, were successively resorted to, but with little effect towards arresting the evil. The age of Louis XIV, by creating a taste for intellectual and refined pleasures, did more to arrest intemperance in France, than all the laws of former rulers.*

* For the evidence of the truth of these statements respecting the history of intemperance, the reader is referred to the accounts

9

It is to the influence which a taste for intellectual pursuits exerts, that we must look to effect and perpetuate a deliverance from sensuality. It was, in fact, increased intelligence and a growing love for intellectual enjoyment that enabled the people of this country to produce the reformation which they have produced, in the use of intoxicating drink. Temperance Societies, to be sure, did much good; but they were an *effect*, themselves, of the more general diffusion and love of knowledge, and could not have been sustained thirty years ago, nor by a people less intelligent.

The cultivation of a taste for intellectual amusements, is a matter of national importance, and deserves all encouragement. Madam De Staël has said that when the amusements of a people become not only harmless but useful, they will be in the right way to attain all the perfection of which they are capable; and we know that on the kind of amusements which young people seek, often depends their future destiny in life. Let, therefore, great attention be given to render the amusements of youth such as will be conducive to mental improvement. They should be seduced, if I may so say, from the haunts of the sensual, by judicious books, pleasing and instructive conversation, well-regulated lyceums, and literary associations; and made to prefer the acquisition of knowledge to the gratification of their appetites. It is thus that I conceive the cultivation of the mind, at a proper time of life, contributes to produce good health, not only by duly

of travellers among the Indians, and in Liberia, Africa, &c. To ancient historians, as Diodorus, Cæsar, Tacitus, Pliny, Plutarch, and others. See also article *Ivrognerie*, Dictionaire Des Sciences Medicales, from which I have selected most of the foregoing facts.

exercising one of the most important organs of the body, but by placing reason and conscience on the throne. Hitherto the conduct of many people, in all countries, has been regulated more by their appetites and passions, than by their deliberate opinions of what was right; but the cultivation of the mind will give men more power to lessen the influence of their sensual propensities.

But to give this power to men, it is not necessary nor proper to commence with the infant, and task his feeble powers of mind and injure his physical development.

It is, in fact, lamentable to see the labor of a *steam engine,* as regards the improvement of the mind, put upon young and delicate children for a number of years; and when they become young men and women, but little or no attention given to their further improvement. It is not uncommon to see those whose early years were almost wholly devoted to study, pass weeks and months, in after life, without attempting to improve their minds by reading or study. They do not attempt *self-education ;* that education which is the best of all, and the only education that is generally of much use, and which every person, by the aid of books, can now obtain. The school-master is abroad, and does much good, but our youth should not suppose that they can learn nothing without his aid. To greater effect, at the present time, is the book-publisher abroad, and tenders to all education, amusement, knowledge and power.

The history of the most distinguished men teaches us, that not to early school education, but to *self-education,* in after life, were they indebted for the development of their great powers. It is surprising, considering the number of such instances, that men have not attached more importance to the last, and less to the former than they have. A late writer,* of superior capacity, has thus alluded to this subject in her remarks on the *Genius of Walter Scott.*

In speaking of his early education, she says, ' Here is a boy lying about in the fields, when he should have been at his Latin grammar ; reading novels when he should have been entering college ; spearing salmon instead of embellishing a peroration. Yet this personage came out of this wild kind of discipline, graced with the rarest combination of qualifications for enjoying existence, achieving fame, and blessing society. Deeply learned, though neither the languages, nor the philosophy of the schools, made part of his acquisition ; *robust* as a ploughman ; able to walk like a pedlar ; industrious as a handicraftsman ; intrepid as the bravest hero of his own immortal works. Here is enough to put us on inquiring, not whether learning, and even school discipline, be good things ; but whether the knowledge usually thought most essential, the school discipline which is commonly esteemed indispensable, be in fact either the one or the other.'

I hope that the view I have taken of mental cultivation, while it may tend to suppress an inordinate desire for acquiring knowledge from books and schools, during infancy and childhood, may serve to stimulate all those who have passed their youth, and possess good health, to apply themselves with great vigor to mental labor and improvement. Although they may have had but little early education, yet they should be encouraged to persevere in the acquisition of knowledge,

* Harriet Martineau.

by the reflection, that the men most celebrated in all departments of learning, had but little education in early life. This is strikingly true of the great and useful men of this country, both of the past and present time.

A taste for reading is one of the most desirable that we ever form, and could we believe, with Montesquieu, that ' reading is a never-failing remedy for all the ills of life,' or with our illustrious Jefferson, that ' but for books, life would scarcely be worth having,' we should none of us neglect cultivating this taste and urging others to do likewise.*

* Since writing the foregoing, I have read the following remarks upon the same subject. in a sermon by the Rev. Robert Hall, On THE ADVANTAGES OF KNOWLEDGE TO THE LOWER CLASSES.

' The acquisition of knowledge, by multiplying the mental resources, has a tendency to exalt the character, and in some measure to correct and subdue the taste for gross sensuality. The poor man who can read, and who possesses a taste for reading, can find entertainment at home without being tempted to repair to the public house for that purpose. He does not lie prostrate and afloat on the current of incidents, liable to be carried whithersoever the impulse of appetite may direct. The man who has gained a taste for books, will, in all likelihood, become thoughtful ; and when you have given the poor the habit of thinking, you have conferred on them a much greater favor than by the gift of a large sum of money ; since you have put them in possession of the *principle* of all legitimate prosperity. I am persuaded that the extreme profligacy, improvidence, and misery, which are so prevalent among the laboring classes in many countries, are chiefly to be ascribed to the want of education.'

SECTION VIII.

INFLUENCE OF MENTAL CULTIVATION IN PRODUCING
DYSPEPSIA IN LITERARY MEN — IRRITATION OF
THE BRAIN THE MOST FREQUENT CAUSE OF THIS
DISEASE.

THE numerous treatises on dyspepsia, published of
late, testify to its general prevalence, and its increase.
That many of these treatises have done some good, I
have no doubt ; that some dyspeptics have been benefited by the directions given in books, is very certain ;
yet I have not seen any work upon this subject, the
writer of which appeared fully aware of what, according to my observation, is the most frequent cause of
this disease in literary men, and consequently the
proper remedies have not always been recommended.
For a great many years, dyspepsia was considered not
only to be a disease of the stomach, but to consist in
' debility of the stomach ; ' and bitters, tonics, and
stimulants were the medicines prescribed to cure it.

But the disciples of a new school in medicine, who
profess to found their opinions upon Pathological appearances, have taught us very different doctrines.
They say that this disease is closely allied to inflammation of the digestive organs, and recommend low
diet, bleeding, &c. as remedies.

No doubt there are cases in which the tonic and stimulating plan is proper and serviceable ; while there are others in which it would be exceedingly injurious — cases in which a directly opposite method of treatment would be beneficial. As a general rule, I am of opinion that the last practice is the best — that more cases of dyspepsia require low, unirritating diet, than bitters and stimulants.

Both kinds of practice are founded, however, upon what I conceive to be an erroneous opinion respecting the origin and most frequent cause of this disease. Dyspepsia is generally considered a disease of the stomach primarily. But I apprehend that in a majority of cases, especially among students, it is primarily a disease of the brain and nervous system, and is perpetuated by mental excitement.

Among the reasons I have for this opinion, independent of my own experience, are the following.

First. A blow or other injury of the head, or a tumor in the brain, frequently produces sickness, irritation of the stomach, and all the symptoms of dyspepsia.

Second. Dyspepsia ' may be produced by mental affections,' says Dr. Parry ; and in this opinion he is supported by numerous observers. Who is there that has not felt the influence of bad news, or mental agitation, in destroying the appetite and deranging digestion, and thus producing dyspepsia for a short time ?

Third. Insanity, or disease of the brain, is usually preceded by the symptoms of dyspepsia, and recovery from mental derangement is often marked by a return of these symptoms.

During the paroxysm or continuance of insanity, the brain alone appears affected ; but at other times, when the brain is relieved, the stomach is affected. I am aware that Broussais and others say, that in such cases the disorder of the stomach is the primary affection, and is truly chronic inflammation of the stomach ; which, after continuing a considerable time, stimulates the brain until madness is produced. But the same able observer says, that the insanity is preceded by long-continued hypochondriasis, and other nervous affections, which I suppose to arise from disease of the brain, and not of the stomach, as he affirms. He refers to instances of melancholy, from nostalgia, unrequited love, loss of fortune, mortified pride, &c. ; but which did not amount to insanity until after long-continued disorder of the stomach. He supposes that in such cases, the violence of the reaction from the disease of the stomach produces insanity ; but to me it appears more rational to suppose, that the irritation of the brain, produced by the *moral* cause, not only caused the disorder of the digestive organs, but by its continuance, increased the disease of the brain to such a degree as to cause mental derangement ; just as we see a blow on the head produce at first, only slight sickness of the stomach, and vomiting, but followed by violent delirium. From the cases which Broussais has given, it evidently appears that slight irritation of the brain from mental or other causes, gives rise to derangement of the stomach, and produces the ordinary symptoms of dyspepsia.*

Mr. Abernethy refers to cases somewhat similar ; but his peculiar and extravagant notion, of the vast influence of the stomach in the animal economy, causes

---

* Broussais, De L'Irritation et De La Folie.

him to overlook that of other organs. He says, however, ' there is no hurt of the head that does not affect the digestive organs ;' but adds, ' if these are not attended to, people will go into a complete state of hypochondriasis, and therefore I am sure the recovery of the functions of the brain mainly depends upon the digestive organs.'* That it is important to attend to the digestive organs, in injuries of the head, or of any other part of the body, I have no doubt ; but I cannot believe that it is as important as to attend to the diseased organ itself. No one rule, relating to the cure of disease, is more important, than that which teaches, to let a diseased organ *rest*. If, therefore, the brain is injured by a blow, or becomes irritated by disease, or excited by passion or mental anxiety, it should be permitted to remain in a quiet state. I have already shown in a former part of this work, that a quiet state of mind is essential to recovery from wounds of the head ; but this state of mind is equally essential when the brain is in an irritable state, from severe study, or from the violence of passion, and it is a neglect of this, which, as I conceive, causes innumerable nervous complaints and diseases of other organs, with which the brain sympathises.

I very much doubt whether *sick-headache* as often arises from disordered stomach, as from irritated brain. I have repeatedly noticed an attack of sick-headache, after indulging in stimulating food and drinks in the evening ; but I have known the headache prevented, by keeping the head *cool* after an evening's debauch.

* Lectures on Anatomy, Surgery, and Pathology, Vol. 2.

Dr. James Johnson says that Mr. Weeks of Jamaica, when intoxicated, always went to sleep with his head in cold water, in order to prevent headache ; and it is a common practice in India, and some other places, after drinking what is called a *musquito dose* of brandy, to sleep with the head on a wet pillow, and thus subsequent headache is prevented. I have known this practice resorted to, and with like effect. But if the pain of the head is caused by indigestion, what possible efficacy can there be in keeping the head cool? I conceive, however, that the increased action of the blood-vessels during sleep, produced by the stimulating food or liquor, determines an unusual quantity of blood to the brain, irritates it, and this irritation of the brain produces the pain of the head, sickness and disorder of the stomach. I have noticed, moreover, that this disease most frequently affects those whose nervous systems are delicate and easily excited ; and I have often known it produced by grief or great mental anxiety ; and it is seldom relieved without rest or long abstinence.

Fourth. Examination of the bodies of those who have died, after long continued dyspeptic symptoms, confirms the opinion I have advanced, that dyspepsia is often a disease of the head, and not of the stomach. Dr. Abercrombie, *On Organic Diseases of the Brain*, says, that 'Symptoms which really depend upon disease of the brain, are very apt to be referred to the stomach.' After mentioning several cases, in which for a long time the prominent symptoms were those of dyspepsia, and in which no trace of organic disease of the stomach was discovered after death, but tumors, or other disease of the brain, he says, ' Many other cases of organic disease of the brain are on record, in which the only morbid appearances were in the head, though some of the most prominent symptoms had been in the stomach. Some of these resembled what has been called sick-headache, others were chiefly distinguished by remarkable disturbances of the digestive functions.' Dr. A. adds this important caution :—' In cases of this class we must beware of being misled, in regard to the nature of the complaint, by observing that the symptoms in the stomach are alleviated by attention to regimen, or by treatment directed to the stomach itself. If digestion be impeded, from whatever cause, these uneasy symptoms in the stomach may be alleviated by great attention to diet, but no inference can be drawn from this source, in regard to the cause of the derangement.'

This last quotation, I think explains a very common mistake — a mistake which is not only made by dyspeptics themselves, but by writers on this disease. They suppose because *low diet*, &c. relieves the principal symptoms in the stomach, that therefore the disease is confined to that organ ; when in fact the disease is in the head, but is manifested only by the stomach, the liver, or some organ with which the brain sympathises, and the *low diet* gives relief, by lessening the too energetic action of the brain.

Dr. Hastings, of England, has called attention to this subject, in the *Midland Medical and Surgical Register* of 1831. He says, that not unfrequently cases occur, which exhibit symptoms of disordered stomach, accompanied by increased determination of blood to the head, alternate flushings and coldness, irregular spirits, &c.; and he states that in all the cases which terminated fatally, under his care, he found thickening of the membranes of the brain, and marks of chronic inflammation within the head. Dr. H. believes that many of the nervous symptoms of which dyspeptic persons complain are produced by slow alteration of the membranes of the brain, in consequence of chronic inflammation; and recommends leeches, cold applications to the head, and issues in the neck, for the relief of such cases. In the *Medico Chirurgical Review* for 1826, is a case, quoted from Dr. Chambers, of a woman treated, at St. George's Hospital, for an affection of the stomach, of which organ she had chiefly complained. After death, no appearance of disease was found in the stomach or bowels, but several tumors, besides other marks of disease were found in the brain.

M. Bayle has published in the *Revué Medicale*, several cases, exhibiting the connexion between disease of the brain and disorder of the stomach. He endeavors to show that disease of the stomach often produces insanity; but he mentions that many of his patients were remarkable for violent temper, or were melancholy, or exhibited some symptoms of nervous irritation, before they were much unwell; then the stomach became disordered, and finally derangement of the mind ensued. On dissection, the brain and its membranes were found diseased; and here I apprehend was the original seat of the complaint, (produced probably by some moral cause,) which first manifested itself in change of temper, or slight nervous affections; then, as it increased, disordered the stomach by sympathy, and finally produced so much disease of the brain as to cause insanity.

Dr. Burrows relates the case of a lady, who had been unwell for several years. She referred all her suffering to the stomach, and often said, that when she was dead, *there* would be found the seat of her disorder. She died rather suddenly with fever and delirium, after exposure in a very hot day ; and on examining the body, no trace of disease appeared in the stomach or bowels, but the brain exhibited marks of *long standing disease.* *

Some cases and observations in a late work of M. Barras,† confirm the opinion I have advanced respecting the cause and seat of dyspepsia, though this writer does not believe, with M. Broussais and others, that it is an inflammatory disease, but that it consists in an affection of the nerves of the stomach, or what Dr. Johnson calls *morbid sensibility* of the stomach, bowels, &c. He considers the disease to be a *gastralgia,* and not gastritis. But what causes this gastralgia, or morbid sensibility of the stomach ? An attentive examination of the cases he has cited, will show that, very probably, the first cause of morbid action was a *moral one.* Most of the patients whose cases he relates, were of an irritable, nervous temperament, and previous to any symptoms of disease of the stomach, they had ' experienced severe domestic affliction,' had been ' melancholy,' or been afflicted by ' great mental suffering,' or had ' studied severely, or been exposed to constant turmoils.' When such cases terminated

---

* Burrows on Insanity, p. 236.

† Traite sur les Gastralgies et les Enteralgies, ou Maladies Nerveuses de l'Estomac et des Intestins. Par J. P. T. Barras, M. D.

fatally, no marks of disease were found in the stomach; but effusion, or other signs of disease were observed in the brain.

M. Broussais has also given much attention to diseases of the stomach, and refers to cases which were characterized by dyspeptic symptoms, which he thinks arose from inflammation of the stomach, but which appear to me to have been produced by mental agitation.* He says himself, that he has often seen diarrhœa, colic, and other disorders of the digestive organs, caused by grief, fright, and mental suffering. He also says, that cerebral ' irritation will produce gastric irritation, and even a certain degree of inflammation of the stomach.' Still he asserts, that ' most encephalic phlegmasiae are usually induced by gastric irritation.' I cannot but believe that this observation is incorrect, and that M. Broussais was led to make it in consequence of certain opinions which he has formed respecting the frequency of gastric inflammation, and its influence in producing sympathetic disease : opinions which I think are not fully supported by facts. From the history which he has given, of cases of supposed gastritis, or inflammation of the stomach, we learn that the disorder of the stomach was often preceded by symptoms of disease o the head, such as slight mental aberration, melancholy, epilepsy, convulsions, &c. Some of his patients had studied severely, others had long been hypochondriacal, while others were homesick ; and as his patients were mostly soldiers, many of them conscripts, it is not improbable that they had experienced severe moral suffering. He

See History of Chronic Phlegmasiae, by F. J. V. Broussais, M. D.

cites the case of M. Beau, as one of acute gastritis ; but states, that the patient, previous to his illness,
had manifested a *great passion for study, to which he
had often sacrificed the hours destined to repose.* This
case terminated fatally, and on dissection, marks of
disease were found in the stomach ; but he says also,
that ' he was struck with the density, as well as with
the injection of the cerebral substance.' Still he refers to this case, as one which ' presents a vivid picture
of the disorder that inflammation of the stomach may
occasion in the functions of the economy.' But to me
this is a case which exhibits the influence of diseased
and over-excited brain, on the system, even according
to his own doctrines. He elsewhere says that ' everything which only exercises thought by requiring a
lively and constant attention, keeps up in the brain
a state of vital erection, by which it is sensibly transformed into a permanent focus of irritation. Such
individuals become exceedingly irritable, and easily
contract inflammations through the influence of food,
drinks, atmospherical vicissitudes, &c.' He has also
abundantly proved, that ' an organ which at first is only
affected by sympathy, may become organically diseased by the effect of pain.' *

This was the case, I conceive, with M. Beau. Long
continued and severe study, especially in the night,
during the time that ought to have been devoted to
rest, produced an irritated state of the brain, which
caused sympathetic disease of the stomach, and subsequent inflammation and disorganization. No doubt
the case was aggravated, as M. Broussais supposes, by

* See his Examination of Medical Doctrines, and Treatise on
Physiology applied to Pathology.

too stimulating regimen; but I apprehend it was not first induced by irritating the stomach by food or drink, but by irritating the brain by too severe study.

Fifth. The fact that dyspepsia is frequently cured by permitting the over-tasked and tired brain to rest, or by changing the mental labor or excitement, is evidence that it is primarily a disease of the head, and not of the stomach. How often do physicians fail to afford any relief by medicines, in what are called '*stomach affections*,' but which are readily cured by travelling, or relaxation in accustomed studies, and freedom from care and anxiety! How often a change of the mental excitement affords relief. It seems as if certain portions of the brain having been unduly excited, became diseased, and were benefited by strong excitement of other portions of the same organ. How often are *stomach* affections cured by inert medicines, aided by the imagination, confidence, hope, &c.

What is it but the influence of the mind that gives efficacy to remedies that are secret, which they do not possess when known? Who now goes to Mr. Halsted for the cure of disease of the stomach, or has recourse to *kneading the bowels* to cure it? but who will deny, that before Mr. H. *unfortunately* published his method of cure, a vast many *nervous* people were relieved and cured by him? By some, the relief which Mr. Halsted afforded, would be considered proof that dyspepsia is certainly a disease of the stomach; but to me, it is evidence that the *stomach complaints* he cures, were affections of the organ of the mind, and which the influence of the imagination, hope, faith, &c., relieved. 'There is nothing new under the sun'—or certainly not in Mr. Halsted's method of curing stomach complaints and nervous affections, by *kneading the bowels.* It is but *Mesmerism* revived and revised. In the very able Report, drawn up by M. Bailly, in the name of a Committee of the Faculty of Medicine and of the Academy of Sciences, appointed by the King, to examine into the reality and utility of *animal magnetism,* of which Committee our illustrious Franklin was a member, it is stated : — ' But more than in any other way, patients are magnetized by the application of the hands, and by pressure of the fingers on the middle and sides of the abdomen, — applications often continued for a long time, sometimes for several hours.' That an immense number were cured of stomach complaints and nervous diseases by this procedure, no one will doubt, who examines the records of *Mesmerism.* But the learned Committee believed these cures were effected by the influence which the mind has upon the body ; for they were magnetized in the same way, but experienced nothing more than ' soreness of the stomach, in consequence of the great pressure made over it.'

Although the secret of Mr. Halsted, as relates to the cure of dyspepsia, is supposed to be published, yet I would recommend to those who wish to learn the *true* secret of his success, to read the report from which I have taken the above extracts.* The same report alludes to a fact which I conceive has a very important bearing upon the disease we are considering. It says, that ' when the attention is arrested for a long time, on some interior organ of the body, it produces heat there, and modifies the state of that organ,

---

* **Du Magnetisme Animal en France, &c., Par Alexandre Bertrand.**

10*

so that new sensations are produced.' Of this I have no doubt. I have seldom known a person very attentive to the sensations that food produced in his stomach, who was not, or did not soon become dyspeptic.

The attention which has been directed to the *state of the stomach,* by several popular works on dyspepsia, has, no doubt, done much to produce morbid action of this organ. It is said that the teachings of Broussais, respecting gastritis, have greatly multiplied affections of the stomach, in Paris; and affections of the heart, real or imaginary, were produced by the lectures of Corvisart on the diseases of this organ.

Sixth. The fact that dyspepsia is a disease chiefly confined to the studious, to those whose minds are much exercised and excited, and to those who, by too early mental education, have had a predominance given to the nervous system, is evidence that the brain is the primary organ affected. * I know it is said that the sedentary habits of students cause this disease; and no doubt exercise is necessary to preserve their health; but it proves beneficial by changing the circulation and

* I might refer to numerous instances of men, gifted in early life with superior mental powers, and who enjoyed for a short time great celebrity, but who were always nervous, melancholy, passionate, or on the verge of insanity. Tasso, at the age of 22, was the author of the finest epic poem of modern times; but he was always melancholy, or else devoured by passion, and died at the age of 32. Pascal also enjoyed premature celebrity as an author, but was always hypochondriacal, ever imagining that he saw a gulf open at his side, and died at the early age of 39. But men of genius are not always distinguished in youth. Roger Ascham has placed among ' the best natures for learning, the sad-natured and hard-witted child.' The youth of Goldsmith was unpromising; and Gesner was considered a very stupid boy. ' The mother of Sheridan, herself a literary female, pronounced early that he was the dullest and most hopeless of her sons. The great Isaac Barrows' father used to say, that if it pleased God to take from him any of his children, he hoped it might be Isaac, as the least promising.'—*D'Israeli.*

determining the blood *from* the head. If they studied
less, exercise would not be so necessary. I have not
observed that tailors, shoe-makers, &c. are particularly
liable to dyspepsia. It often happens that men who
commence study late in life, after having been engaged
for years in some laborious employment, become in a
short time dyspeptic. I conceive that this arises from
too severe labor, put too suddenly upon the brain.
This organ should be gradually exercised, as indicated
at page 62, in order to develope it properly and fit it
for severe labor without injury.

It is often said that intoxicating liquors produce this
disease ; but I have been astonished to see how many
drunkards are free from it.

Good living is said to cause dyspepsia ; but the most
healthy people I have ever known, have been among
those who lived well — who eat freely several times a
day of the most nutritious food. By some it is said
that tobacco, snuff, tea, coffee, butter, and even *bread*,
cause this complaint ; but whoever will make inquiries
on this subject throughout the community, will find
that this is seldom true. In fact, dyspepsia prevails,
according to my experience, altogether the most among
the very temperate and careful — among those who
are temperate and careful as regards what they eat
and drink, and the labor they put upon the stomach ;
but exceedingly careless how much labor they put upon that more delicate organ, the brain. Such people
often eat nothing but by the advice of the doctor, or
some treatise on dyspepsia, or by weight ; nor drink
anything that is not certainly harmless ; they chew every mouthful until they are confident on mature reflection, that it cannot hurt the stomach. Why then are

they dyspeptics? Because, with all their carefulness, they pay no regard to the excitation of the brain. They continue to write two or three sermons or essays in a week, besides reading a volume or two, and magazines, reviews, newspapers, &c., and attending to much other business, calculated to excite the mind.*

To me it is not strange, that such persons have nervous and stomachic affections. The constant excitement of the brain sends an excess of blood to the head, and therefore other organs become weakened; and morbid sensibility is produced, which renders the stomach liable to derangement from very slight causes. ' I tell you honestly what I think (says Mr. Abernethy) is the cause of the complicated maladies of the human race; it is the gormandizing, and stuffing, and stimulating their organs (the digestive,) to excess, thereby producing nervous disorders and irritations. The state of their minds is another grand cause; the fidgeting and discontenting yourselves about what cannot be helped; passions of all kinds — malignant passions, pressing upon the mind, disturb the cerebral action and do much harm.'

This statement should be reversed, I think; it is the *fidgeting and discontenting* ourselves that makes the gormandizing so dangerous. I do not mean, however,

* ' Perhaps the greatest and most general cause of nervous affections, particularly in men, is the great increase of mental employment, or business requiring mental rather than bodily exertion, and too often accompanied by that anxiety, with its occasional attendants or sequels, disappointment, which is the produce of the especial ambition, either as to wealth, or honors, or fame, which denotes the present times.' — *Macculloch.*

No author, whose works I have seen, has written so much and so ably upon the tendency which mental excitement has to cause disease of the body, as the distinguished Dr. James Johnson. See his various works.

to approve of gormandizing; and I know that people in this country, generally, eat more than is necessary; still I do not believe that good nourishment, and abundance of it, cause many of the diseases that flesh is heir to. Nations that are best supplied with food, are the most healthy, live the longest, and have most vigor of body and mind. Children, especially, should be well nourished. Good diet is an essential part of good education. The method of *rearing* children, which some propose, and which I fear some adopt, of restricting them to very light food, that contains but little nourishment, is very reprehensible. Every farmer knows that such a course would stint and ruin his cattle; and it will as assuredly have such an effect on children. The way to make children thrive and do well, is to give them plenty of good food, and keep their minds free from anxiety and chagrin.

Insufficient nutriment weakens the mind as well as the body. Many writers place poor diet at the head of the causes that weaken attention, and debilitate all the faculties of the mind. Thus we often see that disease, which wastes the body, enfeebles the mind also, though this is not always the case; for sometimes the brain does not diminish as the other parts of the body do.*

But to return to the causes of dyspepsia. We do not find this disease prevalent in countries where the people eat most enormously. Travellers in Siberia say that the people there often eat forty pounds of food

* We often see persons in *consumption* exhibit clear and powerful intellects; but, according to the researches of M. Desmoulins, the brain does not decrease in bulk or weight in this and many other chronic diseases. — *Andral's Pathological Anatomy.*

in one day. Admiral Saritchaff saw a Siberian eat immediately *after breakfast*, twenty-five pounds of boiled
rice, with three pounds of butter. But dyspepsia is
not a common disease in Siberia. We do not learn
from Capt. Parry or Capt. Lyon, that their friends,
the Esquimaux, are very nervous and dyspeptic,
though they individually eat ten or twelve pounds of
solid food in a day, washing it down with a gallon or so
of train-oil. Captain Lyon was, to be sure, a little
concerned for a delicate young lady Esquimaux, who
eat his candles, wicks and all ; yet he does not allude
to her inability to digest them.

The influence of the mind in producing disease, appears to be but little regarded in practice, though there
are few who will not acknowledge that this influence is
great. Plutarch says, in one of his Essays, ' Should
the body sue the *mind* before the court of judicature
for damages, it would be found that the mind would
prove to have been a ruinous tenant to its landlord.'
The truth of this, mankind will the more realize as
they become more intellectual, unless great care is tak-
en to develope and exercise the organs of the body
equally and properly.*

It is true, however, that the regular application of
the mind to severe but calm study and inquiry, is not

* Laennaec says that the depressing passions are highly instru-
mental in producing consumption. For ten years he had the care
of a religious association of females, whose rules were excessively severe : their diet was not only austere, but their attention was
constantly fixed on the most terrible truths of religion ; and they
were tried by every kind of contrariety, in order to bring them to
a renouncement of their own proper will. ' During the ten years
I was physician to this association, I witnessed its entire renovation two or three different times, owing to the successive loss by
death of all its members, with the exception of a few who went
out oftener and had fewer religious duties to perform.'

very apt to affect the health unfavorably. The illustrious Kant, who lived and studied, to a great age, says, that ' intellectual pursuits tend to prolong life.' *

But studies that strongly excite the feelings, or awaken the passions, are very apt to injure the health ; and it is probably true that the literary men of this country are generally engaged in the strife of parties and sects, and conseqently their studies are not always those of calm inquiry. But the excitement of the mind produced by the numerous stirring incidents of the times, tends to increase disease, and especially nervous diseases, among all classes of people.† A violent election increases disorders of the digestive organs ; and a *difficulty in the parish*, a phrase well understood in New-England, often multiplies them. ‡

Finally. If dyspepsia is a disease o the stomach, why is it not more frequently cured by attention to diet

* This distinguished philosopher placed great reliance on the power of human reason, as a remedy for disease. He believed that by the force of reason, alone, man is, to a certain degree, able to master his sensations. He says that by the strength of *thought*, he was able to forget the pains of gout, and of other diseases. This mental effort, he says, required great force of the will, and caused the blood to rush to his head, but never failed to afford relief.

† Apoplexy, palsy, and other diseases of the nervous system, have greatly increased in modern times, as the following statement exhibits. During the last four years of the 17th century, from 1696 to 1700, there were 80,586 deaths in London ; and during the four last years of the 18th century, 72,591. But though the deaths during the first four years were most numerous, only 442 were by apoplexy, and 89 by palsy ; while, during the last four years, 912 were by apoplexy, and 363 by palsy. Dr. Graham says it is notorious that stomach complaints have likewise increased. — *Graham on Indigestion.*

‡ The venerable Dr. Perkins, of West Hartford, stated, a few weeks since, in a public discourse, that he had himself attended *one hundred Ecclesiastical Councils* to heal difficulties in the churches during the last sixty years.

than it is? I know that by this method some are relieved, and I also know that those disposed to dyspeptic disease, will not be able to continue their severe
studies, if they are not careful as respects diet. For
if the vital energy is all directed to the brain, and consumed by the act of thought, the stomach will not be
able to digest much food. If, however, they study but
little, they can eat more with impunity. I have not,
however, known this disease cured by a change of diet
alone. I have known many students, and professional
gentlemen, who were afflicted with troublesome stomach affections for several years, during which time they
frequently believed they had discovered a remedy for
their evils. Sometimes they were to be cured by
eating *bran bread ;* at others, by weighing all the food
they eat, or by living on rice, or porridge, or by living
without coffee or tea, or by some trifling change in
diet, about as important as putting a few grains, more
or less, of salt in an egg they eat.*

Most of the methods afford some relief for a while,
and this is usually in proportion to the confidence with
which they are imposed or embraced ; but I do not
know of one solitary cure by any of these means *alone.*

The most instances of cure which I recollect, have
been in those individuals whose *minds* have been permitted to rest from accustomed labors, or have been
directed to new pursuits, or relieved from anxiety and
care. Some have travelled far, and have recovered :
voyages have restored others. Some have become

* 'ARGAN. Monsieur. combien est-ce qu'il faut mettre de
grains de sel dans un œuf?
M. DIAFOIRUS. Six, huit, dix, par les nombres pairs, comme
dans les mendicaments par les nombres impairs.
Le Malade Imaginaire.

husbands, and forgotten their stomach complaints; some have succeeded in business and are well; some are in, or out of office, and thus their minds are freed from long-continued anxiety; while others remain as they were several years since; having just discovered, for the twentieth time, some new, and, as they believe, effectual remedy for their indigestion; but which will assuredly disappoint them, if they do not cease from mental toil, and for a while let the excited brain be quiet.

These views respecting stomach affections so common among the students of this country, will, to many, appear strange, perhaps absurd; but to some, I trust, they will be useful. I feel confident they will be, if they induce those who are worn down by mental labor and anxiety, connected with long-continued disorder of the digestive organs; to throw aside their *bitters, blue pills, mustard seed, bran bread*, &c. &c. and seek bodily health and future mental vigor, in judicious exertion of the body, innocent amusements, cheerful company, ordinary diet, and *mental* relaxation.

TABLE,

EXHIBITING THE AGE ATTAINED BY SOME OF THE MOST DISTINGUISHED LITERARY PERSONS IN ANCIENT AND MODERN DAYS.

Those marked thus * died through violence or accident.

Name.	Age.	Country.
Fulton	50	United States.
* Winckelmann	50	Germany.
Kiel	50	Scotland.
Brumoy	50	France.
Marot	50	do.
* Condorcet	50	do.
Pliny the younger	50	Italy.
Scarron	51	France.
Simson	51	England.
Smollet	51	do.
Tasso	51	Italy.
Virgil	52	do.
Shakspeare	52	England.
Tournefort	52	France.
La Bruyere	52	do.
Clairaut	52	do.
Moliere	53	do.
Cegnard	53	do.
Blarke	54	England.
Descartes	54	France.
Fourcroy	54	do.
Quinault	54	do.
Burlamaqui	54	Italy.
Davila	55	do.
Camoens	55	Portugal.

Hutcheson - -	55	-	-	Scotland.
Gray - - -	- 55	-	-	England.
Tycho Brahe -	55	-	-	Denmark.
* Pliny the elder -	- 56	-	-	Italy.
Dante - - -	56	-	-	do.
Schaunat - -	- 56	-	-	Flanders.
Pope - - -	56	-	-	England.
Helvetius - -	- 56		-	France.
Mendelsohn -	57	-	-	Prussia.
Ovid - - -	- 57	-	-	Italy.
Horace - -	57	-	-	do.
Gibbon - -	- 57	-	-	England.
Spurzheim -	57	-	-	Germany.
Congreve -	- 57	-	-	England.
Tscharner -	58	-	-	Switzerland.
Guiciardini -	- 58	-	-	Italy.
* Bailly -	58	-	-	France.
Ariosto - -	- 59	-	-	Italy.
Kepler - -	59	-	-	Germany.
Racine - -	- 59	-	-	France.
Bayle - -	59	-	-	do.
Demosthenes -	- 59	-	-	Greece.
Saussure -	59	-	-	France.
Lavater - -	- 60	-	-	Switzerland.
Gesner - -	60	-	-	do.
Butler, Joseph -	- 60	-	-	England.
Homer - -	60	-	-	Greece.
Desfontaines -	- 60	-	-	France.
La Mothe Houdart	60	-	-	do.
Montaigne -	- 60	-	-	do.
Mosheim -	61	-	-	Germany.
Galvani - -	- 61	-	-	Italy.
Maupertius -	- 61	-	-	France.
Villaret - -	- 61	-	-	do.
Boccaccio -	61	-	-	Italy.
Charron -	- 62	-	-	France.
Freret - -	62	-	-	do.
Paley - -	- 62	-	-	England.
Scott, Sir W. -	- 62	-	-	Scotland.
Puffendorf -	63	-	-	Sweden.
Burton, Robert -	63		-	England.
Mandeville -	63	-	-	Holland.

Nieuwentyt	- - 63	- -	Holland.
Fenelon	- - 63	- -	France.
Aristotle	- - - 63	- -	Greece.
Cuvier	- - - 63	- -	Germany.
Homberg	- - - 63	- -	Batavia.
Boyle	- - - 64	- -	Ireland.
De Thou	- - - 64	- -	France.
La Harpe	- - 64	- -	do.
Blondel, David	- - 64	- -	do.
Dwight, Timothy	- 65	-	United States.
Bentivoglio	- - 65	- -	Italy.
Hume	- - - 65	- -	England.
Sydenham	- - 65	- -	do.
Tillotson	- - 65	- -	do.
Quevedo	- - - 65	- -	Spain.
Schlichting	- - 65	- -	Poland.
Condillac	- - - 65	- -	France.
Bacon	- - - 65	- -	England.
Milton	- - - 66	- -	do.
Zimmermann	- 66	- -	Switzerland.
J. J. Rosseau	- - 66	- -	do.
Graswinckel	- - 66	- -	Holland.
Huygens	- - 66	-	do.
Walther	- - 66	- -	Germany.
Werner	- - - 66	- -	do.
Montesquieu	- - 66	- -	France.
B. Constant	- - 67	- -	Switzerland.
Mackintosh, Sir James	67	- -	England.
Griesbach	- - - 67	- -	Germany.
Smith, Adam	- 67	- -	Scotland.
D'Alembert	- - 67	- -	France.
Burke	- - - 67	- -	Ireland.
Hevelius	- - - 67	- -	Germany.
Schmeizel	- - 68	- -	Russia.
Fabricius	- - - 68	- -	Germany.
Gresset	- - - 68	- -	France.
Duclos	- - - 68	- -	do.
Blondel, Francis	- 68	- -	do.
Lessius	- - - 69	- -	Brabant.
Erasmus	- - 69	- -	Holland.
Muschenbroeck	- 69	- -	do.
Baronias	- - 69	- -	Italy.

Paul, Jove	- -	69	- -	Italy.
Valisnieri	- -	69	- -	do.
Cervantes	- -	69	- -	Spain.
Berkeley	- -	69	- -	England.
Origen	- - -	69	- -	Egypt.
Scaliger	- -	69	- -	France.
Beaumarchais	- -	69	- -	do.
Abbadie	- -	69	- -	do.
Pelisson	- - -	69	- -	do.
* Ramus	- -	69	- -	France.
Madame Dacier	-	69	- -	do.
Mascaron	- -	69	- -	do.
Dryden	- - -	70	- -	England.
Clarke, Adam	-	70	- -	do.
Temple	- - -	70	- -	do.
Selden	- -	70	- -	do.
Copernicus	- -	70	- -	Poland.
Boerhaave	- -	70	- -	Holland.
Leibnitz	- - -	70	- -	Germany.
Gall	- - -	70	- -	do.
Tissot	- - -	70	- -	Switzerland.
Petrarch	- -	70	- -	Italy.
Stephens, Henry	-	70	- -	France.
Crebillon	- -	70	- -	do.
Nollet	- -	70	- -	do.
Rosseau, Jean B.	-	70	- -	do.
Rabelais	- - -	70	- -	do.
Le Sage	- -	70	- -	do.
Nicole	- - -	70	- -	do.
Lemery	- -	70	- -	do.
Jenner	- - -	71	- -	England.
Dumont	- -	71	- -	France.
Borelli	- - -	71	- -	Italy.
Fracastor	- -	71	- -	do.
Leti -	- - -	71	- -	do.
Casaubon	- -	71	- -	Switzerland.
Linnæus -	- -	71	- -	Sweden.
Gronovius	- -	71	- -	Holland.
Graevius -	- -	71	- -	do.
Lausberg	- -	71	- -	Flanders.
Seneca	- - -	71	- -	Spain.
Racine	- -	71	- -	France.

Diderot - -	- 71	-	-	France.
Dacier - -	- 71	-	-	do.
Chaucer - -	- 72	-	-	England.
Richardson -	- 72	-	-	do.
Robertson -	- 72	-	-	do.
Van Swieten -	- 72	-	-	Holland.
Burnet - -	- 72	-	-	Scotland.
Sannazarius -	- 72	-	-	Italy.
Bourdaloue -	- 72	-	-	France.
Barthez -	- 72	-	-	do.
Malherbe - -	- 72	-	-	do.
Confucius -	- 73	-	-	China.
Bonnet - -	- 73	-	-	Switzerland.
Camden -	- 73	-	-	England.
Locke - -	- 73	-	-	do.
Crabbe - -	- 73	-	-	do.
Lopez de Vega	- 73	-	-	Spain.
Mezerai -	- 73	-	-	France.
La Condamine -	- 73	-	-	do.
Dodart - -	- 73	-	-	do.
Pothier - -	- 73	-	-	do.
De Sacy -	- 73	-	-	do.
D. Stewart -	- 73	-	-	Scotland.
Jenner - -	- 74	-	-	England.
Nelle - -	- 74	-	-	Franconia.
Hamilton -	- 74	-	-	Ireland.
Johnson - -	- 74	-	-	England.
Barros - -	- 74	-	-	Portugal.
Rance -	- 74	-	-	France.
La Fontaine -	- 74	-	-	do.
Destouches -	- 74	-	-	do.
Vauban -	- 74	-	-	do.
Haller - -	- 75	-	-	Switzerland.
Stahl - -	- 75	-	-	Germany.
Heister - -	- 75	-	-	do.
Usher - -	- 75	-	-	Ireland.
Sheffield -	- 75	-	-	England.
Scaliger -	- 75	-	-	Italy.
Reaumur -	- 75	-	-	do.
Bouhours -	- 75	-	-	do.

Perrault	- -	- 75	- -	Italy.
Mabillon	- -	75	- -	do.
Frederic II.	-	- 75	- -	Prussia.
Cardan	- -	- 75	- -	Italy.
Sanctorius	- -	75	- -	do.
Solis	- -	- 76	- -	Spain.
St. Augustin	-	76	- -	Barbary.
Wolff	- -	- 76	- -	Silesia.
Prideaux	- -	76	- -	England.
Mably	- -	76	- -	France.
Lagrange	- -	77	- -	Italy.
Buchanan	-	- 77	- -	Scotland.
Home, Sir Everard		77	- -	England.
Euler	- -	- 77	- -	Switzerland.
Bembo	- -	77	- -	Italy.
Bossuet	-	- 77	- -	France.
Laplace	- -	78	- -	do.
Galileo	-	- 78	- -	Italy.
Cullen	- -	78	- -	Scotland.
Swift	- -	- 78	- -	Ireland.
Roger Bacon	-	78	- -	England.
Flechier	-	- 78	- -	France.
Mallebranche	-	78	- -	do.
Corneille	-	- 78	- -	do.
S. Parr	- -	79	- -	England.
Galen	- -	- 79	- -	Anatolia.
Spallanzani -	-	79	- -	Italy.
Euripides	-	- 79	- -	Greece.
Kircher	- -	79	- -	Germany.
Marmontel	-	- 79	- -	France.
Massillon	- -	79	- -	do.
Menage	- -	- 79	-	do.
Roscoe	- -	80	- -	England.
Kant	- -	- 80	- -	Germany.
Burder, Geo.	-	80	- -	England.
Harvey	-	- 80	- -	do.
Thucydides	-	80	- -	Greece.
Juvenal	-	- 80	- -	Italy.
Young	- -	80	- -	England.
Rollin	- -	- 80	- -	France.
Vertot	- -	80	- -	do.
Plato	- -	- 81	- -	Greece.

Warburton	-	-	81	- -	England.
Mead	- -	-	81	- - -	do.
Buffon	-	-	81	- -	France.
Pestalozzi	-	-	82	- -	Switzerland.
Polybius	-	-	82	- -	Greece.
Huber	-	-	82	- - -	Geneva.
Zenocrates		-	82	- -	Greece.
Duhamel	-	-	82	- -	France.
Fleury	-	-	82	- -	do.
Butler, Charles		-	83	- -	England.
Hopkins, Samuel	-		83	- -	United States.
Goethe	- -	-	83	- -	Germany.
Hoffman		-	83	- -	do.
D'Aguesseau	-	-	83	- -	France.
D'Aubenton		-	83	- -	do.
Herschell		-	84	- -	England.
Bentham	-	-	84	- -	do.
Gleim	- -	-	84	- -	Germany.
Franklin	-	-	84	- -	United States.
Metastasio	-	-	84	- -	Italy.
Raynal	-	-	84	- -	France.
Anacreon	-	-	85	- -	Anatolia.
Newton	-	-	85	- -	England.
Swedenborg	-	-	85	- .	Sweden.
C. Hutton	-	-	86	- -	England.
Halley	-	-	86	- -	do.
Young	-	-	86	- -	do.
Mirabeau	-	-	86	- -	France.
St. Pierre	-	-	86	- -	do.
Cassini	-	-	87	- -	Italy.
Crebillon	-	-	88	- -	France.
Hill, Rowland	-	-	89	- -	England.
Sophocles	-	-	90	- -	Greece.
Saint Evremont		-	90	- -	France.
Hobbes	-	-	91	- -	England.
Huet	-	-	91	- -	France.
Wren, Sir C.	-		91	- -	England.
Hutton, Wm.	-	-	92	- -	do.
S. W. Johnson	-		93	- -	United States.
Wilson, Thomas	-		93	- -	England.
Hans, Sloane	-		93	- -	Ireland.
Fergusson, Adam			93	- -	England.

Vida	- - -	96	- - Italy.
Isocrates	- -	98	- - - Greece.
Simonides	- -	98	- - Isle of Ceos.
*Zeno	- - -	98	- - - Cyprus.
Saadi	- - -	99	- - Persia.
Herodian	- -	100	- - - Greece.
Fontenelle	- -	100	- - France.
Gorgias	- -	107	- - - Sicily.
Hippocrates	- -	109	- - Isle of Cos.

MENTAL HYGIENE.

MENTAL HYGIENE;

OR,

AN EXAMINATION

OF THE

INTELLECT AND PASSIONS.

DESIGNED TO SHOW

HOW THEY AFFECT AND ARE AFFECTED BY THE BODILY FUNCTIONS,

AND THEIR

INFLUENCE ON HEALTH AND LONGEVITY.

BY

WILLIAM SWEETSER, M. D.,

PROFESSOR OF THE THEORY AND PRACTICE OF MEDICINE IN BOWDOIN, CASTLETON,
AND GENEVA MEDICAL COLLEGES, AND FELLOW OF THE AMERICAN
ACADEMY OF ARTS AND SCIENCES.

SECOND EDITION, RE-WRITTEN AND ENLARGED.

NEW-YORK:
GEORGE P. PUTNAM, 155 BROADWAY.
1850.

John F. Trow, Printer,
49, 51 & 53 Ann-st.

PREFACE

TO THE SECOND EDITION.

———

THE previous edition of the following work having been for some years exhausted, and frequent inquiries for it having been made of the author, he has taken advantage of his earliest leisure to prepare a second edition. In doing this he has re-written nearly the whole volume, and added to it a large amount of new matter. The division of the chapters is left the same as in the previous edition,— though each has been more or less enlarged—and the general arrangement of the subjects has not been essentially altered. That this edition will be found improved by the labors bestowed upon it, is a hope with which the author ventures to flatter himself, but on this point it is for others to decide.

Fort Washington, City of New-York,
August 6th, 1850.

INTRODUCTION.

WHATEVER speculative views we may entertain in regard
to mind—however distinct in its nature we may deem it to
be from matter—of the fact that it is essentially involved
with our organic structure, and that between the two a
reciprocation of influence is constantly and necessarily
maintained, we are sufficiently assured. Of the mental constitution and its laws, we have not the faintest knowledge
except as they reveal themselves through the medium of
certain material conformations. Wherever these are discovered we are convinced that mind is, or has been, con-
joined with them. Without such arrangements of matter,
its astonishing phenomena have never been disclosed to us.

The mutual relationship and constant interchange of
action subsisting between our mental and corporeal natures, can scarce have escaped even the most careless
observation. Let the functions of either be disturbed, and
more or less disorder will straightway be reflected to those of
the other. The hardiest frame must suffer under the agita-

tions and afflictions of the mind; and the firmest mind cannot long remain unharmed amid the infirmities and sufferings of the body.

Mind and body ought always to be studied together, and under their mutual and necessary relationships, otherwise our views of the animal constitution will be limited and erroneous. It has been said, that the less we know of the corporeal, the more we fancy we know of the spiritual world; and the contrary is doubtless equally true. He whose researches are altogether physical, or altogether metaphysical, is very liable to become exclusively material, or exclusively spiritual in his views.

The leading design of the present volume, as implied in its title, is to elucidate the influence of intellect and passion upon the health and endurance of the human organization. The character and importance of this influence has, it is believed, been but imperfectly understood and appreciated by mankind at large. Few, we imagine, have formed any adequate estimate of the sum of bodily ills which originate in the mind. Even the medical profession, concentrating their attention upon the physical, are very liable to neglect the mental causes of disease, and thus are patients sometimes subjected to the harshest medicines of the pharmacopœia, the true origin of whose malady is some inward and rooted sorrow, which a moral balm alone can reach.

The work we are introducing will be divided into two Parts. Under the first we shall consider the intellectual operations in view of their influence upon the general functions of the body; but as their effects on the vital economy are less forcibly marked, and less hazardous to its welfare than those belonging to the passions, only the smaller portion of the volume will be embraced by this division.

The Second Part will comprise a view of the moral feelings or passions in the relation which they also bear to our physical nature. Of these we shall, in the first place, offer a general definition, and such a classification of them as will be deemed necessary to our leading design. Next we shall point out their effects upon the different functions of the constitution; and then describe some of the most important of the individual passions belonging to the three great classes—pleasurable, painful, and mixed—into which it is proposed to separate them; thus taking occasion to examine more intimately their physical phenomena, and particular influence on the well-being of the human organism. And then we shall make some remarks upon the effects of the imagination; aiming to show how this faculty of the mind, when uncontrolled and disorderly, tends to weaken the nervous system, and injure the general health. The imagination here acting through the instrumentality of the passions morbidly excited by its licentious operation, such a consideration of it will not be inapposite to the design of the present treatise.

As the work before us is not addressed to any particular class of readers, technical expressions will be carefully avoided, and its matter be rendered as plain and comprehensible as the nature of the subject will allow. And as truth, so far at least as the author can penetrate his own feelings, is its grand aim; all mystical speculations and ungrounded theories, whether of a metaphysical or moral nature, will be scrupulously excluded from its pages.

Such, then, is a summary exposition of the plan and purpose of the present volume, and the author has only to hope that the principles advocated in it may not be wholly unprolific of good, and that it may subserve, in a measure at least, the great end for which it was prepared.

CONTENTS.

PART I.

INTELLECTUAL OPERATIONS.

CHAPTER V.

CHAPTER VI.

CHAPTER VII.

PART II.

PASSIONS.

CHAPTER VIII.

CHAPTER IX.

CHAPTER X.

PART FIRST.

INTELLECTUAL OPERATIONS.

CHAPTER I.

MAN is distinguished from all other known animals, not
only by his peculiar conformation of body—by his erect and
dignified attitude—but by a far higher measure of intellectual endowment, and a consequently greater extension of his
relations with external things. Remarkable, however, as
this superiority of our species certainly is, still may it be
questioned if, through human pride, it has not been something exaggerated, or a broader separation between us and
the lower animals been assumed than Nature herself will
acknowledge. Thus, by some metaphysical writers, all
glimmerings of the higher mental faculties have been denied
to brutes, and all their acts been ascribed to the direct impulse of a resistless instinct. This is evidently wrong;
certainly in the physiological meaning of the word instinct.
The simple animal instincts may be defined to be peculiar,
inward feelings, or sensations originating urgent wants or
desires, which stimulate or call forth certain muscular actions, whose purpose or end is, by satisfying the want, to re-

lieve the sensation that excited it; the series of physical actions produced being always understood to take place independent of education or imitation, and without any foresight of the end to be attained by them. Or, to put the definition in another form : Instincts consist in particular physical conditions, and consequent sensations, impelling to some definite train of muscular movements, which contribute or are essential to the preservation of the individual, or the continuance of the species, and thus grow out of the " stimulus of necessity." Abundant examples illustrative of the foregoing definitions of instincts might be adduced, but the appetites of hunger and thirst will be sufficient for our purpose. These instinctive wants or desires are originated or excited by physical conditions of the stomach, or system at large, which demand the supply of food and drink, and thereby serve as monitors to solicit the co-operative acts requisite to furnish such supply. Hence animals, so soon as born, and independent, therefore, of either education or imitation, go through, and as perfectly as ever afterward, all those complicated muscular movements needful to meet the calls of nutrition. Instinctive feelings, when simple and uncontrolled, almost uniformly elicit instinctive actions.

Simple, undiscerning, undeviating instinct—admitting such an unmixed principle—can obviously only exist in the humblest forms of animal life, as the *invertebrata*. In the lowest, even, of the *vertebrata*, or vertebral animals—those furnished with a spinal marrow and internal bony system— some faint glimmerings of an intelligent principle begin to show themselves, mingling with, modifying and exercising some evident dominion over the mere instinctive operations. It is in this division of the animal kingdom that we begin to discover variations in individual character, in intelligence, in temper, &c. ; and the higher we ascend in it, the greater is the degree of such variations. " Thus every one knows that there are stupid dogs and good-tempered dogs, as there are stupid men or good-tempered men. But no one could distinguish between a stupid bee and a clever bee, or between a good-tempered wasp and an ill-tempered wasp, simply because all their actions are prompted by an unvarying instinct." *

Ascending in this division of animate being, we find the intelligent principle, with the faculty of reasoning, advancing, and apparently in correspondence with the development of the brain.   And in man, whose brain is most fully developed—most complex in its fabric—the intellectual faculties are far more elevated than in any other example, as yet known, in animate nature.   In him the instinctive propensities obviously become subject—though in different degrees in different individuals—to the nobler reasoning powers.

Instinct will, I think, be generally found in the inverse ratio of reason—the latter faculty rendering it less necessary to animal preservation.   It ever seems to be proportioned to the necessities for it.   In the infant, instinct being the more necessary in the absence of reason, we observe more obvious traces of it than in the adult, though feeble compared with what the young of the inferior ani-

* Carpenter's Human Physiology.

mals present. The human female shows undeniable evidences of a necessary instinct, in her strong love for her offspring on the instant of its birth, and sometimes even before its birth; in her impulsive desire to nourish it; her ceaseless care in its preservation, and her indomitable energy in its defence from danger. Unless her nature be perverted by disease, or entirely depraved by vice, the human can at first no more escape such instinctive feelings than the brute mother. But in the latter, they are transient—lasting only while their young need their protection; and, in some, they are evinced merely by the careful preparation for the welfare of their offspring before they come into existence; whereas, in the former, they soon becoming mingled with, modified, widened and strengthened, by feelings and principles far more exalted—of a moral and intellectual character—we have, growing out of such combination, the most devoted, the most enduring, the most self-sacrificing of all human affections—*a mother's love.*

In the savage condition of man, especially as witnessed in the inferior races, the instinctive propensities are more marked, active, dominant, than in his state of civilization and intellectual advancement. In individual men, too, it will appear as a general truth, that the more eminently developed are the higher faculties of the mind, the less will be the instinctive manifestations.

In living nature, all naturalists, I believe, admit, that there exists something like a gradually ascending chain, rising from the humblest plant, passing through the zoophyte, or transition link, to the animal scale, and so upward to man—its highest limit as yet disclosed to human intelligence. In tracing, too, this rising chain of life, it will be seen that structure and function ever advance in a corresponding relation—the general development of the former being an unerring measure of the perfection of the latter. Thus, on reaching the naturalist's second great division of the animal kingdom, *vertebrata*, or that to which belong a brain and spinal marrow, we begin, as I previously remarked, to discover, in addition to the simple instinct which probably alone governs the lower or brainless animals, some faint evidences of powers of a higher mould, and which grow more and more clear, in proportion as the organization, particularly of the brain, approaches nearer and nearer to that of our own. Hence, in the class of animals whose brain and general nervous system most closely resemble man's, do we detect the rudiments of nearly all the human mental faculties, and consequently an approximation, imperfect, to be sure, still an obvious approximation to a rational nature. Although this gradation in the vegetable and animal kingdom—this gradual rise from the humblest to the loftiest organic forms—is sufficiently obvious in its general features, yet it cannot be denied that, in its particular parts, it will sometimes be found less direct and simple than might be inferred from the statements of many naturalists. Still, that there is a general, and mostly an easy advance in organic structure and function, will scarce be contradicted.

A question here presents itself, How widely is man removed from the most manlike of the inferior animals? Do his reasoning powers differ from those of the latter in degree only, or in kind? Is he raised in his nature out of the pale of the animal kingdom? Is there no easy gradation to the human link in the chain of life, or is the breach wider here than at any other point? Or may not the step from the highest race of the ape to the most humble of our own, be really easier than human pride has been generally willing to acknowledge?

The Asiatic orang-outang, *simia satyrus*, both as respects structure and mental powers, would seem to claim as near a kindred to humanity, as any other known animal. It has been, I believe, hitherto found only in the Islands of Borneo and Sumatra, in the Indian Ocean. The Malays believe this animal to possess rational faculties, and the power of speech, which he cunningly avoids exercising lest he should be put to work,—the black races always regarding labor as a great punishment. Cuvier believed, and the opinion is not improbable, that the powerful pongo of Borneo, of whose courageous and manlike acts we have such marvellous accounts, is only the adult *simia satyrus*. The specimens of this animal that have been transported to Europe or the United States, having been all young, and falling victims to an ungenial climate and unsuitable food, before attaining their full physical or mental maturity, our knowledge of the utmost development of its capacities must consequently be but imperfect; still, even under such adverse circumstances as we have been able to contemplate these animals, have they astonished us by their display of the habits and feelings of our own nature. But the accounts given by travellers of the orang-outang in its native condition, and its close imitations of the actions of man, even making the fullest allowance for exaggeration, excite our still higher wonder.

The chimpanzee, *simia troglodytes*, an African ape, would appear, from recent examinations made by naturalists, to approximate in structure and function even closer to the human species than the Asiatic orang-outang, to which we have just been alluding. How near, therefore, these remarkable animals in a propitious climate, and under a well devised plan of instruction, might be brought to the inferior races of mankind, our data are insufficient to warrant an opinion. Placed beside the cultivated European, the distinction both in their structure and mental endowments is broad indeed, but it becomes much lessened when the comparison is made, —and such is the only just one,—with the lowest of our own species, as the savage New Hollander or the Bosjesman Hottentot. But then man differs widely enough even from the most manlike of the brute creation, to warrant naturalists in not merely ranking him as a distinct species, but in placing him in a separate order. No one would now entertain the ridiculous notion of Monboddo and Rousseau, that man is nothing more than an ape, improved under moral and physical influences. Nor should I be willing to admit him, on the system of progressive development of Lamarck, and the author of the Vestiges of Creation, to be but a monkey advanced through this principle of development one step upward in the ascending scale of life; but I would rather choose to regard him as a species, from his primary creation, distinct from that of all other animate beings.

2*

Man would appear, on the evidence of geology, to be among the latest, as he is the most perfect of organic creations. And it would almost seem as though nature, through successive destructions and new creations, had been progressively advancing in her living structures, gradually improving upon her early types, to the occupants of the present and last surface of our earth. According to the distinguished geologist Cuvier, the globe on which we dwell is composed of various layers or strata of rocks, those on which all the others rest being the most ancient, and of course representing the first or internal stratum. On this primitive stratum animals existed, but only of the lowest forms. Then upon this comes another layer, the surface of the primary, with all its inhabitants, having been overwhelmed by some dread convulsion. Here again, in the lapse of time, other living beings succeeded, but as is inferred from their abundant organic remains, of a somewhat more advanced construction. Thus has revolution after revolution been going on, each succeeded by new worlds of life, until we come to the present surface, or the alluvial deposits, —not the result of any grand convulsion,—in which the remains of animals now existing are alone discoverable. These views of Cuvier do not accord in all their points with those derived from more recent geological observations. The primary rocks have been found destitute of organic remains, and hence are called *azoic*, implying absence of life. There must then have been a period in the formation of our globe, when there was an entire destitution of both animal and vegetable life; and furthermore, the organic relics found in some of the earlier geological formations, show a higher animal organization than is consistent with a regular or uniform progressive advancement in the scale of life. Still, it would seem to be true that at each new geological era, nature has made some general improvement on her previous animal structures, and that, therefore, on the present surface of the earth are found the most perfect and complicated, at the head of which stands man, the masterpiece of all earthly creations. He belongs alone to the present face of the globe, no fossil remains of him having ever been found in any of its older strata. He is the latest then, as well as the most perfect of the earthly works of creative power. Millions of ages, for aught we know, may have been spent in reaching the complicated organisms presented in man and other of the mammalia occupying the present face of the globe. And the inquiry cannot but come up in every reflecting mind: Is here the end, the consummation? Is the world finished? Has nature attained the summit of her scale? Have these mighty revolutions of foregone times now ceased, and is man therefore to continue the terrestrial master-touch of his Maker? Or, in the course of ages, may not yet another convulsion arise, desolating the present surface of the earth, and on the new one which succeeds, nature make a still further advance in animal life, and produce a race of beings as much excelling man as he does any prior creation? And yielding a little license to the fancy, may we not imagine the learned naturalists on this new crust, puzzling their wits over the fossil bones of our own proud race, and marvelling to what humble order of beings they could have belonged?

Analogy would certainly favor the belief, that the present face of our globe is at some future time to be swept over by the hand of desolation; when, or through what destroying influence, the human mind can form no conjecture. Thousands of ages may first elapse, or physical causes, of which man can have no prescience, may be now at work in the Universe, preparing the way for a speedy consummation of this dread convulsion. To my mind there appears more evidence for believing that nature has advanced in her scale of animal life through successive destructions, and new and improved creations, than by the system of progressive development, or the gradual transformation of one species into another and of a higher character, put forth many years ago by Lamarck, and recently revived and somewhat modified in that beautifully written, though we are compelled to add, too fanciful work, the Vestiges of Creation. But then this whole subject of cosmogony, or world-making, is so obscure and difficult, so wanting in well established data, that I fear we can make little out of it unless we admit some aid from the imagination.

In conclusion of this somewhat desultory chapter, let us briefly inquire how the mind of man differs from that of the inferior, even the most sagacious of the inferior animal. The human is distinguished from the brute mind in the far higher degree of its intellectual capacities, its unmeasurable improvability, and in the possession of moral sentiments,— but faint evidences of which are exhibited by any of the lower orders of the animal creation. Man alone, too, has speech, a language, or the power of expressing his thoughts and feelings by words or articulate sounds. Many of the inferior species have doubtless some power of communicating with each other through sounds, combined with actions and gestures, but such is widely different from a vocal language, though probably all that their rude faculties and simple feelings require. Several birds, moreover, may be taught to pronounce words and even to repeat sentences; but to associate thoughts with them is altogether above their power. They articulate mechanically, through imitation. Language implies a connected series, an association of ideas, a degree of intelligence which the brute mind cannot attain. It belongs only to the more exalted moral and intellectual capabilities of man, and these capabilities are dependent upon this power of speech for their full exercise and development.

Weeping and laughter, as expressive of certain mental conditions, as sorrow, and mirth, and satisfaction, would appear to be peculiar to our own species. Some animals beside man would seem to shed tears, but whether from grief is a matter of doubt; but none, I believe, not even the most manlike of the apes, ever evince a mirthful state of mind by laughter. Indeed their countenances are always marked even by a ludicrous expression of gravity.

The faculty of reflection, at least to any obvious extent, would appear to belong only to man. By reflection is meant the action of the mind upon itself; or the turning inward, or throwing back, the thoughts upon themselves, and thus creating new mental combinations, or new thoughts out of the ideas obtained through the medium of the senses. And from this compound operation of the mind do we derive an additional and exhaustless spring of knowledge, with new motives to action, and a measureless increase in our relations with external things.

The relations of the brute animal to the objects among which he is placed have reference chiefly, if not solely, to the gratification of his appetites, or the satisfaction of his bodily wants, and his preservation from injury or destruction. His sensual desires pacified, and unthreatened by danger, he commonly falls asleep, or, at least, remains at rest. But such is not true of man, at least of civilized man. With his appetites satisfied, with ample provision for every physical necessity, and exempt from even the remotest apprehension of harm, still actuated by a class of wants above those of his mere animal nature, does he remain awake; observing the objects and phenomena around him; reflecting, perhaps, on his own mysterious nature, its complicated relations, its inscrutable destiny. Or, unsatisfied with the present, is stretching his view far into the dim and misty future, and judging, or trying to judge of its fast-coming events. Nor yet can his expanding mind be bounded by the world in which he dwells, but grasps at the universe and eternity, and space and time are too limited to contain it.

This curiosity, this insatiable appetite for knowledge, or the discovery of new truths, seems an attribute especially of our own nature, and is the stimulus ever urging us forward in the path of intellectual advancement. Scarce has the infant become familiar with the light of heaven; hardly does expression begin to brighten its vacant eye, ere it evinces its incipient curiosity in touching, tasting, smelling, hearkening, and is thus treasuring up ideas of sensation, which are afterward to be compared, abstracted, combined, or, in other words, to be worked up into various new forms, constituting new and inexhaustible sources of mental progress.

It may be proper that I should here mention one other remarkable tendency in man's mind, and so far as we can have any evidence, in his alone, and therefore distinguishing him from all the rest of the animal kingdom;—it is to believe in some superior, invisible, and controlling existence. Various forms and attributes may be ascribed to this power in different conditions, and by different races of man; but I think it must be yielded, although some travellers have endeavored to prove the contrary, that no people or nation —I do not here speak of individuals—have ever been discovered entirely destitute of such belief. And associated with it is the fervent desire and confident expectation of passing after death to the blessed abode of this unseen power, and dwelling for ever amid joys, and among beings far more exalted than any which this earth can afford. How shall we explain such belief in the human mind? Is it innate, or was it implanted there by our Creator? Did it originate in an early revelation to our race, and which was communicated by tradition from age to age? Or was it begotten of man's longing after immortal life and undying bliss? Such questions cannot, of course, receive a categorical answer. At any rate it forms one of the strongest arguments of natural religion—of which I am here only speaking—for man's immortality.

To man, then, in addition to his sensual wants which he holds in common with the brutes, belong those of a moral and intellectual, and I may also add of a religious character; and his external relations being correspondently multiplied, new feelings, new desires, new passions must be generated, which, while they open sources of enjoyment immeasurably exceeding any possessed by the lower animals, may beget a train of moral, and their consequent physical ills, burdening life with sorrow, and almost raising a doubt whether it should be viewed as a gift of mercy, or an imposition of wrath. Thus in the present disposition of things, do we ever find a system of compensation, an attempt, as it were, at a general equalization of enjoyment.

The inferior animal, if his appetites are appeased, and he is exempt from physical pain and the fear of danger, is apparently happy in the simple feeling of existence. But what torture of mind may not our own species endure, even when free from all bodily suffering, safe from every harm, and with resources, even in superfluity, for the gratification of every sensual want? An agony sometimes so terrible as to drive its miserable victim to the horrid alternative of self-destruction, a catastrophe rarely brought about by any amount of physical pain. Fortunately, however, by a judicious education of our intellectual and moral nature, much, very much may be done to avoid such mental sufferings, and the bodily diseases which so generally supervene.

CHAPTER II.

A JUDICIOUS EXERCISE OF THE INTELLECTUAL FACULTIES IS
PROMOTIVE BOTH OF HEALTH AND HAPPINESS.—HUMAN
NATURE MUST ADVANCE THROUGH THE DEVELOPMENT OF
INTELLECT.—EVILS RESULTING FROM MENTAL INACTIVITY.
—INTELLECTUAL PURSUITS DO NOT NECESSARILY ABBRE-
VIATE LIFE.—EXAMPLES OF LONGEVITY AMONG ANCIENT
AND MODERN SCHOLARS.

THAT the noblest powers of our nature should have been
designed for use and improvement, one might think would
be universally admitted; nevertheless, there are not wanting
those, eminent too for their learning, who have contended
that the savage is our only natural and happy condition.
Thus man—for such has been the picture drawn of him—
in the golden age of his early creation, dwelling in a mild
and balmy climate, abounding in vegetable productions
suitable to his wants, lived solitary, naked, savage; roaming
without care or thought the vast forests which he held in
common with the brute, and feasting at will on the roots and
fruits which the teeming soil spontaneously brought forth.
Then was he pure, gentle, innocent; and exempt from all

those multiform and painful maladies which now afflict and shorten his career, his life glided on in a smooth and happy current, and when death at last overtook him, it came, not as at present, fraught with pains and terrors, but like the tranquil sleep that steals over the wearied senses of innocent childhood. Here, free from all those lights and shadows of the soul which spring from cultivated intellect, like the brutes, he was happy in the bare consciousness of existence, —in exercising his limbs—in basking in the sunshine, or cooling himself in the shade,—and in the gratification of his mere animal propensities.

> " Pride then was not, nor arts that pride to aid ;
> Man walk'd with beast, joint tenant of the shade ;
> The same his table, and the same his bed ;
> No murder cloth'd him, and no murder fed.
> In the same temple, the resounding wood,
> All vocal beings hymn'd their equal God."

But that such a primeval state of blissful ignorance, health and purity ever existed, we have no other evidence than what rests on the fancies of poetry, or the dreams of poetic philosophy. The savages of the present day, who, one would suppose ought to come most nearly to this blessed state of nature, present a picture the very opposite of that described.

Some of the ancient philosophers were in the practice of decrying reason, and of asking whether any thing could be given by the gods to man more likely to make him unhappy. Rousseau has advocated with much speciousness and sophistry this unthinking, savage, or what he calls the natural condition of our species. He contends that meditation is opposed to health, and therefore contrary to nature, and so he who gives himself up to a habit of reflection is a degenerated animal. On like grounds he lauds the custom of certain Indian tribes of flattening the heads of their new-born infants, as it saves them from the pernicious effects of genius.

It might, it appears to me, as reasonably be contended that the infant is the natural condition of the individual, as the savage and ignorant that of the species. The tendency of man is obviously to civilization and mental progress; whence the highest moral and intellectual advancement of which he is capable, is the only natural state that can be predicated of him. It is this mental progress that elevates one man, one race, one age above another. To this do we owe all the arts, refinements and comforts of modern life. It is this to which man naturally, I may say instinctively aspires. Intellect is indeed power, no bounds can be fixed to it. The laws of nature, the force of the elements, the swift lightning, are all turned and rendered subservient to its mighty purposes. Whatever man is to attain, must be through his intellectual advancement,—through this lies his destiny upon the present earth. Through the power of his intellect, if our species last, must he at length inherit the earth; all other animal forms must recede before his increase, and all available matter be worked up into his own superior organization. Such period is indeed far distant, if we measure time by our own little span of existence; but if the earth and our species remain undestroyed, it will inevitably come. Human intellect may yet be but in its dawnings; it may have done little, scarce any thing, in comparison with what it is destined to accomplish. Let us not then, with some brain-sick poets and philosophers, presume to undervalue a power so vast, so boundless, so all-controlling,—a power through which our Creator has raised us above every other living creature, and by the advance of which alone we can ascend in the scale of creation. If ignorance is bliss, as is contended by some, then would it be bliss to be a brute.

Furthermore, is it not through a high and proper cultivation of the intellectual, that the moral nature is to be elevated and improved? I hold the belief, though I know the popular arguments that may be brought against it, that the most perfect state of intellect would necessarily imply the most perfect state of morals, inasmuch as it would enable us to calculate the moral with the same precision that we now do the physical laws; for the former, I believe, are just as settled, just as inflexible as the latter, and that any deviation, therefore, from moral rectitude—could we trace it in all its bearings, in all its remote connections—would be found as surely followed by suffering as any mechanical violence done to the body. But in the former case the suffering is generally indirect, removed from, and in consequence not readily traceable by our short-sighted intellect to its true source; while in the latter it is immediate, evident in its relation to its cause, and which is therefore guardedly shunned. No one, in his proper senses, will jump from the giddy precipice; no one, however he may be pained with cold, will lay his hands on the burning embers, for the effect is direct, palpable, and obvious, therefore, to the most common understanding. And were our intelligence sufficiently exalted, it would, I doubt not, discover the same necessary connection between violations of the moral laws, and suffering or punishment; and then man would no sooner swerve from a moral law than he would throw himself from the headlong steep, or touch the living coal. We now rush into evil as the insect does into the blaze of the candle, from stupidity, or our purblind intellect failing to show us the inevitable consequences. A supreme intelligence could not go wrong.

The mind, like the body, demands exercise. That the proudest faculties of our nature were intended for slothful inaction,—that talents were given us to remain buried and unproductive, is repugnant alike to reason and analogy. There is, indeed, no power of the living economy, however humble, but needs action, both on its own account and on that of the general constitution. So closely united by sympathies are all our functions, that the judicious exercise of each one, beside conducing to its individual welfare, must contribute in a greater or less degree, a healthful influence to every other.

Man, as already affirmed, discovers a natural desire for knowledge; and the very exertion necessary to its attainment, and the delight experienced in the gratification of this innate curiosity, diffuse a wholesome excitement throughout the system. There is a pleasure in the exercise of thought, in whose kindly effects all the functions must in some measure participate. Every new acquisition of knowledge,

every new truth brings with it the highest, the purest enjoyment; and, different from our sensual and exciting
pleasures, followed by no wasted health, no moral depression, no regret, no repentance. The man who feels that he
is wiser at night than he was in the morning, feels himself
advanced in the scale of creation, and therefore happier.
Agreeable and well-regulated intellectual occupations are, I
conceive, as essential to the soundness of the mind, as are
judicious exercises to that of the body; and as the health of
the latter, it must be admitted, conduces to that of the former, so, likewise, as it will be my uniform endeavor to establish in the succeeding pages of this volume, does a sound
state of the mind impart a salutary influence to the func-
ti ons of the body.

The mind, then, needs employment, not only for its own
sake, but also for that of the organism with which it is so
intricately involved.   Mental inactivity, in the existing constitution of society, is the occasion of an amount of moral
and physical suffering, which, to one who had never thought
upon the subject, would appear almost incredible.   From
this proceeds that *tædium vitæ*—that dreadful irksomeness
of life—so often witnessed among the opulent, or what are
termed the privileged classes of society, who are engaged in
no active or interesting pursuits, and who, already possessing the liberal gifts of fortune, and consequently the means
of gratifying all their natural and artificial wants, lack the
stimulus of necessity to awaken and sustain in wholesome
action their mental energies.   Hence, although they are objects of envy to those whose straitened circumstances call

for continued and active exertions, yet is their situation oftentimes any thing but enviable. Their cup of life, drugged with the gall and bitterness of ennui, their paramount wish is to escape from themselves—from the painful listlessness of a surfeited existence. The mind must be occupied, else gloomy and discontented, if not wicked feelings, will be likely to enter and abide there. To the enjoyment of retirement, internal resources, a "stock of ideas," such as comparatively few possess, are demanded.

Labor, of some sort, either of mind or body, is appointed to our race. Mother Eve and the Old Serpent are charged with entailing upon us this curse, as it is generally esteemed. But whatever it may have been originally, it has become absolutely necessary both to our moral and physical well-being. With our present constitutions, we should, I imagine, be miserable creatures indeed, with nothing to do but to sit under fig-trees in the garden of Eden. Paradoxical as it may seem, yet is it questionable if a much heavier curse could be imposed on man, with the nature he now possesses, than the entire gratification of all his wishes, leaving nothing for his hopes, desires, or struggles. The feeling that life is without aim or purpose—that it is destitute of any motive to action—is of all others the most depressing, the most insupportable to a moral and intellectual being. Man, at the end, is very apt to lament that existence has been a failure, because he has not reached some point—attained some eminent good—at which he could sit down content and happy, and to which all his hopes and labors had been directed. But we should know—and the earlier we know this the better—that life is a chase, and a chase after something which we never overtake. And, is it not the chase, more than the possession of the game, that brings joy and animation to the huntsman? Let us, then, enjoy the chase, and be satisfied when it is finished, though the game has continued to elude our pursuit.

Men of different constitutions, habits, talents, and education, will, as it might be supposed, require different sorts and degrees of mental action. Such as are endowed with vigorous intellectual powers, and in whose exercise they have been long accustomed to indulge, are exposed to most suffering when their minds are left unemployed. Those, for example, who are fond of study, and have been long used to devote a part of their time to its prosecution, may even sustain a manifest injury, both in their moral and physical health, by a sudden and continued interruption of such habit; a painful void being thus left in the mind, indirectly depressing its feelings, and, by a necessary consequence, all the important functions of life.

It is told of Petrarch, when at Vaucluse, that his friend, the Bishop of Cavillon, fearing lest his too close devotion to study would wholly ruin his health, which was already much impaired, having procured of him the key of his library, immediately locked up his books and writing-desk, saying to him, " I interdict you from pen, ink, paper and books, for the space of ten days." Petrarch, though much pained in his feelings, nevertheless submitted to the mandate. The first day was passed by him in the most tedious manner; during the second, he suffered under a constant headache; and, on the third, he became affected with fever. The bishop now taking pity on his condition, returned him his key, and thus restored him to his previous health.

Those, again, who, while yet in the vigor of life, retire from their wonted business, be it mercantile or professional, and thus all at once break up their habits of mental application, are apt to fall into a painful state of listlessness or ennui, and which, in certain temperaments, will often grow into a morbid melancholy, shading every scene and every prospect with a dismal and hopeless gloom. And sometimes the disgust and loathing of existence become so extreme, that they rid themselves of its hated burden with their own hands. This state of moral depression, if long continued, may also originate painful and fatal physical infirmities, or may pass into some settled form of insanity, especially that of monomania. In some instances it will change into, or alternate with, a reckless and ungovernable excitement; the individual running into wild extravagance, or rash speculations; giving himself up to habits of gambling, or gross intemperance, to relieve the painful void in his purposeless existence.

Elderly persons, who all at once give up their accustomed occupations, and consequently mental activity, and retire to enjoy their ease and leisure, will not uncommonly, especially if they had been previously free livers, experience a rapid breaking up of their mental, and perhaps bodily powers also, passing sometimes into a more or less complete state of what is termed senile dementia.

Under the circumstances of mental *inertia* to which I

3

have been referring, it is often observed that any thing arousing the mind to exertion, even positive misfortunes, will, by reviving the almost palsied feelings, be attended with a manifestly salutary influence. Thus is it that the retired opulent are oftentimes, if not past the age of action, made happier, healthier, and I may likewise add better, by the loss of so much of their property as to render renewed exertions necessary to their subsistence. Retirement from long-established and active duties demands intellectual and moral resources, to which few, in the present condition of society, can claim a title.

A mistaken, though generally received notion exists, that studious habits and intellectual exertions tend to injure the health, and prematurely exhaust the living energies; that they are prosecuted at the expense of the body, and must therefore hasten its decay. Such unfortunate consequences, however, are far from being necessary, unless the mental labors are urged to an unwarrantable excess, when, as in all overstrained exertions, whether of body or mind, various prejudicial effects may be rationally anticipated. I do not mean to assert that those in whom the intellect is chiefly engaged will enjoy the same athletic strength, or exhibit equal muscular development with others whose pursuits are of a more mechanical character,—for nature seldom lavishes upon us a full complement of her various gifts,—but I have no hesitation in believing that under prudent habits of life, and with a naturally sound constitution, they may preserve as uniform health, and live as long as any other class of persons. In support of such belief, abundant instances might be cited, both from ancient and modern times, of men eminently distinguished for the amount and profundity of their mental labors, who, being temperate and regular in their habits, have continued to enjoy firm health, and have attained a protracted existence. Indeed, the observation has been made by some eminent writer, that "one of the rewards of philosophy is long life." Let me illustrate by a few examples. Among the moderns, Harvey lived to eighty-one, Jenner to seventy-five, Heberden to ninety-two, Boerhaave to seventy, Locke to seventy-three, Bacon to seventy-eight, Galileo to seventy-eight, Sir Edward Coke to eighty-four, Bentham to eighty-five, Newton to eighty-five, and Fontanelle to a hundred. Boyle, Leibnitz, Volney, Voltaire, Buffon, and a multitude of others of less note that could be named, lived to very advanced ages. And the remarkable longevity of many of the German scholars, who have devoted themselves almost exclusively to the pursuits of science and literature, is doubtless sufficiently familiar to my readers. Professor Blumenbach, the distinguished German naturalist, died not many years ago at the age of eighty-eight; and Doctor Olbers, the celebrated astronomer of Bremen, in his eighty-first year.

Baron Berzelius, the distinguished Swedish chemist, the magnitude of whose intellectual labors, and the number of whose scientific publications are almost incredible, died recently at Stockholm in his seventieth year.

Of the prominent intellectual men of our own country, many might also be mentioned who attained to very great ages. Chief Justice Marshall and Thomas Jefferson reached

their eighty-fourth year; Doctor Franklin and John Jay
their eighty-fifth; James Madison his eighty-seventh; John
Adams his ninety-first, and John Quincy Adams his eightieth.
Now all these men, it is well known, were, during the greater
portion of their lives, engaged in the most profound mental
labors. Doctor Franklin continued his public services till
he was eighty-two, and his intellectual exertions to near the
close of his life. In a letter to one of his friends, written
when he was eighty-two years old, speaking of his advanced
age he says: "By living twelve years beyond David's period,
I seem to have intruded myself into the company of posterity
when I ought to have been abed and asleep. Yet, had I
gone at seventy, it would have cut off twelve of the most active years of my life, employed too, in matters of the greatest
importance."

The ancient sages, however, seem to have been privileged
in respect to health and longevity, above those of modern
days. Physical education was at their period held in much
higher regard. More of their time was passed in the open
air, and in active, muscular exercise, than is common with
our own scholars. Their studies were often prosecuted
without doors, and not a few of them taught their pupils,
and accomplished even many of their astonishing intellectual
labors whilst walking in the fields and groves. It was in
this way that Aristotle imparted his instructions, whence,
probably, came his disciples to be called peripatetics—the
Greek verb περιπατεω, *peripateo*, meaning to walk about, or
to walk abroad.

Socrates had no fixed place for his lectures, instructing

his pupils sometimes in the groves of Academus, sometimes on the banks of the Ilyssus, or wherever, indeed, he might chance to be with them. The eminent scholars of those days were likewise in the habit of travelling from country to country to disseminate their stores of knowledge.

I will close the present chapter by citing a few out of the numerous and best authenticated examples of longevity among the philosophers and learned men of antiquity. Homer, it is generally admitted, lived to be very old; so also did the philosopher Pythagoras, and the historian Plutarch. Thucydides, the celebrated Greek historian, and Solon, the famous lawgiver of Athens, reached the age of eighty. Plato died in his eighty-first year. Pittacus and Thales, two of the seven wise men of Greece, lived, the former to be eighty and the latter ninety-six. Xenophon, the Greek historian, and Galen, the distinguished physician, the latter of whom is said to have written no less than three hundred volumes, both attained their ninetieth year. Carneades, a celebrated philosopher of Cyrene in Africa, and founder of a sect called the third or new Academy, reached the same age. It is stated of Carneades that he was so intemperate in his thirst after knowledge, that he did not even give himself time to comb his head or pare his nails. Sophocles, the celebrated tragic poet of Athens, died in his ninety-fifth year; and then, according to one account, not in the course of nature, but by being choked with a grapestone. Other accounts have placed his death a little earlier, and referred it to a different accident, but all agree that he exceeded his ninetieth year. Zeno, the founder of the sect of the Stoics, lived to be ninety-eight. Hippocrates expired in his ninety-ninth year, and, as we read, free from all disorders of mind or body. Xenophanes, an eminent Greek writer, and the founder of a sect of philosophers in Sicily called Eleatic, arrived to a hundred, and Democritus to the extreme age of a hundred and nine. I am aware that there is a little discrepancy in the statement of different historians in regard to some of the above ages, but there is no disagreement, I believe, in regard to the fact that all these individuals lived to be very old.

CHAPTER III.

EVIL CONSEQUENCES THAT MAY BE APPREHENDED FROM OVER-
TASKING THE INTELLECTUAL POWERS.—RULES PROPER TO
BE OBSERVED BY STUDIOUS MEN FOR THE SECURITY OF THEIR
HEALTH.—THE ABILITY TO SUSTAIN INTELLECTUAL LABORS
VARIES IN DIFFERENT INDIVIDUALS, AND CONSEQUENTLY THE
PROPORTION OF TIME THAT MAY BE SAFELY DEDICATED TO
STUDY.

THE capabilities of the mind, in like manner with those
of the body, must have their limits. The powers of the brain
may be impaired by extravagant mental, as those of the
muscles by severe corporeal exertions. And so close are the
sympathetic ties uniting mind and body, that whatever tends
to injure the former, must necessarily endanger the soundness of the latter. Hence, if the intellectual faculties are
habitually overtasked, a train of moral and physical infirmities may be induced, imbittering existence and shortening
its term.

Persons who addict themselves immoderately to intellectual labors become particularly exposed to affections of
the brain, or organ overworked. They are liable to head

aches, and an undefinable host of nervous ailments. Inflammation, too, and a variety of organic diseases of the brain are not uncommon with them ; and apoplexies and palsies are apt to assail them as they advance in life. Whenever there exists a predisposition in the physical constitution to apoplexy, close mental application, and, in a particular manner after the middle term of life, is most hazardous.

Epilepsy is another melancholy disease of the nervous system, which a highly active and exalted state of the mind would seem to favor. Many individuals distinguished for their talents and mental efforts, have been the subjects of this pitiable malady ; as Julius Cæsar, Mahomet, and Napoleon ; and of learned men, Petrarch, Columna, Francis Rhedi, Rousseau, and Lord Byron, are familiarly cited instances. Still, how much in these examples may be justly ascribed to the abstract labor of intellect, and how much to mental anxiety, or the undue excitement and depression of the moral feelings, cannot be easily determined.

Extreme mental dejection, hypochondriasis, and even insanity, particularly if there be in the constitution any tendency to such conditions, may sometimes result from the cause I am considering. And, in occasional instances, under their intemperate exertion, the energies of the brain have been consumed, the light of intellect has become extinct, and the wretched victim, in a state of mental imbecility, or even drivelling idiocy, has been doomed to linger out a miserable existence within the walls of a mad-house.

I have stated what may occur in extreme cases, from abuse of the intellectual powers. Still, I conceive that the

diseases of literary men are far oftener to be imputed to incidental circumstances connected with the neglect or abuse
of their physical and animal nature, as their sedentary
habits, injudicious diet, inconsiderate indulgence of their
different appetites, &c., than to their mere mental labors.
But, as being less blameworthy, and more flattering to their
pride of understanding, students generally prefer to charge
their bodily infirmities upon their toils of intellect. I feel
well satisfied that, would studious men, or those whose avocations draw especially on the energies of the brain, but
bestow the requisite attention on the regimen of life, they
might, as before said, enjoy as good and uniform a share of
health as most other classes of the community. But, unhappily for themselves, as they sooner or later discover, the
importance of this they do not generally sufficiently understand, or properly regard. Thus we meet not a few in the
community, who cultivate and adorn, in the most eminent
degree, their intellectual and moral, while they are daily in-
fringing the laws of their physical, nature. They neglect
their needful exercise; they eat and drink as they ought
not to eat and drink; they sleep irregularly, and abuse in
a thousand other ways the welfare of their bodies. They
think only of the mental—the spiritual; the gross vesture
of flesh is beneath their consideration; and thus, heedless
of all admonition, do they continue in their pernicious
course, till their retribution comes in ruined health and premature decay. They are sinners—construe the term as
we will—for they offend against the laws of their Maker, as
evinced in their living organization, and thereby lessen the

3*

sum of their usefulnesss, and shorten the career of their being. We are obviously possessed of a threefold nature—intellectual, moral and physical; and would we secure to ourselves the greatest amount of enjoyment, and raise ourselves to the highest attainable condition of humanity, we must regard, must educate and perfect it, in its threefold relations.

Among the rules of health most essential to be observed by those whose pursuits belong more especially to the mind, we may, in the first place, mention temperance, both in eating and drinking.   Persons of studious and sedentary habits neither require, nor will they bear, the same amount and kind of food as those whose occupations call forth greater physical exertion, and produce, consequently, a more rapid consumption of the materials of the body.   If such, therefore, will persist in eating and drinking like the day-laborer, they must look to experience indigestion, and all its aggravated train of miseries.   Or, even should they escape such, the yet graver ills of excessive repletion, as inflammations and congestions, will be likely to overtake them.

A certain degree, at least, of regularity in respect to meals, is also important to be observed—the stomach, like every other organ of the animal economy, being subject to the influence of habit; and it is furthermore important, that while partaking them, the mind be abstracted as far as possible from all other concerns, and interested especially in the agreeable sensual impressions it is experiencing.   The enjoyment of our food forms one of the best of sauces for the promotion of its digestion.

Eating, furthermore, being an imperious animal duty, sufficient time should always be appropriated to its performance. The habit of rapid eating is exceedingly common among studious men, and is very apt to be acquired at our colleges and boarding-schools—the inmates of which often dispatch their food more like ravenous animals than civilized human creatures. This most disgustingly vulgar practice of gorging our food but half masticated—of hurrying through our meals as though we were just going off in the stage-coach, I believe to have more concern in the production of indigestion among us than has generally been suspected. We read that Diogenes meeting a boy eating thus greedily, gave his tutor a box on the ear; and, also, that there were men at Rome who taught people to chew, as well as to walk. The instruction of some such teachers, both in reference to health and manners, might not be altogether out of place among ourselves.

There are a class of men who, under an affectation of moral and intellectual refinement, assume to regard eating as one of those base animal gratifications to which as little time and thought as possible should be appropriated. But let us remember that we yet dwell in the flesh, and cannot, therefore, become wholly spiritualized. Those actions which Nature has enjoined as necessary to our constitution, are fortunately—indeed the species, with its present laws, could not otherwise have been preserved—associated with enjoyment. It is the part of wisdom, therefore, not to despise, neither slavishly to pursue, the corporeal pleasures, but to accept of them with thankfulness, and to partake of them with prudence. The gratification of all our appetites contributes, both directly and indirectly, to health and happiness; it is their abuse, only, that is reprehensible, and followed by pain and regret. Take from man his regularly returning social meal, and of how many sweet, domestic and friendly sympathies and associations, and consequently of how much human enjoyment, would you not deprive him? There belong to our nature sensual, moral and intellectual wants, and it is to their wise and duly apportioned gratification that we owe whatever happiness existence can afford. Spiritualize an individual, or raise him, through the purity and refinement of his intellect, much above the rest of his species, and he would be entirely unfitted for the sphere of his present being. Warmed by no human sympathies, enjoying no human companionship, he would be alone among his race. Even as it is superior and refined intellect is apt to look upon the ordinary pnrsuits and enjoyments of the would as futile, frivolous, and to become secluded and misanthropic.

It is scarcely necessary, I trust, to insist on the importance to the health of intellectual men of daily exercise in the open air. Without this no one whose employments are of a sedentary character, can expect to maintain sound health. The amount of exercise required will depend something on the constitution, and much on the kind and quantity of the food. From two to four hours of the day should certainly be devoted to active bodily exertions.

Many students, tempted on by the inviting quietude, are in the habit of protracting their labors late into the hours of the night, and at the manifest expense of their physical health. The wan and sallow countenance of the student is almost proverbially associated with the midnight lamp. Few causes tend more certainly to shatter the nervous energies, waste the constitution, and hasten on the infirmities of age, than deficient and irregular sleep. Thus, "to be a long and sound sleeper," we often find enumerated by the older writers among the signs of longevity. Those persons whose occupations, whatever may be their nature, interfere with their necessary and regular repose, are almost always observed to be pale, nervous, emaciated. Even a single night of watching will often drive the color from the cheek, the expression from the eye, and the vigor from the brain. Although so much of evil to mind, body, and estate, is ascribed to the prodigal indulgence in sleep, yet in our own busy and ambitious community we might reasonably doubt whether there is not, on the whole, more detriment from its deficiency than excess. And I am well satisfied that the human constitution would, in general, suffer less from extending than contracting the needful term of repose.

Constitutions will naturally differ in the amount of sleep they require, but most persons have to appropriate to it as much certainly as seven hours of the twenty-four. The slumbers of the forepart of the night affording, there is good reason to believe, most refreshment to the functions, it is advisable that students retire and rise seasonably, and accomplish, if circumstances will permit, their most arduous duties in the early portion of the day; for this is the time, if the body is in health, when the thoughts will generally be most clear and accurate, and the labors, therefore, most profitable. The fittest working hours, indeed, both for mind and body, would seem to be those which intervene between breakfast and dinner, having reference to our own customary hours for these meals. It is the stillness and seclusion of the night which have mostly rendered it so favorite a period for study and contemplation.

Again, those devoted to intellectual application should frequently relax their minds by amusing recreation, by mingling in cheerful society, and joining in its rational diversions; otherwise they are liable to become gloomy, irritable, and misanthropic, states of feeling always at war with our physical well-being. The dignity even of the most erudite and talented, would hardly suffer from occasionally uniting in the innocent frivolities of society, while a gladdening influence would thus be imparted to the whole moral and physical constitution. Among the ancients it seems that the greatest souls did not disdain occasionally to unbend, and yield to the laws of their human condition. Thus the Catos, with all their severity of manners, found relaxation and enjoyment in the ordinary pleasures of life. And it is told of Epaminondas, that amid all his glory and moral greatness, he felt it no detraction to dance, and sing, and play with the boys of the city And that Scipio Africanus amused himself in gathering shells, and playing at quoits on the sea-shore with his friend Lælius. And also that the sage Socrates became the pupil of the captivating Aspasia in dancing, as well as in eloquence, even when he was advanced in life. Montaigne, after extolling the mighty intellect and lofty virtues of Socrates, his patience and forbearance under poverty, hunger, the untractableness of his children and the scratches of his wife, concludes by saying that " he never refused to play at cobnut, nor to ride the hobby-horse with the boys."* I do not mean to imply, however, that our own scholars and distinguished sages should dance with children, or take lessons in dancing of courtesans, or play at cobnut with boys, but only that they should relieve their mental labors by such amusements and recreations, such social enjoyments as, are consistent with their characters and agreeable to their feelings.

As a pure air not only serves to invigorate and sustain the body, but likewise to animate the mind, literary men should always choose for their studies, where so much of their time is passed, large and airy rooms. The narrow and confined apartments which many select for the prosecution of their mental labors, cannot be otherwise than prejudicial to health.

Different individuals, as we should naturally conclude, vary materially in their capability of supporting mental exertions. This may in some cases be referrible to habit, and in others to the native strength or feebleness of the constitution in general, or of the organ of thought in particular. To some persons mental application is always irksome; the task of thinking is the most unwelcome one that can be imposed on them. While in others, just the reverse is observed; the intellectual operations are ever accomplished

* Essays.

with ease and satisfaction, and to the new results of their studies and reflections do they owe the purest delights of existence. In the latter, then, the exercise of mind, being less arduous, and associated also with a pleasurable excitement, will be far better sustained than in the former. Mental occupations for which one has no taste, I scarce need say, are much sooner followed by fatigue and exhaustion, and are consequently more injurious, than such as accord with the inclinations.

I may here remark, though it must be sufficiently obvious to every one, that we can form no correct estimate of the absolute amount of mental labor in different individuals from what they accomplish. For as the giant in body may support his three hundred weight with as little effort as the dwarf his one, so also may the gigantic intellect produce its astonishing results with the same ease that the less gifted mind performs its comparatively insignificant tasks. Many a poetaster has doubtless worked as hard to bring forth a volume of doggerel verses, as Newton did in the production of his Principia.

In relation to the period of time that may be safely and profitably devoted to study, we can lay down no rules which will be universal in their application. Few persons, however, can spend advantageously, and without hazard to the physical health, more than seven, or, at furthest, eight hours of the twenty-four in close mental application. As the brain grows weary, its capabilities must diminish, and its productions in consequence be comparatively feeble, whence they are said to smell of the lamp. Having then regard only to the intellectual results, nothing is really gained by overtasking the mind. It has been truly remarked that " there is scarcely any book which does not savor of painful composition in some part of it; because the author has written when he should have rested."

CHAPTER IV.

THE INTELLECTUAL OPERATIONS ARE NECESSARILY ASSOCIATED,
TO A GREATER OR LESS EXTENT, WITH PASSION.—THOSE
MENTAL AVOCATIONS WHICH ELICIT THE STRONGEST MORAL
FEELINGS ARE MOST DETRIMENTAL TO HEALTH.

THE intellectual operations are seldom if ever altogether
isolated from passion. Indeed, it is oftentimes through the
activity of the passions that the powers of our understanding develope and perfect themselves. Even the mathemati-
cal studies, which would seem so purely to engage the reasoning powers, are not entirely exempt from all moral excitement or commotion. The mathematician may experience
anger or regret if he encounters obstacles or difficulties in
the solution of his problems, and joy and satisfaction under
the opposite circumstances. But then with how many of
our intellectual labors do not the most agitating feelings, as
of hope and fear, envy, jealousy, anger, almost necessarily
blend themselves! Need I instance the deep and terrible
passions so frequently called forth in controversies of a religious and political character, and which have so often lighted
the torch of the bigot, and deluged fields in blood? Where

is the eminent statesman, who, if he be not as phlegmatic as a clod of earth, does not at times, even in the midst of his highest mental exertions, feel himself writhing under the most painfully conflicting emotions?

It will scarce be disputed that the particular motives which are the incentives of our mental labors must serve to determine their influence upon the feelings. If knowledge be pursued for its own sake, or with a benevolent end, its acquisition will generally be associated with a quiet self-complacency, diffusing a healthful serenity throughout the whole moral constitution. But when, on the other hand, the stimulus to its pursuit is selfish ambition or personal aggrandizement, then may the most agitating and baneful passions of our nature be engendered.

We see, then, that it may be no easy matter to decide in each individual instance how much the intellectual operations are immediately concerned in the production of physical infirmities and premature decay, and how far they act indirectly through the emotions. It is not always to the midnight lamp alone, as is so commonly supposed, that the pale cheek and contracted brow of the scholar are due. The ambitious strife so active among literary men, and the anxious desire for success and popular favor, and all the consequent moral agitation and suffering, as of envy, jealousy, anxiety, deferred or defeated hopes, oftentimes do more, far more, to break down the constitution, than would even the most arduous mental efforts in their unblended operation.

The literary labors of Sir Walter Scott, although so persevering, do not seem, until aided by other causes, to have been productive of any injury to his health, which is to be ascribed in a great measure to his peculiarly happy temperament. He appears through his whole career to have enjoyed a remarkable exemption from all those painfully agitating feelings which so wear upon the mind and body of the larger proportion of authors; to have displayed little of that keen sensibility so proverbially characteristic of the aspirants for literary fame. Hence his mental efforts must have been attended with less anxiety, and his moral tranquillity less hazarded by their event than among the more sensitive tribe of writers. It may furthermore be added that he was constant in his habits of exercise in the open air. But in the latter part of his life, when the brightness of his fortune had become overcast by the clouds of adversity; when his mental tasks were mingled with anxiety and broke in upon his needful rest, and his regular and salutary exercise, then did his physical health begin to yield, and fatal disease of the brain soon closed the last and most painfully tragic scene of his conspicuous and worthy career.

Those mental employments then, as it will now be inferred, which have the least tendency to call forth the painful and agitating emotions, will always be found most consonant to health. I may mention, in illustration, those tranquil and innocent studies which are embraced under the various departments of natural history, as botany, horticulture, zoology, &c., studies which rarely fail to bring content and serenity to the mind, to soften asperities of feeling, and to render healthier, happier, and better, those who have become devoted to them.

Studies that exercise especially the reasoning faculties, whose aim is truth, and which are attended with positive and satisfactory results, inasmuch as they afford the most calm and permanent gratification, and favor, therefore, that harmony between the moral and physical nature which has been deemed so important to health and longevity, are most safe and salutary in their influence on body and mind. Hence it is that those engaged in the exact sciences, as the mathematician, the astronomer, the chemist, usually enjoy better health, firmer nerves, more uniform moral tranquillity, and, other things equal, I believe a longer term of existence than those whose pursuits are more connected with the imagination, as the poet, or writer of fictitious narrative. In these latter the deep and varying passions are more frequently awakened; a morbid sensibility is encouraged, and the flame of life, exposed to such continual and unnatural excitement, must burn more unequally and waste more rapidly. Who does not rise with more self-satisfaction, with a more calm, equable and healthful condition of the mind, from studies which exercise and instruct the understanding, than from the morbidly exciting works of romantic fiction? Poetry and romance, then, ever as they wander from the standard of nature, must become the more prejudicial in their effects on the moral and physical constitution. To illustrate this remark I need but refer to the writings of Lord Byron and Sir Walter Scott.

Reason, the noblest gift of our nature, should always reign superior; should always hold in proper subjection the subordinate faculties. Whenever this rightful order in the

mental economy is subverted, whenever reason becomes enslaved to the fancy, and a sickly sentimentality of feeling
usurps the place of the bold impressions of truth and reality,
the vigor of the nerves decays, health languishes, and life is
most commonly abbreviated.

"It is well known," says Dr. Pinel, "that certain professions conduce more than others to insanity, which are chiefly
those in which the imagination is unceasingly or ardently engaged." He informs us that on consulting the registers of
Bicetre, he found many priests and monks, as well as country
people, who had been terrified into insanity by the anticipation of hell torments; also many artists, painters, sculptors,
and musicians; some poets transported into madness by
their own productions, and a great many advocates and
attorneys. But no instances of persons whose professions
require the habitual exercise of the judging faculty;—not
one naturalist, nor a physician, nor a chemist, nor a geome-
trician.

Mr. Madden, an English writer, drew up tables to prove
the influence of different studies on the longevity of authors
and artists. At the head of these we find the natural philosophers with an average term of existence of seventy-five
years. At the foot are the poets, who average but fifty-
seven years, or eighteen less than those engaged in the natural sciences.* It must be admitted, however, that these
data of Mr. Madden are exposed to so many sources of error that no great reliance can be placed upon the inferences
drawn from them.

* Infirmities of Genius.

In conclusion of the present chapter, let me remark, what has been before implied, that all those mental avocations which are founded in benevolence, or whose end and aim are the good of mankind, being from their very nature associated with agreeable moral excitement, and but little mingled with the evil feelings of the heart, as envy, jealousy, hatred, must necessarily diffuse a kindly influence throughout the constitution.

CHAPTER V.

MENTAL labors judiciously varied will, in general, be far better sustained than those of a more uniform or concentrated
character. As the same physical effort soon tires and ex-
hausts the muscles concerned in it, so likewise will the same
mental exertion produce a corresponding effect on the faculties it particularly engages. Hence the manifest relief we
experience in changing our intellectual occupations—just,
indeed, as we do in shifting our postures, or our exercises.

Close and undivided attention to any one object of real
or fancied moment is apt to be followed, earlier or later, according to incidental circumstances, by pains and dizziness
of the head, palpitations and irregularities of the heart's action, general lassitude and prostration of strength, dimin-

ished appetite, impaired digestion, emaciation, a contracted, sallow, care-worn countenance, and a whitening and falling out of the hairs. Or the mind, too ardently devoted to a particular theme, too long and intently engrossed by some solitary and absorbing subject, may at last, as Dr. Johnson has so well illustrated in the history of his astronomer, lose all power of seeing it aright, or in other words, become actually insane in relation to it. The common saying, therefore, that one may tell a lie till he believes it, is not without foundation in truth. Hence extravagant enthusiasm comes hard upon the confines of, and sometimes actually passes into insanity. And there is no community which is not more or less infested with wild bigots, zealots, those swayed by a single idea, and hardly to be distinguished from monomaniacs, who for their own sakes, and that of the community, ought to be subjected to the discipline of a madhouse.

The improvement in the countenance and general aspect of the body, and in the healthful vigor of all the functions, consequent to a relaxation from concentrated mental application, there are few but must have experienced in themselves, or remarked in others.

Change would seem almost essential to our health and happiness.

> " Look abroad through Nature's range,
> Nature's mighty law is change."

If subjected to like influences for long continued periods, they cloy and weary the senses, and we pine for novelty.

4

The same food will after a while pall upon the taste; the
same scenery cease to delight the eye; the same society lose
its early charms, and even the voice of love will fall dull and
unmusical on the ear. Healthful and agreeable excitement
in most of our organs is, to a certain extent, dependent on
variations in their stimuli, and the brain forms no exception
to this rule. It is sameness that begets ennui, or that painful weariness of existence so often witnessed among mankind, urging them sometimes even to self-destruction as a
relief.

"Il est donc de la nature du plaisir et de la peine de se
détruire d'eux-mêmes, de cesser d'être parce qu'ils ont été.
L'art de prolonger la durée de nos jouissances consiste à en
varier les causes. . . . . . . Voyez cet homme que l'ennui
dévore aujourd'hui, à côté de celle près de qui les heures
fuyaient jadis comme l'éclair; il serait heureux s'il ne l'avait
point été, ou s'il pouvait oublier qu'il le fut autrefois."*

The older writers used particularly to recommend the
varying of the habits and scenes of life, as of eating, drinking, exercising, thinking; "to be sometimes in the country,
sometimes in the town; to go to sea, to hunt," etc. Some
of the ancient medical sages even went so far as to advise,
for the sake of change, an occasional slight excess. "To
indulge a little, now and then, by eating and drinking more
plentifully than usual." Most persons will find their account, both as respects health and happiness, in occasionally
quitting old scenes and duties, and interrupting their estab-

* Bichat. Recherches Physiologiques sur la Vie et la Mort.

lished habits and associations, since by so doing they will return to them with refreshed powers, and renewed susceptibilities of enjoyment. The law of mutation is stamped upon, and seems necessary to the harmony and perfection of all the works of creation, and its operation may be equally needful to elicit and sustain the healthful action of our own bodily and mental powers.

Although I have not been disposed to regard even severe mental exertions, of themselves, so common a source of physical infirmity as is generally done, nevertheless I conceive a temperate exercise of the intellect, united with habitual muscular activity, to be most favorable to the general health of the system, to longevity, and, I may furthermore add, to the greatest sum of happiness to the individual.

Man, however, at the present period of the world, rising to power and honor, not as in the earlier ages through feats of strength, or bodily exploits, but by the superior influence of his mental endowments, it is not surprising that our physical should so often be sacrificed to our moral nature ; that mind should be cultivated to the neglect, if not at the expense of the body.

Let me state in conclusion of the present chapter, that body and mind are so closely bound up together, that the slightest physical disease, particularly of the brain itself, may variously affect, or even destroy some or perhaps all the intellectual faculties. It requires but very little material change, but slight compression of this organ, to degrade the loftiest intellect below even that of the most stupid brute. The transcendent mind of Sir Walter Scott was reduced to the most melancholy state of imbecility by a little softening in a limited portion of the brain. The powerful intellect of Dean Swift sunk under the pressure of water upon the brain. For five years prior to his death, he remained speechless and idiotic, "a driveller and a show." But I might cite any number of instances of the most lofty understandings brought to a like pitiable and humiliating condition by some, oftentimes slight, material change in the brain, and sometimes of other organs but indirectly connected with the functions of mind. What then is this our boasted intellect when it takes so little a matter to turn the philosopher into the fool? The memory suffers oftentimes most strangely under certain physical conditions of the brain. The power of remembering recent events is sometimes destroyed, while those long past come up with unusual vividness before the mind. And again the reverse of this is true, daily occurrences being retained while those of older date are lost to the remembrance. Sometimes the memory for words, or even for a particular class of words, as nouns, adjectives, verbs, is destroyed. There may remain a distinct idea of things and their relations, and also of persons, but their names cannot be recalled, nor understood when heard. Thus one thing may be called for another, and sometimes the individual thus affected invents a sort of language of his own, and always using his words in the same sense, it comes to be understood by those in constant attendance upon him.* In some instances not only

* Abercrombie on the Brain.

language, but all knowledge that had been acquired prior to the invasion of the physical malady is effaced from the memory, so that a new education becomes necessary.

In certain conditions, moreover, of the brain, as in dreams, the excitement of delirium, etc., ideas long forgotten, or sensations which produced no idea at the time they were received, may be revived, or brought out in the most distinct and vivid forms. Very many extraordinary and almost incredible cases of this nature might be adduced. Thus languages long forgotten have been spoken fluently under such states of cerebral excitement. Dr. Carpenter cites a remarkable instance "in which a woman, during the delirium of fever, continually repeated sentences in a language unknown to those around her, which proved to be Hebrew and Chaldaic; of these she stated herself, on her recovery, to be perfectly ignorant; but on tracing her former history, it was found that, in her early life, she had lived as servant with a clergyman, who had been accustomed to walk up and down the passage, repeating or reading aloud sentences in these languages, which she must have retained in her memory unconsciously to herself."*

Diseases of other organs beside the brain exercise a remarkable influence upon the powers of the understanding. Thus in disorders, especially of the stomach, liver, bowels, the memory and judgment often become very obviously impaired, and all mental processes are conducted with unusual labor and embarrassment. "He," said Dr. George

---

* Human Physiology.

Cheyne, more than a hundred years ago, "that would have a *clear* Head, must have a *clean* Stomach."*

Full feeding lessens the clearness and activity of the intellectual faculties. An intellectual process which we could carry out with ease before, we might find very difficult and embarrassing after dinner. Hence gluttonous men, those who live under the dominion of their stomachs, are very apt to be stupid in their intellects.

> " Fat paunches have lean pates ; and dainty bits
> Make rich the ribs, but bankrupt quite the wits."†

That the particular nature of our food, as well as its quantity, may also exercise an important influence upon the strength and character of the understanding will, I think, hardly be disputed. But this subject is altogether too wide for the present volume.

* On Health and long Life.   † Love's Labor Lost.

CHAPTER VI.

EVILS TO BE APPREHENDED FROM THE INORDINATE EXERCISE
OF THE INTELLECT IN EARLY YEARS.

PREMATURE and forced exertions of the mental faculties
must always be at the risk of the physical constitution.
Parents, urged on by a mistaken ambition for their intellectual progress, are extremely apt to overtask the minds of
their offspring, and thus may often not only defeat their
own aims, but prepare the foundation of bodily infirmity,
and early decay. Such a course is, moreover, repugnant to
the plainest dictates of Nature, to be read in the instinctive
propensities of the young, which urge so imperiously to
physical action.

Exercise, in early existence especially, is a natural
want, being then essential to train the muscles to their requisite functions, and to insure to the frame its full development and just proportions. So strong, indeed, is this tendency to motion, that few punishments are more grievous to
childhood, than such as impose restraints upon it. The
young, in truth, of all animals of the higher orders, equally
display this necessary propensity. Liberate the calf or the

lamb from his confinement, and what a variety of muscular contractions will he not immediately exhibit in his active and happy gambols? He is herein but discovering the instincts of his nature, just as much as while cropping the grass and herbage. In tasking, therefore, the functions of the brain, and restraining, consequently, those of the muscles, in early life, we act in contravention to the most obvious laws of the animal constitution.

I do not mean that the powers of the mind are to be absolutely neglected at this period. They are certainly to be unfolded, but then prudently, and in just correspondence only with the development of the physical organization. To look for ripeness of intellect from the soft, delicate, and immature brain of childhood, is as unreasonable as it would be to expect our trees to yield us fruit while their roots were unconfirmed, and their trunks and branches succulent. " Nature," as was said by Rousseau, " intended that children should be children before they are men ; and if we attempt to pervert this order, we shall produce early fruit, which will have neither maturity nor savor, and which soon spoils ; we shall have young learned men, and old children. Infancy has an order of seeing, thinking, and feeling, which is proper to it. Nothing is more foolish than to wish to make children substitute ours for theirs; and I would as soon require a child to be five feet high, as to require judgment at ten years of age."*

In all the examples on record, I believe, in which chil-

* Cited by Tourtelle.

dren have reached maturity much earlier than in the common course of nature—as at six or eight years—old age and decay have been correspondently premature. In Dr. Millingen's Curiosities of Medical Experience, is cited "an account of a surprising boy, who was born at Willingham, near Cambridge, and upon whom the following epitaph was written :—' Stop, traveller, and wondering, know, here buried lie the remains of Thomas, son of Thomas and Margaret Hall, who, not one year old, had the signs of manhood; at three, was almost four feet high, endued with uncommon strength, a just proportion of parts, and a stupendous voice; before six, he died, as it were, at an advanced age.' " According to the surgeon who viewed him after death, the corpse presented every appearance of decrepit old age.

But, setting aside the hazard to the physical constitution, nothing is in reality gained, as respects the intellect, by such artificial forcing. On the contrary, the energies of the mind being thus prematurely exhausted, it seldom happens that these infant prodigies, which raise such proud hopes in the breasts of parents and friends, display even mental mediocrity in their riper years. In some cases insanity, or even idiocy, has been the melancholy result of such unnatural exertion of the organ of thought, while yet delicate and unconfirmed.

Furthermore, those even whose minds naturally, or independent of education, exhibit an unusual precociousness, rarely fulfil the expectations they awaken—either falling the victims of untimely decay,—

" So wise so young, do ne'er live long,"—
4*

or else, reaching early the limit of their powers, they stop short in their bright career, and thus, in adult age, take a rank very inferior to those whose faculties were more tardy in unfolding, and whose early years were, consequently, less flattering. That mind will be likely to attain the greatest perfection, whose powers are disclosed gradually, and in due correspondence with the advancement of the other functions of the constitution. It is a familiar fact, that trees are exhausted by artificially forcing their fruit ; and, likewise, that those vegetables which are slow in yielding their fruit, are generally stronger and more lasting than such as arrive earlier at maturity.

"We have frequently seen, in early age," observes a French writer on health, "prodigies of memory, and even of erudition, who were, at the age of fifteen or twenty, imbecile, and who have continued so through life. We have seen other children, whose early studies have so enfeebled them, that their miserable career has terminated with the most distressing diseases, at a period at which they should only have commenced their studies." *

* Tourtelle.

CHAPTER VII.

INTELLECTUAL OPERATIONS, CONCLUDED.—A FEW GENERAL
SUGGESTIONS IN REGARD TO THE EDUCATION OF CHILDREN.
—SEVERE INTELLECTUAL EXERTIONS ARE ALWAYS HAZARD-
OUS IN OLD AGE.

WHEN we consider the injudicious management of childhood, physical, moral and intellectual, so common in the
community, through the fond indulgence, ignorance, or
wickedness of parents, and all the future ills to flesh and
spirit that must result therefrom, we have almost reason,
like the Thracians, to weep at the birth of a child.

In Sparta, while governed by the laws of Lycurgus,
education was wholly under the control of the state; but
its direction was not assumed until the age of seven. Up
to this time, children remained with their parents, who
placed little or no restraint upon their natural actions.
Afterwards they were enrolled in companies, under the su-
perintendence of governors appointed by the public, and
were subjected to a strict and regular course of physical,
moral and intellectual culture. Lycurgus then, who, as
Plutarch says, "resolved the whole business of legislation

into the bringing up of youth," appears to have fixed upon
the age of seven as the proper one to begin the systematic
education.

During the first years of existence, the brain, probably
from its physical condition, is inadequate to the task of reflection, or to the accomplishment of the higher intellectual
functions. It would appear—if I may indulge for a moment
in theory—that the vital forces are now especially required
by the system at large to maintain its necessary development. If, therefore, they are too prodigally expended on
the intellect, or unequally diverted to the brain, it must be
at the cost of the other functions and organs. At any rate,
under such circumstances, the growth is generally retarded,
the muscular system but imperfectly developed, and the
body continues spare and devoid of its fair proportions.
The complexion will, moreover, be pale and sickly, the circulation and digestion feeble, and nervous affections, scrofula,
or other infirmities of the flesh, are likely to supervene,
overburdening existence, and shortening its term.

But little bodily restraint, therefore, certainly for the
first five or six years of their life, should be imposed upon
children. Long and irksome confinement to the sitting, or
indeed to any one position, and especially in close rooms,
cannot but be inimical to the just and healthful development of their physical constitution. On a general principle, too, it is better that they be allowed to choose their
own muscular actions—to run, jump, frolic, and use their
limbs according to their inclinations, or, in other words, as
nature dictates, than be subjected to any artificial system of
exercise.

Let it not be inferred, however, that the mind is to be neglected, or to receive no regard during the term mentioned ; all contended for is, that its systematic education be not entered upon; that no tasks demanding confinement and fixed attention be imposed upon it. Light instructions, adapted to the capacities, and particularly such as can be associated with amusement and exercise, may be advantageously imparted, even on the earliest development of the mental faculties. And then the moral education, as I shall hereafter show, can scarce have too early a beginning.

Whenever a precocity of intellect is displayed, or a disposition to thinking and learning in advance of the years, and to the neglect of the usual and salutary habits of early life, it should be restrained rather than encouraged, since it is far more desirable that children grow up to be sound and healthy men, than as premature, sickly, and short-lived intellectual monsters.

In the first period of our being, the perceptive faculties, and the memory for words, are, more especially, to be called into action. That such is in accordance with the ordina_ tions of nature, the earliest habits and propensities of children clearly reveal to us. While awake, they are constantly, and almost as it were without an effort, learning the sensible qualities of external bodies, and the symbolical sounds by which they are indicated, and thus daily collecting the raw materials of knowledge, to be wrought into various new and wonderful intellectual forms, as the brain and reflective faculties advance to maturity.

In the primary instructions then of children, such

knowledge only is to be imparted, for the acquisition of
which they evince a natural aptitude. We observe them,
for example, catching with interest, repeating, and remembering new words; delighted with, and soon imitating,
harmonious sounds; pleased with pictures, and attempting
rude copies of them. Hence, beside language, music and
drawing might not improperly be introduced into the early
systematic education. The analogy here between the infancy of society, and that of the individual, cannot fail to
strike us. Barbarous people, like children, are particularly
impressed by the sensible qualities of objects, and for the
expression of which, and their own feelings, they have an
imperfect language. They possess, likewise, a rude harmony, painting and sculpture; but no science, no philosophy; scarce any thing to intimate the progress of the reflective powers, or the maturity of the species.

From what has been remarked it will be readily seen
that paintings and drawings, appealing as they do directly
to the senses and memory, must be especially useful as a
means of conveying elementary knowledge to childhood. In
natural history, for example, a good deal of rudimental instruction may in this way be communicated even in very
early life.

As the mind and body ripen, those studies are to be entered upon in which the reasoning faculties are in a special
manner engaged; as the science of numbers, intellectual,
moral, and the various other departments of philosophy.
The period when the more purely intellectual education
ought to be commenced cannot, of course, be precisely fixed,

for the reason that no two minds will be likely to mature in exact correspondence with each other. It is questionable, however, if the more strictly philosophical sciences can be generally prosecuted to much advantage before the sixteenth or seventeenth year.

Although the mind as it becomes more developed may be submitted to a stricter discipline than at first, yet at no period of the scholastic education is it to be rigorously tasked; but agreeable recreations and active exercises should frequently alternate with the labors of study, thus insuring a sound body as well as an enlightened mind. Plato had much to say on the exercises of the youth of his city, as their races, their games, their dances, &c., and seems to have regarded these as of most important consideration in the training of the young to the lettered sciences. That erudition and health are each most desirable is not to be disputed; nevertheless, to the mass of mankind—for comparatively few earn their bread by the efforts of their intellect—a good share of the latter will be likely to conduce far more to their success and happiness in life, than a large and disproportionate amount of the former.

In children of weakly constitutions, severe mental application is in a particular manner hazardous. In such the physical education is ever of paramount regard; the future health—for whose absence life has no recompense—being closely dependent on its judicious management. The practice, unhappily a very common one, of selecting the most delicate child for the scholar, is founded in error; some pursuit demanding physical action and exposure to the open

air is here especially necessary to impart new vigor to the
infirm body.

In view of the physical health of the young, and the proper development of their frames, it is of the highest importance that the apartments appropriated for their instruction
be both spacious and airy, and so planned, also, that any unnatural restraint on the posture of the body shall be avoided.
Breathing the corrupted air of crowded school-rooms, and
long confinement in them under constrained positions, is
even at the present time, under all our improvements in
their ventilation and construction, a not unusual source of
bodily infirmity. Observation has convinced me that children suffer in their health even more than adults from a confined and impure air.

Finally, the instructions of youth should always, as far
as practicable, be associated with pleasure. Children ought
to be allured and encouraged, not forced and frightened to
their mental tasks. Instead of

> "——— creeping like snail
> Unwillingly to school,"

they should go to it cheerfully and merrily as to a place of
enjoyment, and not under the terrifying apprehension of the
rod. "A chaplet of *laurel*," as it has been said, "is worth a
cart-load of *birch*." "How much more decent would it be,"
says Montaigne, "to see the forms on which the boys sit,
strewed with flowers and green leaves, than with the bloody
twigs of willows? I should choose to have the pictures of
Joy and Gladness in the schools, together with Flora and

the Graces, as the philosopher Speusippus had in his, that where their profit is, there might be their pleasure. The viands that are wholesome for children ought to be sweetened with sugar, and those that are hurtful to them made as bitter as gall."

The conduct of education has of late certainly undergone a perceptible melioration ; yet it needs no great stretch of memory to carry us back to the time when the following remarks of the author just cited on the schools of his own period would not have been altogether misapplied to our own. " They are really so many cages in which youth are shut up as prisoners. Do but go thither just as their exercises are over, you hear nothing but the cries of children under the smart of correction, and the bellowing noise of the masters raging with passion. How can such tender, timorous souls be tempted to love their lessons by those ruby-faced guides, with wrath in their aspects and the scourge in their hands?"* The system of corporal punishment in schools is, as it should be, much less common than formerly; but whether, contrary to the opinion of such wise men as Solomon and Doctor Johnson, the rod should be entirely spared, will admit of some reasonable doubt. There are some children so morally obdurate, that there seems to be no other effectual way to act upon them than through their physical sensibilities. Even here flogging should be very rarely resorted to, but when it is done it should be done thoroughly. Nothing can have a worse effect upon a child than frequent

* Essays.

small floggings. The birch then, although its use is properly becoming very much relaxed, will not be likely, for all the arguments in favor of moral suasion and moral influences of the humane, to be wholly dispensed with. It has too many associations, literary, classical and other, to be lightly given up, or easily forgotten. We tingle at the very thought of it. Shenstone has immortalized it in his School Mistress. Its very name (*Betula*, from the Latin *batuo* to beat) recalls to our thoughts the use to which it has been applied from time out of mind. "Its twigs," says Threlkeld, as cited by Dr. Drummond, "are used for besoms and rods; the one for the cleanly housewife to sweep down the cobwebs, and the other for the magisterial pedagogue to drive the colt out of the man."

In the last term of existence, all severe mental efforts become hazardous, in a special manner endangering apoplexies and palsies, to which this period is so peculiarly predisposed. In extreme age, indeed, almost every sort of exertion grows irksome and difficult; and the brain and other animal organs, fatigued as it were by the protracted exercise of life, incline to rest, the condition to which they are so fast approaching. Vitality, now feeble and nearly expended, the most prudent economy is demanded to preserve it to its utmost limits. Both mind and body, therefore, should be suffered to repose from all the cares, and anxieties, and labors of existence, that they may glide easily and gradually into their final sleep.

PART SECOND.

PASSIONS.

CHAPTER VIII.

THE mind, equally with the body, is the subject of numerous feelings, pleasurable and painful, and which, according as they are mild or intense, receive the name of affections or passions.

The term passion comes from the Greek. verb πασχω, *pascho*, and the Latin patior, each meaning to suffer, or to be acted upon, or affected either pleasantly or painfully. In its literal and primitive sense, then, it imports all mental feelings, without respect to their degree, although in common usage it denotes only their deeper shades; the word affection being employed to express those of a more gentle character. Still, a division of this sort must be in a great measure arbitrary, for as different degrees only of moral feeling are implied by affection and passion, it is clear that no definite point can be established at which the former will be just exalted into the latter, or the latter just reduced to the former. In truth, the literal signification of the term affection answers precisely to that of passion.

Some have attempted to make a distinction between passion and emotion, using the former as expressive of passive-
ness, or the simple feeling immediately resulting from the
moral impulse ; and the latter to indicate the visible effects,
or the commotion manifested in the frame. But such a
distinction, certainly in a physiological and pathological examination of the passions, will seldom be found practicable,
since the feeling and physical phenomena are oftentimes so
closely associated as to appear to be but the simultaneous
effects of the primary exciting cause, and both, therefore, to
belong essentially to the constitution of the passion in which
they are displayed.

In the ensuing pages, then, the word passion will be
employed as a general expression for moral feeling, and its
concomitant physical effects, and it will therefore comprehend, and be used synonymously with both affections and
emotions, its degree being denoted, when necessary, by the
adjunction of an adjective. I may observe, however, that it
is only the more exaggerated feelings, or what all agree in
classing as passions, that put in hazard the physical health,
in more particular relation to which we have to consider
them.

As the design of the present volume calls for no detailed
metaphysical disquisition on the passions, our classification
of them will be very general and simple. We shall consider them under three principal heads, viz. : pleasurable,
painful, and mixed, or those in which pain and pleasure are
more or less obviously associated. Not that I regard this
as an unobjectionable division. Like all others, it is in a

measure artificial, yet it seems to us to be the one which will best subserve the grand object of our treatise. The line especially between the two first and last classes, cannot in every instance be nicely defined; for the passions ranked as pleasurable are seldom wholly pure or unmingled with pain. Thus the happiest love is rarely clear from all pangs of jealousy, or the brightest hope from all sufferings of apprehension; and, as though it were preordained that no human enjoyment should be complete, even when at the summit of our wishes, and under the full gratification of our most ardent passions, fears and forebodings of change will almost always sully the purity of our happiness.

The same is in like manner true of the painful passions. Rare indeed is it that we find them wholly unmitigated by those which are pleasurable. Some faint beams of hope will generally penetrate even the deepest moral gloom. It is questionable, then, whether any of the passions, could they be perfectly analyzed, would be found absolutely free from all mixture of their opposite.

A large proportion of the painful passions experienced in society, are the offspring of such as are pleasurable. We suffer, because we have enjoyed. Our present state is darkened by contrasting it with the brighter past. Thus does our happiness frequently depend much less on what we are than on what we have been. The humble peasant in his lowly cot may enjoy as much felicity as the noble in his lordly palace; but reduce the latter to the condition of the former, and he becomes overwhelmed with misery. Diminish the wealth of the rich man to what he would once have

regarded as abundance, and wretchedness, sometimes even
despair, may be the melancholy consequence. Often then
might we be happy had we never been so, or could we bury
in oblivion all remembrance of the past.

The reverse likewise holds true; the pleasurable passions deriving their existence from, or becoming greatly enhanced by, those which are painful. Few, probably, have reflected how large a share of human misery and human happiness derives its existence from contrasts. As we suffer because
we have enjoyed, so also do we enjoy because we have suffered. Indeed, under our present constitution, the sufferings would seem almost as necessary to the enjoyments of
life, as are the toils and fatigues of the day to the balmy
slumbers of night.

Knowledge, too, or the enlargement of our ideas, in
opening to us new fields of desire, and causing new comparisons with our present condition, becomes a frequent
source of discontent, and the various painful passions of
which it is the parent.

CHAPTER IX.

GENERAL REMARKS ON THE EVILS AND ADVANTAGES OF THE
PASSIONS.——THE PHYSICIAN SHOULD INVESTIGATE THE
MORAL AS WELL AS THE PHYSICAL CAUSES OF DISEASE.——
INDIVIDUALS, FROM TEMPERAMENT, EDUCATION, AND VARI-
OUS INCIDENTAL CIRCUMSTANCES, DIFFER VERY STRIKINGLY
IN THE FORCE AND CHARACTER OF THEIR PASSIONS.

THE agency of the passions in the production of disease,
especially in the advanced stages of civilisation, when men's
relations are intimate, and their interests clash, and their
nervous susceptibilities are exalted, can scarce be adequately appreciated. It is doubtless to this more intense and
multiplied action of the passions, in union sometimes with
the abuse of the intellectual powers, that we are mainly to
attribute the greater frequency of diseases of the heart and
brain in the cultivated, than in the ruder states of society.
Few, probably, even suspect the amount of bodily infirmity
and disease among mankind resulting from moral causes—
how often the frame wastes, and premature decay comes
on, under the corroding influence of some painful passion.

It has seemed to me that the medical profession, in
seeking for the remote occasions of disease, are too apt to

5

neglect those existing in the mind.   Thus does it oftentimes happen that, while the physician is imputing the infirmities of his patient to all their most familiar causes, as bad diet, impure air, want of exercise, etc., it is in reality some un- happy and unrevealed passion which is preying on the springs of life.   A knowledge of the secret troubles of the sick would, in many instances, shed new light on their treat- ment, or save them, at any rate, from becoming the subjects, if not the victims, of active medicinal agents.   Plato has been cited as saying, " The office of the physician extends equally to the purification of mind and body ; to neglect the one, is to expose the other to evident peril.   It is not only the body that, by its sound constitution, strengthens the soul; but the well-regulated soul, by its authoritative power, maintains the body in perfect health."

In delicate and sensitive constitutions, the operation of the painful passions is ever attended with the utmost dan- ger ; and, should there exist a predisposition to any par- ticular form of disease, as consumption, or insanity, for ex. ample, it will generally be called into action under their strong and continued influence, as I purpose to illustrate under the head of particular passions.   It is probably true, as was said by Zimmerman, that, " In general, men of a powerful imagination suffer the most from violent sallies of the soul; and they who have more of reason than imagina- tion, suffer most from the slower movements of the mind. Very indolent or stupid people, in general, suffer the least from the passions; but they who unite an enlightened reason to a lively and reflecting genius, are the most agitated by them."* The same view was expressed by Dr. George Cheyne, and from whom Zimmerman copied it. †

The passions, however, although so greatly abused, and the occasion of so large a proportion of the ills we are doomed to suffer, yet when properly trained, and brought under due subjection to the reasoning powers, are the source of all that is great and good in man's nature, and contribute in a thousand ways, both directly and indirectly, to health and happiness. Intellect, without their quickening influence, even could it exist at all, would be but a dull and dreary waste. The soul would have no impulse to arouse it from its senseless apathy. They are the sunbeams which light and cheer our mental atmosphere. The greatest achievements are always accomplished by those of strong passions, but with a corresponding development of the superior faculties to regulate and control them. Sluggish feelings can never be parents to high and generous resolves. It belongs to us then to govern and direct to their proper ends, through the force of reason and the will, the passions which nature has implanted in our breasts. They cannot, nor is it desirable that they should be extirpated.

> " When Reason, like the skilful charioteer,
>   Can break the fiery passions to the bit,
>   And, spite of their licentious sallies, keep
>   The radiant track of glory ; passions, then,
>   Are aids and ornaments. Triumphant Reason,
>   Firm in her seat and swift in her career,

* On Experience in Physic.
† Essay on Health and Long Life.

Enjoys their violence ; and, smiling, thanks
Their formidable flame for high renown."*

Mankind, owing to original differences of constitution
or temperament, vary remarkably in the ardency of their
feelings. Indeed, the external physical characters will
oftentimes pretty clearly indicate the native vivacity and
force of the passions. Thus, who would not at once distinguish, even by the complexion, the sanguine, or warm and
excitable, from the phlegmatic, or cold and passionless ?
With acute moral, we almost, if not always have associated
corresponding physical sensibilities. Hence, if slight causes
affect the mind, so likewise will they the body; or, as it has
been said, " he who suffers extremely from a slight wound,
will suffer equally from a disagreeable idea."

Incidental circumstances operating upon the constitution, will likewise influence the activity and strength of the
passions. Hence it is that the inhabitants of tropical countries are more apt to be hasty and violent in their feelings,
to be agitated by more vivid emotions, and consequently to
become enslaved to their sensual and animal nature, than
those who dwell in colder climes. The unspiritual or carnal
heaven of the Mahomedan is but a semblance of the sensual
feelings inspired by his own voluptuous climate. Indolence and free living have also the effect to aggravate, and
activity and temperance to weaken the operation of the
passions ; whence there are few better antidotes to their
ungovernable violence than simple food and drink, and

* Young.

bodily labor. Fasting has from time immemorial been observed as a religious rite to mortify the flesh and spirit, and subdue inordinate passions. Fasting and prayer are especially urged in our own religion as a security against temptation, or our immoderate and wicked desires.

In some persons the animal or baser nature would appear constitutionally to predominate, the passions readily breaking from the control of reason and the will, and bringing sorrow, shame, and disease upon the unhappy individual. In others the contrary is true; the intellectual nature holding the supremacy, and ever keeping the feelings under a just restraint; and truly fortunate are they,

" Whose blood and judgment are so well co-mingled."

Some, again, appear naturally impressed by the good, and others by the evil passions. We meet individuals, rarely, it is true, yet we do meet such, in whom the amiable affections maintain a distinguished pre-eminence, even from the earliest development of their moral nature. They appear predestined to be good. Their placid and benevolent tempers would seem to be the result of a physical necessity, or of some happy but partial action of creative power. Such, however, are exceptions to the general laws of the species, and are consequently never perpetuated. But here the question will necessarily arise, Can we ascribe any virtue, any merit to such innate goodness, to such constitutional amiableness ? Virtue is essentially active. It is engendered, through the force of the will, out of the contentions between the generous and noble, and the base and despicable passions of the soul. Its very existence depends upon the successful struggle of our fortitude with the evil dispositions that are striving within us. It can only, therefore, be predicated of imperfect natures. Chastity would be no virtue in one without carnal desires, nor clemency in him who was incapable of hatred or anger. The poets glorify their gods by making them war with demons. As the artist heightens and sets off the bright and beautiful colors of his canvas by the dark shades with which he intermingles and contrasts them, and exaggerates the beauty of his angels through the ugliness of his devils, so does nature, on her moral canvas, enhance the lustre and comeliness of virtue by the very shadows and deformities which she throws into the picture. Hence, on the commonly received notions of the character of God,—as the idea has been elsewhere suggested,—although we may call him good, great, just, bountiful, yet we cannot call him virtuous; for his goodness demands no effort, no sacrifice; it belongs to his very essence; is as natural to him as it is to the flower to shed its odors, or the sun its luminous rays.

There is ever a contention going on in the human breast between the pure and wicked passions or dispositions, and herein consists all the machinery of demons, good and bad, in which the different systems of theology so abound. They are typical of the good and evil within us. Their wars for man's salvation or destruction are moral allegories. We resist the devil when we cultivate and cherish the higher, and successfully strive against our vicious sentiments and

inclinations. The evil demon has gained us, when the baser
or animal triumph over the better and higher powers of our
nature. Then has our good angel forsaken us, and we are
left to our doom, to moral and physical ruin.

As it has already been remarked, the good passions
greatly preponderate in some natures, so do the bad in others; and we meet those who scarce ever, even from their
childhood, manifest an amiable or generous feeling. Such
extreme cases, however, are happily rare. Generally, there
exists in our composition, a due mixture of the good and evil
dispositions. " Our virtues would be proud, if our faults
whipped them not; and our crimes would despair, if they
were not cherished by our virtues."

Finally, there are those, who from early existence are
marked by the predominance of some particular passion, as
fear, anger, or ambition; that is, they are constitutionally
timorous, irascible, or aspiring in their tempers. Education, however, may do much, very much, in repressing passions originally in excess, and developing such as are deficient; and herein consists moral culture, so vitally essential
both to our health and happiness. Need I say, then, how
much we must be the creatures of constitution and circumstance? how much of what we are we must owe to our native
organization and predispositions, and those resistless influences which, in the necessary current of events, are brought
to act upon us?

I am aware that views like the preceding will be objected
to by some, as inconsistent with the freedom of our will, or
as tending to the doctrine of necessity, of which many ap-

pear to entertain such needless dread. That we belong to some vast system, the grand purpose of which is hidden from human intelligence, will scarce be gainsaid ; and that our every volition and action may be but infinitesimal and necessary links in the mighty and complicated chain of this great and unsearchable system, it is not irrational to believe. But as I pledged myself in the outset to shun all abstract speculations, I will leave this perplexed subject of fatalism with the remark only that there was true philosophy in that ancient mariner, who, being caught in a great storm at sea, exclaimed thus to Neptune :—" O God, if it is thy will, I shall be saved ! and if it is thy will, I shall be destroyed ! but I'll still steer my rudder true."

CHAPTER X.

THE passions have become so multiplied and modified
through our social wants and relations, that it would be in
vain to attempt a precise and satisfactory philosophical classification of them. The very same passion is often differ-
ently designated according to its intenseness, or as it is
transient or enduring in its character; as fear and terror;
hatred, anger, rage; sorrow, melancholy, despair. And
then, again, many of the passions are so complex in their
nature, or involve such a variety of feelings, that it becomes
a matter of no little perplexity to decide on the particular
denomination to which they rightfully belong. Could each
one, however, be subjected to an accurate analysis, or traced
up to its primal elements, they would probably all be redu-

5*

cible to a few simple ones, grounded on our saving instincts, and consequently having a direct or indirect relation to the preservation of the individual, or the perpetuation of the species.   Like our organic structure, they would be found to have their original types discoverable in the lower departments of life.   Thus in the inferior animal we may see the passions operating in their most simple and necessary forms, as exemplified in fear and anger.

Some writers on the passions have regarded them all but as emanations from the principle of self-love.

> " Two principles in human nature reign,
> Self-love to urge, and reason to restrain ;
> Self-love, the spring of motion, acts the soul ;
> Reason's comparing balance rules the whole."*

Whether such, however, be their essential and primary source, is a question which, interesting as it may be in ethical science, is nevertheless unimportant to the design of the present essay.   Our principal purpose being to show that the passions founded in pleasure are, as an ordinary principle, healthful, and those associated with pain, or in which pain preponderates, the reverse, the aforementioned summary division of them, viz., into pleasurable, painful, and those in which pleasure and pain are obviously commingled, is all that will be needful.

Let me here state the general proposition, which will be sufficiently illustrated in the sequel, that the condition of

* Pope's Essay on Man.

our moral feelings exercises a potent influence upon our physical organs, while that of our physical organs influences in an equal manner our moral feelings. In other words, that mind and body necessarily participate in the weal and woe of each other. Thus passion has been not unaptly defined, "any emotion of the soul which affects the body, and is affected by it." So remarkable is this interchange of influence between the mental feelings and bodily conditions, that by imitating the attitude and general expression of a particular passion, the sense of that passion will not unfrequently be straightway produced in the mind.

The effects of the passions are declared especially in those organs and functions which have been termed organic, or vegetative; as in the heart and general circulation; in the lungs, the stomach, the liver, the bowels, the kidneys, &c. Need I instance the disturbance in the circulation, respiration, digestion, which so immediately ensues under the strong operation of anger, fear, and grief?

So sudden and sensible is the influence of the different emotions upon the viscera of the chest and abdomen, as to have deceived Bichat, and several other eminent physiologists into the belief that in these organs is their primary seat. And to the same origin, in truth, would the figurative language of every people, civilized or barbarous, appear to refer them. Thus, while to indicate thought or intellect the hand of the orator is carried to the head; to express sentiment or passion it is directed, almost as it were instinctively, to the chest, or the pit of the stomach; and who would not be offended by the impropriety of the contrary?

That the passions should be referred to the situation where their physical consequences are particularly felt, is not to be wondered at; still it is not true that they are primarily and essentially in the viscera. They must originate in some condition of the mind, in some peculiar mode of perception, though instantly, many times even with the swiftness of thought, transmitting their influence to one or more of the organs mentioned.

It has been supposed that each emotion has some special organ or organs on which its power is more particularly expended. That some act most obviously on the heart, as fear and joy; others on the respiration, as surprise; and again others, as grief, on the digestive organs. "We shall find," says Dr. Bostock, "a clear indication of this connection in our common forms of speech, which must have been derived from observation and generally recognized, before they could have become incorporated with our language. The paleness of fear, the breathlessness of surprise, and the bowels of compassion, are phrases sanctioned by the custom of different ages and nations."* That certain of the secretions are influenced by particular passions is a well known fact. Thus the tears flow in grief and other strong emotions. Maternal love is well known to promote the flow of milk. Dr. Parry relates an instance of a lady who, long after she had ceased to nurse, would have a secretion of milk on hearing a child cry.† Even girls, old

* Elementary System of Physiology.
† Elements of Pathology.

women, and men, are said sometimes to have secreted milk under a strong desire to furnish it. The idea of savory food stimulates the flow of saliva.

The effects of a passion, however, as will hereafter be shown, are rarely limited to a single organ and function, but more or less of the viscera and their functions, though not usually in an equal degree, are embraced within their influence. But even admitting it to be true that each emotion bears a special relation to some individual organ or organs, our physiological knowledge of the passions is far from having reached that degree of perfection which would enable us in every instance to detect such relation.

It may be proper to remark here, that there exists a reciprocation of influence between the moral feelings and internal organs—that the particular condition of the former may either determine, or be determined by, that of the latter. Indigestion, for example, is well known to be sometimes the consequence, and sometimes the cause, of an irritable and unhappy temper. A sour disposition may be either the occasion or result of a sour stomach. Thus, in some instances, we sweeten the stomach by neutralizing the acerbity of the temper, while in others, we sweeten the temper by neutralizing the acidity of the stomach. Who of us but must have felt our digestion improve under the brightening of our moral feelings? And who of us but must have experienced the brightening of our moral feelings under the improvement of our digestion?

Admitting the above remarks to be true, the reason will be plain why children who, through the ignorance or weak fondness of parents, are fed on indigestible diet, or indulged in improper gratifications of their appetite, other things being the same, require the rod so much oftener than others whose dietetic habits are regulated with more wisdom. An exclusive diet of bread and milk, united with judicious exercise in the open air, will oftentimes prove an effectual means of correcting the temper of peevish and refractory children.

When brought into close and frequent intercourse with particular individuals, we cannot but remark how sensitive, irritable, and disputatious they are apt to become, if unfavorable weather prevents for a few successive days their customary exercise abroad, and, more especially, if they have in the mean while been indulging in rich and indigestible food. The skin, at the same time, will look more dingy, and the eye less clear and bright than natural—circumstances, together, going to show that transient indigestion is the occasional cause of such unhappy state of temper. Under the conditions mentioned, a walk of an hour or two in the fresh air, will, by restoring the health of digestion, not rarely bring about the most agreeable change in the moral feelings.

The condition of the liver is also well known both to receive an influence from, and impart an influence to, the temper of the mind. Thus a sallow complexion, spare body, and the other signs of what is termed a bilious habit, are proverbially associated, either as cause or effect, with an unhappy disposition. I have known not a few individuals of unsteady tempers, in whom their amiable or unamiable fits were almost uniformly announced by the clearness or sallowness of their complexions.

Difficulties in other functions—as those of the uterine system—will likewise often cause a waywardness of temper, rendering the disposition morose and quarrelsome, or, it may be, gloomy and dejected. And the disturbance of the moral feelings, under the action of such physical causes, is sometimes to such extent as to constitute moral insanity, and more especially in those who have naturally weak resolutions, or but little strength of will, or have never been educated to a proper self-control. Shakspeare has said—

" 'Tis in ourselves that we are thus and thus."

And this is true in a physical, equally as in a moral sense. External things take their hue very much from our different physical conditions.

" An hypochondriacal man," says Zimmerman, "whose nerves are weakened and relaxed, will consider, perhaps, the earth as a frightful desert. The moment he feels a transitory relief, the country around him seems to be covered with flowers; he thinks that the sun shines out, and that the birds make the woods resound with their melody." *

The intellectual faculties, as previously shown, do not escape the influence of these physical disorders. Thus, under morbid states of digestion, the memory becomes impaired, the thoughts wander, or are concentrated with difficulty on any particular topic, and all mental exertions become irksome, and unsatisfactory in their results.

* On Experience in Physic.

The well-known moral infirmities of many of the distinguished literary geniuses of modern times, may doubtless have been owing, in a proportion of the cases, at least, to those of a bodily character. "If health and a fair day smile upon me," says Montaigne, "I am a good-natured man; if a corn trouble my toe, I am sullen, out of humor, and not to be seen." That the capricious and unhappy temper of Pope was due, in a great measure, to the imperfection of his constitution, and consequent disorder of his bodily functions, especially of digestion, will scarce, I think, be questioned.

The poet Burns possessed all that moral sensibility, all the acute sensitiveness of feeling, so common in men of superior and erratic genius. He was unsteady and jealous in his temper, subject to great mental despondency, and, like many other men of poetical genius, weak in moral fortitude, or in the resisting or controlling power of his will. Now he is well known to have suffered severely from dyspepsia, and other bodily ailments, even before he became intemperate, and which may have had no small share in the production of his mental infirmities. "Burns had in his constitution the peculiarities and delicacies that belong to the temperament of genius. He was liable, from a very early period of life, to that interruption in the process of digestion, which arises from deep and anxious thought, and which is sometimes the effect, and sometimes the cause, of depression of spirits. Connected with this disorder of the stomach, there was a disposition to headache, affecting more especially the temples and eyeballs, and frequently accompanied by violent and irregular movements of the heart.

Endowed by nature with great sensibility of nerves, Burns was, in his corporeal as well as in his mental system, liable to inordinate impressions—to fever of body as well as of mind." All these morbid tendencies, and associate moral infirmities, were greatly aggravated by the indolent, irregular, and intemperate habits to which he surrendered himself, more especially in the latter part of his melancholy career. " In his moments of thought, he reflected with the deepest regret on his fatal progress—clearly foreseeing the goal towards which he was hastening, without the strength of mind necessary to stop, or even to slacken his course. His temper now became more irritable and gloomy; he fled from himself into society, often of the lowest kind. And, in such company, that part of the convivial scene in which wine increases sensibility and excites benevolence, was hurried over, to reach the succeeding part, over which uncontrolled passion generally presided."* Genius, high mental culture and refinement, generally go with an excitable temperament, with moral and physical susceptibilities, oftentimes even morbidly delicate, and out of which are engendered a host of bodily and mental ailments and infirmities ; and all these frailties are encouraged and nourished by the peculiar habits and pursuits which genius affects. A certain degree of refinement of our sensibilities may be desirable, or, at any rate, other things being the same, must in a measure correspond with moral and intellectual culture ; but, when in excess, is incompatible both with health and happiness, and

* Life of Burns. By Dr. Currie.

unfits us for all the necessary and ordinary duties of life. All our powers are wisely suited to our present sphere of existence, and "no sentient being, whose physical construction was more delicate, or whose mental powers were more elevated, than those of man, could possibly live and be happy here." He would enjoy no society, no interchange of thought, no human sympathies or aspirations, for man would bear to him the relation of an inferior animal. Do not now the nice perceptions, the refined and elevated sentiments, the delicate nervous susceptibilities of superior genius, sometimes approximate it to such unhappy condition? "Is there, then," asks Dr. Currie, "no remedy for this inordinate sensibility? Are there no means by which the happiness of one so constituted by nature may be consulted? Perhaps it will be found, that regular and constant occupation, irksome though it may at first be, is the true remedy. Occupation, in which the powers of the understanding are exercised, will diminish the force of external impressions, and keep the imagination under restraint."*

Lord Byron was remarkable for his morbid sensibility, and to which the weaknesses of his moral character, his capricious, wayward, and frequently gloomy temper, his excessive and unmanly feeling in regard to his lameness which so tormented him, are to be in a great measure ascribed. And all these infirmities were doubtless aggravated by his too free indulgence in strong liquors. The inspirations of his muse are said to have been generally aided by his favor-

---

* Life of Burns.

ite spirit *gin*. Byron exhibited all the infirmities, and experienced all the sufferings which are the so frequent companions of the poetic temperament. Byron attained early
the maturity of his genius and the summit of his fame, for
they were based upon the powers of his imagination, which
may be highly developed at an early age. Poetic distinction
has often been acquired even in boyhood, while in the pursuits
of science or philosophy, which demand the exercise more especially of the higher or reflective faculties, true eminence
is not often achieved before the fortieth or fiftieth year.
The early ripeness of Byron's powers was followed by his
correspondently early decline and death. Thus do we find
him repining over the loss of his youth at the age of thirty-
six.

> " My days are in the yellow leaf,
>   The flowers and fruits of love are gone,
> The worm, the canker, and the grief
>   Are mine alone.

> " If thou regrett'st thy youth, why live?
>   The land of honorable death
>   Is here, up to the field and give
>   Away thy breath."

He died in his thirty-seventh year, an age at which the
man of science has generally scarce entered the lists of fame.

Robespierre was in body meagre, sickly and bilious; and
who can say—for the mightiest events will oftentimes spring
from the most insignificant causes—how much of the horrid

cruelties of the French Revolution may not have been traceable to the vicious physical constitution of this blood-thirsty
monster ?

It is worthy of observation, that diseases of the organs of
the abdomen are more apt to engender the gloomy and painful passions, than such as are confined to the viscera of the
chest. Thus it may be stated as a general truth, that the
dyspeptic will be more uniformly despondent and irritable
than the consumptive subject.

It will now be obvious that a painful mental state having imparted an unhealthy influence to a bodily organ, a
reaction must take place from this latter to the mind, adding
new force to the moral suffering. And, on the other hand,
when bodily disease excites the painful passions, they, in
their turn, react upon and aggravate the morbid physical
condition.

In like manner must the happy and healthful states of
mind and body be constantly contributing to each other.
Thus, sound and easy digestion imparts content and good
humor to the moral feelings, which pleasurable mental condition reacting on the digestive organs, serves to maintain
the health of their functions. It is a familiar saying that we
should ask for favors after dinner. Thus Menenius, in
alluding to the obstinacy of Coriolanus, says—

> " He was not taken well ; he had not dined :
>   Therefore I'll watch him
>   Till he be dieted to my request,
>   And then I'll set upon him."

A knowledge of this action and reaction of mind and body upon each other, should instruct the physician that all his duties to his patients are not comprised under their mere physical treatment, but that he is to soothe their sorrows, calm their fears, sustain their hopes, win their confidence; in short, pursue a vigilant system of moral management which, although so much neglected, will, in many cases, do even more good than any medicinal agents which the pharmacopœia can supply.

CHAPTER XI.

WHEREIN REAL AND IMAGINARY AFFLICTIONS DIFFER FROM EACH OTHER.—INCIDENTAL REMARKS NATURALLY SUGGESTED BY THE MUTUAL RELATIONS AND DEPENDENCIES OF OUR PHYSICAL AND MORAL CONSTITUTIONS.

KEEPING in mind the facts that have been stated in the preceding chapter, we come readily to the distinction between what are called real and imaginary sorrows; terms which, although so familiarly used, do not always carry with them a sufficiently definite meaning. The former, or real afflictions, are referrible to the agency of extraneous causes, operating primarily or immediately on the moral feelings; as loss of property, of relatives and friends, of reputation; and hence are strictly moral in their origin. The latter, or imaginary, are the offspring, for the most part at least, of unhealthy states of some portion of our organization, and their origin is consequently physical. Thus may we have accumulated about us all those blessings of existence which the world so earnestly covet, as friends, kindred, fortune, fame, and yet be even far more miserable than the penniless, houseless, friendless wretch, who is forced day by day to wring his scanty subsistence from the frigid hand of charity. Some morbid condition of the stomach, of the liver, or of the nervous system may, and without causing any well defined or appreciable bodily suffering, so influence the mind as to paralyze all its susceptibilities, dry up all its springs of enjoyment, and overwhelm it with fearful apprehension; or, in the strong language of Dr. Brown, with "that fixed and deadly gloom, to which there is no sunshine in the summer sky, no verdure or blossom in the summer field, no kindness in affection, no purity in the very remembrance of innocence itself, no heaven but hell, no God but a demon of wrath."*

But these imaginary sorrows, as they are called, are real enough to those who experience them, and vain is it to argue that they exist but in the fancy. They have a positive physical cause, constantly operative, and are often infinitely more distressing than any absolute moral affliction, and more frequently lead to despair and suicide.

Our moral have a much closer dependence on our physical infirmities than mankind are generally prepared or willing to admit. It demands, in truth, an exaltation of will, of which few can boast, successfully to combat the morbid influences which the body often exercises on the mind. "He," says Dr. Reid, "whose disposition to goodness can resist the influence of dyspepsia, and whose career of philanthropy is not liable to be checked by an obstruction in the hepatic organs, may boast of a much deeper and firmer virtue than falls to the ordinary lot of human nature."†

* Philosophy of the Human Mind.

† Essays on Hypochondriasis.

The extent, then, to which human happiness, and, it may be added, human virtue, must depend on the integrity of the bodily organism and its functions, can scarce be computed. There are some whose original fabrication is so defective, whose living machinery or individual parts of it are so prone to work wrong, that it would seem almost physically impossible for them to be happy and amiable in their feelings and tempers. While, again, in others, so perfect is the whole organization, and consequently so healthy are all its functions, as to exempt them almost entirely from those multiform and terrible moral sufferings which come primarily from the body. Can we, therefore, escape the conclusion that we may be physically predisposed, I had almost said predestined to happiness or misery? Such, in fact, is implied in the familiar expressions of happy and unhappy constitution or temperament. As, moreover, these vicious constitutions are oftentimes inherited, and must, probably, in the first instance, have grown out of infringements of the organic laws, it becomes a literal truth, that the sins of the parents may be visited on their unoffending children, even to remote generations. " To be well born," then, is a matter of no little importance, " but," as has been wisely said by another, " not in the sense in which that expression is usually employed. The most substantial privileges of birth are not those which are confined to the descendants of noble ancestors.

" The heir of a sound constitution has no right to regret the absence of any other patrimony. A man who has derived from the immediate authors of his being, vigorous and untainted stamina of mind as well as body, enters upon the world with a sufficient foundation and ample materials for happiness."*

The vast importance of a judicious physical education, both to virtue and happiness, cannot now but receive its just appreciation ; for under its influence even a bad constitution, and the moral infirmities which are its almost necessary attendants, may be, in a very considerable measure, corrected. And we can likewise understand how essential is a prudent moral discipline to the good health of the body. In a perfect system of education, as it has been before remarked, the moral, intellectual, and physical natures are each subjects of most important, if not equal regard.

The deduction may, I think, also be drawn from what has gone before, that the practice of medicine must be varied and modified to suit it to different conditions of society. The simple, routine, mechanical practice which might serve well enough in hospitals, dispensaries, and among the rude, unlettered, or mere manual laborers, might be but ill-suited to the refined, cultivated, intellectual and educated classes. Among the latter, the intellectual and moral powers being more developed, and exercising consequently greater influence over the material organization and its functions, demand a more especial regard. Their nervous system also being more susceptible, and its sensibilities more delicate and acute, the means directed to the physical constitution have to be adjusted to suit such modified conditions. The

* Dr. Reid on Hypochondriacal and other Nervous Affections.

6

judicious and intelligent physician, thus learns to shape his practice, not only according to the different diseases, but also the different classes of patients he may be called on to treat. He who has practised medicine only in hospitals and dispensaries, will find he has much to learn when he comes to pursue it among the higher and more cultivated classes of society.

Having learnt how the disposition may be affected by bodily conditions, ought we not to exercise a mutual forbearance, and to cultivate feelings of charity for those infirmities of temper, which even the best of men will occasionally display, and which oftentimes belong more to the flesh than the spirit?

CHAPTER XII.

THE PASSIONS CONSIDERED MORE PARTICULARLY.—THE PLEA-
SURABLE PASSIONS, WITH THEIR EFFECTS ON THE PHYSICAL
FUNCTIONS, SUMMARILY NOTICED.

THE pleasurable passions include love, hope, friendship, pride,
etc. Joy, which is ranked among them, would seem to be
rather a general expression, or consequence, of all this class
of emotions, than in itself a distinct and specific one; therefore are we said to enjoy love, hope, friendship, etc.; consequently the phenomena of the whole of them may be embraced under the general head of joy.

The passions founded on pleasure cause a universal expansion—if so it may be expressed—of vital action. The
blood, under their animating influence, flows more liberally
to the superficies, and playing freely through its capillary
vessels, the countenance becomes expanded, its expression
brightens, and the whole surface acquires the ruddy tint
and genial warmth of health. The body also feels buoyant
and lively, and there is a consequent disposition to quick
and cheerful muscular motions: to run, to jump, to dance,

to laugh, to sing; in short, every function would seem to be gladdened by the happy moral condition. The common expressions, therefore, such as "the heart is light, or leaps with joy," " to swell with pride," " to be puffed up with vanity," "to be big with hope," are not altogether figurative; for the heart does bound more lightly, and the body appears literally to dilate under the pleasurable affections of the mind.

Nothing now contributes more effectually to the healthful and harmonious action of our organism than an equable distribution of the blood to its various parts, and especially the free circulation of this fluid in the extreme vessels of the surface. A full, bright, and ruddy skin is always ranked among the surest tokens of health. The nervous system must also experience a salutary excitement under the agreeable moral emotions. But I need not further dwell on what will be so apparent to all,—the wholesome influence of a happy state of mind upon our bodily functions. " Love, hope, and joy," says the celebrated Haller, " promote perspiration, quicken the pulse, promote the circulation, increase the appetite, and facilitate the cure of diseases."*

As, however, excess of feeling, whatever may be its character, is always prejudicial, even this class of passions, when violent, may be fraught with danger to health and life. Even felicity itself, if it exceed the bounds of moderation, will oppress, and sometimes even overwhelm us. When pleasurable feelings are extravagant, they become transformed into those which are painful. In other words, the

* Physiology.

extremity of pleasure is pain. Great joy is sometimes expressed like grief, by sobbing and tears. And what seems yet more strange, grief is sometimes expressed by immoderate laughter. "Dr. Crichton observes, 'that many (I am almost tempted to say most people) now and then have been inclined to laugh when a person has first begun to relate some misfortune. Nay, a more unaccountable circumstance of this kind is, that many people, when they have to tell of the death of another person, feel themselves often inclined to laugh at the moment they begin to speak of it;' and these individuals, he adds, are possessed of fine feelings. I knew two brothers who had experienced poignant grief from the death of a sister. The day after her interment they walked to her grave, a distance of two or three miles, to indulge their feelings, and on their return were seized with an irresistible propensity to immoderate and loud laughter, which continued for some time."* Laughter and weeping are oftentimes mingled in the expressions of both joy and sorrow, showing an unaccountable, a paradoxical relation between the effects of these two opposite passions in their more acute forms.

Extravagant and unexpected joy unduly excites the nervous system ; increases unnaturally and unequally the circulation, and occasions a painful stricture of the heart and lungs, accompanied with sighing, sobbing, and panting, as in severe grief. Under its influence, too, the visage will often turn pale, the limbs tremble and refuse their support to the body, and in extreme cases, fainting, convulsions,

---

* Laycock on Hysteria.

hysterics, madness, temporary ecstasy, or catalepsy, and even instant death, may ensue. If the subject be of a delicate and sensitive constitution, and more especially if he labors under any complaint of the heart, the consequences of the shock to the nervous system of sudden and immoderate joy will always be attended with exceeding hazard.

I have mentioned insanity as one of the morbid effects of joy. Esquirol, however, a French writer on this disease, of high authority, asserts that the cheerful emotions are rarely its cause; that joy, so excessive even as to destroy life, does not take away the reason; and that on a careful investigation of certain cases of insanity ascribed to joy, he became assured that the cause was mistaken. English writers, however, generally rank extravagant joy among the causes of mental alienation. Dr. Mead affirms, "that immoderate joy, too long continued, as effectually disorders the mind as anxiety and grief," and says:—"I have formerly heard Dr. *Hale*, physician to *Bethleem-hospital*, and of great experience in these matters, say more than once, that in the year MDCCXX, ever memorable for the iniquitous South Sea scheme, he had more patients committed to his care, whose heads were turned by the immense riches which fortune had suddenly thrown in their way, than of those who had been completely ruined by that abominable bubble."* It has been observed that adventurers in lotteries have suffered more serious consequences, as loss of reason, and other physical ills, from the prizes than from the

---

* Medical Precepts and Cautions, by Richard Mead, M. D., &c. London, 1751. pp. 88–9.

blanks that they have drawn.—" An engineer proposed to the committee of public safety in the second year of the republic, a project for a new invented cannon, of which the effects would be tremendous. A day was fixed for the experiment at Meudon; and Robespierre wrote to the inventor so flattering a letter, that upon perusing it, he was transfixed motionless to the spot. He was shortly afterwards sent to the Bicetre in a state of complete idiotism."*

The assertion has been made by some, it was made by Zimmerman, that sudden joy is even more hazardous to life than sudden grief, and that there are more numerous instances of fatal effects from the former than the latter passion.

Diagoras, a distinguished athlete of Rhodes, and whose merit was celebrated in a beautiful ode by Pindar, inscribed in golden letters on a temple of Minerva, died suddenly from excess of joy on seeing his three sons return crowned as conquerors from the Olympic Games.

Dionysius, the second tyrant of that name, is recorded to have died of joy on learning the award of a poetical prize to his own tragedy. And Valerius Maximus has ascribed the death of Sophocles to a like cause.

Chilo, a Spartan philosopher, called one of the seven wise men of Greece, on seeing his son obtain a victory at Olympia, fell overjoyed into his arms, and immediately expired.

It is related that Pope Leo the Tenth, under the influ-

* Treatise on Insanity. By Ph. Pinel, Prof. of the School of Medicine at Paris, etc.

ence of extravagant joy at the triumph of his party against
the French, and for the much coveted acquisition of Parma
and Placentia, suddenly fell sick and died. " M. Juventius
Thalna, on being told that a triumph had been decreed to
him for having subdued Corsica, fell down dead before the
altar at which he was offering up his thanksgiving. Vate-
rus relates, that a brave soldier, who had never been sick,
died suddenly in the arms of an only daughter, whom he
had long wished to see. A worthy family in Holland being
reduced to indigence, the elder brother passed over to the
East Indies, acquired considerable riches there, and returning home, presented his sister with the richest jewels: the
young woman, at this unexpected change of fortune, became
motionless and died. The famous Fouquet died on being
told that Louis XIV. had restored him to his liberty. The
niece of the celebrated Leibnitz, not suspecting that a philosopher would hoard up treasure, died suddenly, on opening a box under her uncle's bed, which contained sixty
thousand ducats."*

Dr. Good tells us of a clergyman, an intimate friend of
his own, who, at a time when his income was very limited,
received the unexpected tidings that a property had been
bequeathed to him amounting to three thousand pounds a
year. " He arrived in London," says Dr. Good, " in great
agitation, and entering his own door, dropt down in a fit
of apoplexy, from which he never entirely recovered."†
Haller made the remark, that " excessive and sudden joy

* Zimmerman on Experience in Physic.
† Study of Medicine.

often kills, by increasing the motion of the blood, and exciting a true apoplexy."*

If the extreme of joy follow unexpectedly an emotion of an opposite character, the danger will be heightened. A story is recorded of two Roman matrons, who, on seeing their sons, whom they had believed to be dead, return from the famous battle fought between Hannibal and the Romans near the lake of Thrasymenus, and in which the Roman army was cut to pieces, passing suddenly from the deepest grief to the most vehement joy, instantly expired.

Examples have likewise happened where culprits, just at the point of execution, have immediately perished on the unexpected announcement of a pardon. We may hence draw the important practical lesson, that the cure of one strong passion is seldom to be attempted by the sudden excitement of another, of an opposite character. Violent emotions are, as a general rule, to be extinguished cautiously and gradually. Rapid and extreme alternations of feeling, and indeed all sudden extremes, are repugnant to the laws, and, consequently, dangerous to the well-being of the animal economy. To endeavor, at once, to eradicate deep grief by excessive joy, is, as I have seen it remarked, as irrational as it would be to expect the restoration of a frozen limb from pouring upon it hot water.

Instances are not wanting where the inflation of pride, or immoderate self-esteem, which must be ranked among the pleasurable feelings, has actually deranged the understand-

* Physiology.

6*

ing. Menecrates, a physician of Syracuse, as we read in classical literature, was particularly famed for his exalted self-conceit, and which at length so disturbed his intellect that he fancied himself to be the ruler of heaven, and, in a letter written to Philip, king of Macedon, styled himself Menecrates Jupiter. The Macedonian-monarch, as the story goes, having invited this physician to one of his feasts, had prepared for him a separate table, on which he was served only with perfumes and frankincense, like the master of the gods. At first this treatment greatly delighted him; but soon growing hungry under such celestial fare, and the temptation of the substantial viands on which the rest were feasting, he began to feel that he was a mortal, and stole away in his proper senses. But then we have no occasion to go back to the ancients for instances of disordered intellect from overweening self-esteem. Thousands in the community have their judgment blinded, and their reasoning powers impaired, through an extravagant and mistaken estimate of themselves. Esquirol places pride among the most frequent moral causes of insanity. And inordinate self-conceit is also a very common attendant on insanity. The insane almost always entertain an unduly exalted opinion of their own powers and consequence. Humility seldom marks their disease.

It will be readily seen, now, how undue praise or flattery may endanger the soundness of a weak and conceited mind; and not always are strong intellects proof against it; even the most vigorous brain may sometimes be turned through the siren influence of adulation.

Another reason why pride, when immoderate, favors mental aberration, is its exceeding liability to become mixed with the painful passions. The proud suffer far more poignantly than the lowly-minded from contumely and humiliating reverses of fortune, which, in this uncertain world, can seldom be altogether escaped. But here pride acts not as a pleasurable feeling, but by arousing and giving force to the painful emotions, the effects of which will engage our future consideration.

The great importance, even in reference to bodily health, of an habitual cultivation of the pure, and generous, and amiable affections of our nature, will now be readily inferred, since they are all fraught with gentle pleasure, and all, therefore, the sources of agreeable and salutary excitement. The mild and benevolent affections necessarily carry with them their own reward, both to body and mind. Under their kindly influence, the heart plays more freely and tranquilly, the respiration is more placid and regular, the food acquires new relish, and its digestion fresh vigor; in short, they animate and perfect every living function, and expand and multiply all the various enjoyments of our being. Without them, the heart would have no summer glow; a cold selfishness would freeze up all its springs of joy, and the earth would become a dismal solitude, not worth inheriting. Sad, desolate, and weary is his lot, who lives but for himself —who has nothing to love! " If we had been destined to live abandoned to ourselves on Mount Caucasus, or in the deserts of Africa, perhaps Nature would have denied us a feeling heart; but, if she had given us one, rather than love nothing, that heart would have tamed tigers, and animated rocks."

The exercise of gentleness and good-will in our various social and domestic relations, not only contributes to our own moral and physical well-being, but also to the happiness, and consequently health, of those about us and dependent upon us. Courtesy, like mercy, carries with it a double blessing,—

" It blesseth him that gives, and him that takes."

The ungentle and churlish in heart and manners, however just they may be in principle, chill the feelings, and poison the happiness of all within the circle of their influence.

Cheerfulness, contentment, hope !—need I say how propitious are their effects on the various functions of the animal economy ? Hope has well been termed a cordial, for what medicament have we so mild, so grateful, and at the same time so reviving in its effects ? Many live almost entirely on its cordial influence. And deprived of its animating incitement few would care to live. " Its characteristic is to produce a salutary medium between every excess and defect of operation in every function. Consequently it has a tendency to calm the troubled action of the vessels, to check and soothe the violent and irregular impetus of the nervous system, and to administer a beneficial stimulus to the oppressed and debilitated powers of nature."* The able

* Cogan on the Passions.

physician well understands the advantage of encouraging this salutary feeling in the breasts of his patients. Hippocrates uttered the opinion, verified by all succeeding physicians, that, other things equal, the practitioner who has the fullest confidence of his patients, will be most successful. Hence it is, that like medicines from a physician of fame, will oftentimes prove more successful than from others of less celebrity. On the same principle may oftentimes be explained the frequent improvement observed in a patient on a change of his physician; and also the benefit not rarely derived from newly-discovered and much-talked-of remedies. It is to the faith and hopes awakened in the credulous minds of the sick by his dogmatical promises, that the empiric owes his chief success in disease. That the patient then should possess faith in medicine, and confidence in his physician, is of no little moment as respects his recovery. "It is of little consequence," it has been remarked, "whether a man be healed through the medium of his fancy or his stomach."

I have previously shown that sudden transports of joy may be attended with serious, and even fatal consequences; is it unreasonable therefore to suppose, that the pleasurable feelings may, in some rare instances, continue to exist with too great ardor, consuming with an unnatural rapidity the mysterious forces of life? I have occasionally met with individuals, and I dare say my readers will call some such to mind, who appeared to live almost continually in an unnatural state of felicity; whose every thought and feeling seemed pregnant with an enthusiasm of delight; who were predisposed, physically predisposed to be happy, intensely happy; and these seemingly favored beings have generally come to an early grave: it appearing as though nature had ordained that none of us should exceed a limited sum of enjoyment, and that in proportion, therefore, as she heightens its intenseness, does she curtail its duration.

The human constitution was manifestly never designed for acute excitements, whether of a pleasurable or painful character; hence its energies soon waste under their too constant operation. Even our good desires, then, may be too impetuous, and our virtuous zeal outrun the limits of healthful moderation. It is an apt saying that "the archer who shoots beyond the mark, misses it as much as he that comes short of it." There is no privilege more to be desired, there is nothing more conducive to health, longevity, and true enjoyment, than a just equanimity of mind, a quiet harmony among the various passions; wherefore it is that most philosophers have made our sovereign good to consist in the tranquillity of soul and body, leaving ecstatic pleasures and rapturous feelings to beings of a different nature from our own.

"A constant serenity," says Dr. Mackenzie, "supported by hope, or cheerfulness arising from a good conscience, is the most healthful of all the affections of the mind." And the same author, in enumerating the natural marks of longevity, mentions a calm, contented, and cheerful disposition.* Haller also, in speaking of longevity, says: "Some

* The History of Health and the Art of preserving it.

prerogative seems to belong to sobriety, at least in a moderate degree, temperate diet, peaceable disposition, a mind not endowed with great vivacity, but cheerful, and little subject to care."

As old age comes on, the pleasurable susceptibilities all become weakened, and the keenness of passion in general is blunted. Not, however, that the aged, as some would seem to fancy, are left destitute of enjoyment, for each period of our being has its characteristic pleasures. They have parted, to be sure, with the eager sensibilities which mark the freshness of existence, but then they have gained a moral tranquillity with which earlier years are seldom blessed. The storms of youthful passion have subsided within their breasts, and if life has passed well with them morally and physically, they now repose placidly amid the calm of its decline.

CHAPTER XIII.

GENERAL PHENOMENA OF THE PAINFUL PASSIONS AS MANIFESTED
IN THE BODILY FUNCTIONS.

THE second class of passions, now to be examined, are distinguished by phenomena very different from those which have just been described. As the emotions based on pleasure determine the blood to the surface, equalize the general circulation and vital action, expand the body, lighten and cheer the heart, and animate all the functions; those founded on pain induce a series of results precisely opposite in their character. Under the active influence of these latter, the whole body appears, as it were, to shrink or contract. The blood abandons the surface, and so being thrown in undue quantity upon the internal organs, there follows that inward oppression, that painful sense of stricture and suffocation, and the consequent desire for fresh air, which always mark the intensity of this class of passions. Hence the frequent sighing under severe grief, which act consists in a deep inspiration, succeeded by a corresponding expiration, and thus by expanding freely the chest, and affording a larger supply of air, it alleviates, in some measure, the heart and lungs of their suffocative load. There are few, however, so privileged beyond the ordinary lot of humanity, but must be well acquainted with that painful sense of tightness and weight at the chest, that panting and struggling of the breath, and laboring of the heart, the certain accompaniments of aggravated sorrow.

As an equable distribution of the blood to the various organs, and its free circulation through the capillary vessels of the surface are, as stated under the pleasurable emotions, salutary to the physical economy; an inequality, on the other hand, in the dispensation of this vital fluid, or partial determinations of it, must always prove detrimental to its welfare. Whenever the blood is disproportionably accumulated upon the internal viscera—which has been shown to happen from the operation of the painful and depressing passions—their functions quickly become disturbed, and even the integrity of their organization endangered.

The painful passions also act immediately on the nervous system, depressing, disordering, expending, and sometimes even annihilating its energies. A morbid concentration of the nervous influence upon the internal organs, has likewise been supposed to take place under the operation of the painful passions, and to which have been referred those distressing internal sensations which they so generally occasion.

The painful and depressing emotions exercise a striking influence on the various secretions—increasing, diminishing, and depraving them. Thus dryness of the mouth, from suppression of the salivary secretion, almost always attends severe and unpleasant affections of the mind. This is proved " by the well-known test, often resorted to in India, for the discovery of a thief amongst the servants of a family—that of compelling all the parties to hold a certain quantity of rice in the mouth during a few minutes—the offender being generally distinguished by the comparative dryness of his mouthful."* But there are few of us, it is to be presumed, who have not experienced that uncomfortable dryness of the mouth and throat, huskiness of the voice, frequent and difficult swallowing, which proceed from moral embarrassment, agitation, and suffering. Even poisonous properties are said to have been imparted to the saliva by violent mental commotions. The secretion of milk is in a particular manner affected by the disturbing and depressing passions, as anxiety, grief, fear, anger, fretfulness, &c. Under their influence it may be diminished, or be entirely suppressed, or become so vitiated as to cause disease, and even death, in the infant. We shall have occasion to recur to this subject— the effect of the moral feelings on the secretions—under the particular passions.

I have stated that the general effect of the painful passions is to induce a contraction or concentration, and a depression of the actions of life, but in their more aggravated forms, they are sometimes followed by a transient excitement, reaction or vital expansion, when their operation becoming more diffused, is necessarily weakened in relation to any individual organ. Under such circumstances, the

---

* Carpenter's Human Physiology.

oppression of the heart and lungs is in a measure removed, and the circulation and respiration go on with more freedom. Hence it is, that when anger and grief explode, or break forth into violent action and vociferation, and tears flow abundantly, their consequences are much less to be dreaded than when they are deep, still, and speechless, for then it is that their force is most concentrated. Thus Malcolm says to Macduff, overwhelmed by the cruel tidings of the murder of his wife and children :—

> " What, man ! ne'er pull your hat upon your brows ;
> Give sorrow words. The grief that does not speak,
> Whispers the o'er-fraught heart, and bids it break."

Let me here repeat the general and important truth, that the pleasurable passions tend to expand or enlarge the sphere of vital action, and to equalize its distribution, and are therefore salutary in their physical effects, whilst those of a painful nature concentrate or contract, and disturb its just equilibrium, and are consequently deleterious. To be convinced of this, we need but contrast the countenance of the happy and confident with that of the sad and despondent. In the former it is bright and dilated, and the blood plays freely in its extreme vessels. In the latter, it is pale, sickly, contracted, and expressive of inward pain.

As, therefore, when we use the familiar expressions,—to be light or buoyant with joy,—to expand with pleasure,—to be inflated with pride,—to be puffed up with vanity, we but express physiological truths ; so do we likewise when we say the heart is oppressed or breaking with grief; or that the body shrinks with fear, or withers under sorrow and despair.

It is, moreover, worthy of remark, that the same spare or contracted state of the body, and sallowness of the complexion, which result from the operation of the painful and depressing passions, are, when constitutional or dependent on incidental causes acting primarily on the physical system, very commonly associated with an unhappy and unamiable disposition. Thus Cæsar, while he put trust in the rosy and expanded face and full-fed sides of Marc Antony, looked with suspicion on the pale and contracted countenance, and meagre frame of Cassius.

> " Would he were fatter !—But I fear him not:
> Yet if my name were liable to fear,
> I do not know the man I should avoid
> So soon as that spare Cassius."

Here, then, we have a further illustration of the statement previously made, that the like bodily condition may be either the cause or the effect of particular passions ; that an interchange of influence is constantly and necessarily taking place between our moral and physical natures.

I will now go on to exhibit somewhat more in detail, the effects of the painful emotions on our bodily functions, under the general heads of anger, fear, grief, envy, jealousy, and shame. I select the three former of these, especially, as being by far the most comprehensive in their character.

In truth they must enter, one or more, into all the numerous varieties of this division of passions; accordingly, the descriptions of their phenomena will necessarily comprise the principal ones of the whole class. Perhaps, indeed, all the painful passions, could they be subjected to an accurate analysis, might be found but modifications of, and consequently be reducible to, anger, grief, or fear.

CHAPTER XIV.

ANGER being founded especially on the instinct of self-preservation, is essential to the constitution of all animate beings. It is aroused by, and at the same time urges us by an instinctive impulse to repel or destroy, all such causes as oppose or threaten our moral or physical ease and security; or, in other words, which bring unhappiness to the mind, or pain, injury, or destruction to the body. Hence it is often directed against the irrational, and even inanimate objects of creation. Modified and abused, therefore, as we find it, it was originally implanted in our breasts as a necessary safeguard alike to our happiness and existence. This passion, although more frequently of a purely selfish nature, may originate in our sympathies with the wrongs and injuries of others, or in the feeling of repugnance toward injustice, or wickedness in general, when, it assuming a more beneficent and dignified character, we often express it by the term indignation.

In an extreme paroxysm of anger, which I will here

describe, the most painful phenomena are exhibited. The countenance becomes distorted and repulsive, and the eye sparkles with a brutal fury. All the vital actions are commonly, in the first instance, oppressed, and are many times nearly overwhelmed. The blood recedes from the surface, leaving it cold and blanched ; and tremors and agitations often come over the limbs, or even the whole body, and sighing, sobbing, and distressing nervous affections, as hysterics, spasms, convulsions, especially where there is a predisposition to such, are of not unfrequent occurrence. The vital fluid, and may-be the nervous influence also, being impelled from the exterior, and thus accumulated on the internal organs, the functions of these become sensibly embarrassed. The motion of the heart is feeble, labored, irregular, and oftentimes painful. The breathing is short, rapid, difficult or suffocative, and a tightness or stricture is felt in the whole chest, in some cases extending to the throat, and causing a sense of choking, impeding, or for a time wholly interrupting the power of speech. Hence, probably, comes the expression, " to be choked with rage."

The organs of the abdomen also come in for their share of the prejudicial influence. Thus distress is apt to be experienced in the situation of the stomach, and the functions of this organ, with those of the liver and bowels, may undergo various disturbances.

Fainting sometimes takes place in violent anger ; and in occasional instances, the system being unable to react under the intensity of the shock, life has surrendered itself almost as to a stroke of lightning ; and the death here, or from such sudden gust of passion, is, according to Mr. Hunter, as absolute as that caused by the electric fluid, the muscles remaining flaccid, the blood liquid, or dissolved in its vessels, and the body passing rapidly into putrefaction. Reaction, however, does for the most part speedily ensue, and many times, even in severe paroxysms, the excitement is manifested from the very beginning. Under the active stage of anger the following train of phenomena will be displayed in greater or less strength.

The heart now aroused, beats quick and forcibly, and the blood rushing impetuously to the head and surface, the brain becomes heated, the face flushed, the lips swollen, the eyes red and fiery, the skin hot, and literally may it be said that we burn with anger. The muscles also contract with a preternatural strength; the fists and teeth often become clinched as in preparation for combat, and the impulses of instinct subduing perhaps altogether the will and reasoning powers, the brutalized slave of passion vociferates, stamps, threatens, is violently agitated, and perceiving and judging in a manner wholly different from what he would in a tranquil state of mind, his character becomes allied to that of the maniac, and thus may he commit acts the bare thoughts or mention of which would strike him with horror under a more rational or unpassionated state of feelings. To this forcible reaction of anger the term rage, or fury, is often applied.

Different individuals, owing to their native temperament, bodily health, and moral education, vary remarkably in their propensity to anger, as well as in the pertinacity with which they cherish it. In some it is sudden and transient, while in others, though perhaps less hasty, it assumes a more deep and lasting character, settling into that malignant feeling called revenge, the most terrible, and oftentimes the most obdurate one that degrades the human soul, so that the poets, the true painters of our passions, have fabled it as immortal. The disposition to anger will, as a general rule, be found greater, and the passion more precipitate and ungovernable in hot than in cold climates.

In many of the inferior animals, when enraged, the various physical phenomena of the emotion under notice, may be seen in all their formidableness. In those of our own species, too, in whom, either from physical organization, or defective moral and intellectual culture, the animal or baser nature is ascendant, we oftentimes behold exhibitions of it equally fearful.

Anger accompanied with paleness of the surface, or in which reaction does not take place, is generally most deep, and its consequences most formidable. Some persons always become pale when under its influence, which may now and then be owing to the mingling with it of a certain measure of fear, which passion has a more depressing operation.

Anger sometimes proves fatal, the severity of its shock at once suppressing the action of the heart, or, as occasionally has happened, causing an actual rupture of this organ, or some of its large blood-vessels ; for the heart, although a strong muscle, is sometimes broken, literally broken by passion. Apoplexy, hemorrhages, convulsions, or other grave

7

affections, may likewise proceed from anger, quickly terminating existence.

Although the danger from this passion is generally lessened by reaction, still, when such is violent, the blood may be so forcibly impelled as to induce fatal apoplexies, or hemorrhages.

The emperor Nerva died of a violent excess of anger against a senator who had offended him. Valentinian, the first Roman emperor of that name, while reproaching with great passion the deputies from the Quadi, a people of Germany, burst a blood-vessel, and suddenly fell lifeless to the ground. "I have seen," says a French medical writer, "two women perish, the one in convulsions, at the end of six hours, and the other suffocated in two days, from giving themselves up to transports of fury."*

If there chance to exist any tendency to apoplexy, as in those of a plethoric habit, and who live generously, or should there be any complaint at the heart, the danger from anger will be much increased. Hence it is that old men, who are more particularly disposed to affections of this sort, offer the most frequent examples of sudden death from passion.

Numerous examples of apoplexy occasioned by anger, are recorded both in ancient and modern works on this disease. Bonetus tells of a lady who, in consequence of a sudden fit of anger, was seized with violent and fatal apoplexy, and in whose brain blood was found largely diffused. "A gentleman somewhat more than seventy years of age, of a

---

* Tourtelle.

full habit of body, and florid countenance, on getting into his carriage to go to his country house, was thrown into a violent passion by some circumstances which suddenly occurred. He soon afterwards complained of pain in his head, and by degrees he became sleepy, and in about a quarter of an hour wholly insensible. He was carried into the shop of an apothecary at Kentish Town, and was immediately largely bled. When I saw him, about an hour afterwards, I found him laboring under all the symptoms of strong apoplexy. In about twenty-four hours he died."*

The distinguished John Hunter fell a sudden victim to a paroxysm of anger. Mr. Hunter, as is familiar to medical readers, was a man of extraordinary genius, but the subject of violent passions, and which, from defect of early moral culture, he had not learned to control. Suffering, during his latter years, under a complaint of the heart, his existence was in constant jeopardy from his ungovernable temper; and he had been heard to remark, that "his life was in the hands of any rascal who chose to annoy and tease him." Engaged one day in an unpleasant altercation with his colleagues, and being peremptorily contradicted, he at once ceased speaking, hurried into an adjoining room, and instantly fell dead. Mr. Hunter ascribed the commencement of his heart-disease to a fit of passion.

The heart receiving immediately the shock of every fit of anger, the life of the passionate man who labors under an affection of this organ, must be held in constant uncertainty.

* Treatise on Nervous Diseases. By John Cooke, M. D., etc.

Nothing does more to protract existence under complaints of this nature than moral serenity.

Various morbid effects of a more or less grave and lasting character are also liable to follow immoderate anger. Thus palsies, epilepsy, hysteria, and mania may be placed among its occasional consequences. Anger, or violent or ungovernable temper, as it is sometimes expressed, holds, according to the reports of different lunatic asylums, both of Europe and America, a prominent place among the causes of insanity. Raving madness is said to be the form of mental derangement which most often results from this cause, though dementia has sometimes been the consequence of its sudden operation. Dr. Good cites the case of Charles the Sixth of France, "who being violently incensed against the duke of Bretagne, and burning with a spirit of malice and revenge, could neither eat, drink, nor sleep, for many days together, and at length became furiously mad as he was riding on horseback, drawing his sword, and striking promiscuously every one who approached him. The disease fixed upon his intellect, and accompanied him to his death."*

Anger destroys the appetite, and checks or disorders the function of digestion. Let one receive a provocation in the midst of his dinner, and he at once loses all relish for the food before him. Dr. Beaumont, who had under his charge a man with a fistulous opening into his stomach, so large that the interior of this organ could easily be inspected, re-

* Study of Medicine.

marked that anger, or other severe mental emotions, would sometimes cause its mucous, or lining coat, to become morbidly red, dry, and irritable ; occasioning, at the same time, a temporary fit of indigestion. Pains and cramps of the stomach and bowels sometimes follow the severe influence of this passion, and the liver may also become implicated in its morbid effects. Thus the flow of bile has been so augmented under its sudden action, as even to occasion a bilious vomiting, or diarrhœa. An old writer relates a case of fatal ileus, from volvulus, caused by a paroxysm of anger. And Dr. Whytt observes of this same passion, that in women it frequently occasions spasmodic contractions in the bowels, and flatulent or hysteric colic.

This, like other emotions when forcible, variously affects the different secretions. Under its influence the saliva becomes diminished, and consequently inspissated, whence its frothy whiteness, and adhesiveness, and the frequent swallowing under its action. Dr. Whytt speaks of it as having been followed by an uncommon excretion of saliva; and we have the statement on various and respectable medical authority that the secretions of the mouth may become poisonous through rage. Dr. Good remarks, " that most animals, when roused by a high degree of rage, inflict a wound of a much more irritable kind than when in a state of tranquillity : and we have numerous examples in which such wound has been very difficult of cure, and not a few in which it has proved fatal; as though at all times, under such a state of excitement, some peculiar acrimony was secreted with the saliva."*

* Study of Medicine.

It has even been affirmed that true hydrophobia may be generated by the bite of an animal when transported by fury ; in proof of which many examples are cited from the older medical writers; and some, where even the bite of a man worked up into fury has produced symptoms of this disease. How far we may accredit these marvellous relations is matter of some doubt, though it would seem hardly reasonable to impugn the truth of all of them, resting as they do on the testimony of such numerous authorities. That some, or even many, were cases of tetanus mistaken for hydrophobia, is altogether probable. Broussais asserts that anger imparts to the saliva "poisonous qualities, capable of provoking convulsions, and even madness, in those persons bitten by a man agitated with it."

The secretion of milk is often very remarkably affected by fits of anger, being rendered so irritating as to cause griping and morbid discharges in the infant. An irritable and fretful temper has been found to diminish its quantity, to render it thin and serous, and so to deprave its quality as variously to disorder the bowels of the child.

Various hemorrhages, as from the nose, lungs, stomach, and inflammations of different parts, as of the skin, the brain, the stomach, the lungs, have occasionally followed severe fits of passion. The author last cited states, that he has seen hæmoptysis, or spitting of blood, and violent pneumonia, or inflammation of the lungs, proceed solely from anger. He relates the case of an elderly man, who, owing to a violent fit of anger, occasioned by a visit from some foreign soldiers, was suddenly affected with an extensive inflammation of the right loin, which terminated in a large and bad ulcer.

Dr. Laycock, in his Essay on Hysteria, reports a case of a young woman, of indolent habits and obstinate temper, becoming affected with hysteria, ecstasy, and sweating of blood, from being angered. Having been much irritated in consequence of some remarks of her parents, she left home in consequence, and after wandering about for some time, she entered a hospital, suffering under violent attacks of hysteria and general convulsions. "After paroxysms which sometimes lasted twenty-four or thirty-six hours, she fell into a kind of ecstasy—her eyes being fixed, and sensibility and motion suspended. Sometimes she muttered a prayer, and blood would exude in drops from the cheeks and epigastrium, in the form of perspiration." Dr. Whytt observes, that anger has been immediately followed by bleeding at the nipples, and a rupture of such vessels as were lately cicatrized.*

I have now and then met with instances of erysipelatous inflammation about the face and neck, induced by paroxysms of passion. Other cutaneous affections, as urticaria, or nettle-rash, lepra, or leprosy, and herpetic eruptions, will oftentimes, especially where any predisposition to them exists, be produced by the same cause. I have known nettle-rash, in some constitutions, to be almost uniformly brought on by any strong mental emotion. And of leprosy, Cazenave remarks, that "one of the most common causes is to be traced

---

* Observations on Nervous Disorders.

to the mental affections; hence it is not rare to see *Lepra vulgaris* supervene on a fit of anger, or violent grief or fear."* Dr. Pettigrew cites a singular effect of anger, in a boy. Whenever he "fell into a passion, one-half of his face would become quite pale, while the other was very red and heated, and these two colors were exactly limited by a line running down the middle of the forehead, nose, lips, and chin. When this boy had heated himself by any violent exercise, the whole face became equally red."†

As substances most prejudicial, and even poisonous, to the healthy organism, may exercise medicinal virtues in certain states of disease, so extreme anger, although generally baneful in its effects, has, by its powerful impulse, occasionally subdued distressing and obstinate maladies, as neuralgia, gout, agues, paralysis, and various nervous affections. Dr. Abercrombie mentions a case of palsy of six years' continuance, where recovery suddenly took place under a violent paroxysm of anger.

* On Cutaneous Diseases.

† Superstitions connected with Medicine and Surgery.

CHAPTER XV.

ANGER, CONCLUDED.—PHYSICAL EFFECTS OF ITS CHRONIC
ACTION.—IT MAY BE EXCITED BY MORBID STATES OF THE
BODILY ORGANS, AND THUS BE STRICTLY PHYSICAL IN ITS
ORIGIN.

HAVING learnt in the preceding chapter how severe and
dangerous are the effects of acute anger on the vital economy, it will create no surprise that, under its more chronic
action, as in habitual irritability or fretfulness of temper,
enmity, hatred, revenge, or other malevolent feelings, as
envy or jealousy, in which anger, to a greater or less degree,
is almost necessarily blended, the bodily health should,
earlier or later, experience a baneful influence. The continued torment of mind proceeding from passions of this
nature, can scarce be otherwise than detrimental to the
physical constitution. In the stomach and liver, their effects are early and clearly evinced. Thus will the appetite
and digestion become impaired, and the hepatic secretion be
variously disordered, and sometimes partially or even entirely obstructed, when the bile, being absorbed into the

7*

system, taints the complexion with that dark and bilious hue which is so characteristic of an unamiable or malignant temper. Wherefore the common expression, to turn black with anger, hatred, or revenge, it is not unlikely originated in just observation. It is a literal truth, although expressed in poetry, that one may

———— " Creep into the jaundice,
By being peevish."

Irritability and moroseness of temper may also occasion various inflammatory and nervous complaints, and those more especially to which there is a constitutional tendency. Gout, rheumatism, hysterics, nervous headaches, tic douloureux, and numerous other painful affections, are liable to be excited, or their fits to be renewed under such prejudicial influences.

Nothing surely can be more desirable, both as it concerns our moral and physical health, than a quiet resignation to the fate decreed us. Fretting and repining under unavoidable evils only adds to their burden, and to the eye of true philosophy shows a temper about as inconsistent as that exhibited by some of the heathen world in flagellating their gods for the calamities befalling them.

The condition of temper now occupying our consideration, is particularly injurious when the system is laboring under disease. It is well known to every observing physician, that fractious patients, other circumstances being the same, recover less promptly, and are more exposed to relapses than those who bear their sufferings with more composure and resignation. And equally familiar is it to the surgeon, that under a bad state of temper, wounds heal less kindly, and when recently healed will even at times break out afresh. Likewise, that external inflammations pass less safely and regularly through their restorative processes, and that the pus of abscesses may be speedily transformed from a healthy to a morbid condition, under such unfriendly moral agency.

Regarding then merely our physical welfare, the importance of cultivating an amiableness of temper, of educating ourselves to meet with tranquilness the little ills and crosses of life, will not be denied. It is, after all, the minor evils, the trifling annoyances, or such as tend but to ruffle or fret our feelings, that are apt to be the least resolutely supported, and that oftentimes do more to mar our happiness, and impair our health, than even absolute and grave calamities. Many who would be impatient under the pricking of a pin, might submit with scarce a tremor or complaint to a grave and painful operation. It is only under strong occasions that the full energies of our nature are called forth. Our powers are aroused in correspondence with the emergencies they have to encounter. Thus it is only in lofty and responsible positions that the human character discovers its full force and dignity. Even the weak and timid soul will often astonish us by its patience and fortitude under great sufferings and dangers. Slight maladies of body, too, will frequently be marked by excessive irritability and unreasonable repining, while those of a more serious character are oftener distinguished by unusual calmness and submission. Death is the most important of all events we are destined to encounter, and it is truly astonishing how the powers of the mind will frequently rise to meet it;— with what composure and resignation even the most timid and sensitive may encounter its approach. In children the moral powers will not rarely seem to be elevated as the physical yield, and the observation was made by Dr. Zimmerman, that they are never more amiable than in their last illness.

" We observe in children, who are sick and in a dangerous situation, a very unusual compliance in every thing, together with a degree of knowledge, which is the fruit only of reflection and experience, and a genius and eloquence far above their years."* It would seem a law of our being then, and truly a beneficent and consolatory one, and from which numerous moral reflections might be drawn, that the energies of the soul should be developed in accordance with the importance of the exigencies to be encountered—should mount above even death itself.

The immediate and annoyful physical effects of mental irritation are strikingly displayed in those of a nervous and sensitive temperament, when disturbed on retiring to rest, by unseasonable noises, as the barking of dogs, crying of children, thrumming of pianos, etc. Under such vexing circumstances, the action of the heart often becomes unnaturally accelerated, and each pulsation of it is painfully

* On Experience in Physic.

sensible. A disagreeable dryness, too, is commonly experienced in the mouth and throat, with feverishness, sometimes itching of the skin, and a general nervous agitation or restlessness, often more harassing than even definite and seated pain, and the health, as might be expected, remains disturbed through the whole of the subsequent day. Under the condition described, the nervous sensibility will sometimes be raised to such morbid acuteness, that the slightest sounds, even the ticking of a clock, will be almost insupportable.

Some persons are constitutionally irritable, and in such the infirmity will be found hard indeed of cure, as persons are seldom entirely reasoned out of their physical predispositions. I have known persons so excessively irritable in their temper, and exercising so little government over it, as to be but slightly, if at all removed, from moral insanity. " We not unfrequently," says Dr. Carpenter, " meet with individuals, still holding their place in society, who are accustomed to act so much upon *feeling,* and to be so little guided by *reason,* as to be scarcely regarded as sane; and a very little exaggeration of such a tendency causes the actions to be so injurious to the individual himself, or to those around him, that restraint is required, although the intellect is in no way disordered, nor are any of the feelings perverted. . . . . . . The habit of yielding to a natural infirmity of temper often leads into paroxysms of ungovernable rage, which, in their turn, pass into a state of maniacal excitement."*

* Human Physiology.

An irritable and fractious temper, whether due to native temperament, or other causes, becomes, necessarily, the instrument of its own punishment:

" Secum petulans amentia certat."

And it furthermore poisons the happiness of all within the circle of its influence.   To so many occasions of annoyance, to so many petty vexations are we all, even the most fortunate of us, exposed, that the happiness of the naturally irritable man must be continually encountering obstacles, and his health consequently be ever liable to injury.   Heavy indeed are the penalties to which we are oftentimes doomed for the native faults of our organization !

It will be seen from what has preceded, how essential it is, on physical as well as moral considerations, that children be timely educated to control their tempers.   Those who have been too fondly indulged, or to whose passions an indiscreet license has been permitted, will be likely to enjoy less uniform good health,—to suffer more frequent disorders of their digestive organs, than such as have been the subjects of a stricter and wiser moral discipline.

" Although," says Dr. Reid, " an evenness and quietness of temper may, in many cases, appear connate or constitutional, equanimity ought not on that account to be regarded as altogether out of the reach of acquisition.   The feelings which have been subject to an habitual restraint will seldom be found to rise above their proper level.   Disproportionate emotions may often, in early life at least, be corrected, in the same manner as deformities and irregularities of bodily shape are, by means of constant pressure, forced into a more natural figure and dimension."* "By too great indulgence and a want of moral discipline, the passions acquire greater power, and a character is formed subject to caprice and to violent emotions: a predisposition to insanity is thus laid in the temper and moral affections of the individual. The exciting causes of madness have greater influence on persons of such habits than on those whose feelings are regulated."†

"We take great care," says Esquirol, speaking of the vicious morals and education of France as causes of insanity, "to form the mind, but seem to forget that the heart, like the mind, has need of education.

"The ridiculous and deplorable tenderness of parents, subjects to the caprices of infancy the reason of mature age.

"Accustomed to follow all his inclinations, and not being habituated by discipline to contradiction, the child, having arrived at maturity, cannot resist the vicissitudes and reverses by which life is agitated. On the least adversity insanity bursts forth; his feeble reason being deprived of its support, while the passions are without rein, or any kind of restraint." The same author relates the case of a lady nineteen years of age, of a sanguine temperament, who, having never experienced the least contradiction, was exceedingly choleric, and of extreme susceptibility. Under the

* On Nervous Affections, etc.
† Prichard on Insanity.

smallest provocation she became so irritated as to give herself up to the most insane acts of anger. She abused her
mother and friends, and threatened both their lives and her
own. After each attack of such fury she fell into a state of
prostration, and was, after a while, restored to calmness of
body and mind. If she attempted to restrain the outbreak
of her anger, she experienced severe sufferings. Her head
became swollen, her face and eyes injected with blood, and
this state was only relieved, by allowing vent to her rage.

Anger in its various degrees and modifications may
grow out of, or the propension to it may be aggravated by
various morbid conditions of our bodily organs. Unhealthy
states of the liver are well known to render the temper suspicious, peevish, or morose; and a large share of our moral
infirmities were ascribed by the ancients to an excess in the
secretion of this organ. Hence comes it that the term gall,
or bile, is used synonymously with anger, malignity, or bitterness of temper. And choleric, which signifies passionate, is derived from the Greek word χολη, *cholee*, meaning
bile.

In many morbid affections of the stomach, the subjects
become exceedingly irritable, venting their spleen upon
every body and every thing about them; and inflammation
of this organ will sometimes induce violent fits of passion.
It is doubtless through the morbid excitement which they
awaken in the mucous or inner gastric coat, that stimulating
food and drinks will, in some constitutions, always enkindle
an irascibleness of feeling. The liberal use of wine or spirit
is, in certain individuals, uniformly followed by fearful out-

breaks of anger. It is said of Lord Byron, that wine made him "savage instead of mirthful." The unhappy state of temper under which most persons awake on the morning subsequent to a debauch is, I believe, mainly owing to the morbid and irritable condition left in, and the depraved secretions acting upon, the delicate lining of the stomach; a part, than which few, if any, in the whole animal economy have closer sympathies with our moral nature. Hence may be derived an additional argument, if such were needed, in favor of temperance both in meat and drink, and one especially applicable to those of excitable feelings.

There are certain conditions of the nervous system attended with uncommon irascibility. In some morbid states of the brain, exceeding irritability, with frequent and uncontrollable outbreaks of anger, are apt to be displayed; as at the commencement of acute hydrocephalus in children, and of other inflammatory affections of this organ. A large proportion of epileptic subjects are morbidly irritable, and liable to strong agitations of passion; or, as said by Esquirol, exceedingly susceptible, irascible, ungovernable.

Insanity, at its commencement, is very often marked by impatience, irritability, and bursts of anger, and in its progress perhaps by maniacal rage or fury, either continued, or happening only at certain times of the day, or monthly, or at particular seasons. Some cases of mania consist of one almost uninterrupted fit of violent anger against every body and every thing. Or the insane person may exhibit a general moroseness of character, or a malignant hatred toward, and a disposition to inflict cruelty and even death upon particular persons, especially such as are most near and dear to him in his rational mind. This strong propensity to fits of rage, and the destruction of life, sometimes constitutes the only evidence of insanity, the mind remaining in all other respects apparently rational, and the case is then classed under that variety of mental aberration termed monomania. A case of this nature is related by M. Pinel, and cited by Dr. Prichard, which was clearly referrible to physical disease, probably of the nervous system.

"A man who had previously followed a mechanical occupation, but was afterwards confined at Bicêtre, experienced, *at regular intervals*, fits of rage ushered in by the following symptoms: At first he experienced a sensation of burning heat in the bowels, with an intense thirst and obstinate constipation; this sense of heat spread by degrees over the breast, neck, and face, with a bright color; sometimes it became still more intense, and produced violent and frequent pulsations in the arteries of those parts, as if they were going to burst; at last the nervous affection reached the brain, and then the patient was seized with the most irresistible sanguinary propensity; and if he could lay hold of any sharp instrument, he was ready to sacrifice the first person that came in his way. In other respects he enjoyed the free exercise of his reason; even during these fits he replied directly to questions put to him, and showed no kind of incoherence in his ideas, no sign of delirium; he even deeply felt all the horror of his situation, and was often penetrated with remorse, as if he was responsible for this mad propensity. Before his confinement at Bicêtre a fit of madness seized him in his own house; he immediately warned his wife of it, to whom he was much attached, and he had only time to cry out to her to run away lest he should put her to a violent death. At Bicêtre there appeared the same fits of periodical fury, the same mechanical propensity to commit atrocious actions, directed very often against the inspector, whose mildness and compassion he was continually praising. This internal combat between a sane reason in opposition to sanguinary cruelty, reduced him to the brink of despair, and he has often endeavored to terminate by death this insupportable struggle."

There are certain states of the functions of the skin, which are accompanied with an extreme fretfulness of temper. In what are familiarly termed colds, and under the influence of our chilling easterly winds on the sea-coast, many persons become excessively irritable. At the commencement of some diseases of the lungs, a similar condition of moral feeling is displayed. And in disorders of the urinary system, a peculiarly anxious and irascible disposition of mind is very frequently discovered.

Anger, arising out of conditions of our physical organization, must, of course, be directed, not to its real cause, but toward things and persons without, and which have no agency in its production. Thus may we suspect and maltreat those nearest and dearest to us, for no other reason than that our stomachs or livers are not executing as they should do their respective offices. And most persons must, I think, have remarked how apt one is to dream of quarrelling with his friends when going to bed on an indigestible supper. It is plain, then, that the cook will often have far more concern in the domestic tranquillity of families, than human philosophy has yet suspected. And would this important functionary but cultivate his art in reference to the facility of digestion, as well as to the gratification of the palate, he might contribute more to the happiness of society than nine-tenths of the boasted moral reformers of the time.

CHAPTER XVI.

FEAR.—ITS DEFINITION.—BEING ESSENTIAL TO SELF-PRESERVA-
TION, IT BELONGS INSTINCTIVELY TO ALL ANIMALS.—DIFFER-
ENCE BETWEEN MORAL AND PHYSICAL COURAGE.—CERTAIN
CONDITIONS OF OUR BODILY ORGANS AND FUNCTIONS BEGET
A MORBID TIMIDITY OF CHARACTER.—CERTAIN INSTINCTS
CONQUER FEAR.—DELICATE AND NERVOUS CONSTITUTIONS
ARE SOMETIMES ENDOWED WITH A REMARKABLE DEGREE OF
COURAGE AND FIRMNESS.

FEAR, like anger, is grounded on the principle of self-preservation, though the preservative acts to which these two passions incite are of a very different nature. Thus while anger
is defensive and offensive, stimulating us to repel or assault
and destroy the causes which threaten our safety or happiness, fear urges to avoidance or flight, and it is only when
escape has become hopeless that our guardian instincts force
us to resistance, or even attack.

Fear being, as already said, based on the instinct of self-
preservation, belongs of necessity to all animals; and it will
commonly be found bearing a direct relation to the feebleness and defencelessness of the individual, circumstances

rendering it the more needful. It may be set down as a general truth, though like most general truths admitting of occasional exceptions, that a sense of weakness begets timidity, while a consciousness of strength imparts boldness of character. Hence it is that fear is more especially conspicuous in the female constitution; I mean in all such circumstances of danger as demand energy of resistance, or strength of physical action, for under real calamities and sufferings, where endurance alone is required, woman will oftentimes display a degree of firmness of which our own stronger sex might well be proud. Woman looks to the strong arm and bold spirit of man for protection and defence, while he turns to her more delicate and passive nature for consolation and support under those ills of life against which his courage is powerless and his strength vain.

Different individuals are by nature more or less susceptible to the action of fear. Some even from their early childhood are notable for their cowardice, while others are equally so for their intrepidity. Habit and education, however, will certainly do a great deal toward conquering a native timorousness of character.

In our own species, courage admits of the distinction, generally recognized, into physical and moral. The former is constitutional, though habit, by its well known influence on the vital organism, operates to increase it. It is frequently called strength of nerve, and answers to the courage seen in the lower animals. The latter, or moral courage, presupposes a supremacy of the higher faculties, and is therefore peculiar to man. Thus the naturally timid,

pricked on by duty, honor, pride, have not rarely become
bold and successful warriors. And the most delicate and
effeminate in body, through the ascendant influence of their
moral nature, have faced dangers and borne sufferings, under which naturally stouter hearts and firmer nerves would
have quailed;—have offered up their lives in the cause of
truth, their honor, or their country. Hence may we account
for the superior firmness always displayed in a just cause.

"Thrice is he arm'd, that hath his quarrel just."

Moral courage belongs more especially to cultivated and
intellectual man. His will, strengthened by new motives,
learns to restrain the trembling nerve, and to subject the
weaker flesh to the dominion of the braver spirit. But in
the uncultivated and ignorant, it is the mere animal or brute
courage that is chiefly exhibited. Therefore it is, that in
difficult and hazardous undertakings, the greatest fortitude
and perseverance are almost always manifested on the part
of the leaders, whose resolution is strengthened by a higher
intelligence and more weighty responsibility.

Fear will oftentimes proceed rather from ignorance, or
mistaken judgment unduly magnifying the hazard, than
from any actual deficiency in fortitude. Familiarity with
any particular danger, conformably to a law of the animal
constitution, serves to lessen the apprehension of it, though
not necessarily emboldening toward others of a dissimilar
nature. The mariner looks calmly on the ocean tempest,
which would strike dismay to the heart even of the consti-

tutionally far braver landsman. The physician, although he may be naturally timid, walks undisturbed amid the desolating pestilence from which the hardiest courage flees in terror. And the delicate female, who would tremble and turn pale at even the sight or sound of a warlike instrument, might bear the pains of sickness and the approach of death, with more serenity and fortitude than the soldier of a hundred battles.

Good health, as a general rule, conduces to boldness, while infirmity of body tends to beget a pusillanimity of character. There are very many morbid states of the system, which may so depress the courage as to transform even the most daring into cowards. Disorders of the stomach and liver are particularly apt to engender false apprehensions, and weaken the natural fortitude, much more so, as a general truth, than more dangerous, or even fatal maladies of the lungs. Agues, and other malarious diseases, almost always render their subjects timid and apprehensive. Dr. Macculloch tells us that fear is so remarkable a character in these affections, that in some parts of the Mediterranean, where they are endemic, the only name by which they are known to the common people, is Scanto, meaning fear or fright. Long continued exposure to the infection of intermittent fevers will oftentimes, of itself, occasion irresoluteness and timidity.

" A gentleman was exposed to the emanations from a drain or sewer, which had become obstructed in his own house in London. He was soon afterwards seized with an ague, although he had not been out of the metropolis for years. The ague was easily cured by the proper remedies; but, for a long time afterwards, it harassed him in quite a different shape—namely, in that of a sudden dread or horror of—he knew not what. It usually recurred at the same hour of the day, and would last from two to three or four hours, during which the individual suffered the miseries of the damned. I know hundreds of people who had been exposed to malaria in hot and unhealthy climates, and who were harassed, for years after their return to this country, by these periodical horrors."* There are some diseases, however, which through the unnatural stimulation they promote in the brain and nervous system, arouse even to a morbid exaltation of courage. There are also certain instincts which completely conquer the passion of fear. Thus the most timid mother, forgetful of herself, will rush into any peril, into fire or flood, to save the life of her offspring. It is said the hare will attack the eagle in defence of her young.

Although, as before said, courage generally attends good health and physical vigor, and is wanting in the delicate, weakly, and sensitive, yet remarkable exceptions to this rule are sometimes encountered. Thus the pale and spare in body, weakly in constitution, and delicate in temperament, will sometimes exhibit the most extraordinary energy, firmness, and boldness of character. Disheartened by no obstacle, dismayed by no danger, they are fitted for the most difficult and daring enterprises. The rash and reso-

* Johnson on Change of Air.

8

lute Cassius, of whom Cæsar stood in such apprehension, is
represented as frail and spare in body, and of a nervous
temperament.   And Cæsar himself is recorded to have been
thin and delicate, of a weakly constitution, and subject to
epilepsy.   The frail, sensitive, nervous female, who would
shudder at the buzzing of a beetle, will sometimes be found
adequate to the most daring acts of courage.   There are
many persons who always seem timid and irresolute under
the ordinary and trifling dangers and difficulties of life, but
display an exalted heroism on occasions of great trial and
peril.   It is a remarkable circumstance in the living actions,
in the functions of mind, as well as body, that while slighter
stimuli or influences are often yielded to, inordinate ones
call forth a powerful and successful resistance.

True courage is a most desirable quality of mind ; it is
promotive of health and happiness, and essential to, and
by the Greeks and Romans was used synonymously with
virtue.   A timid man may be afraid to act right, may not
dare to do his duty when opposed by dangers. and difficulties.   Of this virtue every body is ambitious, and none
more so than the coward, as proved by his vainglorious affectation of it.   Indeed, all of us are prone to assume both
the intellectual and moral qualities in which we are most
deficient.   Thus, the fool affects wisdom, the strumpet
modesty, the knave honesty, the niggard liberality, and the
poltroon bravery.

CHAPTER XVII.

FEAR, like the other passions, is exhibited in various shades
or degrees. It may be slight and transient, or so aggravated
as completely to dethrone the judgment, and jeopard, not
only the health, but even the existence of its subject.

Fear is one of the most painful of the passions, and its
effects, both on the mental and bodily functions are truly
astonishing. Under its powerful influence the fiercest
animals are rendered gentle and subservient to our will and
purposes.

In acute fear, the effects induced on the physical organization and its functions are very remarkable, and oftentimes exceedingly distressing. The respiration becomes
immediately and strikingly affected. Thus, on the first impulse of the passion, owing to a spasmodic contraction of
the diaphragm, a sudden inspiration takes place, directly

succeeded by an incomplete expiration ; the latter being,
as it would seem, interrupted, or cut short by a spasm of
the throat, windpipe, or lungs. Hence arises the irregular
and convulsive breathing so characteristic of extreme fear.
Under its action the respiration almost always grows short,
rapid, and tremulous,—as may be seen in the inferior animals when frightened,—and a painful sense of suffocation
is experienced in the chest. The voice becomes embarrassed, trembles, and, in consequence of the diminution and
inspissation of the secretions of the mouth and throat, is
dry, husky, thick, and unnatural. Even temporary speech-
lessness may be induced under the first shock of this
passion.

" Obstupui, steteruntque comæ, et vox faucibus hæsit."

The heart, likewise, suffers severely from the influence
of acute fear. It becomes oppressed, constricted ; flutters
and palpitates, and is variously agitated ; and the pulse is
consequently small, feeble, rapid, and oftentimes irregular.

The viscera of the abdomen, too, not unfrequently experience disagreeable sensations, unnatural or spasmodic contractions, and a morbid increase of their secretions. Sometimes vomiting, but oftener a diarrhœa, perhaps involuntary,
takes place ; and jaundice has, in occasional instances,
quickly followed its operation. The urine, also, is augmented, pale or limpid, and the desire to void it becomes
frequent, urgent, and many times irresistible.

The blood, as might be anticipated, abandons the surface, the face turns pallid, and the skin becomes universally cold, contracted, and rough, like goose-flesh, and as a consequence of this contraction, the hairs growing from it are elevated, or in the common phrase, stand on end, or if not, they seem as though they did to the affrighted individual. Chills often spread themselves over the surface, or over portions of it, sometimes as it were in streams; and cold sweats, partial or general, not unusually break forth. About the forehead, especially, a cold, dewy sweat will frequently be seen from the influence of great fear.

Partial tremors, as of the limbs, or a general shuddering and shaking, and chattering of the teeth, as under extreme cold, or in the first stage of a paroxysm of ague, are also common phenomena. Ague, in fact, is derived from a Gothic word (*agis*), meaning terror, on account of the similarity of effects between it and this passion. It is worthy to be noted here, that these same symptoms produced by fear, when the result of morbid physical states, are apt to be connected with an unnatural degree of timidity or apprehension. On the effect of agues in producing such conditions of mind I have previously remarked. And I feel well satisfied that we possess less courage if chilled and shivering under the influence of cold, than when the surface is warm and comfortable, and the blood plays freely in its extreme vessels. But to proceed with the physical manifestations of fear:— Under its forcible action the eyes glare wildly, as though they would start from their sockets, and the whole countenance is drawn into a painful and repulsive expression. A convulsive sobbing, accompanied by a profuse secretion of tears, and in delicate and sensitive females even severe paroxysms of hysterics will not rarely ensue. The muscular system may likewise become strongly convulsed, or its energies be temporarily suspended, and the individual be rendered dumb and motionless. In extreme cases the whole chest, with the upper part of the abdomen, or region of the stomach, are affected with an agonizing sense of constriction, and fainting often supervenes.

The depressing effects of fear just described are not uncommonly succeeded by reaction ; anger perhaps being aroused toward the cause of alarm, and calling forth extravagant muscular efforts to repel or destroy it. Few of our passions, in truth, long maintain their simple and original character, but others, and of a different nature, are engendered by, and become blended with them. And that such should be the case would seem, in many instances, to be even necessary to our welfare ; the newly-awakened passion serving to counteract the threatening consequences of the primary one. Thus will the excitement of anger act as a cordial to the depression of fear ; and the depression of fear, on the other hand, as a wholesome sedative to the excitement of anger.

Generally, as was before observed, the first impulse of simple fear, when the muscles retain their powers, is to provoke flight, and which is often precipitated with a degree of force which would have been quite impossible in a more tranquil condition of mind. This act is truly instinctive, and therefore irresistible, except under the counter-working influence of some other passion. But when escape is found

impracticable, then will the individual be often driven to the
most fierce and desperate resistance, and thus even the
greatest cowards have sometimes acquired the fame of
heroes.

> " To be furious,
> Is to be frighted out of fear ; and in that mood,
> The dove will peck the estridge."

Fear, in its most aggravated degree, acquires the name
of terror; and, under certain circumstances, and in certain
constitutions, remarkable results have followed its strong impression on the nervous system.   That peculiar condition
which it has been supposed some animals have the power of
producing in certain others, called fascination, has by many
been ascribed to the agency of terror, which paralyzing, as
is thought, all voluntary muscular action in the victim, renders him an easy prey to his destroyer.

That some species of serpents possess this fascinating
influence over birds—even of forcing them, by a gradual and
irresistible movement, actually to fly into their devouring
jaws—is not merely a popular belief, but has been maintained by those whose names sustain a prominent place in
the annals of science.   The following citation relating to
this subject is from M. Broussais, an author whom I have
before quoted, and whose writings were at one time held in
no ordinary repute by many medical men of high rank, both
in Europe and America.   It certainly shows an easy faith,
and a strange process of reasoning in its support.   It is
brought in under the head of instinct.

"If we examine instinct in the prey threatened by the voracity of the snake, we discover something very extraordinary. What is the power which compels the tomtit, perched upon a neighboring bush, to sacrifice itself for the gratification of the wants of an animal creeping upon the ground, at a distance from it? The reptile obstinately pursues it with its looks. So long as the bird does not perceive the snake' it runs no risk; but if the former rests its eyes for a few moments on those of its pursuer, all is lost, for it will become its prey. The bird is terrified—it cannot abstain from looking fixedly at the snake—it flies from branch to branch, as if with a view of escaping, and yet it gradually approaches its enemy. This latter continues gazing at it, presenting, at the same time, an open mouth, and the victim finally flies of itself into it. These are not mere fables, but facts, which few shepherds have not had occasion to notice. The public papers have lately detailed the manner in which a boa-constrictor, conveyed to Europe in an English or American ship, was fed. The journalist relates, that those who took care of this monstrous snake, when they conceived that it was hungry, opened its iron cage, and presented to it a goat (a number of which had been shipped for its use); as soon as the animal perceived its prey, it unfolded itself, and looked at it fixedly, with open mouth. The goat, after hesitating some time, as if undecided between the instinct of self-preservation and that attracting it towards the monster, precipitated itself head-foremost into the living gulf which was to serve as its tomb."

"I do not see," observes the same author, in relation to

his above cited remarks, "why an animal, destined to be-come the prey of another, should not be compelled to yield itself up, when this latter is deprived of other means requi-site for seizing it. It is generally admitted that a number of animals are born only to be devoured. The end of destruction is as much in nature as that of formation, and the acts of instinct which tend to deliver up a prey to its enemy, are as natural as others, the object of which is to avoid danger, or gratify an appetite. Now it appears evi-dent that, in order to attain these ends, the Author of all things has invariably made use of the same means, namely, instinctive impulses." *

Every other writer on the subject of instincts, so far at least as I am informed, has regarded their final purpose to be preservative only ; but the present author appears to have introduced a new one, leading its possessor into destruction for another's support. In another place, Broussais, in the most unequivocal manner, refers fascination to the influence of terror.

Facts, were their details to be relied upon, are certainly not wanting to substantiate such a fascinating influence in serpents. Scarce a peasant, or even a country schoolboy, but can bring some instance toward its support. That birds are sometimes seen fluttering in apparent alarm about and near these reptiles, will not be disputed. But this is often-times only in defence of their nest which the snake is invad-ing, they being actuated by an instinct whose end is the

* Physiology applied to Pathology,

8*

preservation of the species, instead of one urging them to destruction for the support of their enemy. This power of fascination then, although far from being established, can hardly be ranked among the mere superstitions of ignorance and credulity. The propensity, almost resistless, which some persons feel when on the verge of a precipice, to cast themselves down into inevitable destruction, is equally as strange as that a bird should be impelled by an invincible disposition to fly into the deadly jaws of its devourer.

But to resume my principal topic. Extreme terror will, in certain instances, instead of depressing and paralyzing the nervous power, arouse it into new and astonishing action. We read that it has even caused the dumb to speak, and the paralytic to walk; and that the most painful and obstinate diseases have been known suddenly to yield under its potent influence. It is related in Herodotus that during the storm of Sardis, "a Persian meeting Crœsus was, through ignorance of his person, about to kill him. The king, overwhelmed by his calamity, took no care to avoid the blow or escape death; but his dumb son, when he saw the violent designs of the Persian, overcome with astonishment and terror, exclaimed aloud, 'Oh, man, do not kill Crœsus!' This was the first time he had ever articulated, but he retained the faculty of speech from this event as long as he lived." We have instances enough, however, and of a less apocryphal character, of the remarkable curative effects of extravagant fear. Dr. Whytt observes, that it will frequently put a stop to convulsive motions and spasms, and sometimes succeed after other remedies have failed, and

gives a striking instance in illustration.*   A common method of stopping hiccup is by startling the person affected.
Hemorrhage will sometimes be checked by the action of
sudden fright.

Van Swieten records the case of a man who, under the
influence of sudden terror, recovered from hemiplegy, or
palsy of one half of the body, that had afflicted him for years.
"A woman who had been paralytic from the age of six to
forty-four, suddenly recovered the perfect use of her limbs,
when she was very much terrified during a severe thunder
storm, and was making violent efforts to escape from a
chamber in which she had been left alone.   A man who had
many years been paralytic, recovered in the same manner
when his house was on fire."†   Gout has also immediately
disappeared through the operation of unexpected fright.
An old author relates of one of his patients, suffering under
a paroxysm of this disease, that having his feet and legs
wrapped in cataplasms of turnips, a hog entering his room
and beginning to feed on the turnips, so alarmed him that
he began to run and jump, and all his gouty pains straightway vanished.

Intermittent fevers or agues have likewise disappeared
from the strong impulse of this same passion.   Dr. Fordyce
tells of a man afflicted with a fever of this description, that
his brother having led him to walk by the edge of a mill-
dam, pushed him suddenly into the water ; and which, as he

* Observations on Nervous Diseases, &c.
† Abercrombie on the Brain ; cited from Diemerbroeck.

was unable to swim, naturally put him into a very great fright. He was speedily, however, taken out, and from that time forth had no further paroxysm of his disease.* A gentleman, laboring under an obstinate ague, and who had a great dread of rats, happened to be shut up in a room with one of them, which jumping upon him, caused such fright as completely to expel his ague. Among the remedies of intermittent fevers, Dr. Cullen ranks an impression of horror. The many charms, and hateful and disgusting superstitious remedies which have been so often employed, and sometimes successfully in agues, doubtless operate through the impression of horror, dread, awe, which they produce on the mind. Such are spiders, the chips of a gallows, or the halter of an executed criminal worn round the neck.

"Elias Ashmole, in his Diary, April 11, 1681, has entered, 'I took early in the morning a good dose of elixir, and hung three spiders about my neck, and drove my ague away. Deo Gratias!' "†

How the classical remedy for a quartan ague, of placing the fourth book of Homer's Iliad under the patient's head, operates, I am not prepared to explain.

To show the effect of a superstitious impression,—which must be a modification of fear,—upon the mind in the cure of the present disease, I will venture to cite the following interesting narrative, with which some of my readers are doubtless already familiar. It relates to Sir John Holt, Lord Chief

---

* Dissertations on Fevers.

† Pettigrew's Medical Superstitions.

Justice of the Court of King's Bench, 1709, who in his youth appears to have been extremely wild. " Being once engaged with some of his rakish friends in a trip into the country, in which they had spent all their money, it was agreed they should try their fortune separately. Holt arrived at an inn at the end of a straggling village, ordered his horse to be taken care of, bespoke a supper and a bed. He then strolled into the kitchen, where he observed a little girl of thirteen shivering with an ague. Upon making inquiry respecting her, the landlady told him that she was her only child, and had been ill nearly a year, notwithstanding all the assistance she could procure for her from physic. He gravely shook his head at the doctors, bade her be under no further concern, for that her daughter should never have another fit. He then wrote a few unintelligible words in a court hand on a scrap of parchment, which had been the direction affixed to a hamper, and rolling it up, directed that it should be bound upon the girl's wrist, and there allowed to remain until she was well. The ague returned no more ; and Holt, having remained in the house a week, called for his bill. ' God bless you, sir,' said the old woman, ' you're nothing in my debt, I'm sure. I wish, on the contrary, that I was able to pay you for the cure which you have made of my daughter. Oh ! if I had had the happiness to see you ten months ago, it would have saved me forty pounds.' With pretended reluctance he accepted his accommodation as a recompense, and rode away. Many years elapsed, Holt advanced in his profession of the law, and went a circuit, as one of the judges of the Court of King's Bench, into the

same county, where, among other criminals brought before
him, was an old woman under a charge of witchcraft. To
support this accusation, several witnesses swore that the pri-
soner had a spell with which she could either cure such
cattle as were sick, or destroy those that were well, and that
in the use of this spell she had been lately detected, and
that it was now ready to be produced in court. Upont his
statement the judge desired it might be handed up to him.
It was a dirty ball, wrapped round with several rags, and
bound with packthread. These coverings he carefully removed, and beneath them found a piece of parchment, which
he immediately recognized as his own youthful fabrication.
For a few moments he remained silent—at length recollect-
ing himself, he addressed the jury to the following effect :—
' Gentlemen, I must now relate a particular of my life,
which very ill suits my present character and the station in
which I sit ; but to conceal it would be to aggravate the folly
for which I ought to atone, to endanger innocence, and to
countenance superstition. This bauble, which you suppose
to have the power of life and death, is a senseless scroll
which I wrote with my own hand and gave to this woman,
whom for no other reason you accuse as a witch.'   He then
related the particulars of the transaction, with such an effect
upon the minds of the people, that his old landlady was the
last person tried for witchcraft in that county."*

Epileptic fits—the frequent result of a false or morbid
religious excitement or enthusiasm, aided by the principle

* Pettigrew's Medical Superstitions.

of sympathy, in the feeble-minded and ignorant—may often
be counteracted through the passion of fear. An intelligent
minister of Shetland, in Scotland, being much annoyed, and
the devotions of his church impeded, on his first introduction
into the country, by the frequent occurrence of these convulsions, "obviated their repetition, by assuring his parish-
ioners that no treatment was more effectual than immersion
in cold water ; and as his kirk was fortunately contiguous
to a fresh-water lake, he gave notice that attendants should
be at hand, during divine service, to insure the proper
means of cure. The sequel need scarcely be told. The
fear of being carried out of the church, and into the water,
acted like a charm—not a single naïad was made, and the
worthy minister, for many years, had reason to boast of one
of the best regulated congregations in Shetland."[*]

The cure of these convulsions in the parish of North-
maven, in which they were once very frequent, is said to
have been effected by a rough fellow of a kirk officer tossing
a woman affected with them, and with whom he had been
often troubled, into a ditch of water. She was never known
to be thus affected afterwards, and the disease was kept off
in others by a dread of the like treatment.

Boerhaave appears to have operated successfully with
the passion of fear, in the house of the poor, at Haerlem, in
the cure of convulsions, which, through the force of imitation—a propensity so strong in our nature—had spread to

[*] Quoted in Hecker's Epidemics of the Middle Ages, from Hibbert's
Description of the Shetland Islands, &c.

almost all the boys and girls who were its inmates. All medical treatment having proved unsuccessful in the hands of the physicians of the place, application was made to Boerhaave, who, observing the manner in which the fits spread, determined to try the effects of a remedy which would act strongly upon the imagination. He accordingly had several portable furnaces, on which were placed burning coals, and iron hooks, of a figure suited for his purpose; and then gave directions that, as all medicines had failed, and he knew of no other remedy, the next one seized with a paroxysm, whether boy or girl, should be burnt on the naked arm with the heated iron, even to the bone. All became so much terrified at the thought of this cruel remedy, that they struggled with all their might to keep off the fits, and were completely successful.

Dr. Cooke cites, from the eighteenth volume of the Medical and Physical Journal, the following instance of the disappearance of epilepsy from sudden fright. "A lady in the prime of life, of robust habit, was for four years afflicted with this complaint in a violent degree—the paroxysms returning three or four times a week, continuing for some hours, and leaving the patient in a state of stupor. A variety of medicines had been tried in vain, and the case was considered hopeless, when, on receiving a dreadful mental shock, by the circumstance of her daughter being accidentally burnt to death, the disease entirely and finally left her."

Settled insanity has been removed by immoderate fright. An old remedy, indeed, for this disease, and one of high authority, was to terrify the maniac by throwing him into the water, and keeping him there till nearly drowned. Esquirol relates the case of a lady under his charge, who believed she was damned, and had the devil inside of her, being cured by the threat of cold baths, of which she had the utmost dread, every time she gave herself up to her peculiar insane notions and fears. He also gives instances of the complete cure of furious maniacs, through terror of the red-hot iron, with which, as a remedial measure, they were about to be cauterized.

In the thirty-first volume of the Medico-Chirurgical Review, we read the following case, quoted from a Prussian Medical Journal: "A man, between thirty and forty years of age, had been, from the year 1827 to 1831, affected with an extreme degree of insanity, amounting almost to idiocy, and alternating with periodic fits of raving madness. His condition bordered on bestiality, and none dared to approach him in his maniacal paroxysms. His case was deemed quite hopeless; and, for the two following years, he vegetated, so to speak, in the public lunatic house of the place. A fire having accidentally broken out near his cell, his mental powers, which had so long slumbered, were suddenly aroused; and Dr. Ollenroth, upon visiting him a few days afterwards, found him perfectly intelligent, and assiduously occupied with some domestic arrangements. He had no recollection of his former condition. All that he remembered, was simply that, on the approach of the flames, he felt himself seized with an indescribable sense of terror, that he sprung up from his bed, and that he suddenly regained his intelligence."

Many minor affections are also known to be at once removed or suspended, under the strong impression of fear, as toothache, and other nervous pains; hypochondriasis, sea-sickness, etc.

CHAPTER XVIII.

FEAR CONTINUED.——DEATH IS SOMETIMES THE CONSEQUENCE OF
EXTRAVAGANT FEAR.——VARIOUS PAINFUL DISEASES ARE NOT
UNFREQUENTLY THE CONSEQUENCE OF ITS OPERATION.——
THE TERRORS AND MORBID EXCITEMENTS OF RELIGION ARE
OFTENTIMES FOLLOWED BY THE MOST MELANCHOLY EFFECTS
ON MIND AND BODY.——THESE EFFECTS MAY BECOME GREATLY
EXTENDED THROUGH THE PRINCIPLE OF IMITATION OR SYM-
PATHY.——TERROR MAY OPERATE THROUGH THE MOTHER ON
HER UNBORN OFFSPRING.——ITS EFFECTS ON THE HAIR AND
DIFFERENT SECRETIONS.——THE FEARS AWAKENED IN THE
IMAGINATION DURING SLEEP, WHEN FREQUENT AND IMMODE-
RATE, MAY BE FRAUGHT WITH SERIOUS INJURY TO HEALTH.

TERROR is sometimes instantly fatal, at once destroying
the nervous energy, and suppressing the action of the heart;
or it may bring on hemorrhages or convulsions, quickly terminating in death. Children and females being generally
more sensitive and susceptible in their nervous system, are
most liable to become the victims of fear.

Montaigne informs us, that at the siege of St. Pol, a
town in France, "a gentleman was seized with such a fright,
that he sunk down dead in the breach without any wound."

Marcellus Donatus tells of a child who instantly fell dead in a field on seeing, in the morning twilight, two persons clothed in black suddenly appear by his side. Another child was so frightened by the report of a cannon from a vessel while he was bathing in the sea, that he instantly fell into convulsions, and died in fifteen minutes.

An old writer relates of a nun, that she was so terrified on seeing herself surrounded by hostile soldiers with drawn swords, that the blood suddenly flowed from all the outlets of the body, and she immediately perished in their presence.

Broussais gives the case of a lady, who, on feeling a living frog fall into her bosom from the claws of a bird of prey, while she was sitting on the grass, was instantly seized with such a profuse bleeding from the lungs, that she survived but a few minutes.

A case is told by Pechlin* of a lady, who, upon looking at the comet of 1681, through a telescope, became so affected with terror, that she died in a few days.

Predictions of death are sometimes punctually fulfilled through the influence of fear upon the imagination. Lord Littleton, it seems to be well authenticated, died at the exact moment at which his fancied vision had forewarned him his death would take place. The superstitious subjects of such hallucinations have sometimes been preserved from death, which they believed was to happen at a fixed time, and for which their terrors seemed to be fast preparing them, by putting back the hands of the clock, or, as in the

* Observ. Med., lib. iii, observ. 23.

case related by Dr. Darwin, by administering a dose of opium, so as to cause the person to sleep beyond the predicted period.

It is related of a person sentenced to be bled to death, that though the execution of the sentence was only feigned, by causing warm water, after his eyes were blinded, to trickle down his arm, yet the fearful impression on his imagination that the blood was flowing from his veins, destroyed his life as effectually as if the punishment had been actually accomplished. The fear of the axe, too, has sometimes caused death as surely as its fall. A malefactor, as we read, being condemned to decapitation, a reprieve arrived just as his head had been laid upon the block, but life was found to be already extinguished. " In Lesinsky's voyage round the world, there is an account of a religious sect in the Sandwich Islands, who arrogate to themselves the power of praying people to death. Whoever incurs their displeasure, receives notice that the homicide litany is about to begin ; and such are the effects of imagination, that the very notice is frequently sufficient with these poor people to produce the effect."*

" Some young girls went one day a little way out of town to see a person who had been executed, and who was hung in chains. One of them threw several stones at the gibbet, and at last struck the body with such violence as to make it move ; at which the girl was so much terrified, that she imagined the dead person was alive, came down from

* Cited by Dr. Reid, in his Essays on Nervous Diseases.

the gibbet, and ran after her.   She hastened home, and not
being able to conquer the idea, fell into strong convulsions,
and died."*

The following case from the same author just quoted,
will serve to show the hazard of operating upon the timidity
of children, as a means of punishment :

" A schoolmistress, for some trifling offence, most fool-
ishly put a child into a dark cellar for an hour.   The child
was greatly terrified, and cried bitterly.   Upon returning
to her parents in the evening, she burst into tears, and
begged that she might not be put into the cellar ; the
parents thought this extremely odd, and assured her that
there was no danger of their being guilty of so great an act
of cruelty ; but it was difficult to pacify her, and when put
to bed she passed a restless night.   On the following day
she had fever, during which she frequently exclaimed, ' Do
not put me in the cellar.'   The fourth day after, she was
taken to Sir A. Cooper, in a high state of fever, with delirium, frequently muttering, ' Pray don't put me in the cellar.'   When Sir Astley inquired the reason, he found that
the parents had learned the punishment to which she had
been subjected.   He ordered what was likely to relieve
her, but she died in a week after this unfeeling conduct."

Terror, although, as seen, it may occasion instant or
speedy death, yet is more apt to be followed by various disorders of mind and body, either slight and transient, or
serious and lasting.   Deafness, dumbness, blindness, loss of

* Pettigrew ; cited from Platerus.

memory, dropsies, erysipelas, and various cutaneous eruptions have speedily ensued to fright.

"Some time ago," says Zimmerman, "I had the care of
a poor woman of seventy years of age, who had an erysipelatous fever, which was very long and dangerous in its
course, and was apparently brought on by the dread of an
apparition. This poor woman lived in a lonely house which
had the reputation of being haunted, and she one night
fancied she saw in the person of a large mastiff, the much-
talked-of spirit. Her terror was excessive, she shrieked
out and fell down in a state of insensibility. When she
came to herself she complained of anxiety, sickness at the
stomach, and extreme headache, the next day she had considerable fever, and on the day following her head was exceedingly inflamed, and a great part of it covered with an
erysipelatous eruption."*

Severe fainting fits are not unfrequently its consequence,
and which have continued rapidly succeeding each other
for hours. And in some instances a morbid nervous mobi-
lity will be engendered by it, from which the unfortunate
sufferer never wholly recovers, remaining liable ever after-
terwards to palpitations, faintings, or nervous tremors, on
the slightest alarm, and more particularly if it be of the
nature of that which awakened the primary disturbance.
Operating upon females, it will not unusually provoke paroxysms of hysterics, and even leave a settled disposition to
them in the system.

* On Experience in Physic, vol. 2, pp. 278–9.

Catalepsy, that remarkable and rare nervous affection, in which there is an entire suspension of sensibility and voluntary motion, the limbs at the same time remaining fixed in any position, however restrained, in which they may be placed, has occasionally been produced by terror. In nervous and susceptible females, it has been most often thus excited ; but it has happened even in the more hardy of our own sex, as shown in the following, and striking case, cited by Sir Alexander Crichton, either of catalepsy or ecstasy, affections very similar to each other, differing principally in the inflexible and rigid state of the muscles in the latter. "George Grokatzki, a Polish soldier, deserted from his regiment in the harvest of the year 1677. He was discovered a few days afterwards, drinking and making merry in a common alehouse. The moment he was apprehended he was so much terrified that he gave a loud shriek, and immediately was deprived of the power of speech. When brought to a court-martial, it was impossible to make him articulate a word ; nay, he then became as immovable as a statue, and appeared not to be conscious of any thing which was going forward. In the prison to which he was conducted he neither ate nor drank. The officers and the priests at first threatened him, and afterwards endeavored to soothe and calm him, but all their efforts were in vain. He remained senseless and immovable. His irons were struck off, and he was taken out of the prison, but he did not move. Twenty days and nights were passed in this way, during which he took no kind of nourishment, nor had any natural evacuation ; he then gradually sunk and died."

Chorea, or St. Vitus's dance, is another nervous affection which has sometimes been caused by fright. A peculiar nervous affection was brought on in Mr. John Hunter, by great anxiety of mind (and mental anxiety must be regarded but as a modification of fear). It consisted in a feeling as though he were suspended in the air, "of his body being much diminished in size, and of every motion of the head and limbs, however slight, being both very extensive, and accomplished with great rapidity."

Epilepsy has very often been induced by sudden fright, and a permanent tendency to it been left in the system. A celebrated German physician asserts, that in six out of fourteen epileptic patients under his care, in the hospital of St. Mark, at Vienna, the disease had been caused by terror. A man travelling alone by night, encountered a large dog in a narrow path, and fancying himself seized by the animal, he reached home in extreme terror, and on the following morning was attacked with a violent fit of epilepsy, of which he afterwards had many returns. "A young man, having witnessed some of the dreadful events at Paris, on the horrible tenth of August, became affected immediately with this disorder." A maid-servant of Leipsic, while endeavoring to untie some knots, got the impression that one of them was made by a sorceress, and became so terrified in consequence, that she was immediately seized with a fit of epilepsy.*

In young children, convulsions and epilepsy are brought

* Cooke on Nervous Diseases.

9

on with great facility under the operation of strongly and suddenly awakened fear. Tissot, referring to the foolish and dangerous practice of frightening children in sport, observes: " One half of those epilepsies which do not depend on such causes as might exist before the child's birth, are owing to this detestable custom; and it cannot be too much inculcated into children, never to frighten one another; a point which persons intrusted with their education ought to have the strictest regard to."*

Religion, when perverted from its true purpose of hope and consolation, and employed as an instrument of terror; when, instead of being gentle, peaceful, and full of love, it assumes a gloomy, austere, and threatening tone, may become productive of a train of nervous complaints of the most melancholy and even dangerous nature. Religion, in its widest signification, has been defined, " An impressive sense of the irresistible influence of one or more superior Beings over the concerns of mortals, which may become beneficial or inimical to our welfare." Now, according to the fancied character and requisitions of the Power or Powers it worships, it may be the parent of fear, cruelty, and intolerance, or of trust, charity, benevolence, and all the loftiest feelings that adorn our nature. The austere bigot who owns a God of terror and vengeance, becomes the slave of the direst passions. All who differ from his creed are to be hated as the enemies of heaven, and the outcasts of its mercy; and he may even persuade himself that to inflict upon them bodily

---

* Avis au Peuple, &c.

tortures is an acceptable religious duty. This spirit of
gloomy fanaticism has been one of the severest scourges of
our species. No human sympathy has been able to with-
stand its merciless power. It has set the parent against the
child, and the child against the parent, and has blasted every
tie of domestic affection. Even those naturally possessed
of the most tender dispositions have become so hardened
under the customs of religious bigotry, as to look without
the least feeling of compassion on the pangs of the heretic
amid the flames, and who, in their faith, was to pass immediately from his temporal into the indescribable agonies of
eternal fires. "I was once," says Dr. Cogan, "passing
through Moorfields with a young lady, aged about nine or
ten years, born and educated in Portugal, but in the Protes-
tant faith, and observing a large concourse of people assembled round a pile of faggots on fire, I expressed a curiosity
to know the cause. She very composedly answered, ' I suppose that it is nothing more than *that they are going to burn
a Jew.*' Fortunately it was no other than roasting an ox
upon some joyful occasion. What rendered this singularity
the more striking, was the natural mildness and compassion
of the young person's disposition."*

There is, perhaps, no enthusiastic infatuation which has
been more harmful, both to mind and body, than that of religion. The relentless and fearful passions awakened by a
gloomy and vindictive religion, fraught with unimaginable
future terrors, have been productive, alike in past and recent

* Philosophical Treatise on the Passions.

times, of the most melancholy disorders, both in the moral
and physical constitution. Baron Haller speaks of superstitious piety as a very common cause of insanity, especially in
those who picture to themselves the most terrible notions of
a future state. The mind, especially if of a gloomy and enthusiastic cast, dwells upon these frightful ideas until conviction of their certainty becomes established. "An overstrained bigotry is, in itself, and considered in a medical
point of view, a destructive irritation of the senses, which
draws men away from the efficiency of mental freedom, and
peculiarly favors the most injurious emotions. Sensual
ebullitions, with strong convulsions of the nerves, appear
sooner or later, and insanity, suicidal disgust of life, and in-
curable nervous disorders, are but too frequently the consequences of a perverse, and, indeed, hypocritical zeal, which
has ever prevailed, as well in the assemblies of the Mænades
and Corybantes of antiquity, as under the semblance of religion among the Christians and Mahomedans."*

At the field-meetings that are annually held among us
I have been witness to the most frightful nervous affections,
as convulsions, epilepsy, hysteria, distressing spasms, violent
contortions of the body, not only in females in whom, from
their more sensitive and sympathetic temperament, such affections are most readily excited, but also in the more hardy
and robust of our own sex. Even spectators, such as attend
for the purpose of amusement or merriment, will oftentimes
be overtaken by the same nervous disorders. But such

---

* Hecker's Epidemics of the Middle Ages.

morbid affections are not peculiar to field-meetings; they happen among all sects of religionists, who seek to make proselytes by appealing to the fears, rather than convincing the judgment; affrighting the imagination with

> "—— damned ghosts, that doe in torments waile,
> And thousand feends, that doe them endlesse paine
> With fire and brimstone, which for ever shall remaine."

Females, and, indeed, all persons of susceptible feelings and nervous habits, may suffer serious injury from being subjected to such superstitious terrors. Not only the disorders mentioned, but chorea, and other nervous maladies, and even confirmed insanity, have been their melancholy consequence. Dr. Prichard informs us, that several instances of mental alienation, from the cause we are considering, have fallen within his own sphere of observation. "Some of these," says he, "have occurred among persons who had frequented churches or chapels where the ministers were remarkable for a severe, impassioned, and almost imprecatory style of preaching, and for enforcing the terrors rather than setting forth the hopes and consolations which belong to the Christian religion."*

In the report of the New-York State Lunatic Asylum, for 1847, we find, out of 1,609 patients—being the whole number received—in 173 the disease is imputed to religious anxiety, and in 33 to Millerism, a new cause of religious insanity. It is a remark of Esquirol, in his treatise on Mental

* On Insanity, &c.

Maladies, &c., that insanity caused and maintained by religious notions is seldom cured.   But we have it on the
same authority, that religious fanaticism and terrors, although formerly so frequent causes of insanity in France,
have now lost their influence there, and seldom produce the
disorder.   This, on his own account of the matter, would
seem to be owing to the little religious feeling existing in
France; religion, as he informs us, only coming in as a
usage in the most solemn acts of life; no longer offering
hope and consolation to the afflicted—its morality no longer
guiding man in the difficult paths of life.   Indeed he draws
but a sad picture of his poor country.   All sentiment is absorbed in a cold selfishness.   Domestic affection, respect,
love, authority, mutual dependences, have ceased to exist.
Each lives but for himself, and the present.   Marriage ties
are only pretences, entered into by the wealthy either to
gratify their pride, or as a matter of speculation, and by the
common people are altogether neglected.   The children are
injudiciously educated; their passions are left unbridled, and
licentious; and the women are in no better predicament,
being carried away by an insatiable appetite for romances,
the toilet, frivolities, and so on.

It is said of the Society of Friends, in England, that
they are in a great measure exempt from what is termed religious insanity, which immunity has been explained on the
character of their religion; it being one of peace and charity, they are but little exposed to those fanatical excitements
and superstitious apprehensions which work so powerfully
on the imaginations of many other Christian sects.

Instead of these mystical terrors, or following them, the religious visionary sometimes experiences a sort of ecstatic beatitude ; his morbid and overheated imagination enkindles an infuriated and wasting zeal, an impassioned and consuming holy love, often leading to the wildest extravagances of language and action, and the most melancholy consequences to the nervous system. Under the sacred garb of religion, sensual feelings are, I fear, too frequently concealed. The expressions and behavior of some of these heated enthusiasts, evince to the eye of sober reason, that they are devoured by carnal rather than spiritual fires—that their glowing mystical love is lighted at the flames of earth, not heaven.

" This pretended spiritual love consumes the body more than if the patients really gave themselves up to the appetite of the senses, because the orgasm which excites it lasts continually. I have observed that many of these unhappy people have become hypochondriacal, hysterical, stupid, and even maniacal. One patient after raving with this love, and burning with an inward fire, was sometimes attacked with the most painful spasms, and sometimes with stupor, till at length she spit blood, became blind, dumb, and soon afterwards died. Some have died consumptive, others have become paralytic.

" It is inconceivable how many complaints originate in monastic life, from the religious exercises to which the different orders are subjected. The nuns seem to give into these extravagances much more easily than the men, on account of their greater delicacy and irritability. The effects of these spiritual reflections are a heaviness or dizziness of the head, paleness, weakness, palpitation of the heart, fainting fits ; till at length, when the imagination is disordered to a certain degree, all discernment and judgment seem to be at an end, and these unhappy people become, in the true sense of the word, visionaries."*

Women of an imaginative temperament, and whose reflective and reasoning powers are limited, are most susceptible to fervid and fantastical religious impressions. And it is said that when their charms begin to fade, and they cease to be admired, and their worldly influence is consequently on the wane, they are then most prone to become the subjects of holy reveries ; being either transported by a fervid zeal and enthusiasm, or else—overwhelmed by terror, gloom, despair—they pass into some form of insanity, generally either religious monomania or demonomania. Woman, Esquirol tells us in the work previously cited, is more nervous and imaginative, more operated upon by fear, more susceptible of religious notions, more inclined to the marvellous and more liable to melancholy than our own sex. Having reached a certain age, abandoned by the world, and passing into *ennui* and sadness, she next sinks into melancholy, often religious melancholy; and sometimes—when the mind is prepared by weakness, ignorance, and prejudice, for such a result—into demonomania, or a fancied demoniacal possession. These observations may be literally true of the women of France, but to women in general they will hardly apply without some reservation.

* Zimmermann on Experience in Physic.

That women, as has been remarked, when they grow old and cease to be admired, and worldly excitements are failing them, turn their thoughts heavenward, and seek enjoyment in religious reveries, is doubtless often true. But is it not so with us all? Seldom do we dedicate the first flowings of the cup of life, the sprightly streams of our youth, to religion. Such would be indeed a praiseworthy offering. No! we cling to earth and its joys as long as they will serve us,—till age begins to palsy our powers, and deaden our susceptibilities, and then seek in holy aspirations for the felicity which earthly objects can no longer afford :—In the true selfishness of our nature we get all we can out of the present world, and then turn saints for the sake of what we may get in the next.

The convulsive and other morbid nervous affections, the consequence of religious terrors and fanaticism, have, in different countries, and at various periods of the world, so spread themselves through the power of sympathy or imitation, as to hold a place in history among the important epidemics that have afflicted the human species. Demonomania, which is most commonly connected with the terrors of religion, has, through a sort of moral contagion, or the principle of imitation, become at times so extended as to constitute an epidemic. It is a remark of Esquirol, that delirium usually assumes the character of the ideas prevalent at the period when the insanity breaks forth ; and that demoniacal possession is therefore most frequent when religion becomes the principal topic of interest and discussion, and religious ideas therefore principally occupy the mind.

9*

The mental alienation which affected the *Convulsionaires* of St. Medard, beginning in the year 1727, and becoming so extensive an epidemic in France, lasting for fifty-nine years, had its origin in religious superstition. The history of this sect exhibits human nature in the most ridiculous and humiliating point of view. Sometimes the convulsionists bounded from the ground like fish out of water; "and this was so frequently imitated at a later period, that the women and girls, when they expected such violent contortions, not wishing to appear indecent, put on gowns made like sacks, closed at their feet. If they received any bruises by falling down, they were healed with earth from the grave of the uncanonized saint. They usually, however, showed great agility in this respect, and it is scarcely necessary to remark that the female sex, especially, was distinguished by all kinds of leaping, and almost inconceivable contortions of body. Some spun round on their feet with incredible rapidity, as is related of the dervishers; others ran their heads against walls, or curved their bodies like rope-dancers, so that their heels touched their shoulders. Some had a board placed across their bodies, upon which a whole row of men stood; and, as in this unnatural state of mind a kind of pleasure is derived from excruciating pain, some too were seen who caused their bosoms to be pinched with tongs, while others, with gowns closed at the feet, stood upon their heads, and remained in that position longer than would have been possible had they been in health."* It is said that an advocate—Pinault—who belonged to this sect,

* Hecker's Epidemics of the Middle Ages.

barked like a dog some hours every day, and which barking propensity extended among the believers. I believe there has existed a sect of religionists called *Barkers*. Indeed, any physical acts may be extended by sympathy, under morbidly susceptible states of the nervous system. Thus we read that a nun in a large convent in France set to mewing like a cat; when, straightway, other nuns began to mew also; and at length all the nuns mewed together for several hours at stated times every day, vexing and astonishing the whole Christian neighborhood by their daily cat-concert. This propensity might have extended itself and become epidemic, and a new sect under the name of Mewers sprung up, had not the nuns been apprised that a company of soldiers, provided with rods, had been placed at the entrance of the convent, with directions to whip them till they promised to mew no more, which ended the farce.

Another convent-epidemic, described by Cardan, took place in Germany, in the fifteenth century, surpassing even the caterwauling one in France. "A nun in a German nunnery fell to biting all her companions. In the course of a short time all the nuns of this convent began biting each other. The news of this infatuation among the nuns soon spread, and it now passed from convent to convent throughout a great part of Germany, principally Saxony and Bradenburg It afterwards visited the nunneries of Holland, and at last the nuns had the biting mania even as far as Rome."*

* Cited in Hecker's Epidemics, by the translator, B. G. Babington, M. D., &c.

Laycock, in his Essay on Hysteria, has cited from Wes-
ley's Journal a very curious example of the propagation of
physical actions through the power of sympathy, or imitation.

"Friday, 9th [May, 1740].   I was a little surprised at
some who were buffeted of Satan in an unusual manner, by
such a spirit of laughter as they could in no wise resist,
though it was pain and grief unto them.   I could scarcely
have believed the account they gave me, had I not known
the same thing ten or eleven years ago.   Part of Sunday,
my brother and I then used to spend in walking in the
meadows and singing psalms.   But one day, just as we were
beginning to sing, he burst out into loud laughter.   I asked
him if he was distracted, and began to be very angry, and
presently after to laugh as loud as he.   Nor could we possibly refrain, though we were ready to tear ourselves to
pieces, but we were forced to go home without singing another line."

"Wednesday 21, in the evening, such a spirit of laughter
was among us, that many were much offended.   But the attention of all was soon fixed on L. S., whom we all knew to
be no dissembler.   Sometimes she laughed till almost stran-
gled, then broke out into cursing and blaspheming; then
stamped and struggled with incredible strength, so that four
or five could scarce hold her.   Most of our brothers and
sisters were now fully convinced that those who were under
this strange temptation could not help it.   Only Elizabeth
B. and Anne H. were of another mind, being still sure any
one might help laughing if she would.   This they declared

to many on Thursday, but on Friday, 23d, both of them were suddenly seized in the same manner as the rest, and laughed whether they would or not, almost without ceasing. Thus they continued for two days a spectacle to all, and were then, upon prayer made for them, delivered in a moment."

If we recur to the history of the dancing plagues of the middle ages, the dance of St. John or St. Vitus, which, following close upon the ravages of the black death, spread "like a demoniacal epidemic over the whole of Germany and the neighboring countries to the north-west," and tarantism which swept equally over Italy, and fancied to arise from the bite of the tarantula, a ground spider common in Apulia, where the disease first made its appearance, we shall find abundant illustration of the wonderful influence of sympathy in promoting the extension of nervous and imitative disorders.

Epidemic convulsive affections, most often excited by religious fanaticism, have prevailed much in Scotland, especially in its more northern portions. In the United States of America, they have again and again burst forth under the influence of a morbid religious enthusiasm, and spread with astonishing rapidity through whole communities, and into different States. Some of the Western States, particularly in their early settlement, have been most extensively and severely affected in this manner. The following account of a singular nervous affection which has occasionally appeared in certain portions of our western country, called the *jerks*, and which may not be without interest to my readers, is copied from the Ohio Historical Collections into the New York Journal of Medicine, &c., vol. x. p. 372, whence I quote it.

"In 1803, Austinburg, Morgan and Harpersfield experienced a revival of religion, by which about thirty-five from those places united with the church at Austinburg. This revival was attended with the phenomena of '*bodily exercises*,' then common in the West. They have been classified by a clerical writer, as, 1st, the *falling exercise*; 2d, the *jerking exercise*; 3d, the *rolling exercise*; 4th, the *running exercise*; 5th, the *dancing exercise*; 6th, the *barking exercise*; 7th, the *visions and trances*." The account which follows is that of the jerking exercise, which, it is thought, sufficiently characterizes the remainder.

"It was familiarly called the *jerks*, and the first recorded instance of its occurrence was in East Tennessee, where several hundred of both sexes were seized with this strange and involuntary contortion. The subject was instantaneously seized with spasms or convulsions in every muscle, nerve, and tendon. His head was thrown or jerked from side to side with such rapidity that it was impossible to distinguish his visage, and the most lively fears were awakened lest he should dislocate his neck, or dash out his brains. His body partook of the same impulse, and was hurried on by like jerks over every obstacle, fallen trunks of trees, or, in church, over pews and benches, apparently to the most imminent danger of being bruised or mangled. It was useless to attempt to hold or restrain him, and the paroxysm was permitted gradually to exhaust itself. An additional motive for leaving him to himself was the superstitious notion that all attempt at restraint was resisting the Spirit of God.

"The first form in which these spasmodic contortions made their appearance, was that of a simple jerking of the arms from the elbows downwards. The jerk was very quick and sudden, and followed with short intervals. This was the simplest and most common form, but the convulsive motion was not confined to the arms, it extended in many instances to other parts of the body. When the joint of the neck was affected, the head was thrown backward and forward with a celerity frightful to behold, and which was impossible to be imitated by persons who were not under the same stimulus. The bosom heaved, the countenance was disgustingly distorted, and the spectators were alarmed lest the neck should be broken. When the hair was long, it was shaken with such quickness, backward and forward, as to crack and snap like the lash of a whip. Sometimes the muscles of the back were affected, and the patient was thrown down on the ground, when his contortions for some time resembled those of a live fish, cast from its native element on the land."

The following description is given by an eye-witness, and likewise an apologist, and is probably therefore an accurate one. "Nothing in nature could better represent this strange and unaccountable operation, than for one to goad another, alternately on every side, with a piece of red-hot iron. The exercise commonly began in the head, which would fly backward and forward, and from side to side, with a quick jolt, which the person would naturally labor to sup-

press, but in vain ; and the more any one labored to stay
himself and be sober, the more he staggered and the more
his twitches increased. He must necessarily go as he was
inclined, whether with a violent dash on the ground, and
bounce from place to place like a football, or hop round with
head, limbs, or trunk twitching and jolting in every direction, as if they must inevitably fly asunder. And how such
could escape without injury was no small wonder among
spectators. By this strange operation the human form was
commonly so transformed and disfigured, as to lose every
trace of its natural appearance. Sometimes the head would
be twitched right and left, to a half round, with such velo-
city, and in the quick progressive jerk, it would seem as if
the person was transmuted into some other species of creatures. Head-dresses were of but little account among the
female jerkers. Even handkerchiefs bound tight round the
head would be flirted off almost with the first twitch, and
the hair put in the utmost confusion : this was a very great
inconvenience, to redress which the generality were shorn,
though directly contrary to their confession of faith. Such
as were seized with the jerks, were wrested at once, not only
from under their own government, but that of every one
else, so that it was dangerous to attempt confining them or
touching them in any manner, to whatever danger they were
exposed ; yet few were hurt, except it were such as rebelled
against the operation, through wilful and deliberate enmity,
and refused to comply with the injunctions which it came to
enforce.

From the universal testimony of those who have de-

scribed these spasms, they appear to have been wholly involuntary. This remark is applicable also to all the other
bodily exercises. What demonstrates satisfactorily their
involuntary nature is, not only that, as above stated, the
twitches prevail in spite of resistance, and even more for
attempts to suppress them; but that wicked men would be
seized with them while sedulously guarding against an attack, and cursing every jerk when made. Travellers on
their journey, and laborers at their daily work, were also
liable to them."

Religion, it will be seen from the foregoing observations,
when fraught with the terrors of a gloomy fanaticism, or
employed as an agent to stir up a false zeal, and morbid
emotions in the minds of the weak, ignorant, and susceptible, may be productive of the worst evils both to the mental
and bodily constitution. But it is far otherwise with true
and rational religion; a religion grounded on a firm belief
in a supreme and benevolent Power, who has contrived,
and who directs all things by the laws of wisdom and goodness, and to whose will we can confidently resign our present and future destiny. Such a religion serves to temper
the feelings, secure us against an overstrained enthusiasm,
and morbid nervous excitement; to render us better and
happier in life, and to console and sustain us in the hour of
death.

Fright, no matter from what source, will be found, on
recurring to the reports both of our own and foreign lunatic
asylums, to hold a prominent place among the causes of
mental alienation. Mania, or raving madness, most com-

monly follows this cause, though in some instances dementia, or an incoherence in, or a stagnation, as it were, of all the mental powers, has been the mournful and irremediable consequence.

The statement is made by an eminent French writer on insanity, that many facts have come within his information showing that a strong predisposition to madness in the offspring, has arisen from fright experienced by the mother during pregnancy; striking cases of which nature are said to have happened during the period of the French revolution. That strong impressions acting upon the mind of the mother during gestation, and more especially from terror, may, in some manner, and under some circumstances, influence the physical condition of her offspring, at such time a part of herself, and directly dependent upon her vital actions for its nutrition and life, will, I think, scarce be disputed by any one who has cautiously and candidly considered the subject. Dr. Andrew Combe, in his treatise on the Management of Infancy, has cited from Baron Percy the following account of what occurred in this relation after the siege of Landau, in 1793. In addition to a violent cannonading, which kept the women for some time in a continued state of alarm, the arsenal blew up with a frightful explosion, striking almost every one with terror. Out of ninety-two children born in that district within a few months, sixteen perished at the moment of birth; thirty-three lingered for eight or ten months, and then died; eight were idiotic, and died before they were five years of age; and two were born with numerous fractures of the bones of the limbs, ascribed to the cannonading and explosion. That the popular notion that marks upon and deformities of the infant are ascribable to sudden and strong emotions in the mother, is unfounded, is the general though not unexceptionable belief of modern physiologists. That a strong and persisting impression on the mind of the mother at a certain period, and under peculiar conditions of gestation, may not only be adequate to affect the mental constitution, but, occasionally, even to produce marked bodily deformity in the offspring, I should be unwilling, in opposition to so many recorded and authoritative facts, unreservedly to deny. I will ask the liberty of relating a single striking example of an apparent influence of the imagination of the mother upon her offspring.

A number of years ago, while on a visit at Washington, I was invited by the late Dr. Sewall, Professor in the Medical College of that city, to visit a child having a remarkable congenital deformity, the probable consequence of the mother's imagination. Mrs. ——, a woman of strong sensibilities, when three months advanced in pregnancy, experienced a severe shock to her feelings, from seeing the right hand of one of her young children, a daughter, receive an injury by being caught in the wheel of a hand-wagon, with which she was playing. The hand, slightly lacerated and bloody, appeared to the excited fancy of the mother as though all the fingers had been torn off, and she, consequently, became exceedingly alarmed, and there followed the settled impression that her child would be born with a deformed hand. This belief she expressed to her physician, Dr.

Sewall at the time, and repeatedly afterwards, and could not be persuaded out of it. At her proper time she was delivered of a boy, and the first question to her accoucheur was, "Are the hands perfect?" but, to the astonishment of Dr. S., in the place of the right hand, a mere stump, with two small knobs of flesh arising from it, was only to be seen. I examined this deformity with care, and it appeared as though not only the hand, but even the bones of the wrist were wanting. The above circumstances were first related to me by the woman, and verified by her highly respectable attending physician. It was the right hand, let it be remembered, the one corresponding to that injured in the other child, which was deficient. The mental impression was here early produced, and lasted, with a fixed persuasion that the child would be affected with a particular deformity, through the whole period of gestation, circumstances shown by the cases which have been reported in recent years in different medical periodicals, to be favorable to the above-mentioned result. I am not prepared to affirm, that the event in the case related was any thing more than a mere coincidence, and should so set it down, were it not supported by numerous other and well-attested instances of a like nature.

Palsies, partial or general, have immediately followed the powerful action of fear. The dumbness which has occasionally succeeded its operation may doubtless have sometimes depended on a paralysis in the organs of speech. Permanent disease of the heart has also been known as the induced effect of this same passion.

There are many instances recorded where, through the
influence of great terror, the hair has become quickly
changed, in a single night, or even in a few hours, to a gray
or white—where the head of youth has almost immediately
become blanched as in old age.   Dr. Pettigrew has cited
the following case, among others equally wonderful, "of a
noble Spaniard, Don Diego Osorio, who being in love with
a young lady of the court, had prevailed with her for a private conference, within the gardens of the king ; but by the
barking of a little dog their privacy was betrayed—the
young gentleman seized by the king's guard, and imprisoned.   It was capital to be found in that place, and
therefore he was condemned to die.   He was so terrified at
hearing this sentence, that one and the same night saw the
same person young and old ; being turned gray, as in those
stricken in years.   The jailer, moved at the sight, related
the accident to King Ferdinand, as a prodigy, who there-
upon pardoned him, saying, he had been sufficiently punished for his fault."   M. Rostan, in a French Journal
of Medicine, relates of a female imprisoned during the
French revolution, and threatened with execution, that her
skin, in consequence, underwent a permanent change to the
hue of the less dark negro.

Acute fear influences, often very strikingly, the different
secretions, but perhaps none more remarkably than that of
the milk.   Sometimes it lessens, again, when the fear is sudden and great, it entirely arrests it.   Cows, when under the
influence of this emotion, yield their milk with difficulty ;
and the observation is a familiar one in the country, that

some of these animals, and which is doubtless explainable on the action of fear, will not "give down" their milk to strange milkers. The operation of terror is capable also of so vitiating this secretion as to render it not only prejudicial, but actually poisonous to the child who draws it. Dr. Carpenter cites the following instance as one of the most remarkable on record, of the effect of strong mental excitement on the Mammary secretion. "A carpenter fell into a quarrel with a soldier billeted in his house, and was set upon by the latter with his drawn sword. The wife of the carpenter at first trembled from fear and terror, then suddenly threw herself furiously between the two combatants, wrested the sword from the soldier's hand, broke it in pieces, and threw it away. During the tumult some neighbors came in and separated the men. While in this state of strong excitement, the mother took up her child from the cradle where it lay playing, and in the most perfect health, never having had a moment's illness; she gave it the breast, and in so doing sealed its fate. In a few minutes the infant left off sucking, became restless, panted, and sank dead upon its mother's bosom. The physician, who was instantly called in, found the child lying in the cradle as if asleep, and with its features undisturbed; but all his resources were fruitless. It was irrecoverably gone."*

We have cases recorded of bloody sweat supervening upon fright. Dr. Millingen, in his Curiosities of Medical Experience, cites the following case of a widow forty-five years

---

* Human Physiology.

of age, who had lost her only son. " She one day fancied that she beheld his apparition, beseeching her to relieve him from purgatory by her prayers, and by fasting every Friday. The following Friday, in the month of August, a perspiration tinged with blood broke out. For five successive Fridays the same phenomenon appeared, when a confirmed diapedesis (transudation of blood) appeared. The blood escaped from the upper part of the body, the back of the head, the temples, the eyes, nose, the breast, and the tips of the fingers. The disorder disappeared spontaneously on Friday the 8th of March of the following year. This affection was evidently occasioned by superstitious fears ; and this appears the more probable from the periodicity of the attacks. The first invasion of the disease might have been purely accidental ; but the regularity of its subsequent appearance on the stated day of the vision, may be attributed to the influence of apprehension. Bartholinus mentions cases of bloody sweat taking place during vehement terror and the agonies of torture."

The terrors with which some persons are so often, or almost habitually agitated during their nightly slumbers, can hardly be otherwise than detrimental to the health of the body. A frightful dream will sometimes impair the appetite, and leave the individual pale, melancholy, and with his nervous system in a state of morbid commotion through the whole of the subsequent day. After a night passed amid the agony of fancy-framed terrors, it is not to be expected that the nerves should suddenly regain their composure, that the moral tranquillity should be at once restored.

The different mental feelings, liberated during sleep from the control of the judgment, are in many instances highly extravagant, and altogether out of proportion to the causes exciting them. Hence, in dreams, our fears are often aggravated and distressing, and some persons are in the habit of starting suddenly from their repose, in the greatest dismay, uttering deep and direful cries, their bodies perhaps bathed in sweat, and remaining even for a considerable time after they are fully awake, under the painful impression of the fancy which affrighted them. Even convulsions and epilepsy have been the unhappy consequence of such imaginary terrors. Tissot relates an instance of a robust man, who, on dreaming that he was pursued by a bull, awoke in a state of great agitation and delirium, and, in not many minutes after, fell down in a severe fit of epilepsy.

In childhood, the impression of dreams being particularly strong, so that they are sometimes ever afterwards remembered as realities, and fear being then a very active principle, more injury is liable to accrue from their imaginary terrors than at later periods of life. Some children are apt to rouse suddenly from their sleep, screaming, crying, perhaps springing up on end, or out of bed, in a wild delirium of fright, and it may be a good while before their fears can be quieted, and their minds composed to rest. Those convulsions, too, with which children are occasionally seized at night, may not unfrequently proceed from the same visionary terrors.

If the fears of children, from any particular cause, have

been strongly excited while awake, they will sometimes be renewed, even in a more intense degree, perhaps for several successive nights, during their slumbers, thus multiplying the fearful impressions, and thereby the danger.

CHAPTER XIX.

FEAR CONTINUED.—IN ITS MORE CHRONIC OPERATION IT BE-
COMES THE OCCASION OF VARIOUS PREJUDICIAL EFFECTS IN
THE ANIMAL ECONOMY.—SUPERSTITIOUS FEARS IN REGARD
TO DEATH ARE IN MANY PERSONS A CAUSE OF MUCH SUFFER-
ING BOTH TO BODY AND MIND.—THE MANNER IN WHICH THIS
EVENT SHOULD BE REGARDED.—DANGER OF INDULGING THE
FANCY OF CHILDREN IN TALES OF SUPERNATURAL TERRORS.
—FORTITUDE OPERATES AS A WHOLESOME STIMULUS BOTH
TO MIND AND BODY.

HAVING learnt how serious are the consequences oftentimes
arising from acute fear, we rationally infer that even its
more chronic action may be attended with important injury
to health.

A bold, intrepid spirit may justly be ranked among the
conditions which secure to the constitution its full measure
of physical power. Few causes will more certainly impair
the vigor of the nerves, break down the manliness of the
body, and degrade the energies of the mind, than the habitual indulgence in imaginary fears.

The depressing agency of fear is well known to augment

the susceptibility of the constitution to disease; and especially to the action of contagion, and epidemic influences.
It was observed by an old and distinguished medical writer
(Willis), that they who have the greatest fear of small-pox,
are generally the first to be attacked by it. Hecker, in his
history of the Black Death, a malignant and wide-spreading
epidemic of the fourteenth century, says that many fell victims to fear, on the first appearance of the distemper. And
Dr. Caius, in his account of the Sweating Sickness, another
fatal and extensive epidemic which appeared in England in
1485, advises, among other means of escaping the disease,
to set apart all affections, as fretting cares and thoughts, dole-
ful or sorrowful imaginations, vain fears, foolish loves, gnawing hates, and to live quietly, friendly, and merrily one with
another, to avoid malice and dissension, and every one to
mind his own business. The cholera is well known during
its epidemic prevalence to have been often induced in timid
people through their strong apprehensions of it.

Tarantism, to which I have before alluded, was doubtless
often the effect of imaginary fears of having been bitten by
the tarantula. Thus the bite from any unseen insect would
not unfrequently bring on all the symptoms of this peculiar
affection. "The persuasion," says Hecker, "of the inevitable consequences of being bitten by the tarantula, exercised
a dominion over men's minds which even the healthiest and
strongest could not shake off. . . . Wherever we turn, we
find that this morbid state of mind prevailed, and was so
supported by the opinions of the age, that it needed only a
stimulus in the bite of the tarantula, and the supposed cer-

tainty of its very disastrous consequences, to originate this violent nervous disorder."

Many cases may be found recorded where symptoms of hydrophobia have arisen from the mere apprehension of having been bitten by a rabid animal. The hypochondriac fancies and fears himself the subject of particular diseases, and straightway he begins to feel all their symptoms. Some medical students, of sensitive and nervous temperaments, not only imagine that they have the diseases of which they are studying, but will sometimes actually present more or less of their symptoms.

If the sick yield themselves to the impulse of fear, their chances of recovery will generally become lessened; its depressing influence serving to reduce the reacting or restorative powers of the vital economy. It has been remarked, that the small-pox is particularly apt to prove unfavorable in the young and beautiful, who naturally dread a disease so fatal to beauty. A strong will may do much for us in disease, as well as in health. The timid and dispirited, other circumstances being the same, run down the soonest under disease. I have seen those who appeared to me to continue valetudinarians from mere pusillanimity, from lack of energy or moral courage to be well; a certain force of character being a needful stimulus to the physical, as it is to the mental actions.

Undue anxiety, and superstitious apprehensions in regard to death, which so prey upon the minds of some people, may operate to the serious injury of both the physical and moral health and tranquillity. It is, as I conceive, the sol-

emn trappings, ceremonials, and fancied horrors that are so
generally associated, even in our earliest education, with the
dissolution of the body, and the gloomy and fearful imaginings of what is to come after, which cause the feelings to
revolt from its idea with such dismal forebodings. That we
have an instinctive dread of pain will scarce be disputed ;
but whether we have naturally, or independent of education and association, the same feeling in respect to death,
will, at least, admit of question. Lycurgus, the Spartan
lawgiver, " to take away all superstition, ordered the dead
to be buried in the city, and even permitted their monu-
ments to be erected near the temples; accustoming the
youth to such sights from their infancy, that they might
have no uneasiness from them, nor any horror for death, as if
people were polluted with the touch of a dead body, or with
treading upon a grave."* And we read in Herodotus, that
to keep the mind familiar with the thoughts of death, the
ancient Egyptians, at their entertainments, had a small
coffin, containing a perfect representation of a dead body,
carried round and presented to the different guests in rota-
tion, the bearer exclaiming—" Cast your eyes on this figure ;
after death you yourself will resemble it : drink, then, and
be happy."

Death being the grand goal of life, and that toward
which we are all steadily moving, if its image affrights us, it
must, as it is ever in view,—for struggle as we will we cannot shut it out,—be a source of continual and unmitigated

* Plutarch's Life of Lycurgus.

torment ; a bugbear disquieting our whole existence, and
cutting us off even from the little happiness which life might
otherwise afford. We should strive then, so far as in us
lies, to look on death with a composed and philosophical
spirit,—as one of the great and necessary laws of our vital
organization,—as the last function, the inevitable consummation of our present being ; not permitting its gloomy
shadow to hide the few flowers, and darken the little sunshine of existence. It is well known that the mind may, by
a proper discipline, be brought to view this final event of
our nature without the smallest emotion either of terror or
regret ; and there have been those who, even in the midst
of a prosperous fortune, have experienced a pleasing satisfaction in its contemplation ; have looked forward to it as
the desirable and peaceful repose to the anxious and weary
race of life.

> " Sleepe after toile, port after stormie seas,
>   Ease after warre, death after life, does greatly please."*

It is the part of true philosophy to get from existence
all we can ; to participate, so far as fortune permits, in
all its rational and innocent pleasures,—the enjoyments of
mind, the sweets of virtue,—and yet be willing at any moment to part with it. Such was the philosophy of Epicurus,
and of other of the wisest and best among the ancients, and
which soothed their lives and carried many of them calmly

* Spenser's Faery Queen.

through the most painful deaths. The human mind can scarce reach a state of easy quietude until it has learned to contemplate the image of death with composure.

It often happens, paradoxical as it would seem, that those whose existence has been the most barren of enjoyment, who have tasted little beside the bitterness of life, are the most anxious to live, the most apprehensive of death. Buoyed up by the anticipation of change, by the hope that their turn may yet come, and magnifying the value of joys they have never tried, they will still cling with an unrelaxing grasp to the very shreds of a tattered existence. Like the traveller at his inn, they are unwilling to go to rest till they have had their meal. And on the other hand, they who have been blest with prosperity, who have feasted bountifully at life's table, satisfied that they have had their turn, satiated with pleasures whose worthlessness they have discovered, are frequently the most ready to take their departure.

It is of the utmost importance, both to the physical and moral welfare, that the mind be secured by a proper education against the influence of all supernatural and idle sources of terror,—of yawning church-yards, and their pale inhabitants, of

———"damned spirits all,
That in cross-ways and floods have burial."

The ignorant, and those whose education has been erroneous, and who in early life have been subjected to impro-

per associations, often experience the most aggravated sufferings from fears of such nature, and even death has at
times been their consequence.   No human courage is proof
against the terrors of superstition.   The hero who braves
death in the battle-field, may yet tremble at the croaking of
the raven, or the screech of the night owl.

We can now easily imagine the exceeding hazard of indulging the fancies of children with idle tales of apparitions,
haunted houses, witches, &c., which always afford them such
intense and exciting interest.   Ghost-stories, above all the
absurd creations of superstition, would seem to carry most
terror to the youthful mind.   The idea of the reappearance
of the dead—of the pale, sheeted, stalking ghost of a departed mortal—is ever associated with the most awful gloom,
and agitating fear.

Whether all stories founded on supernatural events
should be denied to childhood, is a question I shall not
here enter upon ; but that all such as serve to engender
imaginary fears ought to be interdicted, few, it is presumed,
will feel inclined to dispute.

All children, but in a more particular manner those of a
delicate and timid nature, are liable to sustain no little suffering of body and mind, when their feelings are frequently
wrought upon by fictitious terrors.   As night approaches,
all their superstitious apprehensions increase, and should
they chance to be left alone for ever so short a period, their
situation becomes pitiable in the extreme.   And then on
retiring to rest, appalled by the darkness and silence, and
dreading lest their eyes should encounter some frightful

spectre, they bury themselves beneath the bed-clothes, and thus lie reeking, perhaps, with sweat, and nearly suffocated from the heat and confinement of the air. Nor even here do they escape from their fearful imaginings. Uncouth phantoms keep rising before their vision, and every little noise, though of the most familiar character, as the gnawing of a rat, the jarring of a door or window, or even the moaning of the wind, is magnified or transformed by the dismayed fancy into some alarming supernatural sound. On their falling asleep these waking fantasies may still be continued in the manner of dreams, creating a yet higher degree of terror, causing them, often, to start abruptly from their slumbers, screaming and wild with affright. In the morning, as would be imagined after a night of such painful agitation, they awake gloomy, languid, and unrefreshed.

Under the continued disturbance of such shadowy fears, the health, certainly if it be not naturally robust, will soon begin to decline. The body grows pale, and emaciates, the appetite diminishes, the stomach and bowels get disordered, and so enfeebled, and so morbidly sensitive may the system at length become, that the least noise, if sudden, or the unexpected presence of a person, or any object, will cause violent palpitations, difficulty of speaking, nervous tremors and agitations, and at times even fainting; and sometimes the nervous system never entirely recovers from the morbid condition into which it has been thus brought.

So deep seated do these fearful associations, engendered in the weakness of childhood, many times become, that darkness and stillness will renew them long after the reason is ma-

10*

tured, and their absurdity apparent; and so may they remain a permanent source of injury to the mental tranquillity, and by necessary consequence to the physical health.
The superstitious weakness of Doctor Johnson,—and it may
be, also, that dread of death which so continually haunted
him, weighing like a nightmare on his moral energies, and
imbittering his existence,—were, in all likelihood, the result
of injudicious associations awakened in the education of his
early years. We read in Plutarch that the Spartan nurses
used the children " to any sort of meat, to have no terrors
in the dark, nor to be afraid of being alone, and to leave all
ill-humor and unmanly crying."*

Sporting with the timidity of children, as startling them
with sudden and uncommon noises or sights, which appears
to afford so much amusement to some inconsiderate people,
cannot be too severely censured. And equally censurable
is the practice of playing upon their natural fears as a mode
of punishment, or to enforce their obedience, as shutting
them up in the dark, threatening them with some of the
many nursery spectres which have been created to help in-
efficient parents in subduing their misgoverned and therefore refractory offspring. The most melancholy consequences,
as convulsions, deafness, idiocy, and even death, have sometimes happened to children from such culpable practices.
Some mothers, to still their children to sleep, are in the habit of indiscreetly threatening them with Rawhead and
Bloody-Bones, or other frightful spectres, thus oftentimes

* Life of Lycurgus.

inducing on their tender and naturally timid minds an impression, deep, lasting, and harmful. If a mother cannot quiet her child to rest in a more innocent way than by working upon its fears, she had better content herself to bear its noise till sleep comes of itself, which it always will do in proper time to the young, healthful, and crimeless. Objections equally forcible may be urged against terrifying and confounding the mind while yet unconfirmed, with the awful mysteries and punishments of religion; subjects which always perplex, and often disorder even the ripest intellects.

Why is it, it may be asked, that so large a proportion of young children, even at the present period of boasted light and philosophy, are afraid to be left a moment by themselves in the dark; are so loth to go to bed, or about the house alone after nightfall, although well assured that there are no earthly dangers to hurt them, but that their fancies have been unwisely wrought upon through the idle tales of superstition?

Children, I am convinced, suffer far more from the influence under notice than most persons are prone to suspect; since ashamed to be thought cowards—and at what period of life are we not?—they will studiously conceal the fears which are preying on their health, and crushing all their moral energies. Hence, bodily infirmities in them, excited and maintained by fear, may often be imputed to a physical origin, and they, in consequence, be made the subjects of medicinal treatment, which weakening yet further the powers of the constitution, and thereby adding to the nervous susceptibility, serves but to aggravate the effect of the secret cause.

We can now unerstand how important it is, both as regards their moral and physical well-being, to keep the young as much as possible from the society of ignorant and superstitious domestics, who are always ready to administer to their eager cravings for supernatural marvels. Parents, to escape the noise and trouble of their children, are too prompt to submit them to the care of servants, so that many really receive a much larger share of their primary education in the kitchen than in the parlor. That such should be the case is certainly to be regretted, it belonging to our imitative nature readily to acquire the habits, manners, and modes of thinking and speaking of those with whom we habitually associate. And more especially is this true in early life, when the mind and body are unfolding themselves, and the brain, soft and delicate, receives with the greatest facility every new impression. Boerhaave relates that a schoolmaster near Leyden being squint-eyed, it was found that the children placed under his care soon exhibited a like obliquity of vision. It has been well observed, that there is a necessity for us either to imitate others, or to hate them.

Fearlessness and self-reliance, let me add, in conclusion of the present chapter, operate at all periods of life as a healthful stimulus alike to mind and body; wherefore such feelings ought ever, and in a more particular manner when the moral and physical functions are undergoing development, to be assiduously nurtured. To such salutary feelings, moreover, good conduct is always most propitious. The opposite being essentially blended with fear and distrust, must, therefore, however it may serve us in respect to mere external goods, be incompatible with the true interests both of our mental and bodily constitution.

CHAPTER XX.

THAT singular mental feeling which we express by the
word horror, consists in a deep and painful detestation, almost always more or less mingled with fear, of particular
and, commonly, familiar objects. This, I am aware, is not
the only sense in which the term is used, but it is the one
to which I shall especially restrict it in the present chapter ;
and, taking its original Latin meaning (a shivering or
quaking, as from fear, or the cold fit of an ague), none certainly could better indicate the physical phenomena of this
afflictive moral feeling.

The manifestations of horror, as exhibited in the physical organization, are mostly the same as those presented in
simple fear—as sudden paleness, coldness, and contraction
of the skin, with the consequent elevation of the hairs ; also
chills and rigors, or general tremors of the body, with panting, and oppression of the heart and lungs ; and, when immoderate, it will give rise to the like train of melancholy

phenomena, which have been already enumerated as the characteristics of exceeding terror; such as fainting, convulsions, epilepsy, palsies, and even instant death.

Horror is distinguishable from ordinary fear, inasmuch as it may be excited, and even in an aggravated degree, by the presence of objects which neither threaten, nor, in fact, cause the slightest apprehension of bodily injury. A reptile, or insect, for example, known to be entirely harmless, may beget such a sense of abhorrence as to bring on fainting or convulsions, even in those who would resolutely encounter the most ferocious animal. The fear, then, mingled in the feeling of horror does not necessarily depend on any real danger apprehended from its object, but upon the suffering which its presence occasions in the nervous system.

Very many people are known to suffer, and oftentimes during their whole lives, under a horror, or as it is more usually termed, an antipathy, toward particular animals or things, and which are often in themselves harmless, and to the generality of persons wholly innocuous. Those of a nervous or sensitive temperament are more especially apt to suffer from antipathies. Indeed there are few of such to whom does not belong some object of horror.

> " Some men there are love not a gaping pig ;
>   Some, that are mad, if they behold a cat."

Germanicus could neither endure the sight nor the crowing of a cock. " I have seen persons," says Montaigne,

" that have run faster from the smell of apples than from gun-shot; others that have been frightened at a mouse; others that have vomited at the sight of cream, and some that have done the like at the making of a featherbed."[*] Broussais says he once knew a Prussian officer who could see neither an old woman, a cat, nor a thimble, without experiencing convulsive agitations; without jumping and screaming, and making unnatural grimaces. Toward honey, cheese, musk, strawberries, and other common, and even generally agreeable articles, I have known such strong antipathies to exist, that the most disagreeable and painful effects would be produced by exposure to their slightest influence. Dr. Whytt tells us that "several delicate women, who could easily bear the stronger smell of tobacco, have been thrown into fits by musk, ambergrease, or a pale rose, which, to most people, are either grateful, or at least not disagreeable." Also that the smell of cheese has in some persons almost always caused a bleeding of the nose. That tansy, cinnamon, celery, even when brought near certain individuals, has caused in them fainting, and general uneasiness. And that such was the antipathy to honey in a lady mentioned by Mr. Boyle, that a little of it put into a poultice, without her knowledge, and applied to a slight wound, threw her into great disorder, which lasted till the application was removed.[†]

Toads, crabs, eels, snakes, and spiders, are very common objects of horror. I once knew a strong, healthy man, who

* Essays. † Observations, &c.

would turn pale and be thrown into extreme nervous agitation by the sight of an eel. And I have seen the most distressing effect produced upon the nervous system by the presence of a spider. "Happening," says Dr. Zimmermann, "to be in company with some English gentlemen, all of them men of distinction, the conversation fell upon antipathies. Many of the company denied their reality, and considered them as idle stories, but I assured them that they were truly a disease. Mr. William Matthews, son to the governor of Barbadoes, was of my opinion, because he himself had an antipathy to spiders. The rest of the company laughed at him. I undertook to prove to them that this antipathy was really an impression on his soul resulting from the determination of a mechanical effect. Lord John Murray undertook to shape some black wax into the appearance of a spider, with a view to observe whether the antipathy would take place, at the simple figure of the insect. He then withdrew for a moment, and came in again with the wax in his hand, which he kept shut. Mr. Matthews, who in other respects was a very amiable and moderate man, immediately conceiving that his friend really had a spider in his hand, clapped his hand to his sword with extreme fury, and running back towards the partition cried out most horribly. All the muscles of his face were swelled, his eyes were rolling in their sockets, and his body was immovable. We were all exceedingly alarmed, and immediately ran to his assistance, took his sword from him, and assured him that what he had conceived to be a spider was nothing more than a bit of wax, which he might see upon the table.

"He remained for some time in this spasmodic state, but at length he began gradually to recover, and to deplore the horrible passion, from which he still suffered. His pulse was very strong and quick, and his whole body was covered with a cold sweat; after taking an anodyne draught he resumed his usual tranquillity."*

There are individuals who experience an indefinable anxiety and distress, sometimes attended with faintness and sweating, from the presence, or vicinity of a cat, and even when undescried by either of the acknowledged senses. We must here suppose the nervous system, or a portion of it, from some unknown modification, to be morbidly sensitive to the subtile effluvia arising from the body of the animal.

Strong antipathies in regard to particular colors are of not uncommon occurrence. Dr. Parry tells us that a lady whom he knew could not bear to look at any thing of a scarlet color; and that another could endure the sight of no light color whatever; on which account the papers and wainscot of her rooms were all tinged with a deep blue or green; and the light was modified by green blinds. "If also at any time," says he, "I visited her in white stockings, I was always at my entrance presented with a black silk apron, with which I was requested to cover these offensive garments."† Dr. Elliotson relates of a patient, that being put in a room with red curtains, she was in consequence rendered so thirsty, that she drank seven quarts in one day.

---

* On Experience in Physic.
† Cases of Tetanus, &c., by Dr. Parry, of Bath.

Certain animals seem to be disturbed, and sometimes even rendered furious by red or scarlet; as bulls, and turkey-cocks and I have known cows who would always run at a female with a red shawl. Horses, too, have, in occasional instances, been affected in a like manner by the same color.

Such antipathies may be innate, that is, dependent upon some original and mysterious condition of the animal organization, expressed by the term idiosyncracy, or may owe their existence to a painful association with the particular object of abhorrence which had been awakened in early life. In the former case, being connected with those intimate laws of our constitution, which are yet, and perhaps will ever remain, unveiled to human knowledge; all attempts to trace them to their primary and essential source will necessarily prove futile. That antipathies, or the peculiar character of organism disposing to them, may sometimes be inherited, can hardly be questioned. The most singular tastes are sometimes inherited, and why may not the same be true of distastes or aversions? The fondness for ardent spirits is doubtless many times derived from parents; and it is recorded in one of the older histories of Scotland, that a Scotch girl retained a decided taste for human flesh, for the crime of eating which her father and mother had been burnt when she was but a year old. I know an individual suffering under a deep antipathy to a spider, which antipathy is traceable to his great-grandfather, on his mother's side; that is, has existed in four successive generations.

It is a popular notion that antipathies often arise from fright or injury experienced by the mother when pregnant, from the particular object of horror. In support of such notion, the singular case of James the First, of England, has been cited. This monarch, though all his family were distinguished for their bravery, was constitutionally timid, even to a most ludicrous extent, and could never look upon a naked .sword without shrinking; and "turned away his head even from that very pacific weapon which he was obliged to draw for the purpose of bestowing the *accolade* on a knight dubbed with unhacked rapier, from carpet-consideration."* Now, it is well known to the readers of history, that David Rizzio was stabbed at the feet of Queen Mary, two months previous to the birth of James.

Dr. Copland relates, that a man-servant in his family, advanced in life, "had so great an antipathy to the sight of a mouse, that he would fly as fast as he was able from the place where one was seen, and become quite frantic at the sight. He stated that his mother, who likewise had an antipathy to mice, had been distressed by one thrown upon her when pregnant of him." † Like instances will doubtless recur to the minds of many of my readers, for they are. of familiar occurrence. But even in cases of this description, the origin of the antipathy can, for the most part, be explained quite as plausibly on the principle of association. Thus James, from his earliest childhood, must doubtless have often heard the recital of all the frightful circumstances connected with Rizzio's cruel death—have observed his

---

* History of Scotland, by Sir Walter Scott.
† Medical Dictionary. Article, Antipathy.

mother express horror, as we might presume she would, of the instrument of the murder; and the deep and fearful impressions thus made on his tender mind, may have served to suppress his natural courage, and have been the occasion of his remarkable aversion to the sight of a drawn sword.

In the other example quoted, the mother would naturally be often telling of, and manifesting her repugnance to, a mouse, in the presence of her child, and thus necessarily create the same dread of it in his infant mind, the impression of which would be indelibly preserved. If a mother has a detestation of any particular insect, as a spider, for example, is it not well known that she will be repeatedly expressing it? every little while crying out to her child, with a fearful shudder, " Take care of that awful spider?" Is it strange, therefore, that the mind of her offspring, thus early imbued with, or, as it were, educated to, a horror of this insect, should ever afterwards retain it? " A man," observes Dr. Zimmermann, " who imbibes any particular idea in his early youth, is so strongly affected with it, that he never gives it up, even in maturer life, if it has been frequently repeated. In good truth, why do we see people so bigoted to some particular error, who are open to conviction in every other respect, and yet are blindly bigoted to this, but that from their infancy they have heard some absurd tale a thousand times repeated, and by these means the idea has been so firmly imprinted in them, that it would be as easy to whiten the Ethiopian as to remove their superstition ?"

Although, then, our antipathies may sometimes be innate, and may possibly, in certain instances, be referrible to the influence of the imagination of the mother strongly excited during some period of gestation, nevertheless I conceive them much oftener to originate in some painful or alarming association with the object of aversion, engendered in infancy or childhood.

Mr. Locke, when speaking of antipathies, says, "a great part of these which are accounted natural would have been known to be from unheeded, though, perhaps, early impressions or wanton fancies at first, which would have been acknowledged the original of them, if they had been warily observed." *

It many times happens that the primary and incidental source of the antipathy is known and admitted. Thus, Peter the Great, when an infant, had a fall into the water on riding over a bridge; in consequence of which, even in mature life, he could neither bear the sight of water, nor the rattling of a carriage upon a bridge.

We can now see how essential it is in the education of children, to avoid, as far as may be, all occasions of erroneous association, or false prejudices,—exciting or cherishing imaginary terrors in relation to any particular object; as from such sources will often grow up aversions causing no little suffering both to body and mind during the whole future existence.

When antipathies already exist, and more especially if

* On the Human Understanding.

toward common objects, or such as we are every day liable to encounter, both health and happiness demand that the most persevering efforts be made to subdue them. They may generally be surmounted, either entirely or to a very considerable extent, by gradually inuring the mind to the presence or influence of the object of horror, the well-known effect of habit being to obtund the feelings. If, however, the repugnance be very strong, a greater share of moral energy than most persons possess will be required to vanquish it. James being naturally timid, and weak in his resolutions, never, that we learn, overcame his aversion to the naked sword. Whereas Peter, of a more bold and determined character, in the end completely conquered his painful dislike to the rattling of a carriage over a bridge, and his dread of the water, by resolutely exposing himself to the former, and repeatedly plunging into the latter.

It is an unaccountable fact in our constitution, that habit will in some cases not merely overcome an antipathy, but will actually beget a fondness for the object of former aversion. Thus does it happen that those who at first experience the greatest horror at the sight of blood, so that they can scarce look upon it without fainting, will, under the influence of custom, not unfrequently become the most bold and devoted surgeons. Nurses, and those females whose business it is to dress and prepare the dead for their last narrow receptacle, although at first perhaps sensitive, delicate, and moved with horror at the mere sight of a dead body, come at length to experience a pleasurable excitement, even a morbid delight among the gloomy scenes and circumstances of their unnatural occupation. Sir Walter Scott, in the following dialogue, has well depicted, and scarcely caricatured the feelings of these crones of the death-chamber.

" ' Ay ! and that's e'en true, cummer,' said the lame hag, propping herself with a crutch, which supported the shortness of her left leg, 'for I mind when the father of this Master of Ravenswood that is now standing before us, sticked young Blackhall with his whinger, for a wrang word said ower their wine, or brandy, or what not—he gaed in as light as a lark, and he came out wi' his feet foremost. I was at the winding of the corpse; and when the bluid was washed off, he was a bonny bouk of a man's body.'

" ' He's a frank man and a free-handed man, the master,' said Annie Winnie, ' and a comely personage, broad in the shouthers, and narrow around the lungies—he wad mak a bonny corpse—I wad like to hae the streaking and winding o' him.'

" ' It is written on his brow, Annie Winnie,' returned the octogenarian, her companion, 'that hand of woman, or of man either, will never straught him—dead—deal will never be laid on his back—make you your market of that, for I hae it from a sure hand.' "*

In many other points in our moral nature, it is truly surprising how extremes may be changed, and not unfrequently in a brief space of time, to those of a directly opposite character. Hence the common saying, that fallen an-

---

* Bride of Lammermoor.

gels make the worst devils; and Old Apollyon himself, as we read, was once an angel of light. The formal and sanctimonious puritan, if he departs from goodness, will often pass to the most hopeless extreme of vice. The coy, prudish, blushing female, may become the most shameless and abandoned courtesan. The homespun clown, going to the metropolis, and casting aside his rustic garb, will not rarely become transfigured into the most laughable caricature of a city fopling. And the needy and low-bred wretch, and the ranting political leveller, on attaining to wealth and power, are apt to become the most arrogant, overbearing, and offensive aristocrats.

In some of our senses, but particularly in the sense of taste, this same principle holds in a very striking manner. Hence many articles which are in the beginning most offensive and sickening to the palate, will, under the power of habit, not only get to be agreeable, but absolutely necessary to our comfort. In tobacco we have a strong and familiar illustration of this remark. It is well known, too, how attached some people become to garlic, though at first so acrid and unpleasant. And even asafœtida, naturally so odious both to taste and smell, was held in such esteem by some of the ancients that they termed it " the meat of the gods." Oftentimes, therefore, while we become cloyed and wearied with, and get even to loathe the objects which were at first most pleasant to us, by a strange perversion of taste do we derive a permanent delight from those which were originally disgusting.

The development of antipathies is ever to be carefully

11

watched, and the mind gradually and cautiously habituated to the impression which awakens them. It is to be regretted, however, that a contrary practice more often prevails; the child either being scrupulously preserved from the object of his repugnance, or what is infinitely worse, his terrors of it are purposely excited, or aggravated, for the idle amusement of those who have not sense enough to comprehend the danger of such sport. The most disastrous consequences have sometimes resulted to children, as well as grown persons, by suddenly subjecting them to the influence of an object of their peculiar horror.

CHAPTER XXI.

GRIEF.—GENERAL REMARKS UPON THIS PASSION.—THE ACUTE
STAGE, OR A PAROXYSM OF GRIEF DESCRIBED, WITH THE
MORBID, AND EVEN FATAL EFFECTS OF WHICH IT MAY BE
PRODUCTIVE.

GRIEF, consisting essentially in moral pain, must therefore
enter to a greater or less extent, into all the passions of the
class we are now considering. It bears, then, to the painful
and depressing, a relation analogous to that of joy to the
pleasurable and exciting passions.

Grief, presenting itself in diverse degrees and modifications, is consequently known under a variety of names, as
sorrow, sadness, melancholy, dejection, &c., all of which induce similar phenomena in the bodily functions. The term
is generally defined to mean the mental suffering arising
from the privation of some good in possession, or the disappointment of some pleasing anticipation. I shall allow it,
however, as will be seen in the sequel, a signification still
broader than this definition implies.

The passion in question may be simple, as is most com-

mon under the loss of kindred and friends; or it may be
united with chagrin, or impatient and angry repinings.
And again, it may grow out of, and hence be blended with
the various malignant feelings of the heart, as envy, jealousy,
hatred, revenge, all of which are more or less fraught with
moral pain.   As it is a law of our constitution that every
good and benevolent affection should bring with it its own
recompense, so likewise is it that every evil one should become the author of its own punishment.   " To love is to enjoy, to hate is to suffer."   In hating we punish ourselves,
not the object of our hate.   Self-interest, therefore, if we are
actuated by no better, should be a sufficient motive for us
to cultivate the amiable, and to suppress the vicious feelings
of our nature.

Grief may be acute and transient, or it may assume a
more chronic or lasting character; in which latter case it is
generally designated by the term sorrow, or sadness.   Other
things being equal, its violence will be proportioned to the
suddenness and unexpectedness of the cause producing it.

I will now go on to describe the effects induced upon
the bodily functions by the acute stage, or what is commonly
denominated a paroxysm of grief; and most of these—for
there is a close relationship among all the passions founded
on pain—will be recognized as nearly resembling those
which have already been depicted under the heads of anger
and fear.

On the first strong impulse of mental affliction, an agonizing sense of oppression and stricture is experienced at
the heart and lungs, accompanied with a distressing feeling

of impendent suffocation ; it oftentimes seeming as though
the whole chest were contracted, or bound with cords. The
want of fresh air becomes at the same time exceedingly urgent, giving occasion to the deep and frequent sighing so
commonly observed in those stricken with calamity. Sighing consists in a long drawn, or protracted inspiration, succeeded by a corresponding expiration, which, beside furnish-
ing an increased supply of air, may, by distending the lungs,
facilitate the passage of blood through them, and thus serve
in a measure to alleviate the painful oppression felt in these
organs and at the heart.

So distinct and remarkable is the suffering at the heart
in deep grief, that it is frequently expressed by the term
heart-ache, and its victims are said to die broken-hearted.
Under its aggravated influence sharp pains even are felt in
the heart, sometimes shooting up to the shoulder, and every
pulsation of this organ is attended with a severe and thrilling distress.

It not rarely happens, particularly in nervous females,
that a sort of spasm affects the throat, causing a sensation as
if a ball was rising in it, and choking the passage of the air.
Hence the familiar expression " to choke with sorrow."
The dryness, likewise, in the mouth and throat, from the
diminution in their natural secretions, adds to, and may
even of itself occasion this choking sensation ; and is moreover the cause, or at least in part, of the frequent and difficult swallowing so often noticed in acute grief.

Speaking, owing to this defect of moisture in the mouth
and throat, as well as to the embarrassment at the heart and

lungs, is attended with a marked effort, and the voice is thick, husky, broken, tremulous, and weak.

The circulation, as would be supposed, feels the influence, in a greater or less degree, of this passion. Thus the pulse is generally weakened, oftentimes accelerated, occasionally becomes intermittent, or otherwise irregular; and the extreme vessels of the surface contracting unnaturally, and unsupplied with their wonted quantity of blood from the heart, the skin loses its customary warmth, and its ruddy tint of health. The energies of the nerves, too, becoming depressed and deranged under the morbid agency of this painful emotion, tremors, with various other of those disturbances which we term nervous, are likely to supervene.

The organs of the abdomen are also implicated in the general suffering. An uneasiness, in many cases quite severe, is referred to the region, or what we term the pit of the stomach. The appetite fails, and the powers of digestion become obviously impaired, and sometimes altogether suspended. Imagine one, while in the midst of the enjoyment of his dinner, to be unexpectedly apprised of some afflictive calamity, and the result scarce need be told. On the instant, as though touched by the wand of a magician, will the dishes before him, even the most savory, cease to delight his palate, and he turns, perhaps, with a painful sense of loathing from the very food which but a moment before he contemplated with the most eager desire. Or should he persist in his meal, every mouthful he tries to swallow seems to stick in his throat, and he is forced soon to abandon what has now become to him so disagreeable a task.

Again, suppose the meal to have been just finished on the abrupt excitement of this painful emotion, then there might ensue the various phenomena of indigestion, and even vomiting, were the mental shock extreme. Shakspeare had in view the particular effect of grief under notice, where he makes King Henry say to Cardinal Wolsey,—

———— " Read o'er this,
And after, this, and then to breakfast with
What appetite you have."

Grief often lessens the secretion of bile, or, by exciting a spasmodic contraction of its ducts, impedes its passage; whence the jaundiced hue of the skin which has been known to follow it. Sometimes it increases the amount, and vitiates the quality of this secretion, and even bilious vomitings have been produced by sharp affliction. Other secretions are in like manner affected by this emotion, being increased, lessened, and vitiated. Misfortune will often greatly diminish, or almost suppress the secretion of milk; or so vitiate its qualities as to render it highly noxious to the infant. Children have been attacked with convulsions, and palsy, on sucking immediately after the mother had experienced some painful calamity. Dr. Carpenter states that " the halitus from the lungs is sometimes almost instantaneously affected by bad news, so as to produce fœtid breath."*

In the young, generally, and in most females, at whatever age, on the first impression of ordinary grief, the visage

* Human Physiology.

suddenly becomes distorted, or drawn into a distressed and
dismal expression, as under bodily suffering, and which is
strikingly significant of the painful internal condition.
With this disfiguration of the countenance, the respiration
assumes a new or modified action. There takes place a
deep, and often sonorous and tremulous inspiration, followed
by an interrupted, or broken and imperfect expiration, con-
joined with the familiar sounds so peculiarly expressive of
both mental and bodily anguish, called sobbing or crying.
The lachrymal secretion being at the same time much increased, the tears overflow the eyes, and roll down the
cheeks. This act of weeping, especially when the tears run
copiously, evinces a moderate or moderated sorrow, and is
associated with a mitigation of the inward distress and oppression, as of the heart and lungs, and thus forms a sort of
natural crisis to a paroxysm of grief, just as sweating does
to a paroxysm of fever. Some persons can never weep,
under afflictions of any character, and such generally experience much keener sufferings than those whose sorrows
find a more ready outlet at their eyes. It is seldom that
an individual dies in a fit of grief when weeping takes place
freely.

Crying, though more particularly significant of grief, yet
is by no means confined to it, but happens in various other
emotions, as of tenderness, joy, anger, fear, &c., and may
serve to lessen the danger of all violent passions.

It has been affirmed by some writers, that man is the
only animal that signifies sorrow by weeping; but the truth
of such assertion is not yet incontestably settled. That

the eyes of the inferior animals do oftentimes overflow with tears, is not to be disputed ; but does this happen as a consequence of moral emotions ? It is said of the orangoutang, that he has been observed to cry, much after the manner of our own species. The keeper of one which was exhibited a number of years ago in this country told me, that when grieved or angry she would cry "just like a child." Some other species of the monkey tribe, and even other animals, as the seal and camel, for example, have been asserted to shed tears under the influence of mental feelings. Extravagant grief is sometimes indicated by loud convulsive laughter. The readers of history will probably call to mind the story of Gelimer, king of the Vandals, told by Mr. Gibbon. The first public interview after he had been forced to surrender himself to Belisarius, "was in one of the suburbs of Carthage; and when the royal captive accosted his conqueror, he burst into a fit of laughter."

Violent outward expressions, or crying and noisy vociferations, by no means mark the deepest inward sufferings.

"Curæ leves loquuntur, ingentes stupent."

The following citation from Herodotus will form an apt illustration of the above remark.

"On the tenth day after the surrender of the citadel of Memphis, Psammenitus, the Egyptian king, who had reigned no more than six months, was, by order of Cambyses, ignominiously conducted, with other Egyptians, to the outside of the walls, and, by way of trial of his disposition, thus treated: His daughter, in the habit of a slave, was sent

11*

with a pitcher to draw water; she was accompanied by a
number of young women clothed in the same garb, and
selected from families of the first distinction. They passed
with much and loud lamentation before their parents, from
whom their treatment excited a correspondent violence of
grief. But when Psammenitus beheld the spectacle, he
merely declined his eyes on the ground : when this train
was gone by, the son of Psammenitus, with two thousand
Egyptians of the same age, were made to walk in procession
with ropes round their necks, and bridles in their mouths.
These were intended to avenge the death of those Mityle-
nians who, with their vessel, had been torn to pieces at
Memphis. The king's counsellors had determined that for
every one put to death on that occasion, ten of the first
rank of the Egyptians should be sacrificed. Psammenitus
observed these as they passed; but although he perceived
that his son was going to be executed, and while all the Egyptians around him wept and lamented aloud, he continued
unmoved as before. When this scene also disappeared, he
beheld a venerable personage, who had formerly partaken
of the royal table, deprived of all he had possessed, and in
the dress of a mendicant asking charity through the different ranks of the army   This man stopped to beg alms of
Psammenitus, the son of Amasis, and the other noble Egyptians who were sitting with him; which, when Psammenitus
beheld, he could no longer suppress his emotions, but calling on his friend by name, wept aloud and beat his head.
This the spies, who were placed near him to observe his
conduct on each incident, reported to Cambyses; who, in

astonishment at such behavior, sent a messenger, who was thus directed to address him: 'Your lord and master, Cambyses, is desirous to know why, after beholding with so much indifference your daughter treated as a slave, and your son conducted to death, you expressed so lively a concern for that mendicant, who, as he has been informed, is not at all related to you.' Psammenitus made this reply: 'Son of Cyrus, my domestic misfortunes were too great to suffer me to shed tears: but it was consistent that I should weep for my friend, who, from a station of honor and of wealth, is in the last stage of life reduced to penury.' "*

The keenest sorrow would appear to concentrate, and, as it were, benumb all the actions of life, and its unfortunate subject—his nervous energies completely overpowered—remains silent, motionless, stupefied; sometimes, as in a state of ecstasy, rigid and stiffened like a statue; whence Niobe, overwhelmed with the suddenness and greatness of her misfortunes, is fabled to have been changed into stone. Dr. Zimmermann has cited from Tulpius the case of a young Englishman, "who having met with a refusal from a lady, became perfectly rigid and motionless, sitting in the same attitude with his eyes open, and appearing rather like a statue than a human being; he continued in this posture till night, and then, on being told that his mistress yielded to his passion, he rose instantly as if from a profound sleep, became more cheerful, and soon recovered."

When grief breaks forth into tears and lamentations, and

* Book iii. 14.

violent muscular actions, as beating the breast, wringing the hands, tearing the hair, it shows an energy of resistance in the system, with a more general diffusion of the influence of the passion, and that we have less, therefore, to dread from its consequences. "The soul," as it has been said, "by giving vent to sighs and tears, seems to disentangle itself, and obtain more room and freedom." Anger, too, is here oftentimes awakened, and mingling with the original emotion, assists in promoting its reaction.

We can now see that it is not those who make the greatest ado about their troubles—who are ever, in season and out of season, forcing them upon the notice of others, that are likely to feel them the deepest. Slight grief is apt to prattle and complain, whereas the most profound is speechless, avoids every allusion to its source, shuns all society, even the intercourse and consolations of friendship, and tears and sighs are denied to it, or come but seldom to its relief.

We may furthermore learn that those persons who are anxious to hide their grief, who struggle to confine it within their own bosoms, must undergo far weightier sufferings than such as yield themselves freely to its impulses. Hence those sorrows which are of a more delicate or secret nature, and under which one is often obliged even to feign a contrary sentiment, produce the sharpest inward torture, and are the most speedily destructive to health and life.

> "What equall torment to the griefe of mind,
> And pyning anguish hid in gentle hart,
> That inly feeds itselfe with thoughts unkind,

And nourisheth her own consuming smart?
What medicine can any leaches art
Yeeld such a sore that doth her grievance hide,
And will to none her maladie impart?"*

Sometimes under the sudden stroke of aggravated grief, the powers of life are so completely overwhelmed that they cannot react, and instant or speedy death is the consequence.

"In the war which King Ferdinand made upon the dowager of King John of Hungary, a man in armor was particularly taken notice of by every one for his extraordinary gallantry in a certain encounter near Buda, and being unknown, was highly commended, and as much lamented when left dead upon the spot. but by none so much as by Raisciac, a German nobleman, who was charmed with such unparalleled valor. The body being brought off the field of battle, and the count, with the common curiosity, going to view it, the armor of the deceased was no sooner taken off, but he knew him to be his own son. This increased the compassion of all the spectators; only the count, without uttering one word, or changing his countenance, stood like a stock, with his eyes fixed on the corpse, till, the vehemency of sorrow having overwhelmed his vital spirits, he sunk stone dead to the ground."† "Almost in the very moment that I am writing," says Dr. Zimmermann, "Prince George Louis of Holstein, having lost his wife, directed her corpse to be removed from the coffin in which it was placed, into another

* Spenser's Faery Queene.
† Montaigne's Essays.

of more costly materials; and when this was done, the prince kneeling down at the side of the coffin, desired his valet de chambre to read to him some pages of a pious book, melted into tears, and soon afterwards died."[*]

Under the sudden shock of grief, the heart and nervous system may become so greatly agitated and disturbed, as to place the life of the individual in much peril. Here a general throbbing is felt throughout the body, and a distinct thrill may be perceived in all the arteries whose pulsations are sensible, and the anxiety and distress are extreme. Dr. Hope records the case of a healthy plethoric young female, who, on receiving the intelligence that her husband had deserted her, fell into a state of almost complete insensibility, "and the violently bounding, jerking, and thrilling arterial throb, together with universal flushing, heat, and perspiration of the surface, resisted every remedy, and only subsided with the wane of life."[†]

Dr. William Stroud, in a volume of four hundred and ninety-six pages, published in London in 1847, on the Physical Cause of the Death of Christ, and its Relation to the Principles and Practice of Christianity, has, by a long series of facts and arguments, endeavored to show that the speedy death of Christ on the cross was owing to a rupture of the heart, produced by his mental agony and fear in the Garden, and upon the cross; and that this mode of death goes to fulfil several prophecies in the Scriptures of the Old Testament.

[*] Experience in Physic.
[†] On Diseases of the Heart, &c.

Apoplexy, or some other equally fatal malady, is occasionally induced by sudden and poignant affliction, speedily terminating existence. Pope Innocent IV. died from the morbid effects of grief upon his system soon after the disastrous overthrow of his army by Manfred.

Severe grief may likewise call into action various nervous diseases of a more or less grave and lasting character; as palsy, epilepsy, catalepsy, ecstasy, St. Vitus's dance, and hysterics accompanied sometimes with convulsive laughter. And settled insanity in some of its forms, even dementia, has been known to follow upon sudden and great misfortune.

Dr. Whytt informs us that he had a patient who, upon the unexpected death of her husband, was seized with frequent fainting fits, generally holding her from five to fifteen minutes. "In these faintings she lay like a dead person, without any apparent breathing, or motion of the breast; only when a candle was held near her mouth, the flame was observed to move a little." In this way she continued for two days, coming out of the fits with sighings and crying, and falling into them again in little more than a quarter of an hour.* "It happened not long ago at London, that an Englishman who attended the funeral of his wife, lost the use of all his limbs, and continued speechless for some time afterwards."†

"Two young conscripts, who had recently joined the

* Observations on Nervous Diseases, &c.
† Zimmermann on Experience in Physic.

army, were called into action. In the heat of the engage-
ment one of them was killed by a musket ball, at the side
of his brother. The survivor, petrified with horror, was
struck motionless at the sight. Some days afterwards he
was sent in a state of complete idiotism to his father's
house. His arrival produced a similar impression upon a
third son of the same family. The news of the death of
one of the brothers, and the derangement of the other,
threw this third victim into a state of such consternation
and stupor, as might have defied the powers of ancient or
modern poetry to give an adequate representation of it."*

---

* Treatise on Insanity. By Ph. Pinel, Prof. of the School of Medicine at Paris, &c.

CHAPTER XXII.

GRIEF CONTINUED.—EFFECTS ON THE ECONOMY FROM ITS MORE
SLOW OR CHRONIC ACTION.

ALTHOUGH, as shown in the preceding chapter, an acute
paroxysm of grief may be fraught with extreme hazard to
health, and even life, yet it is the rooted and stubborn sorrow, from whose burden the heart finds no rest, to which
disease and untimely death are the more frequently to be
ascribed. No constitution is proof against the corroding
influence of seated sorrow.

The deep and settled despondency consequent on a
separation from the happy scenes and associations of one's
native home, termed home-sickness; or the moral suffering
proceeding from defeated ambition, reverses of fortune, the
bereavement of near and dear relatives, or disappointment
in the more tender affections of the heart, will not rarely
engender or excite some serious malady, under whose influence life must speedily yield. And to those of a frail and
delicate constitution, the danger from such unfortunate
sources will be immeasurably enhanced.

Morton entitles one of his species of consumption, *a melancholia;* and Laennec, eminently distinguished for his writings and practical observations on diseases of the chest, is disposed to ascribe the greater prevalence of consumption in large cities, to the numerous and close relations among men, affording more frequent occasions for the development of the gloomy and bad passions of the heart. This latter author records the following remarkable example, which was ten years under his observation, of what he believed to be the effect of the melancholy and depressing passions in the .production of consumption. "There existed, during the time mentioned, at Paris, a recent religious community of women, who, on account of the extreme severity of their regulations, had obtained only a conditional toleration from the ecclesiastical authority. Their diet, though austere, did not exceed what the powers of nature could endure; but the rigor of their religious rules was productive of effects both melancholy and surprising. Their attention was not only habitually fixed on the most terrible truths of religion, but they were tried by all kinds of opposition to induce them, as soon as possible, to renounce entirely their own proper will. The effects of this course were alike in all. At the end of one or two months an important function of their constitution became suppressed, and in one or two months more, consumption was evident. They not being bound by vows, I urged them, on the first manifestation of the symptoms of the malady, to quit the establishment; and almost all who followed the advice were cured, though many of them had already exhibited evident signs of consumption. During the ten years that I was physician to this household, I saw it renewed two or three times by the successive loss of all its members, with the exception of a very small number, composed principally of the superior, the grate keeper, and the sisters who had the care of the garden, the kitchen, and the infirmary; and it is worthy of remark, that those persons were the ones who had the most frequent distractions from their religious austerities, and that they frequently went out into the city on duties connected with the establishment." The same author likwise tells us, that almost all the individuals whom he has seen become phthisical without the signs of the constitutional predisposition, appeared to owe the origin of their malady to deep or long continued sorrow.* I have seen it also remarked by another French writer, that phthisis, in those convents particularly where the discipline is severe, carries off a great number of the nuns. The gloomy state of mind induced by such austerity may, to say the least, operate in aid of other causes in generating or exciting this fatal malady.

Nostalgia, or home-sickness, (*maladie du pays* of the French,) through the deep moral suffering attending it, has not unfrequently called forth diseases of the chest, and particularly consumption. The Swiss, when removed from their own native mountains, are particularly liable to become affected with this malady, and sometimes fall victims

* Traité de l'Auscultation médiate et des Maladies des Poumons et du Cœur.

to it, when the lungs will often be found in a state of disease. But the natives of all countries, removed from the scenes, companions, and domestic associations of their native home, may become its subjects. Soldiers forced into the service often experience it in an aggravated degree, and it not seldom proves fatal to them. The natives of mountainous regions appear to be much more subject to home-sickness than the inhabitants of the plains. Esquirol observes that the mountaineer cannot bear a long absence from the home of his nativity, but continues to mourn, and at last pines away and dies if he cannot return to it. He accounts for this on the assumption that the inhabitants of mountainous districts are less civilized than those who dwell on the plains. But do not the more striking objects belonging to mountain scenery, its wild and varying beauties, its impressive boldness and grandeur, stamp themselves more deeply and indelibly upon the feelings, and so beget stronger and more lasting associations, than the tame, uniform, and artificial scenery of the cultivated plain?

The sorrow attendant on disappointed love, in those of frail and delicate constitutions, romantic and sensitive feelings, and secluded habits, is a not uncommon exciting cause of consumption.

Insanity, certainly where any predisposition exists to it in the system, is very liable to be developed by all such causes as depress and afflict the mind. In turning over the reports of different lunatic asylums, we shall learn that a large proportion of their cases are ascribed to moral afflictions; as unrequited love, great reverses of fortune and pecuniary embarrassments, disappointed ambition, religious despondency, remorse, unhappy marriage and domestic trouble, loss of relatives, home-sickness, &c. We are told that the first question which M. Pinel was in the habit of putting to a new patient, who still retained some remains of intelligence, was, "have you undergone any vexation or disappointment?" and that the reply was seldom in the negative. The causes alluded to being always most influential in civilized life, is regarded as one principal reason why insanity prevails in proportion to the cultivation of society. Domestic trials rank among the most frequent moral sources of insanity, and especially among women. Disappointed affection is also a common cause of this malady, but it excites it much oftener, according to M. Esquirol, in females than in males. Women, he tells us, with whom love is the great business of life, bear with much more difficulty than men, the effects of its disappointment. His tables also show that they more often become insane from jealousy. " I have had occasion," says Dr. Zimmermann, " to see all the great hospitals in Paris, and have distinguished in them three kinds of mad people. The men, who were become so through pride; the girls, through love; and the women, through jealousy. All these people had the appearance of so many furies.

"Among the lunatics confined at Bicetre, during the year 3 of the republic, whose cases I particularly examined, I observed that the exciting causes of their maladies, in a great majority of instances, had been very vivid affections of the mind, such as ungovernable or disappointed ambition, religious fanaticism, profound chagrin, and unfortunate love.

Out of one hundred and thirteen madmen, with whose histories I took pains to inform myself, thirty-four were reduced into this state by domestic misfortunes; twenty-four by obstacles to matrimonial connections which they had ardently desired to form; thirty by events connected with the revolution, and twenty-five by religious fanaticism."*

In those disastrous periods when poverty and reverses of fortune are most common, mental derangement has been observed to become more frequent.

"Anxiety and agitation of mind caused by political events, have occasionally produced a very decided effect on the numbers of persons becoming deranged. M. Esquirol declares that the law of conscription increased the number of lunatics in France, and that at every period of this levy, many individuals were received into the hospitals, who had become insane through the excitement and anxiety occasioned by it; they were partly from the number of those on whom the lot fell, and partly from their friends and relatives. 'The influence of our political misfortunes has been so great,' says the same writer, 'that I could illustrate the history of our revolution, from the taking of the Bastile to the last appearance of Bonaparte, by describing in a series the cases of lunatics, whose mental derangement was in connection with the succession of events.'"†

Monomania is a form of insanity not uncommonly following the chronic action of grief. If an individual of the mel-

---

* Pinel on Insanity.
† Prichard on Insanity.

ancholic temperament sustains some grave misfortune, he is apt to brood over it in painful despondency. His general health, therefore, soon becomes impaired, his moral energy languishes, and no motive can arouse him to wholesome exertion. In time his melancholy gets more deep and settled, his temper often grows morose, irritable, suspicious, misanthropic, and at length some unhappy and erroneous impression fastens upon his imagination, and maintaining despotic sway over all his thoughts and feelings, he becomes a confirmed monomaniac.

Obdurate sorrow has sometimes caused a total wreck of all the powers and affections of the mind, leaving a hopeless dementia as its mournful sequel.

The opulent or higher classes would appear to be more exposed to moral sufferings and their morbid consequences, than those who occupy humbler ranks in society. " Even those superior intellectual advantages of education," says Dr. Reid, " to which the more opulent are almost exclusively admitted, may, in some cases, open only new avenues to sorrow. The mind, in proportion as it is expanded, exposes a larger surface to impression." The rich and cultivated have generally more delicate and refined sensibilities, and are more exposed than the inferior classes to the vicissitudes of fortune, as loss of property, wounded pride, disappointed ambition.

Numerous instances are recorded, both by ancient and modern medical authors, where habitual epilepsy has resulted from the baneful influence of moral calamities.

Palsies, likewise, and other melancholy nervous affections are not uncommonly attributable to the same source.

When we consider how immediate and forcible is the impulse of grief upon the heart, it will excite no surprise that disease of this organ should sometimes proceed from its severe and continued operation. Desault and several other French writers have remarked that during the unhappy period of the revolution, maladies of the heart and aneurisms of the aorta became obviously multiplied. Nothing is more common than for derangements of the function of the heart, indicated by intermissions, and other painful and sometimes dangerous irregularities in its pulsations, to be the consequence of lasting anxiety and mental dejection ; and such functional disorders, when long continued, may even terminate in some fatal change in the structure of the organ.

Examples, indeed, are not wanting where the first indications of diseases of the heart have been referred to the sudden impression of some painful disaster, under which the organ sustained a shock from whose violence it could never recover. We find an interesting case of this description recorded by the Chevalier Pelletan, in a memoir published by him a number of years since, and while he was chief surgeon of the Hotel Dieu, in Paris, on certain diseases of the heart. The subject of this record was an Irishman, thirty-six years of age, and of the most ungovernable passions. Having experienced during the revolutionary struggle various fortunes and sufferings, he at length, on the affairs of France assuming a more favorable aspect, obtained a pension of twelve thousand francs, but which was immediately taken from him on the death of the patron by whom it had been procured. This last misfortune, it would seem, completely overthrew him. "He has told me a hundred times," says the Chevalier, "that on hearing the news of his loss, he immediately felt a dreadful weight in his chest. His respiration became fatiguing, and the palpitations of his heart assumed an irregularity, which had no interruption during the two years and a half that he survived his misfortune."

From the period when deprived of his pension, organic disease of the heart appears to have declared itself, and to have gone on increasing in all its terrible symptoms, until the end of two years and five months, when his strength became subdued, and he obtained relief in death.

On inspecting the body, the heart was found colorless, and its whole substance in a remakable state of flaccidity, such as the distinguished narrator of this case had never before witnessed. " The parietes of the cavities fell together, and the flesh of this organ might be compared to the pale and shrunken muscles of an old woman ; there was an astonishing contrast between the flesh of the heart and that of the other muscles of the body." M. Pelletan concluded that the heart, in consequence of the violent mental shock, was struck with a sort of paralysis, and that death ultimately took place from the complete palsy of the organ. It was manifestly, however, a case of chronic softening of the heart, with loss of color, a peculiar morbid condition which has since been recognized. The individual, at any rate, perished

12

of a disease of the heart, the first indications of which immediately followed a strong impression of grief, and this is all
that is necessary to our present purpose.

Dyspepsia is another complaint exceedingly liable to be
induced under the protracted operation of sorrow.   Dr.
Heberden observes, "there is hardly any part of the body
which does not sometimes appear to be deeply injured by
the influence of great dejection of spirits; and none more
constantly than the stomach and bowels, which hardly ever
escape *unharassed* with pains, an uneasy sense of fulness
and weight, indigestions, acidities, heartburn, sickness, and
wind, in such an extraordinary degree, as to threaten a
choking, and to affect the head with vertigo and confusion."*
And Dr. Whytt also remarks, that "long continued grief
and anxiety of mind weaken the tone of the stomach, destroy the appetite and digestion, occasion thirst, a white
tongue, flatulence, and other complaints."†

Chronic inflammation, and even scirrhus and cancer of
the stomach, will sometimes succeed the deep and prolonged
influence of the passion I am noticing.   Laennec asserts
that the depressing passions, when long operative, seem to
contribute to the growth of cancers, and the various other
accidental productions which are unlike any of the natural
structures of the body.‡

Bonaparte died of an extensive ulceration of the stomach,

* Commentaries.

† Observations, &c., p. 207.

‡ Traité de l'Auscultation, &c.

which the physicians who inspected his body pronounced to be cancerous. Now, that his malady was originated or excited by the sorrow and chagrin arising from his painful reverse of fortune, and the wrongs and unkind treatment which he received, or fancied he received, while on the island of St. Helena, is, to say the least, far from being improbable. The father of Napoleon having fallen a victim to cancer of the stomach, many have thought that a predisposition to this disease was inherited by the Emperor. Admitting such to have been the fact, we can then only regard his complaint as developed and hastened, not as primarily produced, by the depressing passions which tormented the latter period of his existence. No distinct tokens of the ailment which destroyed him, were, at any rate, disclosed till about a year subsequent to his arrival upon the island, when he first began to complain of an uneasy sensation in his stomach and right side. It was not, however, until October of the following year that he was subjected to any medical treatment. From this time the disease went on slowly, though steadily advancing, and on the fifth of May, 1821, as the day was about closing, this extraordinary man yielded to its power, and his mighty spirit rested for ever from its vexations and sufferings.

The liver is also very subject, earlier or later, to participate in the morbid effects of mental dejection. At first its secretion is apt to be diminished or obstructed, whence constipation of the bowels, sallowness of the skin, and a train of symptoms generalized under the familiar term *bilious*, commonly supervene, passing at times even into decided jaundice. Biliary concretions, or gall-stones, are said to be very frequent in such as have experienced long continued moral despondency, and it has likewise been asserted that they are generally found in the gall-bladder of the victims of suicide. M. Pelletan observes that he has ascertained this fact a great many times in subjects who had been induced to self-murder by lasting distress, but never in those who had committed it on account of sudden grief and despair, such as happens after losses in gaming, or from disappointed love.

Even fatal organic changes may sometimes be induced in the liver by the operation of deep and prolonged mental sufferings. Such, however, can scarce be regarded as a common result, unless the individual, through the influence of climate, is disposed to hepatic disease, or, driven on by the weight of his afflictions, adds the morbid effect of intemperance to that of the moral cause.

The depression of sorrow, as of fear, conduces to the action both of contagion, and of epidemic influences, and is also, like that of fear, unfriendly to the restorative processes in all diseases and injuries of the body. Every one knows that the danger of sickness becomes essentially aggravated by mental afflictions. And what judicious surgeon but would feel diminished confidence in the success of an important operation, were the spirits of its subject borne down by the pressure of grief?

When sorrow becomes settled and obstinate, the whole vital economy must, ere a long while, experience its baneful effects. Thus the circulation languishes, nutrition becomes imperfect, perspiration is lessened, and the animal temperature is sustained with difficulty; the extremities being in a special manner liable to suffer from coldness. The skin, moreover, grows pale and contracted, the eye loses its wonted animation, deep lines, indicative of the distress within, mark the countenance, and the hairs soon begin to whiten or fall out. The effect of the painful passions in depriving the hairs of their coloring matter, is many times really astonishing. Bichat states that he has known five or six instances, where, under the oppression of grief, the hair has lost its color in less than eight days. And he further adds that the hair of a person of his acquaintance became almost entirely white in the course of a single night, upon the receipt of melancholy intelligence.*

The sleep of the afflicted is generally diminished, broken, disturbed by gloomy and terrifying fancies, haunted and distressed by a revival, in new and modified forms, of their waking sorrows, and thus is rarely granted to them even the paltry solace of a few hours' oblivion to their sufferings; and repose is oftentimes almost a stranger to the couch of misery.

> " Tired Nature's sweet restorer, balmy Sleep ;
> He, like the world, his ready visit pays
> Where Fortune smiles: the wretched he forsakes ;
> Swift on his downy pinion flies from woe,
> And lights on lids unsullied with a tear."†

* Anatomie Générale.   † Young.

The nervous system, subjected to the depressing influence of which I have been speaking, soon becomes shattered, and soul and body mutually wearing upon each other, the energies of both at last sink into irretrievable decay.

CHAPTER XXIII.

GRIEF CONTINUED.—DESPAIR AND SUICIDE.—GRIEF UNDERGOES
CERTAIN MODIFICATIONS, AND IS MORE OR LESS BLUNTED BY
TIME, ACCORDING TO THE NATURE OF ITS CAUSES.—SEVERE
IS OFTEN BORNE WITH MORE RESIGNATION THAN LIGHTER
SORROW.—IN YOUTH, GRIEF IS APT TO BE ACUTE AND TRAN-
SIENT, IN AGE, CHRONIC AND LASTING.

DESPAIR is the name by which we express that extremity of
moral depression, against which the mind has no power of
reaction. Under this dreadful feeling, no ray of hope, no
sunbeam of joy, breaks in upon the Cimmerian darkness of
the soul. To one who has reached this utter state of despondency, life is no longer desirable; the charms of nature
or of art call forth no throb of delight in his dark spirit, and
the cheerful earth spreads out before him like some gloomy
and barren wilderness.

> "He now no more, as once, delighted views
> Declining twilight melt in silvery dews,
> No more the moon a soothing lustre throws,
> To calm his care, and cheat him of his woes,

But anguish drops from Zephyr's fluttering wing,
Veiled is the sun, and desolate the spring,
The glittering rivers sadly seem to glide,
And mental darkness shrouds creation's pride."*

Despair may proceed from a sense of blasted fame, deep
humiliation, or wounded self-love, under which existence, to
the proud man, becomes an unremitting torture. It may,
in like manner, follow blighted expectations, irretrievable
losses, and suddenly ruined fortune,—as happens often to
the gamester; and it oftentimes attends remorse of conscience, whether for real or imaginary offences, and great
public calamities, as destructive epidemics, unhappy political
revolutions, or other grave national misfortunes.

Remorse sometimes becomes the occasion of the most
hopeless despondence, and frequently where there is no real
cause for it, except in the individual's own morbid sensibility. It has been said, indeed, that "remorse is often
felt most acutely by those who have the least reason for
self-accusation." Some persons become utterly wretched
from the false and idle notion that they have been useless
to the world, have done no good to their fellow-creatures,
have been unfaithful stewards, &c., and this idea, preying
upon an unnatural nervous susceptibility, has even provoked
self-destruction. The most deep wounding and even fatal
stings of conscience sometimes follow, in highly sensitive
natures, upon unfortunate, though unpurposed results of

---

* Merry's Pains of Memory.

actions. "A disastrous result," says Dr. Reid, "not unfrequently reflects the horror of guilt upon that conduct,
which would otherwise have escaped any injurious imputa-
tion, which would have been deemed innocent in its character, had it proved so in its consequences. . . . . A man's
character may be shaded by the accidents, as well as by the
actions, of his life. And perhaps, even conscience itself is
seldom more deeply wounded by the stings of guilt, than it
sometimes has been by the arrows of fortune." He mentions in illustration the singular history of Simon Brown,
"the dissenting clergyman, who fancied that he had been
deprived by the Almighty of his immortal soul, in consequence of having accidentally taken away the life of a high-
wayman, although it was done in the act of resistance to his
threatened violence, and in protection of his own person.
Whilst kneeling upon the wretch whom he had succeeded
in throwing upon the ground, he suddenly discovered that
his prostrate enemy was deprived of life."*

Contrition for absolute guilt when yielded to as a mere
passive, unprolific feeling, is liable to be followed by a deep
and hopeless moral despondence, and to which both mental
and physical enegies at last fall a sacrifice. But when it
takes the character of an actuating sentiment, then do its
sufferings become materially lightened, and its effects are
alike propitious to the individual, and useful to society.
The following reflections on this subject are well worthy the
serious meditation of all repentant sinners.

* Essays, &c.

12*

"Remorse itself is considered, perhaps too indiscriminately, as a compensation for misconduct. When it is an unproductive feeling merely, and not a regenerating principle, instead of mitigating, it can serve only to aggravate our offences. Repentance, sentimentally indulged, often stands in the way of a practical reformation. The pressure of conscious criminality ought to be sufficient to rouse into action, but not so great as to crush altogether the powers of the mind. Contrition is most easily indulged in a state of indolence and solitude; but can be alleviated only by strenuous efforts in the service of society. The errors of our past life are not to be atoned by wasting the remainder of it in a sedentary grief, or in idle lamentations. Every good deed which a man performs, lightens, in a certain degree, the load of recollected guilt. Active duty is alone able to counteract the injury, or to obliterate the stain, of transgression.

"In even aggravated cases of remorse, much may be done towards relief, if the patient have resolution enough to administer to himself; to awaken from the lethargy of a vain regret; and make every atonement in his power for any wrong that he has committed, or any moral law which he has broken. A man may compensate to society, for an injury that is perhaps irreparable to an individual; and by the extraordinary exertions of a penitentiary benevolence, be the means of producing a quantity of happiness that is equivalent to the misery which his former vices or errors may have occasioned."*

* Reid's Essays, &c.

In those especially of timid, gloomy, and superstitious dispositions, despair will not unfrequently result from injudiciously awakened religious terrors; the deluded individual conceiving himself an outcast from God's mercy, predestined to the eternal horrors and torments which mad bigotry has portrayed to his fancy. "There is a kind of *Melancholy*," says Dr. George Cheyne, "which is called *Religious*, because 'tis conversant about Matters of *Religion;* although often the Persons so distempered have little *solid Piety*. And this is merely a *bodily Disease*, produced by an ill *Habit* or *Constitution*, wherein the *nervous System* is broken and disordered, and the *Juices* are become *viscid* and *glewy*. This *Melancholy* arises generally from a *Disgust* or *Disrelish* of worldly *Amusements* and *Creature-Comforts*, whereupon the Mind turns to *Religion* for *Consolation* and *Peace :* But as the Person is in a very imperfect and unmortified State, not duly instructed and disciplined, and ignorant how to govern himself, there ensues *Fluctuation* and *Indocility*, *Scrupulosity*, *Horror*, and *Despair*."*

There is a species of mental despondence, the offspring of great public calamities, which produces a strange effect upon our moral nature; begetting, at times, even a carelessness of existence; and where great numbers, driven on to despair, precipitate the termination of their own existence. Hecker tells us that Lubeck, at that time the Venice of the North, with an overflowing population, was thrown into such

* On Health and Long Life. London, 1734, p. 157.

consternation by the eruption of the plague, or Black Death of the fourteenth century, that the citizens destroyed themselves as if in frenzy.

It is true that man's full energies can only be elicited by great afflictions and great dangers, if they be not so aggravated as to overwhelm, and benumb with despair. They put our self-love and self-denial to the true test, and form the rightful assay both of our moral and intellectual nature. No one has been proved who has not been *tried*. But then as they may bring out the brightest points of human character, so also may they its darkest shades. It seems oftentimes that the more precarious is the tenure by which man holds his existence, the more desperate, wicked, and reckless of life does he become. Hence amid the ravages of war or pestilence, when no one feels secure of his being even from hour to hour, all laws human and divine are often set at defiance, and the most appalling cruelties enacted by the infatuated, despairing people. I will not here speak of great political revolutions where each one's life, and all that renders life dear, are in constant jeopardy—every body knows the black history of crime which marks the progress of these terrible disruptions in human society—but will only cite a few facts corroborative of the foregoing assertions, from the history of one of those fearful pestilences where nature lets loose her destructive influences upon wide regions of the earth. " It speaks," says its historian, " of terrible disasters, of despair, and unbridled demoniacal passions. It shows us the abyss of general licentiousness, in consequence of a universal pestilence which extended from China to Iceland and Greenland."*

In this desolating epidemic—the Black Death, or Black Plague of the fourteenth century—it is stated that at least one quarter of the population of the old world was destroyed in the space of four years; and that some countries, and among them England, lost more than double that proportion of their inhabitants in the course of a few months. Kairo, according to Hecker, lost daily of her inhabitants, when the plague was most violent, from ten to fifteen thousand. China is said to have lost more than thirteen millions. India was depopulated. Tartary, Mesopotamia, Syria, &c., were covered with dead bodies. In Caramania and Cæsarea, none were left alive. Cyprus lost almost all its inhabitants. In the report made to Pope Clement, at Avignon, it was stated that throughout the East, probably with the exception of China, twenty-three millions eight hundred and forty thousand people perished by this plague.

" In many places in France not more than two out of twenty of the inhabitants were left alive, and the capital felt the fury of the plague, alike in the palace and the cot."

" In Avignon, the Pope found it necessary to consecrate the Rhone, that bodies might be thrown into the river without delay, as the churchyards would no longer hold them."

The whole duration of the destructive violence of this pestilence in Europe, was, with the exception of Russia, from the year 1347 to 1350; and the loss of its inhabitants

* Hecker's Epidemics, &c.

by the disease is set down at twenty-five millions. Yet the human race speedily recovered itself from this incredible desolation; the past mortality was soon repaired—as has been observed to happen after all wasting epidemics—by a more rapid reproduction, (for nature, although seemingly regardless of individuals, ever exhibits a provident care of species,) and the world aroused from its torpor and depression to new life, and new power of action.

Under such a general and appalling calamity, with the awful terrors of death menacing every one, surely might it be thought that the human heart would have been softened, sobered, renovated,—awakened to moral and religious reflection. But what says the historian? "Morals were deteriorated every where, and the service of God was, in a great measure, laid aside." The masses of the people, as it appears, became generally hardened, selfish, avaricious, corrupted, and, by a sort of reckless despair, were urged onward to all manner of enormities.

The cruelties enacted at this time on the part of the Chistians towards the Jews, on the alleged ground that the latter had poisoned the wells, are in the highest degree reproachful to our nature. The promise to embrace Christianity, and submitting themselves to baptism, could alone save this unjustly oppressed people from a painful death. Few, however, would accept life on terms like these. At Strasburg, two thousand Jews were burnt alive upon a large scaffold erected in their own burial ground. All the Jews in Basle, whose number was large, were inclosed in a wooden building constructed for the purpose, and burnt together with it, at the mere instigation of the mob. In Mayence alone, twelve thousand Jews were cruelly martyred. "At Eslington the whole Jewish community burned themselves in their synagogue; and mothers were often seen throwing their children on the pile, to prevent their being baptized, and then precipitating themselves into the flames. In short, whatever deeds fanaticism, revenge, avarice, and desperation, in fearful combination, could instigate mankind to perform—and where in such a case is the limit?—were executed in the year 1349, throughout Germany, Italy, and France, with impunity, and in the eyes of all the world. It seemed as if the plague gave rise to scandalous acts and frantic tumults, not to mourning and grief: and the greater part of those who, by their education and rank, were called upon to raise the voice of reason, themselves led on the savage mob to murder and to plunder." " Many breathed their last without a friend to smooth their dying pillow; and few indeed were they who departed amid the lamentations and tears of their friends and kindred. Instead of sorrow and mourning, appeared indifference, frivolity and mirth; this being considered, especially by the females, as conducive to health. . . . . During the prevalence of the Black Plague, the charitable orders conducted themselves admirably, and did as much good as can be done by individual bodies, in times of great misery and destruction; when compassion, courage, and the nobler feelings, are found but in the few; while cowardice, selfishness and ill-will, with the baser passions in their train, assert the supremacy. In place of virtue which had been driven from the earth, wickedness every where reared her rebellious standard, and succeeding generations were consigned to the dominion of her baleful tyranny."*

In his account of the plague at Athens, Thucydides writes, that amid a calamity so violent, and such universal despair, things sacred and holy had quite lost their distinction. The pestilence first gave rise to those iniquitous acts which increased more and more in Athens. " Not any one continued resolute enough to form any honest or generous design, when so uncertain whether he should live to effect it. Whatever he knew could improve the pleasure or satisfaction of the present moment, that he determined to be honor and interest. Reverence of the gods or of the laws of society laid no restraint upon men." Still human nature here, as under all conditions, presents many ennobling traits. Its dark side is set off by many generous, disinterested, and self-sacrificing actions ; but they are performed in private, and known therefore but to the few; while wickedness stalks abroad, and rears its head every where to public view.

To return to my more immediate topic:—Despair consisting in utter moral desolation, or the complete absence of all hope, abandons every exertion for the future. Thus does it either shun altogether the intercourse of man, burying itself in the deepest gloom and solitude, or seeks to lessen the intensity of its misery by violent and undetermined action or dissipation. Sometimes it urges on its reckless

* Hecker's Epidemics, &c.

victim to the most criminal and desperate acts,—to gross intemperance, or some more sudden method of throwing off a hated existence. Those even who are hopeless of God's mercy, and look forward but to everlasting torture hereafter, will often hurry themselves to meet the very worst their imagination can paint, rather than endure the agony of despair produced by their dreadful apprehensions; as one will sometimes leap down the dizzy height, the bare view of which sickened his brain, and filled his soul with terror.

When despair does not impel to such rash deeds, all consciousness of suffering either becomes lost in insanity, or the physical energies soon yield to its overwhelming influence. Existence can rarely last long under the privation of every enjoyment and the extinction of every hope.

Grief, in whatever measure it may exist, will always be most obstinate and dangerous in those unengaged in active pursuits, and who have consequently leisure to brood over their troubles in silence and solitude. Bodily and mental activity, and more especially when the result of necessity, must, by creating fresh trains of association, and diverting the thoughts into new channels, tend to weaken the poignancy of affliction. Nothing, in truth, serves more effectually to lighten the calamities of life, than steady and interesting employment. It is, as I conceive, for the reason that females are generally exempt from the cares and excitements of business, and confined at home to their own relatively tranquil domestic duties, that they so much oftener pine and sicken under wounded affections, than our own more active and busy sex. It is a fact which has been often noted in the history of fleets and armies, that when actively engaged in warlike duties, the troops are comparatively little subject to physical disease or moral despondence. Dr. Good observes that " suicide is frequent in the distress of sieges, in the first alarm of civil commotion, or when they have subsided into a state of calmness, and the mischiefs they have induced are well pondered ; but it seldom takes place in the activity of a campaign, whatever may be the fatigue, the privations, or the sufferings endured. On the fall of the Roman empire, and throughout the revolution of France, self-destruction was so common at home, as at last to excite but little attention. It does not appear, however, to have stained the retreat of the ten thousand under Xenophon, and, according to M. Falret, was rare in the French army during its flight from Moscow."*

The subject of suicide, referred to in the above quotation, involving as it does so many curious facts and inquiries, and being so frequent a consequence of the pressure of grief, a few general remarks upon it may not be deemed irrelevant to our present matter.

Suicide in ancient days, and particularly among the Romans when they were at the summit of their glory, was, under many circumstances, not merely excused, but looked upon as a praiseworthy and heroic act; and it was even held to be base and cowardly to cling to existence under suffering and ignominy The Stoics countenanced it. Many of the noblest of the Roman commanders—among whom Bru-

* Study of Medicine.

tus may be mentioned—when the fortune of war turned against them, chose a voluntary death sooner than bear the disgrace of a defeat; and this was regarded as a glorious consummation of their lives.

Cato the younger has, both in ancient and modern times, been held up as an illustrious example of stern and virtuous patriotism, because he took his own life rather than submit to the dominion of Cæsar. Cato's suicide, as often happened in those days, showed the most determined and desperate resolution, and it has frequently been lauded on this very account. He first stabbed himself, but owing to an inflammation which at the time affected his hand, did not strike hard enough at once to complete the work of death, but falling from his bed in his struggles, his son and friends were alarmed and entered his room, where they found him weltering in his blood, and with his bowels fallen out, but yet alive. The physician, perceiving the bowels uninjured, put them back and began to sew up the wound; but Cato in the meanwhile, coming a little to himself, "thrust away the physician, tore open the wound, plucked out his own bowels, and immediately expired." Great honors were paid to the body by all the people of Utica, and Cæsar himself is reported to have said that he envied Cato his death.*

The Roman Lucretia, because she plunged a dagger into her breast rather than survive her ravished honor, has acquired a fame which will be likely to endure as long as female virtue is regarded. And of Portia, the daughter of

* Plutarch. Life of Cato the younger.

Cato and wife of Brutus, who, being cut off from other means, killed herself by forcing burning coals into her mouth, or, as is commonly told, by swallowing fire, Plutarch says, she "put a period to her life in a manner worthy of her birth and of her virtue."

Plato considered suicide to be justifiable under circumstances of severe and unavoidable misfortune: but for such as committed it from faintheartedness, or a want of moral courage to confront the ordinary chances of life, he directed an ignominious burial. Virgil, however, seems to have regarded it as unexceptionably criminal, having assigned a place in the shades below for all those who have voluntarily taken off their own lives, as appears from the following passage in his Æneid.

> " Proxima deinde tenent moesti loca, qui sibi lethum
> Insontes peperere manu, lucemque perosi
> Projecere animas.   Quàm vellent æthere in alto
> Nunc et pauperiem et duros perferre labores!
> Fata obstant, tristique palus inamabilis undâ
> Alligat, et novies Styx interfusa coercet."*

> " The next, in place and punishment, are they
> Who prodigally threw their souls away—
> Fools, who, repining at their wretched state,
> And loathing anxious life, suborned their fate.
> With late repentance, now they would retrieve
> The bodies they forsook, and wish to live;

* Lib. vi., v. 434.

Their pains and poverty desire to bear,
To view the light of heav'n, and breathe the vital air :
But fate forbids ; the Stygian floods oppose,
And with nine circling streams the captive souls inclose."*

We read that a law of the elder Tarquin forbade the
body of the suicide the right of sepulture.   In Athens, also,
a penal enactment existed in regard to self-murder.   Lycurgus, the famous Spartan lawgiver, justified this act by his
own example.

In certain countries people sacrifice themselves in accordance with the customs of society, as the Hindoo widow,
who is voluntarily consumed on the funeral pile of her husband ; or under the belief that they are performing a religious act acceptable to their gods, as the Indian devotee who
throws himself beneath the car of Juggernaut.

"There are certain governments," Montaigne tells us,
"which have taken upon them to regulate the justice, and
proper time of voluntary deaths."   And he says on the authority of Valerius Maximus, that "a poison prepared from
hemlock, at the expense of the public, was kept in times past
in the city of Marseilles, for all who had a mind to hasten
their latter end, after they had produced the reasons for their
design to the six hundred who composed their senate ; nor
was it lawful for any person to lay hands upon himself, otherwise than by leave of the magistracy, and upon just occasions."†

* Dryden's Translation.
† Essays.

In civilized countries self-murder, although unhappily of so frequent occurrence, finds at the present time few advocates, being generally regarded with sentiments of the deepest horror, and among some people and sects the rites of Christian sepulture are denied to its victims.   To this denial of Christian obsequies Shakspeare has allusion in the scene of Ophelia's burial, in his play of Hamlet.

> "*Laer.*   What ceremony else ?
>
>   1 *Priest.*   Her obsequies have been as far enlarg'd
> As we have warranty : Her death was doubtful ;
> And, but that great command o'ersways the order,
> She should in ground unsanctified have lodg'd
> Till the last trumpet ; for charitable prayers,
> Shards, flints, and pebbles, should be thrown on her :
>
>   *Laer.*   Must there no more be done ?
>
>   1 *Priest.*   No more be done !
> We should profane the service of the dead,
> To sing a *requiem,* and such rest to her
> As to peace-parted souls."

In England, at one period, the body of the suicide was cast into the highway.   In aftertime it was buried where three roads met.   In France there was a time when the household goods of the suicide were given to the proprietor of the soil on which the deed was perpetrated.   Afterwards his body was drawn through the streets upon a hurdle.   At the present day these laws—if they still exist on the statute-book—have become obsolete.   It is said, however, that a law exists in Saxony by which the body of the suicide is given up for public dissection.

One might suppose that nothing short of the most consummate and hopeless misery could overcome the strong feeling that binds us to existence; and it is generally true that only the severest moral afflictions, either real or imaginary, or sudden transports of passion which, for the time, vanquish the reason, can provoke to a deed so rash and unnatural as self murder. Still there are exceptions, nor are they rare, where its causes are of a different and less explainable character. Physical sufferings may sometimes be its cause, though far less often than those of a moral nature.

That, like the different forms of insanity with which it is so frequently associated, it is often hereditary, is now proved beyond question. There are few persons, it is presumed, who will not be able to call to mind examples of the hereditary transmission of a propensity to suicide. It is remarkable, too, that the disposition to it will sometimes be developed in different members of a family at nearly the same period of life. Esquirol relates of a man, whose father and grandfather had destroyed themselves when fifty-three years old, that at the age of fifty he began to experience the temptation to suicide, and was satisfied that he should die as they had done. He also cites from Voltaire an example where a man of good habits, mature age, and a serious profession, committed suicide, and left to the officers of his native city a written defence of the act. His father and brother had before destroyed themselves at the same age with himself. He further cites from Dr. Gall an instance where seven brothers, possessed of large fortunes, in excellent health, honorable in their lives, and held in high and general estimation, all committed suicide when between thirty and forty years of age. Numerous examples might be cited where the whole, or nearly the whole of the members of large families have, one after another, fallen by their own hands. In some cases this hereditary propensity begins to be exprienced at quite an early age.

In the opinion of M. Falret, of all the forms of melancholy, that which tends to suicide is most frequently hereditary; and he gives an instance where all the female members of a family for three succeeding generations committed or attempted suicide.

We read that a club existed in Prussia, comprising six members, all of whom, in accordance with its rules, terminated their lives by their own hands. And of one also in Paris in more recent times, a regulation of which was that one of its number should be selected every year to destroy himself.

Dr. Millingen knew a person who could never drink tea without experiencing a desire to commit suicide, " and nothing could arouse him from this state of morbid excitement but the pleasure of destroying something, books, papers, or any thing within his reach. Under no other circumstances than this influence of tea were these fearful aberrations observed."* Esquirol informs us that M. Alibert attended a lady who always felt a desire to destroy herself

* Curiosities of Medical Experience.

after eating; and that she was often discovered after dinner
in the act of passing a cord around her neck, so that it became necessary to keep a close watch upon her. Here some
morbid condition of the digestive function was doubtless the
exciting cause of the propensity. Persons have killed themselves out of spite, or from malignity. Also from the hopes
of bettering their condition; and to escape their agonizing
fears of death, or future punishment. In some persons
attempts at suicide are always excited by intoxication; and
despair at not being able to conquer the debasing appetite
for intoxicating drinks has been the occasion of self-destruction. Esquirol records an instance of a man, thirty years of
age, and in excellent health, killing himself a few days after
marriage, because his wife did not come up to his high-raised
expectations.

Nostalgia, ennui, or weariness of life, from perverted or
exhausted sensibilities, rank among the not unusual causes
of suicide. Some persons, without any other evidence of ill
health, become affected with an unaccountable torpor and
listlessness, both of mind and body; every effort of either
becoming difficult and irksome to them. They consequently
grow discouraged, fancy themselves useless, or perhaps a
burden to their families and to society, and are thus impelled
to throw off what they deem to be a valueless existence.
There are those who having exhausted all life's resources,
and being left without hopes or desires, and almost without
sensations, experience a fearful sense of desolation, a dreadful void within, which nothing can supply. To such all is
vapid, barren, sunless. They covet and seek death. They

13

have surfeited at life's feast, and hurry themselves inde-
cently from the board.

There are periods in society, when, from causes which
are not always easy of explanation, suicide becomes unusually prevalent, so much so as to be entitled an epidemic.
The state of social morals influences the number of suicides
in a community; and the dissemination of speculative and
mystical opinions in philosophy and religion, may so bewil-
der the feeble-minded and irresolute, that they will sometimes rush into the arms of death to escape the painful perplexity in which their puny intellects have become involved.
The reading of books which defend suicide, have been a
prolific source of that act.   Madame de Staël is cited as saying, that more suicides have been caused in Germany by the
reading of Goëthe's Werther, than by all the women of that
country.

Suicide often owes its origin to the principle of imitation,
and under such influence has occasionally so extended itself
in communities, as to be regarded in the light of an epidemic.   And where, from native organization, or defect of
moral culture, fatal propensities exist, the danger from this
source will be greatly increased.   Instances of the epidemic
extension of suicide from imitation, or sympathy, have been
recorded both in ancient and modern times.   It is related
by Plutarch in his treatise on the virtue of women, that
there was a time when all the girls of Miletus were killing
themselves, and without any apparent cause.   Those who
first destroyed themselves served as examples to others, or
awakened their imitative propensity, and in this way did

the fatal work spread itself among them until counteracted by the stronger influence of shame, it being ordained that their dead bodies should be exposed naked to the people. It is recorded that there was a period in the history of Lyons, when its women threw themselves in crowds into the Rhone, and without offering any reason for the act.

Several years since there appeared in the London Medical Gazette the following account of an inclination to suicide spreading itself in a remarkable manner, and, as was supposed, through the force of imitation.

" For about two months an extraordinary number of suicides, and of attempts at suicide, occurred in London; scarcely a night elapsed but one or more persons threw themselves from some bridge, or from the bank, into the Thames—for that was the favorite mode of self-destruction —till at last the police looked on such an event as a thing to be certainly expected and guarded against. The greater number of persons thus endangering their lives, exhibited no common character of insanity; had not been regarded as of unsound intellect; had no cause of utter despair; had scarcely any delusion or mistaken motive. When their lives were saved, they did not give any extravagant reason for the attempt; at most they had been vexed by some untoward circumstance, had had some domestic quarrel, or were poor, though hardly destitute. The fury of the epidemic— which affected women more than men—was increasing to a truly alarming extent, when one of the city magistrates— Sir Peter Laurie, who had probably had some advice tendered him at Bedlam, of which he is the president—determined to try the effects of punishment on all who were brought before him for attempts at suicide. The plan succeeded admirably; some were punished summarily, some were committed to take their trial for attempts at the felony of self-murder, and in a very short time—a fortnight at most—the rage had disappeared, and suicides became no more than usually common."

The writer of this article relates another remarkable instance of the same sort, and in which a similar remedy was successful. It happened at a garrison, where a strange propensity existed among the soldiers to hang themselves on lamp-posts. "Night after night were suicides of this kind committed, till the commanding officer issued a notice, that the body of the next man who put an end to his life, should be dragged round the garrison at the cart's tail, and then be buried in a ditch. His order was but once put in force, and then the epidemic ceased."

Several persons have committed suicide by throwing themselves from the gallery of the monument in London. And at one time there seemed to be a growing propensity to jump from the Leaning Tower at Pisa; three persons—as I learnt from my guide while on a visit to it—having thus put a period to their existence; on which account visitors could no longer ascend it without an authorized attendant.

A French journal—Archives Générales—records that a boy eleven years of age, being reproved by his father in the fields, went home, put on his suit of holyday clothes, procured from the cellar a bottle of holy water, and placed

it beside him, and then hung himself from the cross-beam
of the bed. It appears that the uncle of this boy had a
short time previously destroyed himself in a similar manner, having also first placed near him a bottle of holy water.

Even the reading of cases of suicide may sometimes call
into action this principle of imitation, and lead, it may be,
to fatal consequences. An instance in illustration occurred
a number of years since in Philadelphia, an account of which
was published at the time by Isaac Parrish, M. D., of that
city. The subject was a girl in her fifteenth year, who had
been carefully brought up, and whose situation in life was
apparently every way agreeable. It seems that early in the
morning of the day of her death, "she had held a conversation with a little girl residing in the next house, in which she
mentioned having lately read in the newspaper of a man
who had been unfortunate in his business, and had taken
arsenic to destroy himself. She also spoke of the apothecary's shop near by, and said she frequently went there."

It appeared that two days prior to her death, she had
purchased half an ounce of arsenic of a druggist in the
neighborhood, for the pretended purpose of killing rats,
which she had used as the instrument of her own destruction.*

It is a fact well known in respect to certain individuals,
especially when of a nervous or sensitive temperament, that
if the thoughts of any particular deed, calculated, from its
criminal or hazardous character, to make a deep impression

---

* American Journal of the Medical Sciences, for November, 1837.

on the feelings, chance to be strongly awakened in the mind, they cannot be banished, but becoming more and more concentrated, a propensity, sometimes too powerful for resistance, to the commission of such deed, will actually follow. Were such an one now to become deeply affected—either from his connection with its subject, or its peculiar circumstances—by the occurrence of a suicide, the idea might continue pertinaciously to haunt his imagination, and an unconquerable inclination to the like unnatural deed be the consequence. And that murders are sometimes committed under the same mysterious and urgent impulse, is a fact too well established for denial. I remember an instance in point, which, many years since, came within my immediate knowledge. A young female, while sitting with an infant in her arms near a fire, over which hung a large kettle of boiling water, suddenly started up, and in a hurried and agitated manner ran to a distant part of the room. On asking her the reason of this, she, after a little hesitation, told me that fixing her eyes on the boiling water, it occurred to her how dreadful it would be should she by accident let the child fall into it. " On this idea crossing my mind," said she, " I instantly began to feel a propensity to throw it in, which soon grew so strong, that had I not forced myself away I must inevitably have yielded to it."

An unnatural and irresistible impulse has sometimes urged on the mother to the destruction of her own offspring. Brute animals, as sows and cats, under a like strange perversion of instinct, have been known to destroy, and even to eat their young.

" A country woman, twenty-four years of age, of a bilious sanguine temperament, of simple and regular habits, but reserved and sullen manners, had been ten days confined with her first child, when suddenly having her eyes fixed upon it, she was seized with the desire of strangling it. This idea made her shudder; she carried the infant to its cradle, and went out in order to get rid of so horrid a thought. The cries of the little being, who required nourishment, recalled her to the house. She experienced still more strongly the impulse to destroy it. She hastened away again, haunted by the dread of committing a crime of which she had such horror; she raised her eyes to heaven, and went into a church to pray.

" The unhappy mother passed the whole day in a constant struggle between the desire of taking away the life of her infant, and the dread of yielding to the impulse. She concealed, until the evening, her agitation from her confessor, a respectable old man, the first who received her confidence, who, having talked to her in a soothing manner, advised her to have recourse to medical assistance."*

The propensity to infanticide in a mother has alternated with an equally strong one to suicide; and the latter deed has been attempted to prevent the perpetration of the former, the impulse to which was felt to be invincible.

The following case was first published among other similar ones by M. Marc. It occurred in Germany, in the family of Baron Humboldt, and has the testimony of this dis-

* Prichard on Insanity, cited from Dr. Michu.

tinguished individual. The mother of the family returning home one day, met a servant who had previously given no cause of complaint, in a state of the greatest agitation. She desired to speak with her mistress alone, threw herself on her knees and entreated to be sent out of the house; giving as a reason, that whenever she undressed the little child she nursed, "she was struck with the whiteness of its skin, and experienced the most irresistible desire to tear it in pieces." Esquirol relates the case of a female who was resistlessly impelled to homicide in order to shed blood, for the sight and taste of which she had exhibited a strong relish even from early life. Hence she would often eat her meat raw; and loved to cut in pieces birds or other animals which fell into her hands.

I have known persons, who on taking a sharp weapon into their hands, would almost always experience a disposition to stab those who chanced to be near them. This homicidal propensity has been experienced even in children, from eight to ten years of age.

In view of such cases as have been cited, and enough of them may be found on record, a form of insanity is now generally admitted, where the afflicted individual, without the slightest apparent disorder of the intellect, or any other discoverable mental aberration, and under a horrid conviction of the atrocity of the deed to which he is blindly impelled, and moreover devoid of all malicious intent, is attacked with a violent, and sometimes insurmountable propensity to take life; often that of some particular individual, a friend, or perhaps one bound to him by the closest ties of kindred. This has been termed homicidal monomania, and homicidal madness, and is brought under a variety of mental disease called moral insanity ; that is, where the moral feelings only become perverted, the intellect or reasoning principle being no further affected than thróugh the influence of their morbid excitement or perversion. There is, however, another variety of homicidal madness, but whose consideration would be foreign to our present purpose, dependent on actual hallucinations, in which the individual is urged on to the commission of murder, under a fancied command from heaven, or some other similar delusion of the imagination.

This homicidal propensity of which I have been speaking is apt to be periodical, and is sometimes connected with marked bodily disorder. Thus it has been preceded by wakefulness, headache, thirst, feverishness, internal heat, constipation, colic pains, and various disorders of the stomach and bowels. A case is recorded where epilepsy, to which the patient had been subject during sixteen years, suddenly changed its character, without any apparent cause, and in place of the fits there occurred from time to time an insuperable desire to commit murder. The approach of these attacks was sometimes felt for many hours, and occasionally for a whole day, before they actually seized the individual, and on such premonition he would entreat to be tied down, to prevent him from the commission of the crime to which he was blindly impelled.

The inclination to homicide exhibits the same remarkable tendency to spread from the force of imitation, as we

13*

have previously shown exists in that to suicide. In proof of this examples enough will be found on record. We read that the trial of Henriette Cornier, in France, for infanticide— it becoming, from its peculiar and deeply exciting circumstances, a subject of very general attention and conversation—occasioned in many respectable females a strong propensity to the same unnatural deed. Esquirol speaks of a woman brought to trial for cutting off the head of a child whom she hardly knew; and remarks that the trial being widely published, produced, through the power of imitation, many cases of homicidal monomania.

It is, in part at least, on this principle of imitation that we are to account for the repeated attempts that were once made on the lives of Louis Philippe and Queen Victoria; and the unavoidable publicity of such attempts, and the factitious consequence into which their miserable authors were often elevated, doubtless contributed to spread the disposition to them.

That unhappy instances do now and then occur, where persons acting under this insane impulse are condemned to the punishment of murder, is scarce to be questioned. Still, such morbid impulses should be admitted with a good deal of caution, or they would be unwarrantably pleaded to shield the murderer. Human justice is necessarily imperfect, and it cannot be otherwise than that some must fall the unmerited victims to its imperfection. But as laws are designed to be preventive, or are instituted for the security of the community, such impulsive homicides should be permanently confined, inasmuch as they are fully as dangerous as the rational assassin, if rationality can be predicated of an assassin. The existence of such a morbid impulse may be reasonably inferred when there is no discoverable motive for the crime committed, and when the perpetrator of it makes no effort to escape or to screen himself from punishment. Sometimes he even appears to experience a relief from prior agitation and suffering; is composed, shows no regret, or even manifests a degree of satisfaction at the deed. We have it on the authority of Esquirol, that the impulse to murder and suicide are to be greatly feared in those who are in dread of eternal damnation, and he refers to cases in proof, recorded by Sauvages, Forestus, and Pinel.

Suicide, as previously said, is in some cases to be ascribed to a like inscrutable impulse as that which urges to homicide, and the disposition to it will at times be found to alternate, or to be strangely blended with that to homicide ; and to be preceded also, or accompanied by manifest physical derangements. Striking changes, too, in the moral character and habits, are apt to forerun attempts at suicide. Thus, those who had before been social, mild, and cheerful, as a prelude to this tragic act, will often become solitary, morose, gloomy, and misanthropic. Oftentimes do they undergo a long and fearful internal struggle, subject to remissions and aggravations, against this reasonless impulse, before the preservative instinct is wholly vanquished, and the unnatural deed is consummated. " A melancholic," says Dr. Pinel, " once said to me, 'I am in prosperous circumstances, I have a wife and a child who constitute my

happiness, I cannot complain of bad health, and still I feel
a horrible propensity to throw myself into the Seine.' His
declaration was too fatally verified in the event."*

There is another strange impulse occasionally witnessed,
and doubtless intimately allied to that which has been the
subject of our attention, urging to acts of mischief—as the
destruction of property—and independent of malevolent
feeling, or in truth of any apparent motive. I have known
persons on taking a watch into their hands, to manifest an
urgent desire to dash it in pieces. And I have seen tum-
blers and wine-glasses actually broken under the forcible
influence of such destructive propensity. Children, in like
manner, will sometimes display an impulsive disposition
to break their trinkets, even those with which they had been
most delighted.

An irresistible propensity to burn, or to set houses on
fire, without any other evidence of insanity, called incendiary
monomania, and pyromania, has been admitted by some
writers on forensic medicine and mental diseases. Esquirol
admits, on the strength of various recorded cases, that there
is a variety of monomania without delirium, marked by an
instinctive desire to burn. A case is cited from Dr. Gall,
of a woman, who immediately on taking any intoxicating
drink began to experience an urgent impulse to set fire to
some building. She had caused fourteen conflagrations before being imprisoned. One case has fallen under my
observation, where a female of about sixteen years of age

* On Insanity.

twice set fire to the dwelling in which she lived, without any motive that could be detected or surmised, and without any attempt to conceal the crime or shun its punishment. This inclination, like that to suicide and homicide, has a tendency to spread through the force of imitation. In Germany, it appears, on the evidence of German physicians, that young girls from nine to twelve, fifteen, and eighteen years of age, form the larger proportion of incendiaries. The same does not hold true in France, and probably not in other countries.

I have heretofore alluded to that propensity which some people experience on looking over the brow of a precipice, to cast themselves down. It is, therefore, not improbable that some of the suicides which have been accomplished by jumping from great heights were unpremeditated, the individual having been suddenly overpowered by the force of such inclination. And may it not also be true, that some of the deaths ascribed to accidental falls, were in reality occasioned by this same insurmountable impulse?

The relative number of suicides is considerably greater in cities than in the country. In Prussia, the city have been ascertained to bear to the rural cases, a proportion of fourteen to four. M. Guerry, in an essay on the moral statistics of France, states that from whatever point we start, the relative frequency of suicide will always be found to increase as we approach Paris. And the same assertion is also made in respect to Marseilles, this town being regarded as the capital of the South. Just the reverse of this, though one would scarcely look for such a result, he found to hold true of murders and assassinations, these consequently, in relation to the number of inhabitants, being the most, where suicides are the least numerous. The number of suicides, in proportion to the population, he ascertained to be much greater in the north than in the south of France; and that one sixteenth of all committed in France, are in the department of the Seine.

Self-destruction is more common in males than females; in France, according to Esquirol, in the proportion of three to one; and in England and America the ratio is probably about the same. In the year 1847 we have reported, for the city of New-York, thirty-two cases of suicide, twenty-eight of which were of men, and four of women. In 1848, thirty-four cases; twenty-five of men, and nine of women. In 1849, thirty-five cases; twenty-three men, and twelve women.

In regard to the temperament, the melancholic and bilious would seem to be most prone to suicide, still it may happen to any temperament; even the sanguine sometimes take off their own lives. Esquirol observes that a srcofulous habit often marks those who terminate their lives, it disposing to apathy, indifference, discouragement, ennui. In respect to the moral character of suicides, the same author remarks that there is nothing consistent; cowards and heroes, women and men, the high and the low, the criminal and the honest man, may all be driven on to self-murder.*

Suicide, although it may occur at almost any period of

---

* On Insanity.

life, yet there are certain ages when it would appear to be more particularly frequent. In a table given by M. Dupin, suicide is shown to happen at all ages trom ten to ninety, but to attain its greatest frequency from forty to fifty, or in middle life, diminishing as we recede from it to either extreme. This has been explained on the supposition, that then, more than at any other period, " the mind is exposed to the disturbing influence of disappointed ambition, of domestic anxiety and distress, and of other causes of chagrin and disquietude ; and that it no longer possesses that elasticity or resiliency of spirit, by which it relieved itself from vexing care in more youthful years.

" The middle-aged man feels, when calamities overtake him, that he is less able than he was wont to be, to struggle against them ; and the mortification at the change of his circumstances, coupled with the slender hope of regaining his former position, is too apt to prey upon his mind until he is driven to commit suicide."*

All the statistics on the subject to which I have had access, go to prove that suicide is most common in the warm, or what are generally regarded as the pleasant months of the year. M. Falret, who has written on suicide and hypochondriasis, believes that a moist, hot, and relaxing atmosphere is conducive to moral despondency, and consequently to self-murder ; and it is stated in confirmation of such opinion, that in the months of June and July, 1806, sixty suicides occurred in Paris. In some of the exceeding hot

* London Medico-Churgical Review, for July, 1837.

and relaxing weather of our own summer months, especially when lasting through the night, and interfering with the needful sleep, a distressing faintness, or sinking, as it is often called, at the epigastrium, or region of the stomach, much like that attendant on acute grief, is experienced, and under the agony of which, the individual, if of a gloomy temperament, may sometimes be driven on to the deed we are considering. This feeling becomes much more intolerable when, in addition to the heat, one is subjected to the tainted air and irritating noises of dirty and crowded cities. The experience of all will teach that a high degree of temperature can be much better borne if the atmosphere be pure, than when it is contaminated with noisome effluvia. Such then as are disposed to suicide, should seek, during the hot season, the unadulterated air of the open country, and more particularly that of the sea-coast.

The months most prolific in self-destruction in France would appear to be May, June, July, and August, and, other things being the same, the instances of it become most numerous in extremely warm summers. In a report of those received during six years, into the department of the insane at the Salpêtrière, after attempting suicide, Esquirol informs us that the attempts were most frequent in the summer and spring, and the least so during the three months of autumn. He also shows that insanity most often makes its attack in the summer.

The opinion has heretofore prevailed, that in England the foggy and gloomy month of November is the one most productive of instances of self-destruction; such a conclusion, however, is not borne out by facts. It appears that of the suicides committed in Westminster, from 1812 to 1824, there were thirty-four in the month of June, while but twenty-two happened in the month of November. And furthermore, that in 1812, 1815, 1820 and 1824, not a case occurred in November.*

It is a prevalent notion that the variable and gloomy weather of the early period of spring, and the latter part of autumn in the more northern portions of the United States, favors in a special manner the disposition to suicide. Such opinion, however, would seem to arise rather from some fancied association between unpleasant states of the atmosphere, and unhappy moral feelings, than to be based on any careful observation of facts. On examining the bills of mortality of the city of New-York for the five years prior to the publication of the first edition of the present work, I found the instances of suicide to have been most numerous in the warm and pleasant season of the year. Thus for the months of summer, during the term specified, there were fifty-nine cases; of spring, fifty three; of autumn, forty-six, and of winter but thirty-five. May, generally a very cheerful and agreeable month in the city of New-York, gave twenty-three cases, while February, almost always bleak and dreary, afforded but seven. March and November exhibited the least number of any months, with the exception of January and February. During the two past years (1848 and 1849), according to the reports of the city in-

* Medico-Chirurgical Review, for April, 1837.

spector, there are for the summer, twenty-four cases of self-murder; for the spring, nineteen; for the autumn, fourteen, and for the winter, twelve. The above data are, to be sure, limited, yet so far as they go, they are in agreement with the observations on the same subject made in France and England, and tending to show that the strongest propensity to self-destruction exists in the warm season.

The cases of self-murder vary materially in their relative number in different countries, as well as in the same country at different periods. In France and Germany, if statistics on the subject are to be trusted, they considerably exceed those in England. This is contrary to the belief formerly entertained, certainly by the French, who looked upon England as the country above all others where suicide prevailed, and ascribed its prevalence there to the humid and foggy atmosphere, and dismal skies. "'The English'— says Montesquieu, 'frequently destroy themselves without any apparent cause to determine them to such an act, and even in the midst of prosperity. Among the Romans suicide was the effect of education; it depended upon their customs and manner of thinking: with the English it is the effect of disease, and depending upon the physical condition of the system.' The propensity to this horrid deed, as existing independent of the ordinary powerful motives to it, such as the loss of honor or fortune, is by no means a disease peculiar to England: it is far from being of rare occurrence in France."*

---

* Pinel on Insanity.

In London, as near as can be ascertained, there happen annually about a hundred instances of voluntary death. And in the whole of England the proportion of cases to the number of inhabitants, is set down as about one in nine thousand. M. Guerry states the suicides registered in France from 1827 to 1830, to be six thousand nine hundred; but as many cases of this nature, either from inadequate data, or the importunity of friends, will always be classed under the deaths from accident, the actual amount must probably be much greater; and has been estimated to exceed, in the ratio of three to one, the number of murders and assassinations. In the department of the Seine, where the greatest proportion occurs, the instances have been shown to be as one in every thirty-six hundred inhabitants; and they seem to be yearly increasing in France. M. Charles Dupin has shown such increase to have been almost regularly progressive in Paris from 1829 to 1836; and later tables prove that the number of suicides throughout France is annually augmenting. Thus, in 1836 there were registered two thousand three hundred and ten cases; in 1837, two thousand four hundred and thirteen; in 1838, two thousand five hundred and fifty-six, and in 1839, two thousand seven hundred and seventeen.—In 1843, the number of suicides in France amounted to three thousand and twenty, which exceeded that of 1842 by a hundred and fifty-four; of 1841, by two hundred and six; of 1840, by two hundred and sixty-three, showing a continued progression from 1829 to 1844.

In the city of New-York, the whole number of deaths

registered from the first of January, 1805, to the first of
January, 1842, a period of thirty-seven years, was 164,976,
of which 809, or one out of $203\frac{749}{809}$ are brought under the
head of suicide.

Suicide in New-York, so far at least as we may judge
from the tables of mortality, does not, as in Paris, appear to
be an increasing vice. On the contrary, it would appear to
be manifestly diminishing, regarding it in relation to the
population. Thus, for the five years from the first of January, 1805, to the first of January, 1810, we have registered
eighty-one cases of suicide; which, compared with the mean
of the. city population for this term, that is, $86,071\frac{1}{2}$, gives
us an average annual proportion of one case in fifty-three
hundred and thirteen and a fraction of the inhabitants.
Now for the same number of years, from the first of January, 1835, to the first of January, 1840, there are reported
a hundred and ninety-one cases, and the mean number of
the inhabitants being 291,399, we have, therefore, for this
time, an average yearly ratio of one instance of self-murder
to every seventy-six hundred and twenty-eight and a fraction
of the population—a very manifest decrease when compared
with the aforenamed period.

For the last three years, 1847, 1848, 1849, the whole
number of deaths in the city of New-York was 55,480; of
which number one hundred and one, or one out of $549\frac{31}{101}$
are reported under suicide.

It can scarce be doubted that in our own, as well as in
other countries, the ratio of mortality from the cause under
notice, is considerably greater than is shown by the reported

cases; since, for reasons which all will understand, many unquestionable cases of self-murder will be placed under the head of casualties, sudden death, visitation of God, &c. Esquirol, however, informs us that in the Paris reports are included, not barely those who are known to have destroyed themselves, whether intentionally or not, but likewise all found dead by the police, without its being certainly ascertained whether their deaths were voluntary, by assassination, or from some accidental cause. Hence he accounts for the greater relative number of reported examples of suicide in Paris than in London—the reports of the latter city embracing under suicide only such cases as afford grounds for believing life was purposely taken off.

The modes resorted to for self-destruction, vary greatly according to age, sex, and various incidental circumstances, and the strangest methods are sometimes resorted to. Monomaniacs sometimes inflict upon themselves cruelties apparently of the most dreadful nature, and oftentimes, too, without experiencing any bodily suffering from them. Women much less often have recourse to the pistol or cutting instruments than men. They more generally choose to hang, drown, poison, suffocate, or starve themselves. Suffocation by means of carbonic acid gas, from burning charcoal, is a common mode of self-destruction in France. But fashion and the principle of imitation exercise in this, as in every thing else, a remarkable influence. Sometimes two, urged on by inordinate passion, as where the course of true love does not run smooth, or by extreme misery from other causes, resolve reciprocally to destroy each other, or to terminate their lives together. And there are those who, unwilling, or lacking resolution to destroy themselves by their own hands, take the life of another that they may be condemned to death. To cases of the latter description has been given the name of homicidal suicide.

The very free internal use of cold water has been regarded by some writers as an almost infallible remedy against the propensity to suicide. Esquirol, in his treatise on insanity, alludes to an account, published by Leroy d'Anvers, of the benefit of cold water as a preventive of suicide, and asserts that many facts would seem to favor the employment of such remedy. He cites the case of a highly distinguished Prussian surgeon, by the name of Théden, who, having been hypochondriacal in his youth, grew at last melancholic, with a strong propensity to the commission of suicide; but through the copious use of cold water—from twenty-four to thirty pints a day—his health was restored. He continued the habit of drinking several pints of cold water daily when at the age of eighty years. Hufeland adduces two cases in support of this remedy. Would not then the hydropathic treatment be particularly suited to those laboring under a disposition to self-murder?

Suicide is peculiar to man. We have no evidence that any other animal, even under the most painful circumstances of suffering, ever voluntarily shortens its own existence. The story of the scorpion stinging itself to death when begirt by fire, is a mere poetic fiction. This unnatural act, then, belongs to reason, or I should rather say, the perversion of reason, never to simple instinct.

Grief becomes modified, and assumes a more or less dangerous character, according to the particular nature of its origin. When caused by the decease of friends and kindred, it is, for the most part, sober, solemn, subdued; and instead of provoking, tends rather to soften and quell the sterner passions of man. And then as death belongs essentially to the scheme of nature, as every human heart is exposed to bleed under its bereavements, it is a law of our constitution that the wounds it inflicts should daily experience the sedative and healing influence of time. To the loss even of the best beloved, the feelings will ultimately get resigned, and the idea of the departed, divested of all the acuteness of its original pain, comes at last to be dwelt upon with that species of soothing melancholy which would scarce be exchanged even for the gayest social pleasures. What a happy serenity will often steal over the feelings, when, withdrawing from the busy cares and unsatisfying enjoyments of the world, we yield ourselves to the fond remembrance of those friends and kindred who rest before us from the toils and sorrows of life! And with what gladness will the mourner, his grief sobered by time's tempering power, often quit the noisy scenes of mirth and pleasure, to linger in silence and solitude at that consecrated spot where rests the object of his dearest recollections! But again, other afflictions, as disappointed ambition, ruined fortune, blighted reputation, are apt to awaken moral sufferings of a far less humble and submissive nature, and to which time less certainly extends its healing balm. Such, too, are much more frequently united with the evil passions of anger, envy, jealousy, hatred, and consequently oftener lead to dissipation, crime, despair, and suicide. In loss of fortune, for example, especially where successful efforts cannot be made to retrieve it, the grief that follows is many times rather aggravated than appeased by the influence of time and new associations. Here the evils are ever present, ever felt. The constant deprivations and painful comparisons, the dreadful apprehensions for the future, and the agonizing sense of wounded pride, or self-humiliation, which there will be such repeated occasions to call forth, oftentimes render existence an almost unrelieved torture. How few, under such reverse of circumstances, can look back on the days of their ease and affluence but with feelings of the most bitter regret! And what cause than this has been more productive of despair and self-destruction?

> " But most to him shall memory prove a curse,
> Who meets capricious fortune's hard reverse;
> Who once in wealth, indulged each gay desire,
> While to possess, was only to require :
> Glows not a flower, nor pants a vernal breeze,
> As in his hour of affluence and ease,
> While every luxury that the world displays,
> Wounds him afresh, and tells of better days."*

Severe afflictions will oftentimes be better supported than the minor ills, or lighter trials of existence. Great misfortunes seem often to strengthen, elevate and purify

* Merry's Pains of Memory.

the soul, and are borne with manly composure, and heroic resignation; while lesser evils render us impatient and irritable, and exercise an unhappy influence on the moral character.

In youth grief generally assumes an acute and transient character; while in age it becomes more chronic and lasting. In early life we are buoyed up and sustained, and our sorrows all assuaged and shortened by the gay hopes that play upon the landscape of the future. But the mind of the aged lives almost entirely upon the recollections of the past; anticipation, with its fond promises, its bright coloring, and all its unreal mockeries, can no longer console and sustain it.

14

CHAPTER XXIV.

GRIEF CONCLUDED.—MENTAL DEJECTION AND EVEN DESPAIR
MAY BE EXCITED BY MORBID STATES OF OUR BODILY ORGANS.
—DIFFERENT INDIVIDUALS, AND EVEN THE SAME AT DIF-
FERENT TIMES, OWING TO INCIDENTAL CIRCUMSTANCES,
SHOW DIFFERENT DEGREES OF SUSCEPTIBILITY TO THE
IMPRESSION BOTH OF MORAL AND PHYSICAL CAUSES.—
IMPORTANCE OF A CHEERFUL AND HAPPY TEMPER TO THE
HEALTH OF CHILDHOOD.—GRIEF IS APPOINTED TO ALL.—
LIFE IS APT TO BE REGARDED AS HAPPY OR UNHAPPY
ACCORDING TO THE FORTUNE WHICH MARKS ITS CLOSE.

MENTAL depression, as has been previously asserted, may
grow out of physical as well as moral causes. The intimate
relation between good spirits and good health can hardly
have escaped even the most common observation. There
are circumstances of the body under which the brightest
fortune can bestow no happiness:—where, in the midst of
every outward comfort, the heart is still heavy; and, discontented with ourselves, tired of existence, disgusted with all
about us, we can find neither joy in the present, nor hope in
the future.

Mental depression, or sadness, was by the ancients

ascribed to a redundancy of that humor of the body denominated by them black bile, and for which the spleen, in
their fancy, served as the special reservoir. Hence have we
the origin of the term melancholia, or melancholy, it being
constructed of the two Greek words, μελας, *melas,* meaning
black, and χολη, *cholee,* bile. And it will also appear how
the word spleen came to be used as expressive of gloomy or
unhappy states of the temper. In persons of the melancholic temperament, a distinctive mark of which is a dark
sallow complexion, this black bile was imagined to exist in
excess over the three other humors formerly assigned to the
body. However erroneous, now, may be these theories, yet
none the less true are the facts which they were contrived
to explain. Although the hypotheses of the ancients were
apt to be visionary, yet shall we generally find their observations to be well grounded. That the condition of the
biliary secretion exercises a material influence upon the
mind's tranquillity; that unhealthy, redundant, or obstructed bile, at the same time that it gives its gloomy tint to the
complexion, may color the moral feelings with an equally
dismal shade, will, in our present state of knowledge, hardly
be contested. Thus, the common expression, "to look with
a jaundiced eye," means, as every one must know, to view
things in their sombrous aspect. We readily conclude,
then, that disordered or diseased states of the liver may be
comprehended among the physical causes of despondency of
the mind. Thus—as will be learnt from what has been
previously said—do they engender the same character of
feelings of which they themselves are also begotten.

Certain morbid, though unexplainable conditions of the nervous system, as well as of other parts of the animal constitution, may in like manner cloud our moral atmosphere in the deepest gloom. That distressing state of mind termed, in medical language, melancholia, in most cases certainly, originates in, or at any rate is soon followed by a derangement of some part or parts of the vital organization. In not a few instances we are able to trace it to its primary source in the body. The dreadful sufferings of the poet Cowper, at times amounting to actual despair, from this terrible physico-moral malady, as it has been not unaptly designated, are familiar to most readers. In early life he became the subject of religious melancholy, believing himself guilty of " the unpardonable sin," and consequently that eternal punishment hereafter was his inevitable doom. So poignant, indeed, was his mental agony, that at one time he indulged serious thoughts of committing suicide. His melancholy, with occasional remissions, and sometimes aggravated into the most acute form of monomania, pursued him through the whole of his wretched existence.

Cowper appears to have exhibited from his infancy a sickly and sensitive constitution, and his native bodily infirmities and morbid predispositions were doubtless also favored by too close mental application, as well as by other circumstances to which he was exposed in early life. It is besides obvious that he must have labored more or less constantly under an unhealthy condition of the digestive organs, his fits of melancholy being generally associated with headache and giddiness. Who that has ever been afflicted with dyspepsy but will be able to sympathize with him where, in one of his letters to Lady Haley, he says, "I rise in the morning like an infernal frog out of Acheron, covered with the ooze and mud of melancholy." Judicious medical and moral treatment united, might doubtless have done much in mitigation of the deep sufferings of this distinguished individual.

A morbid or unnaturally irritable state of the inner or mucous coat of the stomach, will oftentimes transmit such an influence to the mind as to deaden all its susceptibilities of enjoyment, and oppress it with the heaviness of despondency. Now, such an unhealthy character of this inner surface of the stomach being one of the necessary results of an habitual indulgence in exciting and inebriating drinks, the danger of a recourse to it, with a view to elevate the dejected spirits, or drown the remembrance of sorrow, will easily be understood. If the mental depression arises from a physical cause, such injudicious stimulation will be sure to augment it, and if from a moral, a physical one will thus be speedily added to it. There is, indeed, no moral gloom more deep and oppressive than that suffered by the habitually intemperate—whether in the use of distilled spirits, wine, or opium—in the intervals of their artificial excitement. In delirium tremens, a disease peculiar to the intemperate, the mind is always, even in its lightest forms, filled with the most dismal ideas, and a propensity to suicide is by no means unusual. The opium-eater, too, when not under his customary stimulus, generally experiences the most terrible mental sufferings.

There are certain affections of the brain which manifest
themselves especially, and at first almost entirely, by an oppressive moral gloom. A number of years since I attended
a lady with a fatal complaint of this organ, which displayed
itself chiefly in such manner, the physical suffering to which
it gave rise being apparently of but little moment. At
first, and long before any disease was apprehended, she became exceedingly dejected, secluding herself as far as possible from all intercourse with society, and even from the
presence of her most intimate friends. Her melancholy increasing, assumed at length a religious cast, and the idea
that she had forfeited the favor of the Almighty, and was
therefore doomed to eternal punishment, so tormented her
imagination, that at one time she made an attempt at self-
destruction. What was quite surprising, her mind was all
the while apparently rational; she conversed freely of her
feelings, admitted the absurdity of her thoughts, but at the
same time declared that in spite of every endeavor they
would intrude themselves upon her. At length she died,
when, deep in her brain, attached to that part of it which,
in anatomical language, is called *plexus choroides*, a cluster
of vesicles, about thirty in number, and nearly the size of
peas, was discovered. Such was the physical cause of all
her poignant mental distress.

Low, marshy, malarious situations, where intermittent
fevers, or agues, as they are more familiarly named, abound,
through some poisonous influence which they generate, so
act on the physical constitution as to weigh down all the
moral energies, and fill the mind with the darkest gloom.

In observing the inhabitants of such unhealthy spots, even when they have become so seasoned to their infection as to resist the fevers, or acute effects which it produces in strangers, we cannot fail to be struck with their sallow, sickly, and emaciated appearance, and the deep melancholy of their countenances, a melancholy which the cheerful smile of more wholesome airs is rarely seen to relax. The nervous system, the liver, and other organs engaged in the function of digestion, almost always, in such situations, labor under more or less obvious derangement. And here we have yet another illustration of the remark which I have before made, namely, that the like physical states which are generated under the operation of grief, will also, when arising from other causes, tend to awaken this painful passion. Thus, the same spare, nervous, and bilious condition that distinguishes the gloomy inhabitants of the unhealthy sites to which I have just referred, is equally witnessed in those who have long suffered under severe mental afflictions.

In passing those infectious spots so common in the South of Europe, the attention is particularly attracted to the sallow and melancholy aspect of the people. We remark it as we journey over the celebrated campagna on our way to Rome. And in a still more striking manner in the Pontine marshes, so long famed for their noxious influence, on our route from Rome to Naples. In Pæstum, too, and all along the rich and fertile shores of Sicily, where the balmy airs, the placid waters, the brilliant skies, and the teeming soil would seem to invite man to joy and plenty, every thing is shrouded in the deepest moral gloom, and the occasional forlorn inhabitant, with his dark, sickly, and desponding countenance, reminds one of some unblest spirit who has wandered into the favored fields of Elysium. Here may it truly be said,

> " Black Melancholy sits, and round her throws
> A death-like silence, and a dread repose :
> Her gloomy presence saddens all the scene,
> Shades every flower, and darkens every green."

The insect that sports about the gaudy flowers, and regales itself on their inviting sweets, affords almost the only indication of joy in these devoted seats of malaria.

It has been suggested that Cowper's melancholy was probably favored by his long residence in the malarious atmosphere of Olney.

Frequent attacks of ague, probably by inflicting an injury on some one or more of the viscera of the abdomen, are very apt to leave the mind a prey to imaginary sorrows, imbittering the present, clouding the future, and at times leading even to despair and all its terrible consequences.   Dr. Johnson tells us that he has known hundreds of people who had suffered under agues, or who had been exposed to malaria in hot and unhealthy climates, and who were harassed for years afterwards by all manner of horrors and sufferings. " I know many," says he, " who are affected with a periodical propensity to *suicide*, which generally comes on during the second digestion of food, and goes off when the process is

completed. Several instances have come within my knowledge, where individuals have been so well aware of the periodical propensity to self-murder, that they always took pre-
cautions against the means of accomplishing that horrid act,
some hours before the well-known hour of its accession."*

The well-known influence, especially in sensitive individuals, of different conditions of the atmosphere on the
temper of the mind, must be produced through the medium
of the physical organization. There are some persons who
almost uniformly feel dejected when the air is damp and
thick, the alacrity of their spirits returning on its becoming
dry and clear. Both ancient and modern physicians have
dwelt on the remarkable effect exercised by the state of the
atmosphere on our moral and intellectual feelings, and faculties. A dry and temperate climate, with a pure and clear
air, is peculiarly adapted to those of a melancholy turn of
mind.

The reader will now, it is to be presumed, have no difficulty in understanding that the like moral causes may, in
different individuals, and even in the same at different times,
call forth very unlike degrees of moral suffering. In those
of a naturally sensitive temperament, or whose nervous susceptibility has been morbidly elevated through bodily infirmities, a trifling mischance may be felt as keenly as a really
serious affliction in such as enjoy firmer nerves and sounder
health. In one afflicted with what we call weak nerves,
almost every thing that is in the least displeasing irritates

* On Change of Air.

14*

and vexes the mind, and a life of unhappiness is the not uncommon consequence of such physical imperfection.   The
coloring of external things depends far more on the character of the internal constitution, than has hitherto been generally suspected in man's philosophy ; and truly, therefore,
has it been said, that " the good or the bad events which fortune brings upon us, are felt according to the qualities that
we not *they* possess."   We are the creatures of constitution
as well as of circumstance, and with respect to our happiness, it may be said to depend even more upon the former
than the latter.   There are some who seem to be destined
through their faulty organization, no matter what may be
their fortune in regard to external goods, to be miserable ;
while others, on the contrary, are so physically constituted
that they can scarce be otherwise than happy.

Similar observations will also apply to our physical sensations, their degree being no certain and constant measure
of the absolute importance of the cause producing them.
Indeed, as has been before remarked, keen moral and keen
bodily sensibilities generally go together.   He who feels
keenly mentally, will be likely to have correspondently acute
physical feelings.   Now to the person concerned, of what
moment is it whether a moral or corporeal source of pain be
augmented, or only his susceptibility to its effect?   As different material bodies, either from their peculiar nature, or
through the help of incidental causes, are more or less com-
bustible, so also are different human beings more or less
excitable.   And with as much reason, therefore, might we
wonder that one substance should be kindled into a flame

by a little spark that causes no impression on the next, as that one man should suffer and complain under an influence to which another appears wholly indifferent. As there are ears so nicely strung as to hear sounds of such exquisite acuteness as to be wholly inaudible to others, so are there minds tuned so delicately as to perceive and feel what in others would raise no sensation, call forth no response. It is recorded of the ancient Roman ladies, that they were so exquisitely sensitive in their nervous systems, that even the odor of flowers would cause them to faint; and the same is said to be equally true of many of the modern ones; so that to

"Die of a rose in aromatic pain,"

may have some mingling of truth with its poetry. Some women are said to possess such exceedingly nice susceptibilities, that fainting will be produced by the mere touch of certain substances, as a peach, velvet, satin, &c. We are too prone, all of us, to assume our own sensibilities as a standard for those of the rest of mankind; hence is it that we so often hear expressions like the following, meant for consolation: "Why, how is it possible you can let such a little thing trouble you? I am sure I shouldn't mind it." As well might the blind man say to him that had vision, Why do you let such objects of sight disturb you? I am not affected by them. Some persons are so phlegmatic, have such thick skins, and leaden nerves, that scarce any thing will arouse their feelings; and in these, what we dignify with the name of firmness, is in reality but the result of dulness or insensibility.

In connection with this comprehensive passion of grief, let me briefly urge the high importance of preserving in children a cheerful and happy state of temper, by indulging them in the various pleasures and diversions suited to their years. Those who are themselves, either from age or temperament, grave or sober, will not unfrequently attempt to cultivate a similar disposition in children. Such, however, is in manifest violation of the laws of the youthful constitution. Each period of life has its distinctive character and enjoyments; and gravity and sedateness, which fond parents commonly call manliness, appear to me quite as inconsistent and unbecoming in the character of childhood as puerile levity in that of age.

The young, if unwisely restrained in their appropriate amusements, or too much confined to the society of what are termed *serious* people, may experience in consequence such a dejection of spirits as to occasion a sensible injury to their health. And it should furthermore be considered, that the sports and gayeties of happy childhood call forth those various muscular actions, as laughing, shouting, running, jumping, &c., which are, in early life, so absolutely essential to the healthful development of the different bodily organs.

Again, children when exposed to neglect and unkind treatment, for to such they are far more sensible than we are prone to suspect, will not unusually grow sad and spiritless, their stomach, bowels, and nervous system becoming enfeebled and deranged, and various other painful infirmities, and even premature decay, may sometimes owe their origin to such unhappy source.

Childhood, moreover—for what age is exempt from them?—will often have its secret troubles, preying on the spirits and undermining the health. The sorrows of this period are, to be sure, but transient in comparison with those of later life, yet they may be the occasion of no little suffering and injury to the tender and immature system while they do last. And then again many of the baleful passions, as envy and jealousy, in which grief is always more or less mingled, may agitate the human bosom long before they can be exhibited in language. Disappointed ambition, too, may wound the breast and disturb the health even in our earliest years.

Children, varying as they are known to do in their temperaments, will be affected in unequal degrees by the moral influences to which I have referred. When delicate and possessed of high nervous sensibility they will feel them far more keenly, and the danger from them will be correspondently enhanced.

Grief, let me add in conclusion of this subject, is a passion from which every human heart is destined to suffer. Affliction, in the continually recurrent vicissitudes of life, must fall upon us all; no one can hope to shun it, though the fates measure it out in very different quantities to different individuals, and to some so abundantly, that, like the Thracians, they might well weep at the birth of a child and rejoice at the funeral of their friends. Life is generally regarded as happy or unhappy according to the fortune which marks its close. We are apt to repine against fate if adversity overtakes us near the end, however great may have been the prosperity of our preceding years. Solon, the famous lawgiver, and one of the seven wise men of Greece, counted no man happy till the manner of his death was known. "Futurity carries for every man many various and uncertain events in its bosom. He, therefore, whom Heaven blesses with success to the last, is in our estimation the happy man. But the happiness of him who still lives, and has the dangers of life to encounter, appears to us no better than that of a champion before the combat is determined, and while the crown is uncertain."* But could we justly complain of a repast where all the dishes were good and plentiful except one or two at the end? Or, on the other hand, praise it if all were poor and scanty but a few of the last? The closing scenes of Sir Walter Scott's career were indeed melancholy; nevertheless, his feast of life, as a whole, was far richer and more abundant than is allotted to most men.

* Plutarch. Life of Solon.

CHAPTER XXV.

ENVY AND JEALOUSY.—SIMILAR IN THEIR NATURE.—SECRET AND DANGEROUS IN THEIR OPERATION.—MANIFEST THEMSELVES EVEN IN INFANCY.—INJURIOUS EFFECTS OF THESE PASSIONS UPON HEALTH. — SHAME. — ITS NATURE. — THE PHENOMENA WHICH ATTEND IT.—WHEN EXTREME MAY BE FRAUGHT WITH DANGER TO HEALTH AND EVEN LIFE.—A FREQUENT SOURCE OF SUFFERING AND DISEASE IN A STATE OF SOCIETY.

ENVY and jealousy are closely allied in their nature, and are oftentimes used indiscriminately for the same mental feeling. The only distinction between these two contemptible passions, is, that jealousy is felt toward a competitor who is, or we apprehend is, rising to our own rank or condition, and likely therefore to interfere either with our present or anticipated fortunes and enjoyments; whereas envy is directed toward those who already, as we conceive, enjoy something more and better, as respects internal or external gifts, than belongs to ourselves. They are each, however, attended by corresponding effects, and as is true of all malignant feelings, become equally the authors of their own punishment, physical as well as moral. They are both secret and degrading passions, and when long and deeply indulged wear equally upon soul and body—prey like a hidden canker on the inmost sources of health and happiness. We may writhe and madden under, but dare not acknowledge the sting they infix in our bosom. "Saw of the soul" was fitly applied by an ancient writer to the wasting feeling of envy.

The manifestations of envy and jealousy, are witnessed even in infancy. "Envy," it has been said, "exerts its baneful effects on us even from our cradle. Children are observed to look sickly, and lose their flesh, if they see other children more indulged than themselves." "I have seen," says a French writer, "a jealous child, who was not yet able to speak a word, but who regarded another child who sucked with him, with a dejected countenance and an irritated eye." Esquirol observes that jealousy sometimes destroys all the delights of early life, and causes a true melancholy with delirium ; and that some children, jealous of the fondness and caresses of their mother, grow pale, emaciate, and die.* In children who are educated together, this feeling of jealousy will be constantly appearing, however anxiously they may strive to dissemble it. An indiscreet partiality on the part of parents or teachers is especially apt to awaken it, and may thus produce the most unhappy effects both on the mind and body of youth.

Dr. Zimmermann observes that there are many persons

---

* Treatise on Insanity.

in the world who really owe their diseases to the passion of
envy, and which diseases are the more dangerous, from their
cause being very often unknown. " The silent, melancholy air
we so often see in our patients, and the uneasiness and distress
that do so much harm in diseases, very often arise from no
other cause than a secret envy, which preys upon the heart,
and disturbs all the operations both of the mind and body."*

There is another form of jealousy beside that noticed, I
mean sexual jealousy; which, for the reason that it is often
blended with the pleasurable emotion of love, I shall class
under the mixed passions.

Shame consists in wounded pride or self-love, and presents itself in every degree, from that which passes away
with the transient blush it raises on the cheek, to the painful mortification of spirit, to the deep and terrible sense of
humiliation which prostrates all the energies of mind and
body, and renders life odious. Such extremes of mortified
pride, it is true, are not ordinarily included under the present passion, still if we carefully consider them, they will be
found to be legitimately reducible to it.

Shame, in its primary and most commonly observed operation, affects, in a striking manner, the circulation of the
extreme, or capillary vessels of the head and neck. Thus,
in many persons, no sooner is it felt than the blood flies to
the face, and not unusually to the neck and ears, suffusing
them with a crimson and burning blush. The eyes, too,
will oftentimes participate in it, and the vision in conse-

* On Experience in Physic.

quence, become partially and transiently obscured. This sudden flow of blood towards the parts mentioned, is not, as might at first seem, owing to any increase of the heart's action, but, in all ordinary cases, at least, is referrible to the immediate influence of the passion on this particular portion of the capillary circulation. Many of the other passions are also known to produce analogous local effects in the circulatory function.

Blushing takes place with remarkable facility in the young and sensitive, and in all persons of fair and delicate complexions, as in those of the sanguine temperament; and still more so if the nervous be ingrafted upon it, forming that compound temperament which has received the name of sanguineo-nervous. Here blushing will be constantly occurring, and on the most trivial occasions.

In certain disordered states of the system, owing probably to a morbid exaltation of the nervous sensibility, blushing happens far more readily than in sound health. In indigestion, for example, the face, under every little emotion, is liable to become flushed and heated.

Shame, when strongly excited, is productive of very striking phenomena, both in the mind and body. Under its sudden and aggravated influence, the memory fails, the thoughts grow confused, the sight becomes clouded, the tongue trips in its utterance, and the muscular motions are constrained and unnatural. Consider, for illustration, a bashful man making his entrance into an evening assembly. Every thing there appears to him in a maze. The lights dance and grow dim in his uncertain and suffused vision.

He perceives about him numerous individuals, but all seem mingled into one moving and indiscriminate mass. He hears voices, but they are indistinguishable, and convey no definite impressions to the mind. His face burns, his heart palpitates and flutters, and, his voluntary muscles but imperfectly obeying the will, he totters forward in the most painfully awkward manner, feeling as though all eyes were upon him, until reaching that transitorily important, and to him fearful personage, the mistress of the ceremony. He now bows like an automaton, or as if some sudden spasm had seized upon his muscles, and either says nothing—shame fixing his tongue, and sealing his lips—or if he makes out to speak, his voice is tremulous and agitated, and scarce knowing what he says, he stammers forth some most inapposite remark, just such, perhaps, as he should not have made,* and then, overwhelmed with confusion, staggers away, stumbling, perchance, over a chair or table, or running against some of the company, and is only relieved of his embarrassment on finding himself mixed with the promiscuous crowd. Now, the moral pain experienced under the circumstances described, is oftentimes of the most intense nature, and the abashed individual would be glad to transport himself to almost any other situation, and might prefer rather to face the cannon's mouth, than endure a repetition of such a distressing scene. Here, however, the pas-

---

* I remember a very sensible and well educated gentleman, who, at a wedding party, on paying his respects to the bride said, " I wish you many happy returns of this evening."

sion is, in most cases, but temporary in its operation, passing
off with the occasion that excited it. But sometimes the
individual continues to suffer under the effects of wounded
self-love ; remains nervous, agitated, unsocial and depressed
through the evening ; has no relish for the refreshments
before him, and even a disturbed and sleepless night may
follow. Such severe effects are more particularly apt to
ensue in those whose nervous sensibility is in excess, or in
the subjects of what we denominate the nervous temperament.

We witness, in a very obvious manner, the operation of
the passion I am noticing, in the intercourse between
the young-of the opposite sexes, some of whom, especially
such as have been educated in a retired manner, can hardly
look at, or speak to one another without blushing the deepest scarlet. May not this sudden rush of blood toward the
head also affect the brain, and thus aid in producing that
confusion of thought so remarkable in those under the present emotion ?

Shame, when habitually manifesting itself in the common intercourse with society, as we see it particularly in
the young, is denominated bashfulness, which occasions to
many persons, even through life, no trifling amount of inconvenience and suffering. There are those who can never
encounter the eye of another without becoming sensibly
confused. For the most part, however, this infirmity readily
wears off under frequent commerce with the world, and as
one extreme often follows another, the most bashful will not
rarely come to be the most bold-faced and shameless.

Bashfulness and modesty, although so frequently confounded, have yet no necessary connection or relationship, and either may exist without the presence of the other. The former, or shamefacedness, as it is often called, is a weakness not unfrequently belonging to the physical constitution, and of which every one would gladly be relieved. It may be a quality of those even who are most impure in their feelings, and, when unrestrained, most immodest in their conversation. Modesty, on the other hand, pertains especially to the mind, is the subject of education, and the brightest, indeed it may almost be said, the rarest gem that adorns the human character. That awkward diffidence so frequently met with in the young of both sexes, is of a nature often very little akin to modesty.

Shame, in its ordinary operation, is not a frequent source of ill health. It is generally too transient in its workings seriously to disturb the bodily functions. Under its severe action, however, headaches, indigestions, and nervous agitations are not of rare occurrence, and even insanity has sometimes followed its aggravated influence. Injured self-love, as is proved by the reports of various lunatic asylums, is by no means an unusual cause of mental alienation. A case is related on the authority of Baron Haller, where deep shame brought on a violent fever, followed by death, in a young female. "It is related," says Dr. Zimmermann, "of Diodorus Chronos, who was considered as the most subtile logician of the time of Ptolemy Soter, that Stilpo one day in the presence of the king proposed a question to him, to which he was unable to reply;

the king willing to cover him with shame, pronounced only
one part of his name and called him ovos, ass, instead of
Chronos. Diodorus was so much affected at this as to die
soon afterwards." Others have told the story a little differ-
ently, yet it appears from all authorities that he died of
shame from not being able to answer a puzzling question
put to him by the philosopher Stilpo. So painful is this
passion in its extreme degree, that to escape it, the guilty
mother is sometimes driven on, in opposition to the strongest instinct of her nature, to the murder of her own
offspring.

Sensitive young children more often suffer under this
passion of shame than has generally been considered.
When strongly impressed by it, they are apt to grow dull,
gloomy, sad; to lose their appetite, and become disordered
in their digestive organs. The effect on the appetite is, in
a particular manner, sudden and remarkable, so that any
child whose feelings are at all quick and delicate may easily
be shamed out of his dinner. To any family disgrace they
become early and keenly sensible, and their sufferings from
such source are more deep and painful than we are prone to
suspect; and especially when—as is most usually the case
—it is made the occasion of reproach and derision to them
by their companions.

The cruel practice of ridiculing the young, making them
the subject of contemptuous merriment, and more particularly of reproaching them with, or mocking their bodily
imperfections, cannot be too severely censured, not only as
deeply wounding their moral sensibilities, but as serving,

also, by an unavoidable consequence, to injure their physical
health. It is generally known that Lord Byron, even in his
earliest years, was most painfully sensitive to his lameness,
and we are told that,—" One of the most striking passages
in some memoranda which he has left of his early days, is
where, in speaking of his own sensitiveness on the subject
of his deformed foot, he described the feeling of horror and
humiliation that came over him when his mother, in one of
her fits of passion, called him a 'lame brat.' " Such an
expression will be acknowledged by all to have been unfeeling and injudicious in the extreme ; and yet how common
is it to hear parents upbraiding their children with those
infirmities of which they may be the unfortunate subjects,
thus awakening in their breasts the most poignant, and
oftentimes injurious sense of mortification, and causing
them to feel their unavoidable physical defects with all the
shame and vexation of some inflicted ignominy.

Some persons would seem to be naturally very susceptible to the passion under notice ; even the slightest causes
are sufficient to provoke it, and in such it becomes a frequent
source of suffering alike to mind and body.

As an agent in the moral discipline of the young, no
passion than that of shame is more frequently, and I may
add, perhaps, successfully brought into requisition ; but
even here it should be resorted to with a good deal of
prudence, or it may tend to crush, instead of correcting the
spirit, and thereby to repress the wholesome energies of the
constitution. A certain measure of self-esteem is a necessary stimulus equally to our mental and bodily functions,

and we should therefore be careful that this sentiment be not too much reduced by the counterworking of shame.

I have met with several instances where a morbid and more or less lasting redness of the skin, would often follow the passion in view. Thus, under its operation, a deep blush would spread itself over the face, extending perhaps to the neck, or even down the chest, and instead of passing off, as is usual, would remain to a greater or less extent, resembling a cutaneous inflammation, sometimes even for several days. These examples were witnessed in females of a delicate complexion, and mostly of a nervous temperament. Different eruptions upon the surface, and particularly those to which a predisposition may exist, will at times be produced by this same passion.

The different secretions may become affected through the agency of shame, as through that of the other painful passions. Dr. Carpenter remarks that the odoriferous secretion of the skin, which is much more powerful in some individuals than in others, is increased under the influence of bashfulness, as well as of certain other of the mental emotions.*

Under an aggravated sense of humiliation the mind experiences unutterable anguish, and the body cannot long remain unharmed. Insanity, convulsions, and even sudden death may be the melancholy result of such painful moral condition. What feeling can be imagined more overwhelming to the proud and lofty spirit, than that of deeply morti-

* Human Physiology.

fied self-love? Under its oppressive influence existence itself is felt to be a cruel burden. How many face death in the battle-field to save themselves from the shame of cowardice, or hazard their lives in single encounter to shun the like reproach, or to wipe, as they believe, some humiliating stain from their honor!

In a state of society, where mankind are necessarily exposed to so many, and oftentimes severe mortifications, and subject to such frequent and painful vicissitudes of fortune, the suffering and disease emanating from wounded pride can scarce be adequately estimated.

CHAPTER XXVI.

MIXED PASSIONS DEFINED.——SEXUAL JEALOUSY.——ITS MORBID
EFFECTS UPON MIND AND BODY.——BEARS A DIRECT PRO-
PORTION TO THE STRENGTH OF THE LOVE ON WHICH IT
IS BASED.——AVARICE.——THE PLEASURABLE AND PAINFUL
FEELINGS BELONGING TO IT.——EFFECTS ON THE PHYSICAL
SYSTEM.——INCREASES WITH AGE.

If we regard man in the spirit of unbiassed philosophy, we
shall find little of unmingled good either in his moral or
physical nature. Evil, in our limited view, would seem to
be absolutely provided for in his constitution. In the very
springs of his enjoyment, health, and life, flow also the
elements of suffering, disease, and dissolution. Consider
our appetites, the source of so much of human happiness, and so indispensable to our preservation both as
individuals and a species, and what a fearful sum of
sorrow, sickness, and death, shall we not find traceable to
them? Look at the law of inflammation! How curious
and wonderful appear the processes instituted by it for the
restoration of injuries, and how essentially requisite do we
find it to the safety and integrity of the vital fabric! And
yet out of this very law, the wisdom and benevolence of

whose final purpose have afforded so frequent a theme to the medical philosopher, will be found to originate the most agonizing and fatal maladies that afflict our race. Indeed, nature would seem to employ inflammation as her favorite agent in the violent destruction of human life.

Those passions now, with which we have been hitherto engaged, although brought under the classes of pleasurable and painful, yet seldom, if ever, can we expect to meet perfectly pure, or wholly unmingled with each other. Rarely, and perhaps I may say never, does it happen to us, under any circumstances, to be completely blessed, but the good we enjoy must constantly be purchased at the price of some evil.

> " Two urns by Jove's high throne have ever stood,
> The source of evil one, and one of good:
> From these the cup of mortal man he fills,
> Blessings to these, to those distributes ills;
> To most he mingles both . . . . .
> The happiest taste not happiness sincere,
> But find the cordial draught is dash'd with care."*

Scarcely indeed can even the most prosperous count upon a single moment of unsullied felicity. Or, supposing a passion to be in the first instance purely pleasurable, yet is it sure almost immediately to engender some other of an opposite shade, our very joys becoming the parents of our sorrows. The elation of hope alternates with the depression

* Iliad.

of fear, the delights of love beget the pangs of jealousy, and
out of even our happiest fortunes there will almost necessarily grow some apprehension of change.   Thus Othello,
when under the full fruition of all his heart's desires,
exclaims,

> " If it were now to die
> 'Twere now to be most happy ; for I *fear*,
> My soul hath her content so absolute,
> That not another comfort like to this
> Succeeds in unknown fate."

So, too, may it be said of our painful passions,—seldom
are they altogether unrelieved by those of a contrary
nature.   Through even the darkest night of the soul some
gladdening beams may penetrate.   Hope, at least, in our
very worst conditions, seldom entirely forsakes us.   Nature
diverts us with it amid the pains and disappointments of
life, as the mother soothes her child, under the bitter drug
or the surgeon's knife, by holding before it some gilded
trinket.   Although each day is betraying its futility, yet
does its false light continue to allure and cheer us, often
even to the hour of our dissolution.   We read in Eastern
allegory of a traveller, who in his flight from a dragon that
he discovered pursuing him, rushed over a fearful precipice;
but was hindered in his fall by seizing upon a slender twig.
Sustained by such weak and uncertain support,—the dragon
glaring upon him from above, the deadly abyss yawning for
him below,—looking upward he saw some tempting fruit,
when, forgetful of the impendent dangers, he plucked and

devoured it. And is it not oftentimes the same with us in life? With evils and dangers in pursuit, and terrors and destruction before, do we not,—held by the equally frail and treacherous support of hope,—continue to pluck, and feast ourselves with the joys of existence? Divested of the principle of hope, it is doubtful if the human race, with its present constitution, could possibly have been preserved. Even in the severest extremities, it still holds us to existence.

> " To be worst,
> The lowest, and most dejected thing of fortune,
> Stands still in esperance, lives not in fear."

It will be understood, then, that particular emotions are assigned to the classes pleasurable and painful, not that they are absolutely unmingled, but because pain or pleasure is their obviously predominant and striking feature. Now in this third class, or what we designate as mixed, both the happy and unhappy passions are distinctly blended, and each, even to the most superficial observation, is rendered plainly apparent.

The deleterious consequences, proceeding from the mixed emotions, will, it scarce need be said, have a direct relation to the preponderance of the unhappy feelings which enter into their constitution. And their operation may, furthermore, be greatly aggravated by sudden contrasts; adverse passions, when alternating or contending, always serving to heighten one another, and thus to produce the most agitating and dangerous effects. The fear, anger, and hate, for example, of sexual jealousy, are each enhanced by the love with which they alternate, or are so paradoxically united. Of the hazard of awakening in the mind disturbed by one strong emotion, another of an opposite character, I have before had occasion to speak. We can perceive, therefore, why it is that a knowledge of the very worst will generally be better borne than an anxious incertitude, under which the feelings are constantly tossed and racked by the painful struggles and oppositions of hope and fear.

We will proceed now to illustrate the mixed passions by a concise account of sexual jealousy, avarice, and ambition.

SEXUAL JEALOUSY, an exceedingly complicated passion, is based on the pleasurable emotion of love, and while this and hope continue blended in its constitution, it will properly come under the present division of mixed passions. But when these feelings have become extinguished, and despair, wounded self-love, hate, and a burning revenge, alone occupy the heart, then will its place be with the painful passions.

Sexual jealousy combining within itself a variety of contending emotions, as hope, fear, anger, suspicion, love, when extreme, few passions are more agitating and harassing, more blinding to the eye of common sense, more perversive of the judgment and moral feelings, or tend to more fearful results. Under its unhappy influence the appetite fails, the flesh wastes, the complexion grows sallow, often tinted with a greenish shade, and the sleep becomes broken, disturbed, painful, filled with all sorts of vague and dismal imaginings, and, in extravagant cases, is almost wholly interrupted. Well, therefore, might Iago exclaim, when he had raised in the breast of Othello a doubt of Desdemona's faith,

> "Not poppy, nor mandragora,
> Nor all the drowsy syrups of the world,
> Shall ever medicine thee to that sweet sleep
> Which thou ow'dst yesterday."

The nervous system also experiences violent perturbations, and even a state of frenzy sometimes supervenes, and life itself is jeoparded. That it becomes a not unfrequent cause of settled insanity, we have abundant evidence in the reports of the lunatic asylums of all countries. This species of jealousy calls up the most terrible and dangerous passions of the heart, and frequently leads to the most cruel and unnatural acts. It often turns even the gentlest nature into that of a fury, or demon. Let every one beware of it. Its breath sheds a deeper, a deadlier venom than that of the fabled dragon of old. If it once enters a dwelling, all peace, all joy, flee for ever before its baleful presence.

> "O, beware, my lord, of jealousy;
> It is the green-eyed monster, which doth mock
> The meat it feeds on. That cuckold lives in bliss,
> Who, certain of his fate, loves not his wronger;
> But, O, what damned minutes tells he o'er,
> Who dotes, yet doubts, suspects, yet strongly loves!"

Other things being the same, sexual jealousy will bear a direct proportion to the intensity of the love upon which it is based. It is where the latter emotion is deepest, that the former becomes most destructive. Hence may it be understood why the opposite sexes are so fond of exciting the feeling in question, by a thousand little artifices, in the breasts of each other, it being a test of their affection, and flattering, consequently, to that strongest of all sentiments, self-love.

AVARICE is another passion manifestly reducible to the class I am now examining. The pleasure of avarice consists in accumulating and hoarding up treasures; in computing and gloating over them; in a feeling of the power which they bestow; and, likewise, in the consciousness of the possession of the means, though there be no disposition to employ them for the purposes of enjoyment; and finally, it may be presumed, in the anticipation of future gratifications they are to purchase, since even in the most inveterate miser there is probably a sort of vague looking forward to the time when his superfluous stores will be brought into use, to administer, in some way, to the indulgence of his wants, and the consequent promotion of his happiness, although such a period never arrives.

The painful feelings mingled in avarice, are gloomy apprehensions for the safety of its treasures, with uneasy forebodings of exaggerated ills which would result from their privation. Hence, fear, suspicion, and anxiety, serve to counterbalance the pleasure arising from the contemplation and consciousness of possession of the soul's idol.

And then, in addition, there is the unhappiness accompanying every little expenditure, even for the common wants of life, — the misery, oftentimes truly distressing, of parting with even a fraction of that wealth to which the soul is so indissolubly bound.

There are numerous passions of a far more guilty character, and whose consequences to the individual and to society are vastly more pernicious, but few are there more despicable, more debasing, more destructive of every sentiment which refines and elevates our nature, than avarice. Nothing noble, nothing honorable can ever associate with the sordid slave of this unworthy feeling. It chills and degrades the spirit, freezes every generous affection, breaks every social relation, every tie of friendship and kindred, and renders the heart as dead to every human sympathy as the inanimate mass it worships. Gold is its friend, its mistress, its god.

In respect to the physical system, avarice lessens the healthful vigor of the heart, and reduces the energy of all the important functions of the economy. Under its noxious influence, the cheek turns pale, the skin becomes prematurely wrinkled, and the whole frame appears to contract, to meet, as it were, the littleness of its penurious soul. Nothing, in short, is expanded either in mind or body in the covetous man, but he seems to be constantly receding from all about him, and shrinking within the compass of his own mean and narrow spirit. He denies himself not merely the pleasures but the ordinary comforts of existence ; turns away from the bounties which nature has spread around him, and even

15*

starves himself in the midst of plenty, that he may feast his imagination on his useless hoards. The extent to which this sordid passion has in some instances reached, would appear almost incredible. An old writer tells of a miser, who, during a famine, sold a mouse for two hundred pence, and starved with the money in his pocket.

Avarice does not, like most other passions, diminish with the advance of life, but, on the contrary, seems disposed to acquire more and more strength in proportion as that term draws near when wealth can be of no more account than the dust to which the withered body is about to return. Old age and covetousness have become proverbially associated. Not unfrequently, indeed, will this sordid inclination remain active even to the end, outliving every other feeling, and gold be the last thing that can cheer the languid sight, or raise the palsied touch. Thus have we examples of misers who have died in the dark to save the cost of a candle. Fielding tells us of a miser who comforted himself on his death-bed " by making a crafty and advantageous bargain concerning his ensuing funeral, with an undertaker who had married his only child." I well remember an old man, who —having reached the extremity of his existence, and in a state of torpor and apathy to all around him—would almost always be aroused, and a gleam of interest be lighted up in his dim eye, by the jingling of money.

Even the sudden and most appalling aspect of death will not always banish this base sentiment from the heart. Thus, in cases of shipwreck, persons have so overloaded themselves with gold, as to sink at once under its heavy

pressure. In excavating Pompeii, a skeleton was found
with its bony fingers firmly clutched round a parcel of money. "When,"—says Dr. Brown, speaking of the miser,—
"when the relations, or other expectant heirs, gather around
his couch, not to comfort, nor even to seem to comfort, but
to await, in decent mimicry of solemn attendance, that moment which they rejoice to see approaching, the dying eye
can still send a jealous glance to the *coffer*, near which it
trembles to see, though it scarcely sees, so many human
forms assembled, and that feeling of jealous agony, which
follows, and outlasts the obscure vision of floating forms that
are scarcely remembered, is at once the last misery, and the
last consciousness of life."*

Although avarice can scarcely be set down as a very
prolific source of disease, still, the painful feelings mingling
with it when extravagant, must exercise a more or less morbid and depressing influence on the energies of life. The
countenance of the miser is almost uniformly pale and contracted, his body spare, and his temper prone to be gloomy,
irritable, and suspicious,—conditions rarely going with a
perfect and healthful action of the different bodily functions.
The miser is, moreover, especially as age advances, very apt
to fall into that diseased and painful state of the mind in
which the imagination is continually haunted by the distressing apprehension of future penury and want. This is
a variety of monomania, and .certainly a strange one, inasmuch as it almost always happens to those possessed of

* Philosophy of the Human Mind.

means in abundance to secure them against the remotest
prospect of such danger ; and usually, also, at an advanced
period of life, when, in the ordinary course of nature, wealth
must soon become valueless.

CHAPTER XXVII.

MIXED PASSIONS CONCLUDED. — AMBITION. — GENERAL CONSID-
ERATION OF IT. — ITS NATURE DEFINED. — EVILS GROWING
OUT OF IT WHEN INORDINATE. — THE PECULIAR POLITICAL,
AS WELL AS OTHER CIRCUMSTANCES OF THE AMERICAN
PEOPLE, CONTRIBUTE GREATLY TO THE GROWTH OF AMBI-
TION. — HEALTH AND HAPPINESS MOST OFTEN FOUND ASSO-
CIATED WITH THE GOLDEN MEAN.

AMBITION, although we are so constantly admonished of
its vanity and danger, would seem to acquire new force
— additional motives being offered to it — with the moral
and intellectual advancement of society. The moralist
who writes, and the preacher who declaims, against it,
could they rightly analyze the motives which actuate them,
would probably find this passion to be one of the most
efficient; — that their endeavors are often stimulated less
by a desire for the good, than the applause of mankind.
The busy efforts of philanthropy are oftentimes incited
mainly by the spur of ambition. Humility even, paradoxical as it may appear, will not unfrequently have its secret
sources in the same passion; and religion itself, stretching

its ambitious views beyond the present life, aspires to glorious distinctions in a world of spirits.

Ambition—such is its tenacity and power—will often
cling to, and buoy us up under the severest trials, amid
bodily sufferings of the most aggravated character, quitting
us only with the last conscious throb of our being. Nerved
by his desire of glory, the Indian endures without a murmur
all the most cunningly devised tortures of his enemies;
the martyr experiences the same animating influence amid
the fires which persecution has lighted for him ; and the
felon on the scaffold, while his confused vision wanders
over the assembled multitude below him, becomes stimulated by a hero's pride, and dies with a hero's fortitude.

With the evils and sufferings of ambition, both to individuals and society, every one must be familiar, for all
history is little else than a record of its enormities and
penalties. In its extreme degree it would appear to swallow up, or, at least, to render subservient to itself, all
other passions of the soul. It vanquishes even the fear
of death ; and love itself, however ardent, must submit
to its more potent sway   Nor can it be bounded by the
narrow limits of our existence, but there is an eager longing that our names and deeds may still live in the remembrance of posterity, when our forgotten bodies have returned to the elements whence they sprung.

" Of all the follies of the world," says Montaigne, " that
which is most universally received, is the solicitude for
reputation and glory, which we are fond of to that degree,
as to abandon riches, peace, life, and health, which are

effectual and substantial goods, to pursue this vain phantom, this mere echo, that has neither body nor hold to be taken of it. And of all the unreasonable humors of men, it seems that this continues longer, even with philosophers themselves, than any other, and that they have the most ado to disengage themselves from this, as the most resty and obstinate of all human follies." *

We may define ambition to be that anxious aspiration, so characteristic of the human species, to rise above our respective stations, or to attain to something loftier, and, as fancy pictures, better than what we now enjoy. It implies, therefore, dissatisfaction with the present, mingled, generally, with more or less elating anticipations for the future. Strictly speaking, it embraces emulation, or the desire which we all feel of a favorable estimation of self, when measured with our compeers. Pride and self-love, then, enter essentially into its constitution, and the rivalships and competitions which necessarily grow out of it, almost always lead to the painful feelings of envy and jealousy.

This passion, consisting, as it does, especially in the wish for superiority over our own particular class, or those with whom we are brought into more immediate comparison, must operate alike upon all ranks of society. Hence, servants pant for distinction above servants, just as kings do for pre-eminence over kings. And the tailor who excels all others of his craft in fitting a coat to a dandy's

* Essays.

back, may feel his ambition as highly gratified as the
proud statesman who has equally outstripped all his com-
petitors.

"Philosophy," says Doctor Paley, "smiles at the con-
tempt with which the rich and great speak of the petty
strifes and competitions of the poor; not reflecting that
these strifes and competitions are just as reasonable as
their own, and the pleasure which success affords, the
same." *

The aims of ambition will differ, and its aspects become
essentially modified, according to the temperament, education, and habits of its individual subjects, and the various
incidental circumstances under which they may chance to
exist. Thus, wealth, literary, political, and military fame,
or even mere brute strength,—in short, almost any thing
that can distinguish us from the crowd, may, under different influences, become the object of our aspirations. The
cynics, or dog-philosophers, while they ridiculed those who
were ambitious of wealth and worldly display, were themselves equally ostentatious of their poverty,—equally proud
of their filth and raggedness. Hence the remark of Socrates to the leader of this sect,—"Antisthenes, I see thy
vanity through the holes of thy coat." And Diogenes, so
distinguished among these currish philosophers, was probably as much the votary of ambition, while snarling in
his dirty tub, as Alexander, when directing his mighty
armies; and on making his celebrated reply to the friendly

* Moral Philosophy.

inquiry of the latter, who had condescended to visit him, "If there was any thing he could serve him in?" "Only stand out of my sunshine," felt, it is not unlikely, as much pride in his singularity and impudence, as did his illustrious and more courteous guest, in all the glory of his conquering power. Well, therefore, might the ambitious monarch exclaim,—"Were I not Alexander, I should wish to be Diogenes." And then, again, so much may the bent of ambition depend on adventitious circumstances, that he who, under some conditions, would pant to excel as a robber, might, under others, be full as eager for excellence as a saint.

> " The fiery soul abhorr'd in Catiline,
>   In Decius charms, in Curtius is divine ;
>   The same ambition can destroy or save,
>   And makes a patriot as it makes a knave."

Among the worst evils of inordinate ambition is its continual restlessness: its dissatisfaction with the present, and its implacable longings for the future. Honors are no sooner achieved than their vanity becomes apparent, and they are contemned, while those which are not possessed hold out the only promise of enjoyment. The ardor of love—and the same is true of most other strong passions—will be quenched, or at least weakened, by fruition ; but the appetite of ambition can never be satiated, feeding serves only to aggravate its hunger. No sooner, therefore, has the ambitious man gained one eminence, than another and yet loftier swells upon his view, and with fresh and more eager efforts and desires he strains forward to reach its summit. And so does he go on, surmounting height after height, still looking and laboring upward, until he has climbed to the utmost pinnacle. But alas! even here he meets but disappointment and unrest. The same ambitious cravings continue to haunt and agitate him, and, deprived of the cheering influence of hope, and the animating excitement attendant on the struggles of pursuit, he is even less content and less happy than on first starting in the race. He has been chasing, as he finds, a phantom; been laboring but to labor; has enjoyed no hour of pleasing respite, and has in the end, perhaps, found only a hell in the imaginary paradise he had framed to himself. Though the rich fruit has ever seemed to wave above him, and the refreshing stream to play before him, yet has he been doomed to an unceasing and a quenchless thirst.

It is certainly a great pity that we do not strive rather for a contented spirit,—to enjoy the good already in possession, instead of wasting ourselves in the pursuit of things which owe all their beauty to the distance at which they are removed from us.

Cineas, the friend and counsellor of Pyrrhus, king of Epirus, with a view to wean the latter from his ambitious designs on Italy, drew him artfully into the following conversation: "The Romans have the reputation of being excellent soldiers, and have the command of many warlike nations; if it please Heaven that we conquer them, what use, sir, shall we make of our victory?" "Cineas," replied the king, "your question answers itself. When the Romans are once subdued, there is no town, whether Greek or Barbarian, in all the country, that will dare oppose us; but we shall immediately be masters of all Italy, whose greatness, power and importance, no man knows better than you." Cineas having paused a moment, continued, "But after we have conquered Italy, what shall we do next, sir?" Pyrrhus, not yet perceiving his drift, replied, "There is Sicily very near, and stretches out her arms to receive us, a fruitful and populous island, and easy to be taken. For Agathocles was no sooner gone, than faction and anarchy prevailed among her cities, and every thing is kept in confusion by her turbulent demagogues." "What you say, my prince," returned Cineas, "is very probable; but is the taking of Sicily to conclude our expeditions?" "Far from it," answered Pyrrhus, "for if Heaven grant us success in this, that success shall only be the prelude to greater things. Who can forbear Lybia and Carthage, then within reach, which Agathocles, even when he fled in a clandestine manner from Syracuse, and crossed the sea with a few ships only, had almost made himself master of? And when we have made such conquests, who can pretend to say that any of our enemies, who are now so insolent, will think of resisting us?" "To be sure," said Cineas, "they will not; for it is clear that so much power will enable you to recover Macedonia, and to establish yourself uncontested sovereign of Greece. But when we have conquered all, what are we to do then?" "Why, then, my friend," said Pyrrhus, laughing, "we will take our ease, and drink and be merry." Cineas, having brought him thus far, replied, "And what hinders us from drinking and taking our ease now, when we have already those things in our hands, at which we propose to arrive through seas of blood, through infinite toils and dangers, through innumerable calamities, which we must both cause and suffer ?"*

The passion under notice, existing as it does, to a greater or less extent, in every human breast, would seem to be a necessary element in our moral constitution. Some, even, of the inferior animals, exhibit undeniable manifestations of its influence. It cannot, therefore, nor is it desirable that it should be altogether suppressed. When moderate, and wisely regulated, it may prove an agreeable and wholesome stimulus alike to the mental and physical economy, and contribute in various ways both to individual and social good.

It is when ambition is extravagant, and especially if it be at the same time ill-directed, that we witness all its pernicious effects on mind and body. He who has once surrendered himself to the thraldom of this passion, may bid farewell to that contentment and tranquillity of the soul, in which exist the purest elements of happiness. The heart thus enslaved will be ever agitated by the harassing contentions of hope and fear, and if success is unequal to the wishes and anticipations—and how seldom is it otherwise? —then come the noxious feelings of disappointment and regret ; humiliation, envy, jealousy, and frequently even despair, infusing their poison into all the healthful springs of life. The sallow and anxious brow, the dismal train of

* Plutarch's Lives.

dyspeptic and nervous symptoms, and the numerous affections of the heart and brain so often witnessed in the aspirants for literary, political, or professional fame, proceed not rarely from the painful workings of the passion under examination. And could we always trace out the secret causes of ill health and premature decay, disappointed ambition would probably be discovered to hold a far more prominent place among them than has hitherto been surmised. How few are adequate, either in their moral or physical strength, to bear up under the blighting of high-reaching expectations, and yet of how many is such the doom! In those, especially, of delicate and susceptive constitutions, the powers of life may soon yield to the disheartening influence of the painful mortification which is the inevitable consequence.

It is a mistake, I conceive, in our education, that the principle of ambition is so early and assiduously instilled into, and urged upon us as the grand moving power of our lives—that great men, not happy ones, are held up as patterns for our imitation. In truth, from the first dawning of our reasoning powers, there is a continued endeavor to nurture within us an aspiring, and consequently discontented spirit, and, by a strange contradiction, while the preacher and the moralist are constantly admonishing us of the vanity and danger of the pursuits of ambition.

The ambition, it may here be observed, which aims at moral excellence, or whose ends are generous and benevolent, serving to promote, instead of interfering with the success and advancement of others, and meeting, conse-

quently, but little opposition or rivalship, will enjoy a preponderance of the pleasurable feelings, and will therefore
be salutary in its effects alike on mind and body.

Our own peculiar circumstances as a people are especially favorable to the growth of ambition. Hardly as yet
emerged from our infancy, with a widely extended territory,
and an almost unparalleled national increase, with so much
to be accomplished, so much in anticipation, every one finds
some part to act; every one sees bright visions in the future, and every one therefore becomes inflated with a proud
sense of his individual importance. The field of advancement, moreover, is alike free to all, our democratical institutions inviting each citizen, however subordinate may be his
station, to join in the pursuit of whatever distinctions our
forms of society can bestow. Hence, as might be expected,
the demon of unrest, the luckless offspring of ambition,
haunts us all, agitating our breasts with discontent, and
racking us with the constant and wearing anxiety of what
we call *bettering* our condition. The servant is dissatisfied
as a servant; his heart is not in his vocation, but pants for
some other calling of a less humble sort. And so it is
through all other ranks—with the mechanic, the trader, the
professional man—all are equally restless, all are straining
for elevations beyond what they already enjoy; and thus do
we go on toiling anxiously in the chase, still hurrying forward toward some visionary goal, unmindful of the fruits
and flowers in our path, until death administers the only
sure opiate to our peaceless souls. That the people of every
country are, in a greater or less measure, the subjects of

ambition, and desirous in some way of advancing their fortunes, it is not our purpose to deny; yet, for the reasons stated, the foregoing remarks are particularly applicable to ourselves. These same political circumstances, too, which so conduce to the increase of ambition, render us extremely liable to great and sudden vicissitudes of fortune, which are always detrimental both to moral and physical health.

Mental occupation—some determinate and animating object of endeavor, is, as I have previously said, essential to the attainment of what we are all seeking—I mean happiness. Yet if the mind is not allowed its needful intervals of relaxation and recreation,—if its objects of desire are prosecuted with an unintermitting toil and anxiety, then will this great aim of our being assuredly fail us. Now, may it not reasonably be doubted if our own citizens, under their eager covetings for riches and preferment, under their exhausting and almost unrelieved confinement to business, do not mistake the true road to happiness? Absorbed in their ardent struggles for the means, do they not lose sight of their important ends? As a people we certainly exhibit but little of that quiet serenity of temper, which of all earthly blessings is the most to be desired.

When loitering in the streets of Naples I have contemplated the half-naked and houseless lazzaroni, basking in indolent content in the gay sunshine of their delicious climate, or devouring with eager gratification the scant and homely fare of uncertain charity, and watched their mirthful faces, and heard their merry laugh, and then in fancy have contrasted them with our own well-provided citizens, with their hurried step and care-worn countenances, or at their plenteous tables, dispatching their meals scarce chewed or even tasted—every where haunted by their restless and ambitious desires—I could not but ask myself, Are *we* really any nearer the great purpose of our existence than these heedless beggars in their "loop'd and window'd raggedness?" and when each have attained the final goal, is it impossible even that the latter may have actually had the advantage in the sum total of human enjoyment? The casual pains of cold and hunger which make up their chief suffering, will hardly compare with those which continually agitate the discontented breast.

To the force of the same passion, to the uneasy cravings of ambition is it that the rash speculations so common among us, and so destructive to peace of mind and health of body, are in a great measure to be ascribed. This commercial gambling—for such it may be rightly named—will oftentimes be even more widely ruinous in its consequences than that more humble sort to which our moral laws affix a penalty of so deep disgrace. For while the private gamester trusts to the fall of a die, or the turn of a card, but his own gold, the gambler on change risks on the hazards of the market, not what belongs to himself only, but, many times, the fortunes of those who had reposed their confidence in his integrity, and may thus involve in one common ruin whole circles of kindred and friends. And yet such are the ethics of social life, that whilst the latter is respected, courted, and elevated to high places, civil and religious, the former is shut out of all virtuous society.

No truth, perhaps, has been more generally enforced and admitted, both by ancient and modern wisdom, while none has received less regard in practice, than that happiness is equally removed from either extreme of fortune,—that health and enjoyment are most frequently found associated with the *aurea mediocritas*, the golden mean.

CHAPTER XXVIII.

An ill-regulated and unbridled imagination, united, as it always is, with strong and varying emotions, must be inimical to the health both of body and mind. In respect to their consequences, it is of little moment whether the passions have their incentive in the creations of fancy, or the sterner truths of reality.

"It was undoubtedly the intention of nature," says Professor Stewart, "that the objects of perception should produce much stronger impressions on the mind than its own operations. And, accordingly, they always do so, when proper care has been taken, in early life, to exercise the different principles of our constitution. But it is possible, by long habits of solitary reflection, to reverse this order of things, and to weaken the attention to sensible objects to so great a degree, as to leave the conduct almost wholly under the influence of imagination. Removed to a distance from society, and from the pursuits of life, when we have been long accustomed to converse with our own thoughts, and have found our activity gratified by intellectual exertions, which afford scope to all our powers and affections, without exposing us to the inconveniences resulting from the bustle of the world, we are apt to contract an unnatural predilection for meditation, and to lose all interest in external occurrences. In such a situation, too, the mind gradually loses that command which education, when properly conducted, gives it over the train of its ideas; till at length the most extravagant dreams of imagination acquire as powerful an influence in exciting all its passions, as if they were realities."*

There is a class of individuals always to be met with in society, who, unsatisfied with the tameness of real life, create for themselves new conditions, and please themselves with impossible delights in the worlds of imagination; who riot amid the false hopes and unnatural joys of entrancing day-dreams, till at last the unreal acquires absolute dominion over their minds—till wholesome truth is sacrificed to sickly mockeries:

" And nothing is,
But what is not."

* Philosophy of the Human Mind.

Such persons are apt to be characterized by a certain sentimental melancholy, mingled with a deep and romantic enthusiasm; by morbidly refined sensibilities; an impassioned and fervid, though often disorderly imagination; and are not unfrequently distinguished by brilliant mental endowments, particularly by a genius for poetry, whose license is to range at discretion through fancy's boundless and enchanting fields. They are prone, also, to become misanthropical and secluded in their feelings and habits.

There are few of us, indeed, even of the most sober imaginations, but must sometimes have experienced the ecstasy of revelling among the delights of the unreal; of forgetting our own dull and unsatisfying sphere, and indulging in dreams of unearthly felicity—dreams, alas! which must soon be dispelled bv some stern reality; leaving us, like the child who has been enrapt by some theatrical fairy show, only the more dissatisfied with our actual condition.

Of Rousseau, who affords a strong example of the unhealthy character of the imagination I am describing, and of the unhappy nervous infirmities which so constantly go with it, Madame de Staël says, " He dreamed rather than existed, and the events of his life might be said more properly to have passed in his mind than without him." Picturing his own morbid excess of sensibility, when at Vevay, on the banks of the Lake of Geneva, he says, " My heart rushed with ardor from my bosom into a thousand innocent felicities; melting to tenderness, I sighed and wept like a child. How frequently, stopping to indulge my feelings, and seating myself on a piece of broken rock, did I amuse myself with seeing my tears drop into the stream !"

The description which Byron has given of Manfred in his youth, was designed to be one of himself, and affords a true picture of the imaginative temper of mind with which we are engaged :

> " My spirit walk'd not with the souls of men,
> Nor look'd upon the earth with human eyes ;
> The thirst of their ambition was not mine ;
> The aim of their existence was not mine.
> My joys, my griefs, my passions, and my powers,
> Made me a stranger.   Though I wore the form,
> I had no sympathy with breathing flesh.
> My joy was in the wilderness—to breathe
> The difficult air of the iced mountain's top,
> Where the birds dare not build, nor insect's wing
> Flit o'er the herbless granite ; . . . . or
> To follow through the night the moving moon,
> The stars, and their development ; or catch
> The dazzling lightnings till my eyes grew dim ;
> Or to look listening on the scatter'd leaves,
> While autumn winds were at their evening song.
> These were my pastimes—and to be alone ;
> For if the beings, of whom I was one—
> Hating to be so—cross'd me in my path,
> I felt myself degraded back to them,
> And was all clay again."

Sir Walter Scott has given us, in the character of Wilfrid, in his poem of Rokeby, a well-drawn picture of this same imaginative temperament.

Such a disposition of the imagination may have its origin in a variety of causes : as native peculiarity of tempera-

ment, delicate health, injudicious education, habits of solitary
reflection, and in the young especially, will oftentimes be
the fruit of an extravagant indulgence in the works of fictitious narrative; too many of which abound in that mawkish
sentimentality, so peculiarly unfriendly to moral and intellectual health. It appears that Rousseau was, in his youth,
a great reader of novels. In sensitive and secluded individuals, this sort of reading, when carried to excess, has
sometimes so wrought upon and disturbed the fancy as to
bring on actual insanity. Esquirol refers the frequency of
insanity among the women of France, to the vices of their
education ; as the preference given to mere ornamental
acquirements, the reading of romances, which incites in the
mind a precocious activity and premature desires, with the
imagination of excellences never to be realized—the fre-
quenting of theatrical exhibitions, and society, and the abuse
of music. He records a number of cases of insanity which
were referred to the reading of romances. Erotic melancholy, or monomania, is the form of insanity most usual
from this cause. The history of the renowned Knight of
La Mancha is doubtless but an exaggerated picture of
cases of hallucination, which in those days were frequently
happening from the general passion for tales of chivalry and
romance. " The high-toned and marvellous stories," says
Dr. Good, "of La Morte d'Arthur, Guy of Warwick, Ama-
dis of Gaul, the Seven Champions of Christendom, and the
Mirror of Knighthood, the splendid and agitating alterna-
nations of magicians, enchanted castles, dragons and giants,
redoubtable combatants, imprisoned damsels, melting min-

strelsy, tilts and tournaments, and all the magnificent imagery of the same kind, that so peculiarly distinguished the reign of Elizabeth, became a very frequent source of permanent hallucination." *

The chivalrous spirit which followed the crusades greatly multiplied erotic melancholy. But as this form of mental aberration is apt to be associated with a disorderly and romantic imagination, and to be excited by an unreasonable indulgence in novel-reading, a few words of explanation in regard to it, will, I trust, not be deemed irrelevant to my present subject. Erotic monomania, or erotomania, as some writers have termed it, means literally love-madness. It is implied in common language by the terms *love-crazed*, or *love-cracked*. Love may consist in a sort of sentimental melancholy, which delights in solitude and soft reveries. Such does not reach insanity, although it oftentimes comes close upon its confines. Shakspeare, however, classes all lovers with lunatics.

> " The lunatic, the lover, and the poet,
> Are of imagination all compact:
> One sees more devils than vast hell can hold ;
> That is the madman : the lover, all as frantic,
> Sees Helen's beauty in a brow of Egypt."

But it is when the passion is so extravagant as to bring the judgment quite under its subjection, to absorb all

---

* Study of Medicine.

other feelings, that it becomes unquestionably a mental disease. The assertion is doubtless true, that nearly all forms of insanity have their primitive type in some of the passions; and erotic monomania is but the exaggeration or extremity of the passion of love.

Galen asserted love to be the occasion of the worst of both physical and moral disorders. The old, the young, the learned, the unlearned, the wise, and the foolish, are all exposed to its maddening influence. Sappho, for the love of Phaon, threw herself from the Leucadian promontory, so celebrated for lovers' leaps, into the sea. Tasso, Abelard and Heloise, Petrarch, and others of countless numbers, and of all conditions, have been the subjects, and many of them the victims of this monomania.

This insane love is sometimes felt for beings created by the imagination; and it has even fixed itself upon the beautiful productions of the sculptor. Alchidas, of Rhodes, became enamored of the Cupid of Praxiteles; and we have instances in more recent times, where the flame of love has been enkindled by the cold marble. Most usually, however, this sentiment, in all its shades, is felt for living flesh and blood, being either sudden, or of slower growth.

The subjects of erotic monomania, like other monomaniacs, have their thoughts and affections all centred upon a single object, and the more they are opposed, the more fixed and obstinate do they become. They are ready to abandon all that is dear in life, as friends, kindred, rank, fortune, social propriety, and even character itself, and to attempt the most hazardous and difficult acts, under the influence of their one controlling sentiment. Hope, fear, joy, rage, jealousy, may alternately, or together, agitate the breasts of these unfortunate beings. Or raving mania even may occasionally supervene, leading, in despair of obtaining the beloved object, to suicide, or homicide, and sometimes to both.

This form of monomania, however, is not always thus apparent, but strives to conceal itself through a deceptive guise, and then it becomes even the more dangerous and fatal in its consequences. Here its subjects grow sad, melancholy, silent; lose their appetite and complexion, emaciate, fall into a sort of hectic, ending perhaps in death. The following familiar lines of Shakspeare well depict this secret and wasting form of erotic melancholy:

> " She never told her love,
> But let concealment, like a worm i' the bud,
> Feed on her damask cheek: she pin'd in thought;
> And, with a green and yellow melancholy,
> She sat like patience on a monument,
> Smiling at grief."

Concealed erotic melancholy is not rare in those of delicate, susceptive and romantic natures, and whose education has been effeminate and voluptuous, and in such will sometimes prove fatal, either directly, or, what is more common, by exciting into action some other disease, as consumption, to which there had existed a prior disposition.*

* Esquirol, in his treatise on Insanity has described this love-

16*

Dr. Zimmermann tells us that love properly belongs to the melancholy passions, and says it "acts suddenly and with violence, because of all passions it is the most impatient, and the least susceptible of control; sometimes, however, it is more slow in its progress, and, like intense grief, gradually undermines the constitution. The more general effects of this tender passion are a tremulous pulse, deep sighs, an alternate glow and paleness of the cheeks, dejection, loss of appetite, a faltering speech, cold sweats, and watchfulness, which gradually terminate in consumption, or perhaps occasion insanity."*

The subjects of this morbidly refined and romantic imagination—to resume my principal topic—are generally characterized by strong and excitable feelings, but which are, for the most part, more ready to respond to ideal than real influences. Truth, in its naked guise, unpurified from the feculencies of the world, is too homely and offensive for such spiritualized beings. The squalid and unromantic beggar, perishing of cold or hunger in his wretched hovel, is an object quite too gross and disgusting to harmonize with their fastidious sensibilities. It is elegant, refined, and sentimental misery only, that can elicit their artificial sympathies. Their love, too—a passion to which, as I have before intimated, they are so exceedingly susceptible—discovers the same exquisite refinement, and is therefore most

madness, under the name of erotomania, and to his account of it, I have to acknowledge myself not a little indebted.

* On Experience in Physic.

apt to fix itself on some ideal model of beauty and excellence. Or should their affections become linked to a
carnal nature, such attachment will most commonly proceed
from the false coloring and bright associations with which
the imagination clothes it. Hence the well-known fickle-
ness and caprice of such persons, and their disappointment
with all veritable objects on familiarity, since all must fall
short of their high-wrought fictitious standards. Many a
poet, through his whole life, has remained constant in his
devotion to some peerless idol of his own beautiful imagination. How, indeed, can it be expected that one accustomed
to dwell on the pure and transcendental creations of a delicate and sublimated fancy, can contemplate with pleasure,
or, I may even say without disgust, the coarseness and
imperfection which so necessarily appertain to our earth-
born nature?

The feelings, unduly excited, as they always are, by
the wild dreams of the imagination, react with a morbid
influence on the various functions of the body, and if
the habits are at the same time sedentary and recluse, a
train of moral and physical infirmities, generalized under
the name of nervous temperament, will, in all likelihood,
be the result. The subjects of this unhappy temperament,
are commonly irresolute, capricious, and unnaturally sensitive in their feelings. Their passions, whether pleasurable or painful, are awakened with the greatest facility,
and the most trifling causes will often elate them with
hope, or sink them in despondency. A deep enthusiasm
generally marks their character, and they not unfrequently

display a high order of talent, and a nice and discriminating taste, yet mingled with all those uncomfortable eccentricities which are so apt to accompany superior endowments. The poet, the painter, the musician—for their pursuits have all a kindred nature, and all work on the feelings and imagination—are more especially the subjects of this peculiar temperament. The nervous sensibility of poets has been proverbial even from the remotest time, and it is therefore that they have been styled, genus irritabile vatum. "The occupations of a poet," says Dr. Currie in his life of Robert Burns, "are not calculated to strengthen the governing powers of the mind, or to weaken that sensibility which requires perpetual control, since it gives birth to the vehemence of passion, as well as to the higher powers of imagination. Unfortunately the favorite occupations of genius are calculated to increase all its peculiarities, to nourish that lofty pride which disdains the littleness of prudence and the restrictions of order ; and by indulgence to increase that sensibility, which, in the present form of our existence, is scarcely compatible with peace or happiness, even when accompanied with the choicest gifts of fortune."

The physical functions in this temperament are almost always weak, and pass very readily into disordered states. Its subjects are particularly liable to indigestion, and to sympathetic disturbances in the nervous, circulating, and respiratory systems. Thus, under sudden excitements, palpitations, flushings of the face, tremors, embarrassment in the respiration, with difficulty of speaking, are apt to occur, and even syncope or fainting will sometimes take place. The body, moreover, is generally spare and feeble, frequently with an inclination forwards; the face is pale and sickly, though, under excitement, readily assuming a hectic glow, and its expression is usually of a pensive character.

The most melancholy nervous affections, as epilepsy, for example, have sometimes been brought on through the workings of an unnaturally exalted and ungoverned imagination. And, in turn, the most enravishing conceits of fancy have at times been experienced while laboring under such disorders. It is in fits of epilepsy, and ecstatic trances, that religious enthusiasts have had their celestial visions, which their distempered minds have often converted into realities. The visits of the angel Gabriel to Mahomet, and the journey of this prophet through the seven heavens, under the guidance of the same angel, might not unlikely have taken place in some of the epileptic paroxysms, to which he is well known to have been subject.

The imagination, then, exercising so decided an influence on our moral feelings and conduct, and by a requisite consequence, on our health and happiness, we perceive how important it is that this faculty be wisely disciplined, or regulated according to the standard of nature,—that it be maintained in strict obedience to the judgment and will, and those delusive fancies in which the human mind is so prone to indulge, be carefully suppressed: since not only do they withdraw us from the rational ends and practical duties of life—thereby rendering us less useful both

to ourselves and to society—but tend also to break down
the physical energies, and prepare the constitution for the
ingress of disease, and for untimely dissolution. The mind,
as well as the body, let it be remembered, may be feasted
too voluptuously. The delights of a fantastic paradise
have little harmony with our present nature. The spirit,

> ——" whilst this muddy vesture of decay
> Doth grossly close it in,"

must forego the raptures of supernal visions, and accommo-
date itself to its material relations—to the circumstances
and necessities of its earthly dwelling-house.

We unfortunately meet with some writers, who, being
themselves the subjects of this fanciful temperament, would
persuade us to seek enjoyment in the cultivation of morbid
sensibilities, to the exclusion of the more wholesome realities of life. Thus, says that popular and exquisitely sentimental author, Zimmermann, "To suffer with so much
softness and tranquillity ; to indulge in tender sorrow without knowing why, and still to prefer retirement ; to love
the lonely margin of a limpid lake ; to wander alone upon
broken rocks, in deep caverns, in dreary forests ; to feel
no pleasure but in the sublime and beautiful of nature,
in those beauties which the world despise ; to desire the
company of only one other being to whom we may communicate the sensations of the soul, who would participate
in all our pleasures, and forget every thing else in the
universe ; this is a condition for which every young man

ought to wish, who wishes to fly from the merciless approaches of a cold, contentless old age." *

Among the best securities against this prejudicial ascendency of the fancy, and those uncomfortable nervous infirmities which so generally attend it, may be advised a life of active and regular employment, directed to some interesting object. It would seem, indeed, necessary to the health and contentment of the human mind, at least in its cultivated state, that it should be constantly actuated by some prominent and engaging motive,—by the feeling that existence has a determinate purpose. The subjection, also, of the impulses of the imagination to a wise restraint; and the strengthening of the judgment and powers of volition by the prosecution of the exact or demonstrative sciences, such as have truth for their great and ultimate aim ; and, in addition, all those means which tend to sustain and elevate the bodily health, and thus to impart vigor to the nervous system,—as pure air, muscular exercise, cold bathing, and temperance in its widest acceptation.

Finally, to guard ourselves from the aforenamed moral infirmities, and their concomitant physical ills, we should cultivate a contented spirit, confining our wishes and expectations within the limits of reason ; and especially striving against the morbid growth of ambition, which, when from the temperament, or other circumstances of the individual, it does not impel to active efforts for its gratifica-

* On Solitude.

tion, will cause the mind to be ever wandering amid vision-ary scenes of wealth and honor, and thus wholly disqualify it for its appointed sphere of action and enjoyments. Avoiding all eccentricities—keeping along in the beaten track of existence—pursuing with regularity, and a suita-ble degree of interest, the duties which belong to our sev-eral stations,—such is the course which would, probably, on the whole, be most conformable to physical and moral health, and enjoyment. The burs and briers of life are oftenest encountered when we wander from its trodden paths.

CHAP. XXIX.

GENERAL CONCLUSION.—THE INTELLECTUAL OPERATIONS A FAR
LESS FREQUENT OCCASION OF DISEASE THAN THE PASSIONS.—
EXAMPLES ILLUSTRATIVE OF THE INFLUENCE EXERCISED BY
THE MIND UPON THE BODILY FUNCTIONS.—CASE OF COL.
TOWNSHEND, WHO COULD DIE AND COME TO LIFE AGAIN
AT PLEASURE.—OUR PHYSICAL INTEREST DEMANDS A VIR-
TUOUS REGULATION OF THE MORAL FEELINGS.—SELF-RE-
LIANCE AND STRONG VOLITION ESSENTIAL TO THE PERFEC-
TION OF HEALTH AND CHARACTER.—MORAL EDUCATION OF
CHILDREN SHOULD BE EARLY COMMENCED.—DUTIES OF PA-
RENTS.—CONCLUDING REMARKS.

I HAVE maintained in the first part of this volume, that
the exercise of the intellectual functions, abstractly considered, does not tend, on a general principle, to favor disease,
or shorten life. Yet exceptions arise where simple intellectual labors are urged to an injurious degree. In the reports
of lunatic asylums we almost always find some of the cases
ascribed to excess of study. I am convinced, however, that
a larger share, both of mental and bodily ills, than rigorous
truth will warrant, is referred to immoderate exertion of the
intellect; the reasons of which error have been previously

explained. Thus, our intellectual efforts are, at the present day, almost always associated with those habits of life, as undue confinement, insufficient and irregular sleep, and other like incidental circumstances, which are well known to be detrimental to health. And furthermore, as knowledge is seldom pursued for its own sake, but for some ulterior advantage, either of fame, or pecuniary profit, mental labors are rarely unaccompanied with the workings, even the strong and painful workings of passion. Intellectual men, it must be admitted, are, either by nature or the force of circumstances, particularly prone to ambition, and are consequently exposed to those various evils and sufferings, already mentioned, which attend upon this passion when it becomes a ruling one in the human breast. If moderate and obedient to reason, and its aims guided by wisdom, it may, as I have previously said, serve as an incentive to call into useful and wholesome exertion the different powers of our nature; but when inordinate, as it is so apt to become, then will feelings of the most painful and destructive character unavoidably grow out of it.

Our own literary and scientific men, those of the learned professions, for example, will furnish ample illustration of the truth of the preceding remarks. How restless, often, and anxious, are their struggles in pursuit of a little ephemeral notoriety ! To what various expedients do we not see them resorting for the sake even of that brief and equivocal fame derived through the columns of the periodical press ? But, then, as the flattery of success may not always reward their endeavors ; as they may meet the shafts of censure where they looked for the blandishments of praise, frequently must the painful and noxious passions, born of defeated hope and wounded pride, such as anger, hate, jealousy, grief, humiliation, take possession of the soul, marring all life's moral peace, and calling forth a host of physical ills, as indigestions, nervous disorders, palpitations, and all sorts of irregularities of the heart's action, rendering existence burdenous, and shortening its term.

The intellectual exertions themselves, then, we rationally conclude, are less a source of evil than the incidental circumstances so commonly united with them; and that those mental labors are always the most harmless which have the least tendency to call forth deep and morbid feeling.

It is, however, to the moral feelings that we are to look for a strongly marked—an undeniable influence on the bodily functions; for this reason have we appropriated to their consideration so much the larger share of the present volume.

The mind is never agitated by any strong affection without a sensible change immediately ensuing in some one or more of the vital phenomena; and which, according to its nature, or the circumstances under which it occurs, may be either morbid or sanative in its effects, in the same manner as in the action of strictly physical agents—the various medicaments for example. Mental emotions, when curative, operate mostly, it is to be presumed, on the principle generally admitted in medical science called revulsion; that is, by calling forth new and ascendant actions in the animal

economy, they repress or destroy the distempered ones already existing. It is no more strange, then, that the passions should, through their influence on our physical organization, be capable of engendering or subduing morbid
phenomena, than that agents essentially material in their
nature should possess such power. We have instances on
record, where, by the simple effort of the will the heart's
action could be directly arrested, and restored again by the
same power of volition; in other words, where the individual could, to all appearance, die, and revive again at his
pleasure. One of the most remarkable and best authenticated examples of this direct power of the mind over the
vital functions, is that of the Hon. Colonel Townshend,
related by Dr. George Cheyne, which, as it may not be familiar to the general reader, I will venture to cite in the present connection.

Colonel Townshend, being affected with a nephritic complaint, was attended by Dr. Cheyne and Dr. Baynard. One
morning he sent early for his physicians to visit him, who
waited upon him with Mr. Skrine, his apothecary. "We
found," says Dr. Cheyne, " his senses clear, and his mind
calm ; his nurse and several servants were about him. He
had made his will and settled his affairs. He told us he
had sent for us to give him some account of an odd sensation he had for some time observed and felt in himself:
which was, that composing himself, he could die or expire
when he pleased, and yet by an effort, or somehow, he could
come to life again ; which it seems he had sometimes tried
before he had sent for us. We heard this with surprise,

but as it was not to be accounted for from now common principles, we could hardly believe the fact as he related it, much less give any account of it, unless he should please to make the experiment before us, which we were unwilling he should do, lest in his weak condition he might carry it too far. He continued to talk very distinctly and sensibly above a quarter of an hour about this (to him) surprising sensation, and insisted so much on our seeing the trial made that we were at last forced to comply. We all three felt his pulse first; it was distinct, though small and thready; and his heart had its usual beating. He composed himself on his back, and lay in a still posture some time; while I held his right hand, Dr. Baynard laid his hand on his heart, and Mr. Skrine held a clean looking-glass to his mouth. I found his pulse sink gradually, till at last I could not feel any, by the most exact and nice touch; Dr. Baynard could not feel the least motion in his heart, nor Mr. Skrine the least soil of breath on the bright mirror he held to his mouth; then each of us by turns examined his arm, heart, and breath, but could not, by the nicest scrutiny, discover the least symptom of life in him. We reasoned a long time about this odd appearance, as well as we could, and all of us, judging it inexplicable and unaccountable, and finding he still continued in that condition, we began to conclude that he had indeed carried the experiment too far, and at last were satisfied he was actually dead, and were just ready to leave him. This continued about half an hour, by nine o'clock in the morning, in autumn. As we were going away, we observed some motion about the body, and upon examination, found his pulse and the motion of his heart gradually returning : he began to breathe gently and speak softly : we were all astonished to the last degree at this unexpected change, and after some further conversation with him, and among ourselves, went away fully satisfied as to all the particulars of this fact, but confounded and puzzled, and not able to form any rational scheme that might account for it. He afterwards called for his attorney, added a codicil to his will, settled legacies on his servants, received the sacrament, and calmly and composedly expired about five or six o'clock that evening." *

Hundreds of instances might be adduced to prove the force of the imagination, or, more properly, of the moral feelings which it awakens, in altering and controlling physical actions. Such influence, it seems to me, was strikingly illustrated by the novel surgical operation which, some years since, excited so strong, though transient an interest, for the cure of stammering. The different operations that were tried in this country, for the removal of such imperfection, were acupuncturation, or the passage of several slender needles transversely through the tongue; the excision of a portion of the uvula, and also of the tonsils ; the division of the frænum of the tongue ; and, lastly, and the one most trusted to, the separation of the genio-hyo-glossus muscle at its origin from the lower jaw. I repeatedly witnessed the trial of each of these operations, and the sudden and surprising relief which usually followed. Stammerers of

---

* English Malady, p. 307 et seq. London : 1733.

the worst class, so soon as the operation was finished, would frequently talk and read with scarcely any, and, in some instances, not the slightest hesitation or embarrassment. In truth, the success of the experiment was, as I thought, most remarkable where the impediment was the greatest. Unfortunately, however, for the credit of experimental surgery, although some submitted to each of the operations, and even to their repetition, the benefit resulting was merely temporary, and in no instance that came within my knowledge, was there a decided and lasting cure. May we not, now, ascribe the remarkable effects of these bloody experiments chiefly, if not entirely, to the strong influence which they exercised upon the mental feelings ?

Dr. Paris in his Pharmacologia has recorded an instance related to him by Mr. Coleridge, strongly illustrative of the physical effects of the imagination. When the peculiar action of the exhilarating gas (protoxide of nitrogen, or nitrous oxide) upon the nervous system was first discovered, it was inferred by Dr. Beddoes that it must necessarily be a specific for palsy, and a patient was therefore selected for the trial, and the management of it intrusted to Sir Humphrey Davy. " Previous to the administration of the gas, he inserted a small pocket thermometer under the tongue of the patient, as he was accustomed to do on such occasions, to ascertain the degree of animal temperature, with a view to future comparison. The paralytic man, wholly ignorant of the nature of the process to which he was to submit, but deeply impressed, from the representation of Dr. Beddoes, with the certainty of its success, no

sooner felt the thermometer under his tongue than he concluded the talisman was in full operation, and in a burst of
enthusiasm declared that he already experienced the effect
of its benign influence throughout his whole body. The
opportunity was too tempting to be lost; Davy cast an in-
intelligent glance at Coleridge, and desired his patient to
renew his visit on the following day, when the same ceremony was performed, and repeated every succeeding day for
a fortnight, the patient gradually improving during that
period, when he was dismissed as cured, no other application having been used."

I have known persons from breathing atmospheric air,
under the impression that it was nitrous oxide, to experience
the same effects as though they had actually inhaled the
latter. Let one direct his attention strongly and exclusively to a particular part of the body, and an uncomfortable sensation will not rarely be felt in that part. It is
through the power of his fancy that the hypochondriac
suffers such various and changeful morbid sensations in
different portions of his frame. Chills and shuddering will
many times begin to be experienced on the bare thoughts of
an ague-fit through which one has recently passed. The
phenomena of mesmerism, the subjects of which have generally feeble wills, and great nervous susceptibility, are
doubtless often produced, like hysteria and other kindred
nervous disorders, through the influence of the imagination.

Having regard but to the laws of our present organization, it seems to me that no truth can be more plain than

that pure and well-regulated moral affections are essential to the greatest good of the whole animal economy,—that the turbulent and evil passions must necessarily corrupt the sources of our physical, moral, and intellectual health, and thus be followed by heavy penalties to the general constitution. Even our physical interest, separate from any other motive, demands the cultivation of the good, and the restraint of the evil passions of our nature.

"He," says an old medical writer, "who seriously resolves to preserve his health, must previously learn to conquer his passions, and keep them in absolute subjection to reason; for, let a man be ever so temperate in his diet, and regular in his exercise, yet still some unhappy passions, if indulged to excess, will prevail over all his regularity, and prevent the good effects of his temperance. It is necessary, therefore, that he should be upon his guard against an influence so destructive."*

Nor did this close connection between a virtuous regulation of the moral feelings and the health of the body, escape the observation of Doctor Franklin's sagacious intellect. "Virtue," says this sententious writer, "is the best preservative of health, as it prescribes temperance, and such a regulation of our passions as is most conducive to the well-being of the animal economy; so that it is, at the same time, the only true happiness of the mind, and the best means of preserving the health of the body."

* The History of Health, and the Art of Preserving it. By James Mackenzie, M. D., &c.

17

The ancient sages who wrote upon the philosophy of
health, dwelt especially on the importance of a prudent government of the affections.　Galen urged that the mind
should be early trained up in virtuous habits, particularly
in modesty and obedience, as the most summary method of
insuring the health of the body in future life.

It has been said, and truly said, that a soul which maintains a certain empire over the body it animates, may also
be of infinite use in preserving life and health.　It is self-
reliance, now, united with a strong will, that gives this dominion to the soul, and thereby contributes a wholesome
influence to all the functions of our being.　Were it required
of me to determine the mental qualities which should be
particularly fostered and strengthened, in reference to
health, happiness, and the force and perfection of human
character, I should name self-reliance and volition ; for if
these are feeble, weakness and effeminacy, moral and physical, are the almost unavoidable consequences.　But are they,
let me ask, sufficiently encouraged and enforced in the present times ?　Is it not according to the spirit of the age to
resign, in too great a measure, our own self-dependence, and
to blend and confound ourselves with the collective masses?
Have we a proper sense of our individuality ?　Do we not
act too much in the aggregate—live too much under the
direction of general ideas ?　It certainly appears to me
that in this age we do not rely enough on our particular
judgment and energies.　We fear to stand on our own independent footing, as units,—self-acting, self-thinking units.
We must have the support of authorities, of public senti-

ment; we must ascertain, not whether our thoughts and our acts are right or wrong, but whether they square with the opinions and conduct of the world. Foregoing our own individuality, we become dependent and subordinate parts of the aggregative body. "Amidst the progress of public liberty," as an eminent French writer has observed, "many seem to have lost the proud and invigorating sentiment of their own personal liberty." Such may have, and doubtless has had some advantages, yet it is not without its evils, opposed, as it must be, to the concentration of individual power—individual endeavors. Has any thing truly great, supremely excellent, ever been accomplished in the world,—has any really important discovery ever been made in the arts and sciences,—any master-works in literature ever been produced, unless mainly as the offspring of single minds? Newton discovered the laws of gravitation—wrote his Principia, not as one of a collective assembly, but by the force of his own unaided intellect. Bacon called in the assistance of no other mind in the composition of his Novum Organon. Harvey, of himself—not as one of a joint company, or convocation, or committee of a convocation—discovered the circulation of the blood. The unrivalled productions of Shakspeare were the outpourings of his own unhelped genius. And Franklin alone first drew the lightnings of heaven down to earth. And so do I believe that every thing of magnitude, every discovery that is destined to elevate man's nature, and man's condition, is to proceed from the strength of individual genius—individual intellect.

We should never learn to walk securely if we always leaned on others; we should never reach the fulness of our powers while we trusted to foreign aidance; and little could we ever bring to pass, if afraid to think and act for ourselves.

Let me here for a moment urge the importance of beginning early (it can scarce be commenced too early) the moral education of children. Every day that this is neglected will the baneful feelings of their nature be acquiring additional force and obstinacy. It is in their very germ, in the weakness of their birth, that these are to be successfully combated. We are, as previously alleged, the subjects of moral feeling, and therefore of moral discipline, at an age by far earlier that is usually imagined. That many children suffer in their health, and oftentimes to no slight extent, under the repeated and severe operation of passions which parents have neglected to reprove, is a truth too plain for contradiction. And not only have they to undergo present suffering from such unpardonable remissness, but not unfrequently does it become the cause of an afflictive train of infirmities, both of mind and body, in their future years; and experience, it may be of the most painful nature, must teach them to bring under control feelings which should have been repressed in the impotence of their origin. "We frequently," says Mr. Locke, "see parents, by humoring them when little, corrupt the principles of nature in their children, and wonder afterwards to taste the bitter waters when they themselves have poisoned the fountain."*

* On Education.

No duties or obligations have been more often or eloquently enforced both by the moralist and divine, than those
of the child to the parent ; and I would not say aught that
might serve in any degree to weaken their deep and binding
character. Still, it appears to me, that those due from the
parent to the child are really of a paramount nature, and
that more serious consequences will be hazarded by their
omission. Our parents bestow, or impose existence upon
us, and are therefore bound, in the most solemn duty, to
spare no sacrifice, to omit no efforts, which may contribute
to render that existence a blessing. If, through their culpable neglect and mismanagement, they entail upon us a host
of mental and bodily ills, we owe them little gratitude for
the life with which they have burdened us.

When we consider the carelessness and misjudgment so
often exhibited in the early training of the young—how
many children are literally educated by example, if not by
precept, to falsehood, hypocrisy, pusillanimity, and intemperance in its broadest sense ; in short, how many moral
and physical vices are allowed to ingraft themselves in the
constitution even in the dawn of its development, we are led
almost to wonder that human nature does not grow up even
more corrupt than we actually find it.

In concluding the present volume I would again urge
the high importance, to the whole living economy, at all
periods of our existence, of a prudent government of the
moral constitution. Man, unrestrained by discipline, or
abandoned to the turbulence of unbridled passion, is
pitiable and degraded indeed. The fountains of his health

and enjoyment are corrupted, and all that is comely and
elevated in his nature marred and debased. His whole life,
in short, becomes but a succession of painful mental and
physical strugglings and commotions,—a torment equally
to himself and all around him.

> " Of all God's workes, which doe this worlde adorne,
>   There is no one more faire and excellent,
>   Than is man's body both for powre and forme,
>   Whiles it is kept in sober government ;
>   But none than it more fowle and indecent,
>   Distempred though misrule and passions bace."

But although the passions appointed to us, are so prolific
of evil—so fruitful a source of disease, sorrow, and ignominy—yet fortunately they are the subjects of education,
and, as when uncontrolled they become the bane and reproach of our nature, under a wise restraint and watchful
culture they may be rendered our richest blessing and
fairest ornament.

E N D .

HINTS

FOR THE YOUNG

IN RELATION TO THE

HEALTH OF BODY AND MIND.

Fourth Stereotype Edition.

BOSTON:
GEORGE W. LIGHT, 1 CORNHILL.
1840.

NOTE.

A PART of the matter now published in the following pages, appeared in the Boston Medical and Surgical Journal, in 1835. The papers, in this way, had an extensive circulation among medical men, and they were written originally for professional gentlemen only. Other benevolent individuals, however, read them, and they were copied into newspapers, and thus reached many persons in the community. Since that time the writer has been frequently solicited to publish them in a more popular form, or to prepare something appropriate on the subject, and give it extensive circulation among parents, teachers and youth, to prove a PREVENTIVE as well as a CURE.

That the evil is wide spread and exceedingly injurious to the young, cannot be denied, or doubted. Its effects upon physical strength and constitutional stamina, are very prejudicial

Its influence in prostrating the mind is no less appalling. Consumptions, spinal distortions, weak and painful eyes, weak stomachs, nervous headaches, and a host of other diseases, mark its influence upon the one—loss of memory and the power of application, insanity and idiotism, show its devastating effects upon the other.

It is equally opposed to moral purity and mental vigor. It keeps up the influence of unhallowed desires ;—it gives the passions an ascendency in the character—fills the mind with lewd and corrupt images, and transforms its victim to a filthy and disgusting reptile.

The evil is common ; its danger little known. Let the young beware of it, and those who are in the way of danger, abandon it forever !

HINTS FOR THE YOUNG.

CHAPTER I.

It can hardly be said that the attention of parents, teachers, or even the members of the medical profession, is duly awakened to the dangers which arise from the habit of Masturbation. Even at this time many doubt the expediency of bringing the subject before the public in any form, believing that diffusing information may be the cause of greater evil to the young, than the benefits which may arise from a knowledge of those dangers to all.— Those who hold to these opinions are hardly aware how extensively known the habit is with the young, and how early in life it is sometimes practised. I have never conversed with a lad of twelve years of age who did not know all about the practice, and understand the language commonly used to describe it. It is certainly

1*

quite too common an opinion, that it is safe and
harmless, and may be indulged with impunity
to a certain extent. Till recently, I had supposed that this view of masturbation was confined to the ignorant and vulgar only; lately,
however, I have seen a prescription from a physician of some reputation, in a case of spontaneous emission of semen, in which he directs
that the patient practise it twice a week as a
means of cure! Supposing that the patient
might have some doubt of the propriety of the
remedy, he proceeds to urge him to the practice
as affording the surest mode of relief! Religious principles, conscientious scruples, and
the common sense of the patient, led him to
very different views of his case; he was not
ready to resort to a practice for a *cure,* which
he well knew to be the *cause* of all his affliction.
By pursuing a course quite opposite to the one
recommended, he is, in all respects, improving;
he has the satisfaction of preserving both his
health and moral purity—a consideration of no
small value to the virtuous mind.

If the apprehension of physical evil is not
sufficient to deter from a practice fraught with
so disastrous effects, the conscientious scruples,
and religious principles of every virtuous youth

should be awakened to deter him from the practice, or lead him to abandon it in future.

It is a vice which excites, to the greatest activity, the strongest and most incontrollable propensities of animal nature; and these are rendered more active by indulgence, while the power of resistance and restraint is lessened by it in a tenfold degree. The moral sensibility becomes so blunted as to retain no ascendency in the character, to control and regulate the conduct. Under such circumstances, the best resolutions to reform, and the firmest determination to abandon the habit, fail of accomplishment. In spite of himself, the victim sinks deeper and deeper in pollution, till he is overwhelmed at last in irretrievable ruin and disgrace.

Can a practice be innocent which so prostrates all the powers of body and mind, which corrupts the very fountain of moral virtue, and entails imperfection and imbecility on unborn generations?

From the hand of God himself we receive the noble attributes which distinguish us from the animals around us. This vice reduces us below their level. To Him are we responsible for this abuse of faculties which are given us to improve and to cultivate for our own happiness and that of our fellow creatures. We cannot, with impunity, violate the laws of our being. This organic law of our formation, is imperative and abiding—no abuse of it will go unpunished—suffering will follow, if it be not scrupulously obeyed.

The propensity which leads to the evil in question, is ever active, and perhaps more frequently leads the young astray than any other; it should, therefore, be more effectually restrained and more carefully controlled. Indulgence, instead of giving relief to its excitement, always increases it. Just in proportion to the gratification, will be the increase of desire. This is true of all the animal appetites and feelings.

There would be the same propriety in directing the intemperate man to resort to spirituous liquors to remove the appetite which his habit had created, as to recommend self-pollution to remove any symptom of disease which had previously arisen from it, or which had, in any other manner, become excited.

To those who doubt the corporeal or mental suffering from indulgence in this vice, I would commend the perusal of the following letter :

DEAR SIR :—Nothing but my deplorable situation would induce me to trespass upon your mind and patience in this esoteric manner. I am well aware that I ought to apologize for thus obtruding myself upon your notice, but I am equally confident that if you could realize the full extent of my misery, you would deem no other apology necessary. Trusting, therefore, in your well known sympathy and benevolence, I have ventured to lay before you my real condition, hoping that if it be in your power to relieve me, you will afford me the benefit of your medical skill and experience.

From the age of fourteen till within two years past, (I am now twenty-three,) I indulged in the frequent habit of self-pollution, like too many others, unconscious of the evil I was bringing upon myself. During this period I was occasionally subject to involuntary emissions, but not so often as to cause any alarm, till about two years since, when the occurrence became so frequent as to cause me much uneasiness. I was then led to reflect seriously upon my course, and to read on the subject, and resolved to abstain from my vile practice. This resolution had often been made before, but had as often been violated ; for the strength of the habit of

masturbation is such as none can estimate who
has never been under its overpowering influence. At last, however, I was enabled to conquer it—but alas! too late—I was held an unwilling captive. The spontaneous emissions of
semen still continued, and have occurred almost
every night since that time, and sometimes
twice in the same night, and even sometimes
when running for a short distance, or in riding.
Having endured so long under this blighting,
withering curse, my constitution, naturally *very*
strong, is broken down, and my mind, as well
as body, completely enervated. I am haunted
day and night with lascivious thoughts and
dreams; suspicious of my friends and disgusted
with myself. My memory has lost its power—
unable to fix my attention—my mind is filled
with terrible forebodings—fear of insanity, and
at times it has cost me a continual effort to retain my reason. It is with difficulty that I walk,
or stand, or even sit erect. An inclination to
lie down and sleep, which desire I am sensible
I have indulged too much:—my sleep never re-
freshes me;—I rise in the morning weak and
weary, to drag out another miserable day. O
how often have I wished for death, or rather oblivion, or any thing to terminate my woes. I

have of late been much annoyed with constant little twitchings or spasms in various parts of my body, and frequently in my face. Sometimes, however, they are so violent as to affect the whole limb with a sudden convulsion.

But more particularly my right eye is rapidly failing; whether the disease be the cataract or amaurosis, I am at a loss to decide; it seems to have some of the peculiar characteristics of both. About two years ago I first noticed several small spots or bubbles floating before my eyes; these have gradually become larger and more numerous, until my eye-sight is very much clouded. These "cobwebs" constantly floating before my eyes when I read, or walk, or look, annoy me excessively, and should they continue to increase at this rate, it cannot be many months before the result will be total loss of vision. My eyes, particularly in the morning, are affected with a burning sensation, which renders it almost impossible for me to use them for several minutes after rising—they seem to be full of sand;—the light is very oppressive;— I usually keep the blind closed to my room at all times of the day.

I am confident this disease of the eyes is the direct result of my venereal complaint, although

a very respectable physician, to whom I stated
my case about a year since, laughed at the idea
of there being any connection between the two.
With this exception I have suffered in silence,
not knowing where to go for advice or assistance.   I am now alone in this city—away from
home, and in fact I am alone in the world—
none to whom I dare communicate the cause of
my distress, although I fear at times that my
friends suspect it or something worse.   Various
reasons have conspired to prevent me from
seeking medical aid :—the want of money to
pay their charges—shame for my situation—a
hope of recovery without the expense, which I
can poorly afford ; for I am without funds except a small salary I am, for the present, receiving, and am in debt for my academical education, which I completed not long since at one
of the New England colleges.   I am looking
forward to the profession of ——— O, I cannot
name it, vile and guilty as I am.   *Would to
God I had known what I now know when first
tempted to this life, health and soul-destroying
vice.*   I feel that I cannot hold out much longer,
either mentally or physically.   I have dieted
myself—abstaining for a while from all animal
food—then giving up tea and coffee.   I experi-

enced no benefit from the change, and resumed them. I have tried violent and moderate and no exercise, (the last of which is altogether more congenial to my feelings, although not to my natural temperament.) I have, for a few weeks past, been making use of Port wine; but nothing seems to affect my disease. I have not, it is true, pursued any regular systematic course of regimen, for I have not known what to do. A few days since, I read a little tract on this subject, written, I believe, by you; but I find nothing in it *particularly* adapted to my case. If your experience in such unhappy cases can suggest any thing, do, sir, have pity on me. Can you give me any *particular* advice as to medicine, diet, and exercise, &c.? What shall I do for my eyes?

Can you direct me to any physician in this city, from whose experience and skill I might hope for assistance? Had I better apply to an oculist, or will it do no good to doctor for my eyes, while my health is in such a state?

If you condescend to notice this, do, dear sir, answer it as soon as your convenience will allow. I am expecting to leave town in about a fortnight, to be absent for several weeks, and if I could hear from you before leaving, it would

2

be esteemed a great favor, and ever be gratefully
remembered by an obliged sufferer.

———   ———

"*Would to God I had known what I now
know, when first tempted to pursue this life,
health and soul-destroying vice,*" is the emphatic
language of this unhappy sufferer, whose physical distress, great as it is, is far less than his
mental anguish. Such is the language of almost
every young man, who seeks relief from his
medical adviser from the disastrous consequences of indulgence in this evil habit. Is not
this an effectual answer to the caviller who
would never teach the young the danger of this
vicious indulgence? I have never yet found
the youth who did not commence this vice
ignorant of its consequences, and even of its
moral turpitude. I have rarely found one who
retained his reason who did not abandon it on
being admonished of its danger. Many an
individual, when insane, has been so impressed
and satisfied of its impropriety and sinfulness,
as to abandon it, and recover ; while hundreds
on whom moral influence could make no impression, go on recklessly to the ruin of mind
and body.

Much experience has taught me that this is an important and necessary subject of education; that information should be diffused upon it; that the young should be admonished, and the whole community enlightened, so that no one shall himself suffer or witness the ravages of the vice upon those around him, without being able to detect it, and avoid it before it be too late.

A hint from a parent who understands the case, may be sufficient. A tract extensively circulated, may do much good as a preventive and a cure, before serious injury is done to health or intellect. In schools of all grades, and manufactories, indeed, in all places where the young are congregated, they should sleep in separate beds, understand the danger of the least indulgence in this vice, and scrupulously avoid every thing which shall tend to it. Lascivious books, pictures, company and conversation should be discarded. I am constrained to believe that the fondling of young persons, the embrace of individuals of the same sex or different sexes, and many of the familiarities which the custom of society admit, while they may be entirely innocent in a thousand cases, awaken propensities in others which should lead to their universal abandonment. I am aware that these views may be considered extravagant and absurd. I can only say that facts, numerous and incontrovertible, coming to my knowledge almost daily, impress me most forcibly of their truth. The propensities should never be educated ; they are always active and easily excited, and require the constant restraints of the moral and intellectual powers, or they gain too much ascendency in the character, and too much influence over the conduct. Whatever circumstances resulting from the intercourse of the young shall awaken to increased activity these feelings of our nature, should be scrupulously avoided.

Nothing can be more commendable in the young, or more approved in the sight of our Maker, than purity of character and high moral influence. Nothing can be more debasing in itself, nothing more repugnant to the pure feelings of uncorrupted youth, nothing more wicked in the sight of Him whose purity is as transcendent as his power is infinite, than those vicious practices which blot out the intellect, debase the moral feelings, blast the rising hopes, and prostrate the physical energies which God has given to man, to elevate him in the scale of being, fit him for usefulness in this life, and immortal happiness hereafter.

CHAPTER II.

THE pernicious and debasing practice of masturbation is a more common and extensive evil with youth of both sexes, than is usually supposed. The influence of this habit upon both mind and body, severe as it has been considered, and greatly as it has been deprecated, is altogether more prejudicial than the public, and, as it is believed, even the medical profession, are aware.

It is perhaps as common with persons of apparently fair moral character, as with the openly vicious. Such persons are often surprised that it should be considered a vice, or a cause of disease, having supposed it quite harmless.

The indications by which parents and friends may be led to suspect this vice, are ill health, especially debility, paleness, with a downcast look, and a disposition to retirement and seclusion, a jealousy and suspicion of those in whom they used to place confidence, and who were former associates and friends. In the progress

2*

of the disease, the victim of it becomes apprehensive that friends dislike and avoid him, that
he is the subject of ridicule and censure, and is
an object of inspection, marked by every one
who comes into his presence, or passes by him
in his walks.   Hence he retires from society,
and chooses to be alone—while alone he sometimes talks to himself, and often laughs much
and frequently, and sometimes aloud.

A great number of the evils which come upon
the young at and after the age of puberty, arise
from this habit, persisted in, so as to waste the
vital energies and enervate the physical and
mental powers of man,   Nor less does it sap
the foundation of moral principles, and blast
the first budding of manly and honorable feelings which were exhibiting themselves in the
opening character of the young.

Many of the weaknesses commonly attributed
to growth and the changes in the habit by the
important transformation from adolescence to
manhood, are justly referable to this practice.

This change requires all the energy of the
system, greatly increased as it is at this period
of life, which, if undisturbed, will bring about
a vigorous and healthy condition of both the
mental and physical powers.

If masturbation be commenced at this period, it cannot fail to interrupt, essentially, this important process; and if continued, will inevitably impress imbecility on the constitution, not less apparent in the body than the mind, preventing, as it will not fail to do, the full development of the powers of both.

The individual becomes feeble, is unable to labor with accustomed vigor, or to apply his mind to study ; his step is tardy and weak, he is dull, irresolute, engages in his sports with less energy than usual, and avoids social intercourse; when at rest, he instinctively assumes a lolling or recumbent posture; and if at labor or at his games, takes every opportunity to lie down or set in a bent or curved position. The cause of these infirmities is *often* unknown to the subject of them, and *more generally* to the friends; and to labor, or study, or growth, is attributed all the evils which arise from the practice of this secret vice, which, if persisted in, will hardly fail to result in irremediable disease or hopeless idiocy. The natural consequence of indulgence in this, as in most other vices, is an increased propensity to pursue it. This is particularly true of masturbation. In my intercourse with this unfortunate class of individuals, I have

found a large proportion of them wholly ignorant of the cause of their complaints; and if not
too far gone, the abandonment of the habit has,
after a while, removed all symptoms, and resulted
in confirmed health.

One young man now under my care, was first
arrested in his career by reading the chapters
on this subject in the Young Man's Guide. For
many months he has totally abstained from the
practice, and yet he is feeble, depressed, irresolute, and unable to fix his attention to any subject, or to pursue any active employment. But
he is steadily convalescing, and will doubtless
recover.

If the symptoms above enumerated do not
lead to apprehensions of danger, and are not
followed by a discontinuance of the habit, other
symptoms, more formidable, and more difficult
of cure, will present themselves. The back becomes lame and weak, the limbs tremble, the
digestion is disturbed, and costiveness or diarrhœa, or an alternation of them, takes place.
The head becomes painful, the heart palpitates, the respiration is easily hurried, the
mind is depressed and gloomy, the temper becomes irritable, the sleep disturbed, and is
attended with lascivious dreams, and not un-

frequently nocturnal pollutions. With these symptoms the pulse becomes small, the extremities cold and damp; the countenance is downcast, the eye without natural lustre; shamefacedness is apparent, as if the unfortunate victim was conscious of his degraded condition.

The stomach often rejects food, and is affected with acidity and loathing; the nervous system becomes highly irritable; neuralgia, tabes dorsalis, pulmonary consumption, or fatal marasmus, terminate the suffering, or else insanity and deplorable idiocy are the fatal result. Long before such an event, the mind is enfeebled, the memory impaired, and the power of fixing the attention lost. These are symptoms which should awaken our attention to the danger of the case, and which should induce us to sound the alarm, and, if possible, arrest the victim from the inevitable consequences of persisting in the habit.

There seems to be a strong influence from this secret vice upon the eyes. A learned professor informed me that he had never seen a case of *gutta serrena* that was not attributable to this practice, or excessive indulgence of the sexual propensity. Weak eyes, and particularly neuralgia of the eyes, or a pain in the eyes without apparent inflammation or local disease, probably often arise from it. I recently saw a cataract forming in both the eyes of a young female, whose general health had been greatly impaired by self-pollution.

The following extract of a letter dated Aug. 22, 1838, from a young man who has for some months past had a distressing pain of the *eyes* and *head*, which has made him a great sufferer, and almost incapacitated him for business, shows the influence of self-pollution, and the evils which result from it in producing these diseases.

" When I was between *thirteen* and *fourteen* years of age, and I do not know but between *eleven* and *twelve*, I think, however, it is the latter, I was induced by a young man with whom I slept, to follow the practice of masturbation, though not without some threats on his part, and indeed was forced to by him. After a while I needed neither forcing nor threatening, but did it voluntarily from three to twelve times a week, till I was between seventeen and eighteen, when I became convinced it was sinful, and abandoned it ; and never, to my knowledge, have practised it since, no, not even once, as I made it a matter of conscience ; but I have had the spontaneous or involuntary emissions, and the nocturnal pollution more or less ever since, especially in lascivious dreams; and sometimes in female company, the involuntary emissions have troubled me greatly. For years, I never harbored the thought that it was injuring my health; but since my eyes have troubled me, which is between two and three years, I have sometimes thought it might be owing to this cause. I am now about twenty-one years of age."

In females, leucorrhœa or fluor albus is often induced by masturbation, and I doubt not incontinence of the urine, stranguary, prolapsus uteri, and many other diseases, both local and general, which have been attributed to other causes.

It is often difficult to obtain information on the subject of masturbation. Where it is suspected by the physician, the friends are wholly ignorant of it, and the individual suffering is not ready to acknowledge a practice which he is often conscious is filthy in the extreme, although he may have had no suspicions of its deleterious influence upon his health.

It is not sufficient that we know the consequences of masturbation, for these are often

irremediable disease; we ought to know the
symptoms of its commencement, of the incipient stages of those diseases which result from
it, as well as the influence of the moderate practice of it upon the physical and mental stamina
of the man—for it is not too much to say, that
the practice cannot be followed by either sex,
even in a moderate way, without injury.

Nature designs that this drain upon the system should be reserved to mature age, and even
then that it be made but sparingly. Sturdy
manhood, in all its vigor, loses its energy and
bends under the too frequent expenditure of
this important secretion ; and no age or condition will protect a man from the danger of un-
limited indulgence, legally and naturally exercised.

In the young, however, its influence is much
more seriously felt; and even those who have
indulged so cautiously as not to break down
the health and the mind, cannot know how
much their physical energy, mental vigor, and
moral sensibility have been affected by the
indulgence.

*Nothing short of total abstinence from the
practice can save those who have become the victims of it.* In this indulgence, no half way

course will ever subdue the disease, or remove the effect of the habit from the system. Total abstinence is the only remedy. If the constitution is not fatally impaired—if organic disease has not already taken place, this remedy will prove effectual, and must be adopted, especially in all cases in which the effects are visible, or the consequences cannot fail to be ultimately fatal.

This means of cure may be seconded by others, which may be found necessary to remove the effects of the habit upon the physical system. Suffice it to remark here, that total abstinence, in an aggravated form of masturbation, is not easily effected. Slight irritation will produce an expenditure of the secretion quite involuntary, and spontaneous emissions and nocturnal pollution may, for a long time, prolong the danger, and prevent that renovation of the powers which would otherwise be the result of the good resolution of the victim of the habit.

In a subsequent chapter we may consider the influence of masturbation upon the mind, as a cause of insanity and idiocy, and suggest some remedies for the removal of its effects upon the health.

3

CHAPTER III.

No cause is more influential in producing insanity, and in a special manner perpetuating the disease, than masturbation. The records of the institutions give an appalling catalogue of cases attributed to this cause; and yet such records do not show nearly all the cases which are justly ascribable to it. For it is so obscure, and so secret in its operation, that the friends in almost all cases are wholly ignorant of it. It is in a few cases, only, where the practice of the vice becomes shamefully notorious, that friends are willing to allow its agency in the production of any disease, particularly insanity; and yet no cause operates more directly upon the mind and the feeling. The mental energies are prostrated by the habit in innumerable cases, long before the delusions of insanity appear. Indeed, there are many cases in which insanity does not intervene between the incipient stages of that mental and physical imbecility, which comes early upon the victim of masturbation, and the most deplorable and hopeless idiocy, in which it frequently results.

This is perhaps peculiar to this cause of idiocy. I know of no other which does not produce the ravings and illusions of insanity, or the gloomy musings, agitations and alarms of melancholy, before the mind is lost in idiotism. But the victim of masturbation passes from one degree of imbecility to another, till all the powers of the system, mental, physical and moral, are blotted out forever.

This is not, however, always the case. In some individuals there is all the ravings of the most furious mania, or the deep and cruel torture of hapless melancholy, before the mind is obliterated, and the energies of the system forever prostrated.

False hearing is often one of the first symptoms of insanity from this cause. The jealousy which had marked the character and conduct previously, now becomes greatly increased, and the suspicion of being the subject of remark and ridicule, is confirmed by hearing voices, opprobrious accusations and censure, which confirm all former belief, and establish the truth of what was before only suspicion. With the jealousy and apprehension which had previously

existed, the illusions always coincide, and some
individual, often a female for whom there has
been some attachment, becomes the object of
particular suspicion. Her voice is heard in
every direction—her image presents itself in his
dreams. In his reveries, which are frequent, he
sometimes suspects that all around him, or particular individuals, know his thoughts. He
hears them utter, as they move about, what was
passing at the same instant of time in his mind.

There are circumstances attending the insanity from masturbation, which renders this
the most distressing form of mental disease. I
allude to the difficulty of breaking up the habit
while laboring under this malady. When insanity is once produced by it, it is nearly hopeless, because the cause of disease is redoubled
and generally perpetuated. The libidinous desires are generally increased, and the influence
of self-restraint cannot be brought sufficiently
into action to prevent the constant, daily, and I
might say almost hourly recurrence of the practice. Thus the cause is perpetuated ; and in
spite of every effort, the disease increases, the
powers of body and mind fail together, and are
lost in the most deplorable, hopeless, disgusting
fatuity ! And yet the practice is not abandoned

All the remaining energies of animal life seem to be concentrated in these organs, and all the remaining power of gratification left, is in the exercise of this no longer secret, but loathsome and beastly habit.

Those cases of insanity arising from other known causes, in which masturbation is a symptom, are rendered more hopeless by this circumstance. It is a counteracting influence to all the means of cure employed, either moral or medicinal; and coinciding as it does with whatever other causes may have had an agency in producing disease, renders the case almost hopeless. Of the number of the insane that have come under the observation of the writer, (and that number is not small,) few, very few have recovered, who have been in the habit of this evil practice; and still fewer, I might say almost none, have recovered, in which insanity or idiocy has followed the train of symptoms enumerated in a former chapter, indicating the presence of the habit, and its debilitating influence upon the minds and bodies of the young.

Most of the cases of insanity from this cause, commence early in life; even confirmed and hopeless idiocy has been the melancholy con-

3

sequence, before the victim had reached his twentieth year.

Of eighty males, insane, that have come under the observation of the writer, and who have been particularly examined and watched, with reference to ascertaining the proportion that practised masturbation, something more than a quarter were found to practise it; and in about ten per cent., a large proportion of which are idiotic, the disease is supposed to have arisen from this cause.

The proportion is probably somewhat less in the other sex.

On a former occasion I observed that the absolute abandonment of the practice, even in those whose minds were unaffected by insanity, was not easily effected. If no *voluntary* practice is continued, the habit may be so far established, and the susceptibility to the complaint be so great, that slight irritation will produce it, and that often for a long time after the danger is appreciated, and the victory over the propensity achieved so far as cautiously avoiding known and intentional indulgence. Nocturnal pollution and involuntary emissions come from slight causes and trifling irritation, but perpetuate, for a long time, all the train of unhappy

influences that have been heretofore detailed.
The unfortunate subject of this detestable vice,
whose mental energy is unimpaired, and whose
moral feelings are susceptible of impression,
can be persuaded to abandon it, if the danger
is set before him in its true light; but hundreds
can bear me testimony, that the effects of it are
long felt, and the involuntary excitement produced by dreams, lascivious companions, warm
beds, and improper intercourse with corrupt
society, has for a long time had its influence
in retarding complete recovery to health. With
the insane we can have no such hopes, and no
such prospects of cure. They will rarely form
resolutions on the subject, and still more rarely
adhere to them. Reason, the balance wheel of
the mind, being denied them, they are obnoxious to the influence of all the propensities in a
high degree.

After the practice of masturbation as a voluntary habit is entirely suspended, long and persevering efforts will be required to remove the
effects from the system, and restore it to vigor
and soundness. The individual himself must
exercise great self-denial, and resolve to persevere with the means and overcome all obstacles
that may be in his way, however formidable and

difficult. The regimen to be adopted must be strictly adhered to on all occasions. As the inebriate would probably never conquer his appetite for alcoholic drink if he indulged once a month only—so in this habit, the occasional ind lgence will thwart the whole plan of cure. The diet should be simple and nutritious; the exercise should be moderate and gentle; indulgence in bed should not be allowed, and the individual should always sleep alone. A mattrass is better than a soft bed. He should rise immediately upon waking, and never retire till the disposition to sleep comes strongly upon him. The cold bath is a valuable remedy; a sea bath is better, and the shower bath is often superior to either.

CHAPTER IV.

AVOIDING, as I intended, all consultation of authors on the diseases which follow masturbation, I shall only detail cases which have come under my own observation, and remedies of which I have seen the good effects. I commenced by remarking that the symptoms attending the early indulgence of the habit can always be cured, if the practice be wholly discontinued. From the apprehension that the cause of these symptoms is often overlooked by the best physicians, it is conceived that the history of the first impression of the habit upon health and intellect is of the greatest importance. Whenever, therefore, a train of symptoms, such as was described in a former paper, takes place at a time of life most obnoxious to the injurious influences of masturbation, the cause not being apparent, the patient should be closely questioned as to this habit; and but too often, the whole mystery of the cause, so long unknown to the patient, parent and physician, will be developed.

Case 1. A respectable young gentleman, of one of the learned professions, was out of health for a long period; his head and eyes suffered exceedingly, and he was in a state little short of insanity. He placed himself under the care of one of the most eminent men in the metropolis, and followed his prescriptions a year, but without benefit. He then called upon another, who asked him if he was addicted to masturbation, to which he answered in the affirmative. The advice given him was principally to abstain from the indulgence, and his health gradually improved, and is now re-established.

Case 2. D., aged 20, had ill health for a year or more; he was pale, feeble, nervous—lost his resolution—had no appetite—took to his bed much of the time, and became dull, almost speechless, and wholly abstracted and melancholy. His brother was his physician; but not ascertaining the cause of the symptoms, he gained no advantage over the disease, and the unhappy young man was constantly losing strength and flesh. After a while he came under the care of the writer. He was in the most miserable condition conceivable; emaciated, feeble, pallid—had night sweats, diarrhœa, or costiveness, total loathing of all food; his heart beat, his head was painful, and he felt no desire, and would make no effort to live. Suspecting masturbation, I found, upon strict inquiry and watching, that my suspicions were well founded. I pointed out the danger of the practice, assured him that it was the cause of all his sufferings, and that he might be restored to usefulness and health again, if he would strictly adhere to the course prescribed for him. He took bark and iron alternately for a long time, pursued a course of gentle exercise and invigorating diet, and gave up at once the vicious indulgence. After a long time he wholly recovered, and is now a healthy and valuable citizen.

Case 3. W., aged 27, called for advice in the summer of 1834, having had ill health for some eighteen months or two years. He complained of confusion in the head and pain in the eyes, indigestion, palpitation of the heart, and difficulty of respiration. His sleep was disturbed, his temper irritable, and he felt dissatisfied with himself, and greatly inclined to gloom and melancholy. He complained of listlessness and indisposition to any bodily efforts, and of inability to fix his mind upon any sub-

ject, or give his attention to any business. His
hands were cold, countenance pale and dejected, pulse frequent, and his whole system in
a state of great irritation. It was ascertained
that for two or three years he had been in the
daily habit of masturbation. For eight or nine
months past he has discontinued it; he is, however, occasionally subject to nocturnal emission, which had thus interfered with his recovery; but he is better, and under the use of
tonic remedies, exercise and generous diet,
feels confident of recovery, having gained his
spirits and appetite.

Case 4. F., aged 20, was for a long time in
the habit of masturbation. He was for years
confined to the house, and much of the time to
his bed. By long indulgence, the habit had
become irresistible, and the consequences truly
deplorable. His mind was as fickle and capricious as that of an infant, and his health
wholly prostrated. For five or six years he was
the most wretched being imaginable. Nocturnal pollution, spontaneous emission, and all the
evils resulting from unrestrained indulgence,
were presented in this truly unhappy young
man. He had been apprised of the danger
which the continued practice would bring upon

him, and was sensible that all his trials had
their origin in this vice; and yet the propensity
had become so strong that he could not resist
it; and if he did, the consequence had become
such that little benefit was derived from his
good resolution.   In his intercourse with his
friends he was covered with shame and confusion, and seemed to feel conscious that every
individual he met with knew, as well as himself,
the height and depth of his degradation.   In this
condition, in a fit of desperation, he attempted
to emasculate himself, but succeeded in removing one testicle only.   After he recovered from
the dangerous wound which he inflicted, he began to get better; and after two years he recovered his health and spirits.   He has since, at
the age of 45, *married* a very clever woman,
and they live in peace and harmony.

Case 5.   W., a young man 20 years of age,
had been feeble and dejected for two years.
He was pale, torpid, irresolute, and shamefaced
in the extreme—so much so, that I could not
catch his eye during a sitting of an hour.   He
complained of his head, of short breathing and
palpitation of the heart, and of extreme debility.
His extremities were cold and damp, his muscular system remarkably flabby, and his snail-

4

like motions evinced great loss of muscular
strength. His father, who accompanied the
young man, said that he had consulted many
physicians without benefit. The moment that
he came into my room, I was strongly impressed
that he was the victim of this solitary vice.
I questioned him some time without ascertaining the cause of the disease. His father was
wholly ignorant, and the physicians had not
suspected it, or inquired concerning it. I requested a private interview—told him the danger
of such habits, the importance of ascertaining
the true cause of disease, and my suspicions
that he was in this habit, and that if so, he
would fall a victim to its influence. He then
acknowledged that he was in the daily practice
of masturbation, and had been for three years—
that he often also had spontaneous emissions,
&c. He had never suspected that it had any
influence upon his health. This young man
afterwards became insane and idiotic. He is
now a most disgusting, filthy idiot, and will
probably never recover.

The symptoms which follow masturbation,
viz., nocturnal pollution and spontaneous emission, often continue after the victim of the vice
is made sensible of the danger of voluntary

indulgence. These require distinct and separate consideration. In some cases they become very obstinate; and in spite of every effort, continue to make such a waste of vital energies as to prevent a recovery of the health—and the new form of disease continuing, the same fatal results follow which took place from a continuance of the habit. The local irritability of the organs of generation often becomes so great, that the ordinary evacuations of the bowels and bladder produce an emission; and even lascivious ideas, riding on horseback, or other equally slight irritations, have the same effect. Such cases require the utmost care to afford any chance of recovery.

In such cases, the regimen must be strict, the diet should be simple and nutritious, and sufficient in quantity; it should be rather plain than light and abstemious; no stimulating condiments should be used, the suppers should be particularly light, and late suppers should be wholly avoided.

All stimulating drinks, even strong tea and coffee, should be discarded; cider and wine are very pernicious—tobacco in all its forms not less so.

The exercise should be such as to induce

the most quiet repose, and never so great as to produce exhaustion and such fatigue as to prevent quiet rest.

Labor is the best exercise, and if it can be in the open air it will be most beneficial. If in self-pollution or spontaneous emission, the patient be reduced beyond the power to labor, the case is little less than hopeless. Every care should be taken to make the sleep quiet and undisturbed.

A mattrass is indispensable ; feathers must always be avoided. The hours allotted to sleep should be short, and the patient should never retire till quite sleepy, and should rise on waking, let the time be ever so short. If it be too early to dress and go to business, he should throw open his bed, walk his chamber, and thus insure quiet sleep again when he resumes his bed. Dreams almost always attend spontaneous emissions ; these are only avoided by promoting quiet sleep. Light suppers greatly conduce to this. All excitements should be avoided in the evening, especially such company and conversation as is calculated to excite the propensities upon which this evil so greatly depends. If this course is not effectual to remove the habit, and the circumstances of the patient will admit of it, marriage should be the next step. On this remedy I rely with great confidence, believing it indispensable to the cure when other means fail. It is proper, always, under such circumstances, to consult a physician who has given his attention to the subject. This little manual is not designed to direct remedies or supersede medical advice—its object is admonitory and not remedial; there are remedies that promise much in cases like the foregoing; they must be presented in each case by those who have made the disease a study, and know the condition of the system in which they can be used with propriety and safety. To the writers of the following letters I recommended marriage.

DEAR SIR:—I have been laboring for four or five years past under a disease which has caused me much concern, but which, hitherto, has baffled all my efforts at removal. I am subject to nocturnal emissions of semen, which have occurred without the least interval two or three times every night for several years past. The cause of these emissions was removed long ago. I have had recourse at various times during this period to the advice of many

4*

physicians, and have tried the remedies which they proposed, but all to no purpose. I have reduced my diet—living mostly on vegetables— exercised much in the open air—used the cold bath and friction of the skin—have taken tincture of iron—have taken astringent pills, camphor, &c., and have carefully avoided every excitement and irritation, mental and physical; but all in vain. I am at present, with only this exception, in perfectly good health—but this is the bane of my existence; and if there are any means whatever by which I can rid my constitution of this curse, I am extremely anxious to know them. If as soon as convenient you will favor me with a line upon my case, you will very much oblige,   Yours, &c.

Eleventh mo. 5th, '37.

Esteemed Friend :—Nothing but self-diffidence, arising from a consideration of the character of the person I am about to address, has for some time prevented me from indulging the desire to do so, since the ends to be answered thereby are not only to add another to the innumerable lessons of human nature and human misery with which the life of a physician so much abounds, and to afford to a sufferer the

consolation of unbosoming himself, and of dis-
closing the evils which he has brought upon
himself, and which nothing but the interposition
of a Divine Providence can remove, but also
to afford an opportunity of acknowledging the
attention thou hast bestowed upon him. For
my first acquaintance with thee I am indebted
to ——, whose kindness and ingenuous conduct
towards me I can never forget while I have the
recollection of any thing. But the conscious
ness of having done all in your power must be
your reward, as you cannot have the satisfaction
of witnessing a successful effect of your exer
tions. My complaint refuses to yield to the
most skilful treatment or the most efficacious
remedies.

All that I suspected or anticipated when I
last saw thee, has since been realized; and
having been repeatedly defeated, have neither
faith or hope to make farther attempts. I am
resigned to my fate, and entertain no saddening
reflections on the past, or anxious thoughts for
the future. There is, however, one consideration so entwined about the heart that it can
never be obliterated while it continues to throb,
that is, the relation which necessarily exists
between me and the respectable family to which

I belong, and the obligations I owe to my
parents, who have passed the allotted age of
man, and who need that attention which they
could expect only from a son. But another and
the greatest end I can hope to effect is, to prevent others from following my footsteps to ruin.
This I think would be accomplished if thou
could be prevailed on to write a book on the
subject, and thus pour into the bosom of national youth that knowledge which would prevent its thousands, and tens of thousands, from
reposing ignorantly and innocently under the
seemingly safe but destructive shade of the
Bohon Upas of Onanism, which is like the lap
of Delilah, in which the mighty Samson slumbered and was shorn of his power. A physician, necessarily so familiar with distress, is not
susceptible of the sympathy which one of my
situation must feel for his fellows, but thou
very well knowest, that if the sordid practice to
which I allude does not destroy both the physical and mental powers of all who come under
its influeuce, it is because they are both originally strong. It must at least relax and weaken
the most robust body and vigorous intellect.

Thou hast doubtless already suspected who I
am from the description of my case; and as my

name is unknown to thee, the addition of it
will be useless. And as I must conclude as
abruptly as I began, I trust that, should I exhibit a confidence unbecoming the occasion,
thy benevolence will not fail to ascribe it to the
ardor of my feelings.

In haste, but with due respect, I subscribe
myself,   Thy friend.

Let me not be misunderstood; I do not recommend marriage to the masturbator; by no
means. If he has not strength of principle to
abandon the practice after he has learned its evil
consequences, he should be doomed to perpetual
celibacy, and not contaminate offspring with
his moral pollution and physical imbecility. I
have no advice for him but to abandon his evil
practices and abstain from the degrading sin.

To those who may have been led astray in
youth, and when informed of the danger and
satisfied of the sinfulness of the practice have
abandoned it, but have suffered from spontaneous emissions afterwards, I have, if other means
fail, recommended marriage. I speak of it as
a *remedy*, only. In all instances in which I
have known of such advice being followed, the
remedy has been effectual.

CHAPTER V.

THE following cases are added to those published in the Journal.

Case 6. When on a journey in a neighboring state, I was consulted in the case of a young gentleman of education, who is now a member of one of the learned professions. He had passed reputably through his college course, and proved a ready scholar in his profession—a gay, social, agreeable young man. He was not successful in business, and returned and secluded himself. From this time his character was changed;—he became shy, suspicious and reserved; apprehended that his presence annoyed every person with whom he associated; he retired almost wholly from the observation of the public, and shut himself up in his father's house; he was even jealous of some members of his own family. In one instance he was persuaded to attempt teaching—in a week his resolution failed him; and although he appeared competent and ready as a teacher, and was popular with the school, yet he abandoned his charge. He had lost his self-respect, and he believed that he was the subject of jest and ridicule of all his acquaintances. At this time his friends consulted me in his case. I saw and conversed with him;—his condition was most unhappy; timid and irresolute in the extreme, he had no confidence in himself, and none in his friends and mankind. I inquired if he was not in the practice of masturbation. He did not admit it, but rather evaded the question. I gave him a general caution on the subject, prescribed diet and regimen for him, but little or no medicine. When I returned from my journey, I found a letter from him of a full sheet, and afterwards received another, acknowledging that he was a victim of this practice, and that it was doubtless the cause of all his calamities. In a few months he became insane, and went into one of the institutions in New England. He became exceedingly imbecile, both in mind and body. After some months he improved; but when I last heard from him, he was far from well, and gave very little promise of ever being useful.

Case 7. A young man, a graduate of one of the New England Colleges, commenced this

practice early in life. While in college, he
pursued it to so great a degree, as to bring upon
him all the nervousness, irritability of temper,
and suspicion of associates which characterizes
the aggravated effects of this pernicious habit.
After he left college, he commenced the study
of a profession, but made little progress, and
finally abandoned it. Since that time he became decidedly insane ; he was for a time violent and dangerous. I was consulted by his
friends, and suggested to them the probable
cause of all his difficulties. Upon investigation,
it was found that he had pursued the course
before alluded to, and was still in the practice
to an extent quite uncommon. In this state he
came under my care. He was the most shamefaced and degraded looking human being conceivable ; it was next to impossible to catch his
eye ; he stooped and walked as tottering as a
man of ninety. So conscious did he seem of
his degraded state, that he covered his head in
his coat, drawing it over his head, and remaining in this situation the whole day, and almost
constantly for the many weeks that he was
under my care.

Fully satisfied in this as in all such cases,
that medication is of no avail without moral

influence, I made unusual effort to excite in his mind self-respect, and some ambition to be useful and active in life. It was all in vain; he declared that he would never abandon the practice—and he never did. This is a most melancholy case; a young man of respectability, of good education, of respectable connexions, of fine talents, reduced to a condition of the utmost degradation, probably wholly in consequence of the want of admonition from some friend who understood his difficulty, at a time when such an effort would have had its influence upon him.

Case 8. About two years ago, a young woman, aged 22 years, came under my care, in a state of the worst form of insanity. She was furious, noisy, filthy, and apparently nearly reduced to idiocy. She had been in this condition many months, and continued so for some time while with me. She was pale and bloodless, had but little appetite, frequently rejected her food, and was reduced in flesh and strength. Finding her one day more calm than usual, I hinted to her the subject of masturbation, and informed her that if she practised it she could not get well—if she abandoned it, she might. She did not deny the charge, and promised to

5

follow my advice strictly. In two or three
weeks from this time, she was perceptibly better ; her mind improved as her health gained ;
and both were much better in the course of a
few weeks. The recovery was very rapid in
this case. At the end of six months she had
excellent health, was quite fleshy, and became
perfectly sane, and has continued so, as far as
we have known, to this time.

Case 9. In the spring of 1837, I was consulted by the father of a young woman who
had, for four years, been in the worst possible
condition of health. She had consulted many
eminent physicians, who had prescribed remedies and regimen for her without benefit. On
first seeing the patient, I was impressed that
the cause of her illness had not been understood, which had rendered all remedies unavailing. Upon inquiring of the patient, I found
that she had been the victim of self-pollution.
I cautioned her to abandon the practice, prescribed some remedies, and saw her no more.

More than a year from the time of seeing
her, I heard directly from her parents, who sent
me word that she had entirely recovered her
health and energy of mind, and that my prescriptions had entirely cured her.

Case 10. Not long since a case of periodical insanity came under my observation, the subject of which was a young lady. The disease had existed ten years without any material change. Suspecting that masturbation was the cause, I directed her mother to ascertain, if possible, and inform me. Some months after, I received intelligence that my patient was better, and that my suspicions of the habit were confirmed by the observation of her friends; the case is not without hope, although so long standing, if the cause is removed.

Three or four similar cases have been under my care recently, in which individuals of the same sex have been reduced to the same degraded state. They are now, and will continue to be while life remains, a melancholy spectacle of human misery, without mind, without delicacy or modesty, constantly harassed by the most ungovernable passion, and under the influence of propensities, excited to morbid activity by a vice far more prevalent than has been supposed, with both sexes.

A large proportion of the "bed ridden" cases, of which there are so many in the community, will be found to have originated in this cause. I never see a pale, sickly lad from 15 to 20, especially if he be shy, shamefaced and retiring, but what I suspect him of this vice; and among a hundred that I have questioned, I have rarely been mistaken.

Case 11. The following case illustrates this fact, and shows also the ignorance of friends and even physicians, of the cause of disease in many aggravated cases. A young man was brought from a distant part of the commonwealth by his brother, who was a physician of more than common intelligence, and placed under my care. The first impression which I received from his appearance was, that he was a victim of this solitary vice. His brother gave me a history of his situation, which was nearly as follows:—When about 13 years of age, he was feeble, sickly, and unable to labor : he had continued in this state four or five years, and gradually got better, so that during the summer previous to his consulting me, he had labored on a farm, and appeared in comfortable health. Late in the fall, he became again listless, stupid and feeble. In the winter, he was decidedly insane. Insanity was followed suddenly by a torpor of the mental and physical powers, perhaps in some measure to be attributed to the medication which had been prescribed for him.

While his brother remained, I suggested to him the probable cause of the malady. He denied the possibility of it, said that he had never suspected it, and that he had lived in the house with him from the time of his first indisposition, and did not believe that he was given to the practice.

In the morning after he left, I examined the patient, and he told me his plain unvarnished story. When about 17 years of age, a hired man of his father's, taught him the practice of self-pollution : he continued it till his ill health came upon him, and for some time after. Towards the close of this period of ill health, he abandoned the practice, and soon improved ; after a while he got so well as to labor, and ultimately quite recovered. Some months before he came under my care, he recommenced the practice, and continued it more than ever ; in a few months he became ill again, and the insanity followed. This was his own story. He remained under my care but a short time, and returned to his friends much in the same condition as he left them, probably ruined for life.

Case 12. The case of a lad of 16, who at an early age exhibited talents and intelligence

5*

quite superior to young men of his age in
general. He was dismissed from one or two
academic institutions in consequence of the
practice of this vice. During the last year,
by his imprudence, he was reduced to the
worst possible condition. Whenever the con-
tents of the bowels or the bladder were evacu-
ated, the seminal fluid passed with it. He was
stupid and imbecile in the extreme; would
stand hours perfectly still, regardless of any
thing around him. He was apparently unconscious of his evacuations, which passed from
him as he stood, or as he lay in his bed, without his regarding them. In this state he came
under my care. For a long time the case
seemed utterly hopeless; no impression was
made upon him, excepting that his habits of
cleanliness improved. Every opportunity was
taken to impress upon the wreck of mind which
remained, the necessity of an abandonment of
the habit, even to the continuance of his life.
In a month or two, there was considerable improvement of his health, and very perceptible
increase of mental vigor. At present he is far
better, and considerable hope is indulged that
he may be restored to his friends and to usefulness, if increasing vigor does not induce him

again to return to the practice, which nearly
cost him his life.

Case 13. Is a respectable young man from
one of the colleges in New England. While
in the seminary, he became jealous of his
friends, and suspicious of all around him, and
left the institution. He had been in the practice of masturbation till his health had become
delicate, and his nervous system very susceptible. He became convinced of the pernicious
influence of this practice, and abandoned it;
but alas! it was too late. His mind became
alienated, partly perhaps in consequence of the
continuance of nocturnal pollution, after the
voluntary practice had been abandoned. In
this state of mind, he made a serious assault
upon the person of a friend, to revenge some
imaginary insult, or supposed injury. In consequence of this he was thrown into prison.
After a while, he came under my care. He had
mind and feelings the most acute and sensitive;
he was conscious of the cause of his calamity,
and very anxious to be cured; such was the excessive irritability of his system, and the excita-
bility of his feelings, that the occurrence of
this spontaneous emission would render him
almost frantic; he was jealous of every body

around him, suspected all his associates of plots to injure, and of words and gestures to insult and abuse him; in more than one instance, he rushed from his room, and made an assault upon the most innocent individual of his associates; he even suspected me, from some smile or hint, of plotting mischief to ensnare him. Such was the state of his mind at one time, and so frequently did he make these assaults, that we were constrained to confine him for a short period.   He was constantly sensible of the cause of his condition, and very solicitous for the removal of it; he was even desirous to be emasculated, believing that this would terminate his misery and afford him an opportunity of usefulness again.

Since writing the above, I received a letter from this young gentleman, dated Jan. 16, 1838, and another from a patient under my care, which exhibit, in a strong light; the jealousy, suspicion and disposition to seclusion, which is so often spoken of in such cases.

DEAR SIR :—When I left —— under your care, it was with no sanguine expectations of ever enjoying much happiness without.   But I thought that at least I would try in what manner

I should be treated by my fellow men, after so long and melancholy a confinement. I hoped it would be thought that the time for showing me mercy had come, and that mercy would be universally extended to me.

But my situation has been more disagreeable than I expected. Persecution has not yet ceased, even though I lived for several months last summer near half a mile from any neighbors, and am now, in the depth of winter, living in solitude. But what is worse to me, even, than contemptible insult, my health has for some time been failing. The bowel complaint, which has troubled me so long, and was relieved by the constant use of opium, induced me to adopt the use of that drug; and I have continued it ever since. Whether it is owing to that or to other causes, (I have no doubt myself that it is owing to that,) my digestive powers have become greatly weakened. I am subject to frequent and very painful attacks of the colic, which leave me in a very debilitated state. To struggle with such a disease all alone, in a cold and uncomfortable dwelling, is certainly a lot not to be desired. I need some other person to be with me; but I have none, and fear I can get none.

In these circumstances you will probably not be surprised that I should wish to obtain admittance somewhere, where, if I must die, I can die in peace; and if there is any chance of my getting better by the use of means, means can be employed.

I have been at —— already, and returning thither would not be likely to add to my uncomfortable notoriety, as would be the case, if I went to ——. I hope that these considerations, together with your own knowledge of the unquestionable unhappiness of my case, will have an influence over your decision as to the propriety of my re-admission. I was glad to get away last spring, and shall now be glad to return. For,—I am unfit for the world without.

With regard to the length of time which I should wish to spend there, it would, if I should live and be tolerably comfortably situated, be several years at least. With regard to the means of defraying my expenses, perhaps some employment might be obtained for me which should be sufficient for that purpose, and at the same time keep me properly screened from notice.

I should wish to go on immediately, if your decision is favorable to my application.

I am, sir, very respectfully, yours, &c.

DEAR SIR :—Trust me—give me presently
an honorable discharge—and after all that has
been said and done, I will acknowledge nothing
amiss in it. Let me once more go abroad in
the world—let me see my friends again—my
father, an affectionate mother and sisters, and I
will truly affect no complaint which shall hinder
me from gaining an honest livelihood. Have
pity upon my mother—she will die herself of
grief at my loss—if I am lost. Oh no, say not
that I am. Deliver me—make record that I
am cured—and when I am dismissed—I call
upon God to witness my sincerity in this my
last declaration—I will be as one dead to any
other statement than that I was handsomely
treated whilst I was here. Oh, who shall I appeal
to if not to God to witness the truth of what
I now say. Believe me, Doctor, my conduct
here—the various accounts that I have delivered
of myself—are not worthy of a final judgment
against me. I was influenced to say and do
what I have, by sentiments entirely foreign to
my natural disposition. Oh, there are those that
I love, and dearly—and I think there are those
who have grossly misrepresented my true feelings. O, Doctor, I am aware that even now,

and at my elbow, there is one writing things
against me, which are as false as ill advised.
He knows me not—nor nothing that evinces
the probability that I deserve the chastisement
which he, from a wretched conceit, would be
transported to see immediately inflicted on me.
O, Doctor, he does not merit your confidence.
Place none in him. 'T is ——. What he
says is false—basely so. He would, I am satisfied, hurry me to my long account—and I know
from his reckless conversation, that no falsehood,
however black, he would omit to conjure up,
to despoil me of life.

Perhaps he has even looked over what I am
now writing to you. He is writing himself, and
I am unfortunately so situated that he can look
over my shoulder. He may be writing that
even now himself which shall decide my fate.
Oh, trust not to *him*, if any other of his companions. I shall be missed truly—no one of my
relations who know me will believe, for a moment, that I should be so rash as to destroy
myself, let me be where I will. It has undoubtedly been told you, that I contemplated it.
It never entered into my heart. Oh, think yourself only for a day more. How could I commit
suicide, while my mother, who sets more by me

than any other of her children, could not survive the intelligence a day. Let not ——, nor
no one else here, prejudice you against me.
'T is false that I am prepared to die. Oh let me,
while under the control of the head of his institution, escape the unmerciful thing. Look
about you, Doctor, consider well whence I came,
who I am, and those who busy themselves in
informing against me. Grant me but to go
away as well as I came, and there shall not let
slip a day when I will not think of you as an
individual for whom I should feel willing to
undergo, as proof of my gratitude, any penance
short of life. I know not what to add—I cannot bear to think of my mother. O, Doctor, I
beseech you let me escape. Have you not
warrant, if there is no faith in man, that I
should still be at your mercy, and thus devoted
to the science, if it were possible for me to have
that ingratitude and folly as to presume to say
aught, if I knew any, to the disparagement of
those things which it was my misfortune here to
become associated. Oh, I must be safe after all.
These things dwelt in my imagination, before
thus actually intimidated. Therefore here is
no disclosure to my prejudice. It is not necessary, because I have solved the riddle, as in

6

the case of Pericles of Tyre, to forfeit my life
perchance. 'T is nothing new to me, this necessary resource of science. Think of me—
are there not others who deserve this horrible
chastisement more than I? There are those
who would not be missed—*I shall be.* There
are few that *despise* me where I am truly
known. Then know me yourself, Doctor, for
something more worthy.

What shall I say? Alas! I can develope
nothing with any assurance now. Has the cup
passed? The mischief is not in me. It has
been bred in the hearts of those who are stone
to their own kin. Have not I brothers and
sisters too? O, Doctor, you are greatly misin-
formed, if it is said that I do not love them
like a brother. They love me, and will mourn
my loss severely. See my father's family—behold my mother, brothers, sisters, and all—and
if you have the sympathy of a parent too—I
am delivered. I am sure you would deliver me
at once, if you was acquainted with every thing
which has a bearing upon my case. It must be
that you are ill advised. —— has done me
mortal injury, and so has Mr. ——, I am convinced. There is no uprightness in those who
have pretended to describe my character.

I dare not repeat what I have good reason to believe has been said of me. There are two or three who urge me to let them see what I write to you—which is as much as to say that their own reputation for truth is concerned. Take particular notice of this, Doctor, I have never uttered a single syllable which might be construed into any manner of a threat, (harsh as the word is.) I am innocent of all such charges. I should not deserve my liberty, if I had said or conceived any thing of such hideous character. I tremble to think of the effect of such a terrible falsehood.

I must close. I cannot compose my mind to develope the matter as it should be. I am terrified beyond measure. Give me an opportunity only to confront the man who has so misrepresented me—then I must be safe.

Most respectfully yours.

I have purposely selected a class of most respectable individuals who have been the victims of this vice, because I believe that in our High Schools, Academies and Colleges, the evil is as alarming, or more so, than among an equal number of young men in any of the humble walks of life. I am confident that the sedentary and inactive are more commonly its victims than the laborious and active. The idle, sedentary, and those who pursue light employments, have more frequently come under my observation, and are most likely to suffer serious injury. Young men who congregate together more than those who labor secluded from associates—students, merchant's clerks, printers and shoemakers, more than those young men who labor at agricultural employments or active mechanical trades. Labor in the open air conduces to sound sleep, and invigorates the physical powers; in this way tends to prevent the practice, and in some measure fortify the constitution against its effects;—at least the same indulgence will produce less perceptible influence; but no means will secure any person from danger, *for no class of the young is exempt from the most melancholy and fatal results, who are, to any extent, in the habit of this secret vice.*

I am aware that full credence is not given by all to the extent of the evil which results from this cause. My own knowledge is almost exclusively derived from observation. I was not sensible of the *extent* and *frequency* of the practice, nor of the disastrous effects which followed it, till circumstances placed me in the way of extensive experience. I was obliged to believe, however reluctantly, what was constantly before my eyes.

For the last four years, it has fallen to my lot to witness, examine and mark the progress of from ten to twenty-five cases, daily, who have been the victims of this debasing habit, and I aver, that no cause whatever, which operates upon the human system, prostrates all its energies, mental, moral and physical, to an equal extent.

I have seen more cases of idiocy from this cause alone, than from all the other causes of insanity. If insanity and idiocy do not result, other diseases, irremediable and hopeless, follow in its train; or such a degree of imbecility marks its ravages upon body and mind, as to destroy all the happiness of life, and make existence itself wretched and miserable in the extreme.

6*

MENTAL ILLNESS AND SOCIAL POLICY
THE AMERICAN EXPERIENCE

AN ARNO PRESS COLLECTION

Barr, Martin W. Mental Defectives: Their History, Treatment and Training. 1904.

The Beginnings of American Psychiatric Thought and Practice: Five Accounts, 1811-1830. 1973

The Beginnings of Mental Hygiene in America: Three Selected Essays, 1833-1850. 1973

Briggs, L. Vernon, et al. History of the Psychopathic Hospital, Boston, Massachusetts. 1922

Briggs, L. Vernon. Occupation as a Substitute for Restraint in the Treatment of the Mentally Ill. 1923

Brigham, Amariah. An Inquiry Concerning the Diseases and Functions of the Brain, the Spinal Cord, and the Nerves. 1840

Brigham, Amariah. Observations on the Influence of Religion upon the Health and Physical Welfare of Mankind. 1835

Brill, A. A. Fundamental Conceptions of Psychoanalysis. 1921

Bucknill, John Charles. Notes on Asylums for the Insane in America. 1876

Conolly, John. The Treatment of the Insane Without Mechanical Restraints. 1856

Coriat, Isador H. What is Psychoanalysis? 1917

Deutsch, Albert. The Shame of the States. 1948

Dewey, Richard. Recollections of Richard Dewey: Pioneer in American Psychiatry. 1936

Earle, Pliny. Memoirs of Pliny Earle, M. D. with Extracts from his Diary and Letters (1830-1892) and Selections from his Professional Writings (1839-1891). 1898

Galt, John M. The Treatment of Insanity. 1846

Goddard, Henry Herbert. Feeble-mindedness: Its Causes and Consequences. 1926

Hammond, William A. A Treatise on Insanity in Its Medical Relations. 1883

Hazard, Thomas R. Report on the Poor and Insane in Rhode-Island. 1851

Hurd, Henry M., editor. The Institutional Care of the Insane in the United States and Canada. 1916/1917. Four volumes.

Kirkbride, Thomas S. On the Construction, Organization, and General Arrangements of Hospitals for the Insane. 1880

Meyer, Adolf. The Commonsense Psychiatry of Dr. Adolf Meyer: Fifty-two Selected Papers. 1948

Mitchell, S. Weir. Wear and Tear, or Hints for the Overworked. 1887

Morton, Thomas G. The History of the Pennsylvania Hospital, 1751-1895. 1895

Ordronaux, John. Jurisprudence in Medicine in Relation to the Law. 1869

The Origins of the State Mental Hospital in America: Six Documentary Studies, 1837-1856. 1973

Packard, Mrs. E. P. W. Modern Persecution, or Insane Asylums Unveiled, As Demonstrated by the Report of the Investigating Committee of the Legislature of Illinois. 1875. Two volumes in one

Prichard, James C. A Treatise on Insanity and Other Disorders Affecting the Mind. 1837

Prince, Morton. The Unconscious: The Fundamentals of Human Personality Normal and Abnormal. 1921

Putnam, James Jackson. Human Motives. 1915

Russell, William Logie. The New York Hospital: A History of the Psychiatric Service, 1771-1936. 1945

Sidis, Boris. The Psychology of Suggestion: A Research into the Subconscious Nature of Man and Society. 1899

Southard, Elmer E. Shell-Shock and Other Neuropsychiatric Problems Presented in Five Hundred and Eighty-Nine Case Histories from the War Literature, 1914-1918. 1919

Southard, E[lmer] E. and Mary C. Jarrett. The Kingdom of Evils. 1922

Southard, E[lmer] E. and H[arry] C. Solomon. Neurosyphilis: Modern Systematic Diagnosis and Treatment Presented in One Hundred and Thirty-seven Case Histories. 1917

Spitzka, E[dward] C. Insanity: Its Classification, Diagnosis and Treatment. 1887

Supreme Court Holding a Criminal Term, No. 14056. The United States vs. Charles J. Guiteau. 1881/1882. Two volumes

Trezevant, Daniel H. Letters to his Excellency Governor Manning on the Lunatic Asylum. 1854

Tuke, D[aniel] Hack. The Insane in the United States and Canada. 1885

Upham, Thomas C. Outlines of Imperfect and Disordered Mental Action. 1868

White, William A[llanson]. Twentieth Century Psychiatry: Its Contribution to Man's Knowledge of Himself. 1936

Willard, Sylvester D. Report on the Condition of the Insane Poor in the County Poor Houses of New York. 1865